D0893538

RAILROADS AND AMERICAN LAW

RAILROADS AND AMERICAN LAW

James W. Ely, Jr.

University Press of Kansas

© 2001 by the University Press of Kansas
All rights reserved

Published by the University Press of Kansas (Lawrence, Kansas 66049),
which was organized by the Kansas Board of Regents and is operated
and funded by Emporia State University, Fort Hays State University,
Kansas State University, Pittsburg State University, the University of
Kansas, and Wichita State University

Library of Congress Cataloging-in-Publication Data

Ely, James W., 1938–
Railroads and American law / James W. Ely, Jr.
p. cm.
Includes bibliographical references and index.
ISBN 0-7006-1144-4 (cloth : alk. paper)
1. Railroad law—United States—History.   2. Railroads and
state—United States—History.   I. Title
KF2289 .E45 2002
385′.0973—dc21
2001003122

British Library Cataloguing in Publication Data is available.

Printed in the United States of America

10 9 8 7 6 5 4 3 2 1

The paper used in this publication meets the minimum requirements of
the American National Standard for Permanence of Paper for Printed
Library Materials Z39.48-1984.

CONTENTS

PROLOGUE

Few aspects of American society were untouched by the coming of the railroad. "The fact is," one newspaper aptly commented in 1882, "that the railroad has revolutionized everything."[1] The railroad was indeed an agent of change, forging a national market for goods, linking city and countryside, facilitating passenger travel, and knitting together distant regions. During much of the nineteenth century the construction of railroads was a consuming passion for Americans. "No enterprise," *Poor's Manual of Railroads* declared in 1900, "is so seductive as a railroad for the influence it exerts, the power it gives, and the hope of gain it offers."[2] Although beneficial in many respects, the railroad was also unsettling to established social and economic patterns. Railroads uprooted people, threatened local economic autonomy, and posed dangers to railroad employees and the communities through which the tracks ran.

Not surprisingly, the advent of the railroad had a profound impact on the evolution of American law. The railroad industry raised a host of novel problems and placed unprecedented demands on the legal system. Railroads helped shape, and were in turn shaped by, legal institutions. As America's first big business, the railroad industry compelled the formulation of new legal rules governing corporate charters, industrial accidents, interstate commerce, eminent domain, the duties of common carriers, government promotion of private enterprise, labor relations, regulation of private property, the reach of federal judicial power, taxation of property, and the reorganization of insolvent businesses. One observer even attributed the growth of law schools after the Civil War to increased travel made possible by railroads.[3] Furthermore, the railroad forced Americans to confront such divisive social issues as racial segregation, work on Sunday, and treatment of Indians in a new context.

Legal questions arising from the operation of railroads became a major preoccupation first of the states and secondarily of federal lawmakers. Consequently, railroads were the topic of a vast outpouring of legislation. Railroad companies soon became frequent litigants in both state and federal courts. As early as 1857 the *American Railroad Journal* observed: "Litigation on this subject has, of course, accumulated proportionally to rapid extension of railroads and the increase of railroad travel in this country."[4]

In that year both Edward L. Pierce and Isaac F. Redfield published treatises on railroad law, the first of a number of specialized volumes devoted to the complex legal problems of the rail industry. By the beginning of the twentieth century, court cases involving railroads dominated judicial dockets. Between 1891 and 1906 almost 25 percent of appeals heard by the Ninth Circuit Court of Appeals concerned railroads.[5] Clearly, railroad companies were major players in shaping the legal environment.

Of course, historians have documented many aspects of railroad history. I have drawn heavily from this literature. Still, there has been no comprehensive legal history of the rail industry. This volume is an effort to illustrate how the advent of railroading affected American legal culture. It is a story of change and innovation, as the legal system endeavored to respond to novel challenges. It also shows that the legal history of railroads is more than an account of statutes and judicial decisions. Because railroads touched nearly every facet of American life, economic issues, sectional rivalry, business practices, technological advances, popular aspirations and fears, and changes in public policy all helped to mold the legal parameters of railroading. The law of railroads did not evolve in a vacuum, but reflected the goals and concerns of American society. Since railroads were the first major industry to experience extensive regulation, the work gives particular attention to the effect of such controls.

Mindful of John Phillip Reid's warning against viewing an untidy past through the lens of grand theories,[6] I am reluctant to impose a thesis on the intricate and sometimes contradictory legal history of railroading. Certainly, there is much evidence to support Leonard W. Levy's conclusion that railroads "were objects of the law's solicitude."[7] But to explain the immense body of railroad law simply as a reflection of the legislative desire to promote business enterprise is misleading. From the earliest period not all developments in rail law served the interests of the industry at the expense of landowners, shippers, and injured parties. Some jurists expressed impatience with railroad claims, and in 1874 a Wisconsin judge lambasted carriers as the "spoiled children of legislation."[8] In reality, then, legislators and judges struggled to balance the rights of contending interests. By the end of the nineteenth century railroads were subject to extravagant criticism and were eventually saddled with a far-reaching regulatory regime. Some railroad historians have attributed the decline of the industry to such stringent regulations. The crucial point is that no easy generalizations will capture the diverse ways that railroading impacted on law.

A prominent legal historian has asserted that judges played a key role in promoting economic growth during the nineteenth century, and that judicially fashioned policy was more influential than legislation in the rise of large-scale enterprise. The implicit thesis is that judges superseded legislators as the primary source of legal doctrine and became allies of the capitalists.[9] Railroad legal history does not bear out this contention. Responding to public sentiment, legislators consistently took the initiative in crafting railroad law. At first lawmakers emphasized promotion of rail enterprise, but later shifted their focus to controlling railroad companies. Although the contribution of the judiciary to railroad law was not unimportant, in most areas of law, courts were broadly supportive of the legislative lead.

This is a work of synthesis. It seeks to integrate all aspects of railroad law and to sketch the interaction of legal developments with the history of a vital industry. I am aware that much has been omitted. The legal history of railroading is an enormous topic, and this book moves rapidly over many issues that deserve more extended treatment. The book is primarily organized on a chronological basis moving from the advent of railroading to the present. But certain discrete topics, such as labor relations and tort law, are treated in separate chapters. This framework seemed best calculated to highlight the varied dimensions of railroad law in an accessible manner.

I have received the support and encouragement of many friends and colleagues over the years that I have labored on this project. The reference librarians at the Massey Law Library of Vanderbilt University have located obscure sources and documents with skill and good humor. Special thanks in this regard go to David Bachman, Martin Cerjan, Janet Hirt, Howard A. Hood, and Stephen Jordan. I am indebted to Jon W. Bruce, David L. Callies, Adrienne D. Davis, John Goldberg, Paul Kens, Robert K. Rasmussen, and John F. Stover for reading and offering valuable comments on the manuscript. In addition, I presented some of my research at the annual meeting of the Pacific Coast Branch of the American Historical Association and at a workshop at Cumberland School of Law. I benefited from the intellectual exchange that these occasions made possible. Nan Paden and Kelley Walker typed the many revisions of the manuscript with efficiency. Mike Briggs of the University Press of Kansas was supportive and helpful throughout the years required to bring this volume to fruition. My wife, Mickey, was unfailing in her love and encouragement as I tackled this lengthy project.

All of these people have my deepest appreciation and thanks. I am, of course, solely responsible for any shortcomings in this book.

1

The Emergence of the Railroad

The decades following the War of 1812 produced sweeping changes in American economic life, spearheaded by developments in the field of transportation.[1] Americans envisioned enormous benefits for all interests from improved avenues of trade. As the nation expanded westward, they also stressed the importance of having commercial ties between the new settlements and the seaboard. Initially, much of this enthusiasm was focused on the construction of canals. The success of the Erie Canal, which opened in 1825, strengthened the position of New York City as the dominant eastern seaboard port.[2] Other cities responded with transportation schemes designed to make them competitive and capture western commerce. Pennsylvania, for example, built its own canal, the Main Line System, finished in 1834.[3] Ohio also experimented heavily with canals.[4]

Overshadowed by well-established rivals, the upstart city of Baltimore was instrumental in pioneering a novel mode of transportation. Hoping to make Baltimore competitive with other eastern ports, business interests promoted the grant of a corporate charter to the Baltimore and Ohio Railroad in 1827.[5] Construction of the line began two years later.

At first, some supporters of internal improvements were understandably skeptical about the efficacy of railroads. They represented, after all, a new and unproven means of travel. These early doubts, however, were soon dispelled. In spite of some persistent criticism, by the 1830s Americans had developed a passion for railroads. The reasons for this rail fever have been well documented by historians. Railroad enthusiasts helped to mold public opinion by ceaselessly trumpeting the advantages of rail travel.[6] The *American Railroad Journal*, founded in 1832, was a leading advocate for the fledgling industry.

Several themes predominated in the drive for railroads. Municipal leaders hoped that railroads would increase commercial activity and divert trade from rival cities. It was widely believed that railroads would raise land values and create new wealth. Moreover, promoters maintained that railroads would strengthen the bounds of national unity and facilitate defense in the event of attack. To many, then, railroads were synonymous with progress, the key to economic and social growth. The formative era of railroad law was shaped by this popular desire for rail transportation.

Courts shared the prevalent railroad enthusiasm. Judges repeatedly stressed the commanding advantages of transportation by rail. A New York court in 1852 characterized railroads as "one of the greatest improvements of modern times."[7] Likewise, the Supreme Court of Tennessee optimistically proclaimed: "Activity, industry, enterprise and wealth seem to spring up as if by enchantment, wherever the iron track has been laid, or the locomotive moved."[8] A South Carolina judge pictured railroads as "a new moral cement of the American Union, as well as the useful vehicles of our vast and increasing internal commerce."[9] Courts continued to emphasize the importance of the railroads in the late nineteenth century. Thus, the New Jersey Chancery Court observed in 1892: "Railroads afford speedy and comfortable passage to and from divers parts of the country, carry produce of mines, farms and factories to markets, distribute industries throughout the land, feed the multitudes in populous cities, and accomplish many other beneficent ends."[10] Such sentiments were often invoked to justify the grant of special privileges to railroads.

In order to harness this zeal lawmakers had to resolve a number of threshold issues that had a lasting impact on railroad history. Foremost was the relationship between railroads and government. For most of the antebellum era, the federal government played a relatively passive role in formulating transportation policy. As evidenced by President Andrew Jackson's Maysville Road veto in 1830, the federal government generally adopted the position of not aiding internal improvements.[11] Consequently, the states took the lead in chartering railroads and developing railroad law. With few exceptions, railroads were incorporated under state law. Prominent state jurists, such as Lemuel Shaw of Massachusetts, were pivotal in fashioning early railroad law.[12] Rail policy remained state-centered until the end of the nineteenth century.

Another question concerned the decision to utilize private corporations rather than state ownership as the primary vehicle for railroad projects. Transportation had long been seen as a public function. Many early canals were built directly by the states, and the same model might well have prevailed with respect to railroads. Indeed, a debate over public ownership versus private investment raged in jurisdictions as diverse as Massachusetts and Texas.[13] Many railroad backers favored public construction, reasoning that rail projects needed government support. Others expressed concern that private railroad companies would exercise undue economic power over individuals and localities. Public ownership seemed more compatible with republican government. Samuel B. Ruggles of New York, a proponent of state ownership, asserted in 1838 that "the very idea of employing a private company to construct and manage a public work involves a political absurdity and a paradox in terms."[14]

A few jurisdictions, in which private capital was inadequate to secure improved transportation, took over the construction of railroads. Michigan, for instance, financed the building of the Central Railroad during the 1830s, only to sell the line to private interests in 1846.[15] As discussed later in the chapter, southern states were especially inclined to assume the role of entrepreneur and build rail systems with public funds.

But generally the states relied on private corporations to accomplish the task of railroad building. There were a number of reasons why the states favored private enterprise. Antebellum state governments were low-budget operations. Any proposal to raise a public revenue through higher taxes faced intense political opposition. J. Willard Hurst has pointed out that "through most of the nineteenth century government found it impracticable to command sizable resources by taxation in a chronically cash-scarce economy."[16] State officials therefore preferred to encourage internal improvements by mustering private energy and resource. Moreover, a number of states had heavily invested in canals. Not only had some of these projects proven a financial disappointment, but railroads threatened the continued economic viability of state-owned canals. Similarly, private canals and turnpikes often struggled to make a profit. All of this naturally made lawmakers skittish about substantial public investments in high-risk railroads.

It was also politically difficult for legislators to support any rail ventures that served only one geographical section of the state while ignoring other interests. Regional interests posed a barrier to any consistent program of state-owned railroads. Further, many doubted the ability of state government to manage projects of such scale and insisted that the private sector could construct railroads more efficiently.[17] As the prominent treatise writer Thomas M. Cooley observed: "the general sentiment is adverse to the construction of railways by the State, and the opinion is quite prevalent, if not general, that they can be better managed, controlled, and operated for the public benefit in the hands of individuals than by the State or municipal officers or agencies."[18]

The upshot was that the construction and management of railroads was largely left in private hands. This decision did not rule out state and local government financial assistance to railroad companies. Yet in the last analysis most rail ventures were the product of private initiative rather than state planning.

Competition with Canals and Turnpikes

From the outset, railroads were in competition with existing canal and turnpike systems. The intense rivalry between canals and railroads over traffic gave rise to numerous legal issues as canals battled tenaciously to protect their market. Canal interests endeavored to block the issuance of railroad charters,[19] to dispute rights-of-way, and to restrict the right of railroads to carry freight. As the Ohio canal commissioners explained in 1850: "We have felt it to be our duty to resist by all means at our disposal every intrusion by railroads upon the canals which impaired the navigation and traffic of the latter."[20] In particular, the advent of the railroad forced courts to reassess the extent to which canal and turnpike grants were inherently exclusive. This struggle between railroads and older modes of travel had a profound impact on both constitutional law and the later growth of the rail network.

Canals were quick to assert a general priority based upon earlier charter grants. The potential force of this argument was illustrated by *Chesapeake and Ohio Canal Company v. Baltimore and Ohio Rail Road Company* (1832).[21] The railroad acquired rights-of-way along the projected route of the canal through the Potomac River valley. Both the railroad and the canal had authority to purchase land, but there was no express provision conferring exclusive rights on the canal. It might well have been argued that the first party to acquire the land should prevail. Instead, the canal maintained that it was entitled to a priority in the selection of routes by virtue of its older charter. The Court of Appeals of Maryland, by a sharply divided vote, upheld this contention. The court reasoned that the prior canal grant conferred a vested franchise to select the most suitable land, and that no other corporation could legally acquire any right-of-way to the land over which the franchise extended. As a result of this decision, the railroad faced the unhappy prospect of finding a new and more expensive route. Recognition of expansive rights in older corporate charters, moreover, threatened new rail ventures. Perhaps sensing this threat, the Maryland legislature engineered a compromise under which the canal and railroad shared disputed mountain passes and at places constructed their lines side by side.

The underlying rationale of *Chesapeake and Ohio Canal*—that original charters contained privileges not directly expressed—was rejected by the Supreme Court in the famous case of *Charles River Bridge v. Warren Bridge* (1837). Writing for the Court, Chief Justice Roger B. Taney insisted that corporate charters must be strictly construed and did not confer any implied rights. Taney further asserted that acknowledgment of implicit corporate rights would stymie improvements in transportation. He astutely pointed out:

> If this court should establish the principles now contended for, what is to become of the numerous railroads established on the same line of travel with turnpike companies; and which have rendered the franchises of the turnpike corporations of no value? Let it once be understood that such charters carry with them these implied contracts, and give this unknown and undefined property in a line of traveling, and you will soon find the old turnpike corporations awakening from their sleep, and calling upon this court to put down the improvements which have taken their place. The millions of property which have been invested in railroads and canals, upon lines of travel which had been before occupied by turnpike corporations, will be put in jeopardy. We shall be thrown back to the improvements of the last century, and obliged to stand still, until the claims of the old turnpike corporations shall be satisfied, and they shall consent to permit these States to avail themselves of the lights of modern science, and to partake of the benefit of those improvements which are now adding to the wealth and prosperity, and the convenience and comfort of every other part of the civilized world.[22]

Although upsetting to some private investors, the *Charles River Bridge* decision greatly benefited railroads. It did much to prevent established turnpikes and canals from blocking the establishment of new railroad lines.

Reflecting a changed judicial attitude, the Maryland Court of Appeals in *Washington and Baltimore Turnpike Road v. Baltimore and Ohio Railroad Company* (1839) rebuffed a claim by the turnpike company that construction of a rail line from Baltimore to Washington impaired an implied obligation by the state not to encourage a diversion of turnpike traffic. The liberating dimension of *Charles River Bridge* was also illustrated in *Thompson v. New York and Harlem Railroad Company* (1846). The proprietors of a toll bridge over the Harlem River sought to enjoin the railroad from operating trains over an adjacent bridge. Plaintiffs argued that the railroad seriously diminished their tolls and violated their franchise. Brushing aside this contention, the court emphasized that the bridge proprietors had no implied right to any exclusive privilege. Noting that new inventions might destroy the value of older modes of travel, the court declared:

The influence of the railroad on the complainant's profits from their bridge is more analogous to that which has been effected in respect of many branches of business, by the astonishing improvements of the last thirty years. The Erie Canal broke up and destroyed the long lines of heavy teams which formerly monopolized the transportation west of Albany, and diminished more than one half the profits of the turnpike companies between Albany and Canandaigua. The line of railroads which succeeded drove from the road the throng of stage coaches, which were profitably employed in the conveyance of passengers to and from the great west. Yet neither the army of teamsters thrown out of business, nor the turnpike corporations, ever claimed compensation from the State in respect of the Erie Canal; nor did the stage owners claim redress against the railroad companies, which destroyed their business and diminished one half the value of their capital.[23]

Similarly, in *Board of Trustees of the Illinois and Michigan Canal v. Chicago and Rock Island Railroad Company* (1853) the Supreme Court of Illinois ruled that a canal charter did not prevent the state legislature from subsequently authorizing a railroad, the effect of which was to divert business from the canal.

Another dispute arose when railroads sought to construct their lines over canals and turnpikes. In states with powerful canal interests, such as New York, some early railroad charters prohibited building lines across canals without permission of the canal commission.[24] The issue, however, was not so easily resolved. A successful railroad building program necessitated the crossing of many canals and turnpikes.

The conflict over the right of railroads to cross canals came to a head in *Tuckahoe Canal Company v. Tuckahoe and James River Rail Road Company* (1840). The railroad proposed to cross the Tuckahoe Canal at two points. Concerned that the erection of rail bridges would obstruct navigation, the canal company maintained that the railroad had no right to cross its works and that such action would interfere with the franchise of the canal. Rejecting this argument, the Virginia Court of Appeals emphatically denied that incorporation of one company implied any exclusive rights. "If these pretensions are listened to," the court warned, "there will soon be an end of the necessary improvement of the country."[25] Since the legislature had not expressly contracted to confer exclusive transportation privileges on the canal company, the legislature was free to charter rival companies. The court concluded that the railroad was authorized by its charter to locate its line wherever desired.

Likewise, the right of railroads to cross privately owned turnpikes was challenged in *Newburyport Turnpike Corporation v. Eastern Rail Road Company* (1839). The railroad planned to construct its line over the turnpike at grade, and to accomplish this, the railroad planned to raise the turnpike above its existing level at the point of intersection. Giving a broad interpretation to a state statute authorizing railroads to cross turnpikes, the Supreme Judicial Court of Massachusetts brushed aside the objections of the turnpike company. Revealingly, the court observed that "it is important, and often necessary, that the rail road should be kept on a given level and not be varied so as to adapt it to the existing levels of other roads."[26] In short, other modes of transportation must adjust to the needs of the railroad.

In time the authority of railroads to cross canals and turnpikes was made clear by legislation. The influential New York general railroad act of 1850 empowered railroads to cross any canal or turnpike, provided that the railroad did not impair the usefulness of the other modes of travel.[27] Illinois enacted a similar measure.[28] Vermont and Pennsylvania gave railroads the right not only to cross turnpikes, but to raise, lower, or alter the course of such roads.[29] Ohio linked the bridging of canals to compliance with rate regulations. An 1852 law required that all railroads operating in the vicinity of any state-owned canal post a tariff of freight rates. The Board of Public Works was directed to allow companies adhering to such rate schedule to construct bridges across canals, so long as the bridges did not block navigation.[30] Following the Civil War, state general railroad laws typically empowered railroads to build over highways and canals.[31]

Another attempt employed to curb railroad competition was to restrict the transportation of freight. This was a sharply contested issue in antebellum New York. The Erie Canal was highly successful, and lawmakers were anxious not to jeopardize canal revenue. For this reason, many early railroad charters in the Empire State contained diverse clauses limiting the shipment of freight. The charter of the Utica and Schenectady Railroad Company, for instance, prohibited carrying anything but passengers and their baggage.[32] The 1836 act incorporating the Auburn and Rochester Railroad Company similarly directed that the company "shall not take and transport merchandize or property in such a manner as to lessen the income on the Erie canal during the time when the canal is navigable."[33]

Other lines were authorized to carry freight but obligated to pay to the canal fund the same tolls on goods as if they were transported on the canal. In 1844 all railroads paralleling the canal system were allowed to transport freight when canal navigation was suspended during the winter, on condition that they pay equivalent tolls.[34] Three years later the railroads won the right to transport freight all year, but the tollage requirement remained. The public was increasingly more interested in lower railroad charges than in protecting canal revenues. Critics pictured the tolls as an unfair tax designed to cripple railroads and monopolize traffic for the canal,[35] and in 1851 the legislature abolished railroad tolls.[36]

Fueled by suspicion of the newly formed New York Central, and by concerns about mounting canal deficits, canal advocates during the 1850s agitated for the restoration of tolls on railroads. The governor urged this step in 1855, and again in the early 1860s. The legislature, however, declined to act.[37] Defenders of the canal then instituted a suit challenging the constitutionality of the repeal act. In *People v. New York Central Railroad Company* (1862) the New York Court of Appeals ruled that railroad tolls were not "canal revenues" under the state constitution, and that the legislature could eliminate tolls on railroad freight. This decision, coupled with the outbreak of the Civil War, marked the end of railroad tolls as an issue in New York.

A levy on railroad freight was also a significant factor in Pennsylvania, a state that witnessed a dramatic triumph of railroads over canals. Beset by financial difficulties in the 1840s, state officials sought to sell their ambitious canal system, the Main Line of the Public Works. Amid rising popular resentment of government involvement with transportation, this policy was approved at a public referendum in 1844. It proved impossible for years, however, to find any purchasers at the asking price. In the meantime, the Pennsylvania Railroad, incorporated in 1846, constructed a competing line from Philadelphia to Pittsburgh. In order to indemnify the state for probable losses to the canal system, the charter of the company mandated the payment of a duty on the tonnage of freight carried throughout the warm weather months. During the 1850s the legislature passed several acts authorizing disposal of the Main Line, and lowering the asking price. An 1857 act for the sale of the Main Line provided that if the Pennsylvania Railroad purchased the canal, the company would be discharged forever from the payment of tonnage taxes and state levies on its property. This generous exemption was included in the sale act out of fear that the railroad would otherwise not buy the canal works.[38] Asserting a duty to protect the public works, the canal commissioners brought suit for an injunction to block the entire sale. They raised a number of objections, but particularly stressed the argument that the tax exemption provision was unconstitutional.

In *Mott v. Pennsylvania Railroad Company* (1858) the Supreme Court of Pennsylvania sustained the sale but struck down the proposed tax exemption. Chief Justice Ellis Lewis, in the principal opinion for a unanimous court, decried the partial nature of a tax break available to only one particular bidder and suggested that such a discriminatory provision undermined the public sale. He then broadly ruled that the legislature did not have the constitutional authority to abridge the power of taxation by entering into a contract that bound succeeding legislatures. Lewis reasoned that governments could not exist without revenue and that a state could not "commit political suicide" by contracting away the tax power. Noting the close relationship between vigorous government and railroads, he pointedly observed: "From the extensive nature of their operations, the power to take private property for the construction of their works, and their continual collision with each other's interests, and with the interests of individuals and municipal communities, they require the constant and energetic protection of the strong arm of the government."[39] Lewis emphasized that the legislature was free to grant tax exemptions, or to eliminate the tonnage duties, but not to prevent repeal by future legislatures if public interest so required. Finding no objection to the sale of the Main Line, the court merely prohibited disposition upon terms that released the Pennsylvania Railroad from taxes, and otherwise permitted the sale to the highest bidder. In June the railroad purchased the Main Line at auction.

Once the Pennsylvania Railroad owned the canal system that the tonnage tax was designed to protect, continued payment of the levy made little sense and burdened the cost of transportation. The railroad's refusal to make further tonnage payments sparked another round of litigation. The state courts sustained the constitutionality of the tonnage tax against a commerce clause challenge.[40] In 1861 the legislature accepted a payment from the railroad in commutation of the tonnage tax and repealed the levy. The company was obligated to reduce freight charges in an amount equal to the repealed tax.[41]

As vividly demonstrated by the experience in Pennsylvania, efforts to retard the growth of railroads by the erection of legal barriers proved futile. Unable to compete with the speed, dependable service, and relatively inexpensive rates of the railroads, canals steadily lost traffic. Lawmakers were caught between the desire to protect state investments in canals and the public clamor for improved transportation. Not surprisingly, the better technology prevailed. By the mid–nineteenth century, competition between modes of transportation was viewed as desirable, and any resulting loss the inevitable price of progress. As the New York Court of Appeals explained:

Railroads destroy the business of stage proprietors, and yet no one has ever thought a railroad charter unconstitutional, because it gave no damages to stage owners. The Hudson river railroad will soon drive many fine steamboats from the river; but no one will think the charter void because it does not provide for the payment of damages to the boat owners.[42]

Although driven in part by nostalgia, canal champions did raise a vital matter—suspicion of the private economic power of railroad companies. In 1859 Ruggles asked: "Cannot the tax-payers of the State perceive that the canal is the only power adequate to keep such a rival within the bounds of moderation?"[43] The hope was that canals, by providing alternative transportation, would serve as a means to regulate railroad charges. In short, canal advocacy was a surrogate for anti-monopoly sentiment and anticipated concerns that would find different expression in the later nineteenth century.

Monopoly Privilege

Even as railroads struggled to defeat the claims of canals and turnpikes, they were prone to seek exclusive privileges for themselves. This led to conflict between competing railroads over monopoly status. Adhering to the *Charles River Bridge* decision that corporate grants conferred no implied rights, courts generally took the position that grant of a railroad charter did not prevent legislatures from subsequently authorizing other railroads that would compete for business.[44] Only an express grant by the legislature could establish an exclusive right. At the same time, however, the power of states to confer exclusive privileges was not questioned in the early nineteenth century.

Courts insisted on strict construction of any express privileges. At issue in *Richmond, Fredericksburg and Potomac Railroad Company v. Louisa Railroad Company* (1851) was language in an 1834 Virginia charter that the legislature would not for thirty years "allow any other railroad to be constructed" between Richmond and Washington, "the probable effect of which would be to diminish the number of passengers." Despite this provision, in 1848 the legislature authorized another line to build into Richmond. Alleging that the 1848 act impaired its contract with the state, the Richmond, Fredericksburg and Potomac Railroad brought suit to enjoin its rival from extending tracks to Richmond. The Supreme Court ruled that the monopoly was limited to passengers, and that the charter contained no guarantee that the state would never allow another railroad to be constructed over any portion of the route. Consequently, the 1848 act did not impair the terms of the original charter.

From New England to the lower South, however, states were often persuaded to grant monopolies of traffic to fledgling railroads for a period of time.[45] "Some of the early railroad charters were exclusive," Thomas Cooley explained, "and gave a complete monopoly within certain prescribed limits."[46] Notwithstanding a deep-seated aversion to monopolies, several reasons militated in favor of exclusive privilege. Shielding newly formed railroads from competition was seen as a powerful inducement for investors to place capital in risky ventures. Moreover, some jurisdictions extended exclusive charters on condition that the company pay a portion of its earnings to the state. This allowed the legislature to hold down the level of taxation. In the initial era of railroad building, a number of states found the monopoly model an attractive technique to encourage development.

Where the grant of monopoly status was clear, courts displayed little hesitation in upholding the exclusive privileges. The 1830 Massachusetts act creating the Boston and Lowell Railroad provided that no other railroad would be authorized for thirty years between Boston and Lowell. Pointing to an 1852 state statute, two rival lines asserted the right to combine operations and transport passengers and freight by a different route from Boston to Lowell. In *Boston and Lowell Railroad Corporation v. Salem and Lowell Railroad Company* (1854), the plaintiff sought an injunction against such operations and an accounting for lost revenue. Chief Justice Shaw observed that the conferral of exclusive rights was a matter of legislative policy and one that served developmental needs:

> With this want of experience, and with an earnest desire on the part of the public to make an experiment of this new and extraordinary public improvement, it would be natural for the government to offer such terms, as would be likely to encourage capitalists to invest their money in public improvements; and after the experience of capitalists, in respect of the turnpikes and canals of the Commonwealth, which had been authorized by the public, but built by the application of private capital, but which as investments had proved in most instances to be ruinous, it was probably no easy matter to awaken anew the confidence of moneyed men in these enterprises.[47]

He stressed that the legislature possessed the authority to grant exclusive rights, and that the terms of the 1830 charter constituted a contract binding the state. It followed that the rival railroads had no right to combine operations and infringe the monopoly of the Boston and Lowell Railroad.

The most important and lasting rail monopoly was that granted by New Jersey to the Camden and Amboy Railroad. In 1832 the Camden and Amboy secured a concession that no other railroad would be permitted to transport passengers or goods across New Jersey between New York City and Philadelphia. Since the original charter of the company was to expire thirty years after the opening of the railroad, the monopoly provision would be in force for decades. For its part, the Camden and Amboy transferred a block of capital stock to the state and agreed to pay, in lieu of other taxes, a transit duty on passengers crossing the state. The Camden and Amboy was immediately a financial success, and the payment of dividends and transit duties constituted the principal source of revenue in the state budget. This meant that the public indirectly benefited from the monopoly provision since the legislature did not need to levy a property tax in the years before the Civil War. Not surprisingly, the Camden and Amboy Railroad became a dominant force in the politics of antebellum New Jersey.[48]

Notwithstanding its sizable contribution to state revenue, the Camden and Amboy over time was subject to increasing criticism. There were complaints about overcharging, lax safety standards, and poor service. Some felt that the monopoly grant retarded railroad development elsewhere in New Jersey. Another concern was the impact on interstate commerce, because the transit duties fell heavily on nonresidents crossing New Jersey. The *American Railroad Journal,* a proponent of rail competition, repeatedly denounced the Camden and Amboy monopoly.[49] During the 1850s there was an unsuccessful move in Congress to construct a competing rail line from New York to Washington. There were also several state legislative investigations, but the monopoly survived. Indeed, in 1854 the New Jersey legislature confirmed the exclusive privileges of the company but determined that the monopoly period would terminate in 1869.

Despite the political controversy, New Jersey courts acted to protect the Camden and Amboy's enjoyment of its exclusive franchise. The court of chancery enjoined two other railroads from combining services in such a manner as to provide a continuous line of transportation between New York City and Philadelphia. The chancellor emphasized the positive role of monopoly grants in fashioning transportation policy:

> In this state great works of internal improvement, requiring large outlays of capital, have been almost universally constructed by private capital and private enterprise, aided in some instances by public bounty. Bridges, turnpikes, railroads, and canals, have been thus constructed. It has been neither the disposition of the people, nor the policy of the legislature, to incur the hazards of such enterprises, and experience elsewhere has fully demonstrated that the policy of the state, in this regard, is a wise one. If these works are entrusted to private enterprise, the inducements held out for their execution must rest in legislative discretion.[50]

Concluding that the wisdom of conferring an exclusive franchise was a matter for the legislature, the court upheld the validity of the grant.

Shortly before its exclusive privileges were slated to end, the Camden and

Amboy protected its dominant position by consolidating with a potential rival line. In 1871 the company was leased on a long-term basis to an emerging rail giant, the Pennsylvania Railroad, which was seeking access to New York City. The Camden and Amboy story suggests the advantages and perils of the monopoly model of development.

A feature of the formative era of rail development, monopoly concessions for set periods of time arguably served the legitimate purpose of securing private investment in doubtful ventures. In an economy lacking adequate capital markets, this was no small benefit. Yet, in operation, exclusive privileges had antidevelopmental consequences, tending to stifle innovation and to retard enhanced railroad capacity. They soon became a source of contention. It should be emphasized that most states relied on competition, not monopoly status, to encourage rail development. As private capital formation matured, the rationale for the early monopoly grants was undermined, and the states moved to embrace open access to the industry.

Impact of State Parochialism

Although the pattern of private ownership and competition gained dominance, rivalry between cities, and eventually between states, was often a driving force in shaping railroad law. Recall that the first railroads were typically financed by local investors, with the aid of state and local governments, for the purpose of increasing the commerce of particular regions. Consequently, investors and government officials had a proprietary expectation that "their" railroad would primarily serve local economic interests. It was just a short step to treating private railroad companies as instruments of state commercial policy. Nowhere in the antebellum era was this protectionist attitude more evident than during the colorful "Erie War" in Pennsylvania.[51]

Concerned that trade with the West was slipping away to New York City, Pennsylvania enacted statutes, forfeited a corporate charter, and even condoned extralegal violence to prevent railroads chartered in the state from making through connections in the Erie area with out-of-state lines. This policy had two objectives: (1) to benefit business interests in Erie by making railroads break bulk in that city, and (2) to capture some of the western trade for Philadelphia. By virtue of Pennsylvania's unique geographic position, rail lines from northeastern cities to the West had to cross the northwestern portion of the state. Pennsylvania initially sought to control the track gauge in such a way as to compel a stop in Erie. There was a wide variety of gauges in use on railroads before the Civil War. Generally, the question of which gauge to adopt was determined by individual railroad companies. In 1851, however, the Pennsylvania legislature directed that tracks west of Erie had to match the gauge prevalent in Ohio, while that east of Erie should conform to New York's usual gauge.[52] The effect, of course, was to prevent through connections. A year later the lawmakers required all railroads thereafter constructed to adopt the same gauge as those on lines built by the state.[53] By establishing a uniform gauge throughout the state, lawmakers hoped to curtail entry to Pennsylvania markets by New York–based railroads.

The Supreme Court of Pennsylvania endorsed the state's approach in *Commonwealth v. Franklin Canal Company* (1853). Alleging a breach of its corporate charter, the attorney general moved to restrain the company from constructing a track between Erie and the Ohio state line in order to connect with a railroad running to Cleveland. The court stressed the doctrine of strict construction of charters, and declared "that no railroad company can connect with a foreign railroad which meets it at the state line, unless expressly authorized by its charter." Further, the court observed that the proposed rail connection violated "the spirit if not the letter" of the 1851 gauge act. Employing martial language, the court spoke darkly of perverting privileges to aid rival states and described the 1851 statute as "intended to guard the territory of the state against lawless invasions." The court concluded that under its charter the company had no right to build a line to the Ohio border.[54]

In 1853, however, the Erie War entered a new phase. The Pennsylvania legislature abruptly changed course, repealing the gauge laws and authorizing railroads to determine track width.[55] When the Erie and North East Railroad began to alter its gauge to conform to adjacent Ohio and New York lines, Erie faced the prospect of being bypassed. Desperately, the city council adopted an ordinance prohibiting a change of gauge. In December 1853 the mayor led a crowd to tear up some of the newly laid track. This action precipitated a series of violent incidents between Erie citizens and railroad employees. The federal circuit court issued an injunction against interference with the gauge change. By January 1854 the Erie War was a national concern, and President Franklin Pierce considered a proposal to dispatch federal troops.[56]

The governor sympathized with the people of Erie, declaring that "it is the right and the duty of the State to turn her natural advantages to the promotion of the views and welfare of her own people."[57] Some judges shared this states' rights sentiment. For instance, Judge Walter H. Lowrie warned against "a Quixotic and impracticable cosmopolitism" and urged that state pride should "not be frittered away by the mere American feeling."[58] These remarks made plain the conflict between local economic interests and the need for a national transportation network. Already a more nationalistic understanding of railroads was gaining ascendancy. "The lines of our railroads," the *American Railroad Journal* proclaimed in 1854, "pay no attention to the boundaries of the *States*. They are co-extensive with the *whole* country."[59] From this perspective, the insistence upon a break of gauge at Erie was an indirect means of levying duties upon goods from other states and a threat to commercial unity. It also raised the unhappy prospect that other communities could attempt to sever rail connections.

Meanwhile, the Pennsylvania legislature abrogated the charter of the Franklin Canal Company pursuant to an 1849 general railroad act authorizing revocation of railroad charters for abuse of privileges. In February 1854 the governor seized the embattled line.[60] Subsequently, the Franklin Canal Company was sold to a railroad that was chartered in Ohio and authorized to connect with other lines in Erie. Complicated litigation and legislative maneuvering ensued. In *Commonwealth v. Erie and North East Railroad Company* (1854–1856), the Supreme Court of Pennsylvania found that the company, which formed part of the continuous line through Erie, had violated its charter in several respects, and ordered remedial steps. Yet when Erie officials continued to resist the right to maintain a through rail connection, the court in supplemental opinions sharply denounced the use of physical force to resolve legal issues. Eventually, the railroads won the right to connect their lines on condition they construct a sidetrack to Erie's harbor.

Several points emerge from the Erie War. The legislature pursued a seemingly inconsistent course with respect to rail connections. The incident underscored the difficulty of controlling railroad commerce through state legislation. Playing a secondary role, judges endeavored to follow what they perceived to be state policy. Judges were prone to construe corporate charters strictly, but they also stressed that rail policy was for the legislature. There were later attempts in other jurisdictions to prevent gauge changes by legislation,[61] but the drive to establish uniform gauges and connections with interstate lines was too strong to resist effectively. Although the citizens of Erie ultimately lost the struggle to prevent the adoption of connecting gauges, the underlying conflict between local interests and interstate transportation would later resurface in other forms and heavily impact the development of railroad law.

Another legal device used by various states for local advantage was to refuse franchise grants to railroads chartered in other jurisdictions. Here, too, the experience in Pennsylvania is illuminating. The Baltimore and Ohio Railroad struggled for years to secure the right to construct a line to Pittsburgh. Rebuffed by the Pennsylvania legislature during the 1840s, the Baltimore and Ohio obtained control of the Pittsburg and Connellsville Railroad, a small Pennsylvania chartered company with authorization to build to the Maryland state line. By this means, the Baltimore and Ohio hoped to reach Pittsburgh. In 1864, however, the legislature revoked the charter of the Pittsburg and Connellsville on grounds the company had abused its privileges. Lawmakers made no secret of their desire to keep a foreign enterprise out of Pennsylvania. A series of complex lawsuits in both state and federal courts followed.[62] The crucial judicial action was a quo warranto filed by the attorney general asserting that the Pittsburg and Connellsville had no legal existence. In a revealing argument, the attorney general maintained that by accepting a Maryland charter the company acted in a manner inconsistent with its allegiance to Pennsylvania. He likened such an act to treason.

On this issue, the Supreme Court of Pennsylvania was unimpressed with the state's protectionist policy. In *Commonwealth v. Pittsburg and Connellsville Railroad Company* (1868), the court emphasized that the legislature was not the final judge of alleged abuse of a corporate charter. Finding no violation of the railroad's charter, the court dismissed the action. A chastened legislature promptly repealed the 1864 act, and in 1871 the Baltimore and Ohio finally reached Pittsburgh. It should be noted that Pennsylvania was not alone in refusing to grant access to railroads incorporated in other states. Only gradually did states accept the evolving role of railroads as a mainstay of national economic life rather than as a servant of local interests. The enactment of general railroad laws finally put an end to the policy of state exclusiveness.

Corporate Law

The initial tendency of courts to read railroad charters narrowly, as demonstrated in Pennsylvania, reflected suspicion and uncertainty about business corporations generally. The Jacksonian movement aroused attacks on grants of corporate status as a type of special privilege. But the organizational advantages of the corporate form were so obvious in the case of large-scale enterprise that little criticism was directed against railroads on this score.[63]

Nonetheless, uncertainty existed about the legal nature of railroad companies. Railroads emerged when the distinction between public and private enterprise was cloudy. They were typically constructed and operated by private corporations. Although state and local aid was sometimes crucial in the early stages of a project, railroads secured the bulk of their capital from private investors.[64] Organization of railroads was motivated in part by the hope of pecuniary gain. By the 1850s certain railroads were attracting a sizable amount of European investment.[65] Even where state governments purchased stock and became part owners, the states generally deferred to private decision making. States were reluctant to vote their stock in ways that intruded upon the administration of the private managers.[66]

Yet railroads were clearly not treated as ordinary private enterprises. The creation of railroads by special charter from the state legislature reinforced the notion that these corporations were expected to perform some duties of a public character. A number of these charters declared that railroads were to be regarded as common carriers, a status that had long entailed particular obligations.[67] Both individual railroad charters and general railroad incorporation acts contained regulatory features. Further, general railroad legislation often expressly spelled out the public aspect of the roads. The Pennsylvania act of 1845 provided that "upon the completion of any railroad . . . , the same shall be esteemed a public highway."[68] The New York act of 1850 authorized individuals to organize a rail corporation "for public use."[69] This view was embodied in state constitutions after the Civil War. The Illinois Constitution of 1870, for instance, proclaimed that railroads "are hereby declared public highways."

Courts also recognized the public dimension of railroading. Although railroad companies were private in form, courts repeatedly emphasized that railroads were carrying out the public function of improved transportation. As Chief Justice Shaw described one railroad in 1842, "it is manifest that the establishment of that great thoroughfare is regarded as a public work, established by public authority, intended for the public use and benefit, the use of which is secured to the whole community, and constitutes therefore, like a canal, turnpike or highway, a public easement." Shaw added that the property of the company "is in trust for the public" and must be used "in a particular manner, and for accomplishment of a well defined public object."[70] Other judges echoed this opinion. Thus, the Supreme Court declared in 1872: "That railroads, though constructed by private corporations and owned by them, are public highways, has been the doctrine of nearly all the courts ever since such conveniences for passage and transportation have had any existence."[71] Indeed, as discussed later in the chapter, courts routinely pointed to the public character of railroading as a basis for upholding municipal financing schemes and the delegation of eminent domain. It should be noted, however, that judicial pronouncements about the public nature of railroads usually appeared in decisions sustaining the unique privileges accorded the roads.

Antebellum railroad corporations, therefore, can best be understood as a sort of hybrid organization, combining both private and public features. Courts and commentators frequently characterized railroads as quasi-public enterprises, suggesting their dual nature. As one treatise explained, "railroads, by whomsoever constructed or owned or operated, are quasi public works."[72] But the characterization of railroads as quasi-public, however convenient, served to mask fundamentally different conceptions of railroads. Well before the Civil War, railroad spokesmen began to stress the essentially private nature of rail enterprise. In 1846 the *American Railroad Journal* maintained that "railroads are built by companies of individuals, with their own capital—and they are managed for the mutual benefit of those who *build* and those who *use* them."[73] Following the Civil War, companies put increased weight on the private aspects of railroading in the face of mounting state regulation. Courts therefore gradually developed an understanding of railroads as private property. In 1875, for example, the Supreme Court of North Carolina observed that a railroad company "is created also for private benefit, and in respect to those purposes it is a private corporation and its charter is a contract."[74] The implications of this stress on the private character of railroads would be worked out during the rate regulation debates of the late nineteenth century.

Railroads were a major force in shaping early corporation law. Because corporations were seen as a delegation of sovereign power to private individuals, state legislatures at first doled out charters to petitioners on an individual basis. As hostility to corporate organization dissipated and the popular clamor for railroads mounted, lawmakers granted railroad charters generously. In 1835 alone, for instance, Tennessee incorporated eight railroads.[75] Similarly, Ohio granted forty-seven rail charters between 1830 and 1850,[76] while South Carolina passed twenty-one acts of incorporation before 1850. Not to be outdone, the Illinois legislature incorporated fifty-five railroad companies in 1857.[77] Many of these lines, of course, were never built. But the profusion of rail charters shows the legislative receptivity to such enterprise.

As the volume of railroad petitions steadily increased, so did objections to the individual charter system. There were two basic concerns. First, the consideration of individual charter requests consumed a great deal of legislative time and proved inefficient. Second, the passage of special charters opened the door to favoritism. Existing companies could use their political clout to block the award of charters to possible rivals. Moreover, competing groups could in effect bargain with the legislature over the terms in their charters. Examination demonstrates that railroad charters in particular states tended to follow a pattern and to contain many common provisions, but there was room to secure concessions and special arrangements through the legislative process. Indeed, some special charters were tailored to meet particular circumstances.

Starting in the 1840s, states began to shift away from special charters and to enact general railroad laws. These measures reflected the premise that free entry to the industry was desirable. Under general railroad acts, the organization of a railroad corporation was made generally available without the need for an application to the legislature. This not only saved legislative time but ensured that all promoters were on an equal footing. Although the general railroad acts were modeled upon the earlier general incorporation laws, they were potentially more sweeping because all lines formed under these acts enjoyed the power of eminent domain.[78] Lawmakers would henceforth rely on competition and private economic ordering to determine where and when lines would be built. Courts had no difficulty in sustaining legislative authority to incorporate railroads by general act.[79]

Some jurisdictions did not accept open incorporation of railroads until after the Civil War. Only in 1873, following expiration of the Camden and Amboy monopoly, did New Jersey enact a general railroad law. Likewise, North Carolina resisted general incorporation of railroads until 1871, when the lease of the state-sponsored North Carolina Railroad marked a new era in the transportation policy of that state. Eventually, the unrestricted entry of new rail lines would be seen as problematic, but lawmakers of the mid–nineteenth century put their faith in private entrepreneurship.

Financial Aid to Railroads

Another set of legal issues emerged from widespread state and local government assistance to railroads. As discussed earlier, states for the most part relied on private enterprise to construct railroads. Yet even with far-reaching legal privileges, railroading was an expensive and speculative venture. Promoters often found it difficult to attract sufficient private capital, and a large number of railroad projects proved abortive. At the same time, governors and civil leaders voiced concern that their states and cities were falling behind other jurisdictions in the building of railroads.[80] Public subsidy for internal improvement projects was not a new policy. States had previously provided money for river navigation and turnpike companies, and made stock subscriptions in such enterprises. Consequently, the persistent pressure for public financial assistance to railroads to hasten the pace of construction built upon a widely shared commitment to improved transportation.

Reflecting this booster sentiment, a number of state constitutions adopted during the 1830s required the legislature to promote transportation projects.

The Tennessee Constitution of 1835 contained typical language: "A well-regulated system of internal improvement is calculated to develop the resources of the State, and promote the happiness and prosperity of her citizens; therefore, it ought to be encouraged by the general assembly." To meet this obligation and satisfy the public's clamor, states such as Illinois and Michigan appropriated funds for extensive programs of canal and rail building. These ambitious schemes, however, outstripped public resources and were impossible to implement.[81] Disillusionment soon set in. To compound matters, the panics of 1837 and 1839 left many states saddled with debt for which there was little to show. As a result, the public turned sharply against continued state aid for internal improvements. Starting with New York in 1846, states began to amend their constitutions to prohibit any pledge of state credit to private companies. The Michigan Constitution of 1850, for instance, barred the state from owning stock in any corporation and from being a party to any internal improvement projects. By the time of the Civil War, most northern states had constitutional provisions preventing state aid of internal improvements.[82]

In practice, however, these constitutional restrictions did not close the door on the use of public funds to assist rail construction. The willingness to help railroad companies financially waxed and waned, but popular enthusiasm revived upon the return of good times. Local governments, and those states not inhibited by constitutional provision, devised a variety of techniques to extend support to railroads. In Tennessee, for instance, the state lent its credit by guaranteeing the bonds issued by railroad companies into the 1850s.[83] Many jurisdictions, moreover, enacted laws authorizing local governments to use tax revenue or to borrow money in order to purchase stock in railroad companies. There was typically little opposition to such measures in state legislatures. In Ohio, for example, subscription to railroad stock was viewed as a question for localities to decide.[84] Once state constitutions banned state assistance, railroads turned to local government for support. Anxious to induce companies to build through their communities, cities and counties commonly issued bonds to finance rail construction. The railroad company typically received the bonds as payment for a stock subscription, and then negotiated the bonds to third parties in order to raise money for construction. Other localities endorsed bonds issued by the railroads, employed tax revenue to obtain stock, or made outright donations to railroad companies.

The city or county decision to subscribe to railroad stock was ordinarily ratified by public referendum. Although occasionally a community voted against extending aid, the referenda usually saw a decisive margin in favor of the subscription proposal. Thus, in 1852, Yelobusha County, Mississippi, backed a rail stock subscription by a 5-to-1 vote, while a year later the city of Milwaukee voted 746 to 16 to extend municipal credit to a local line.[85] These referenda underscore the broad extent of public support for the policy of assistance to railroads.

Nonetheless, individual taxpayers frequently sought to enjoin either the issuance of bonds or the collection of taxes to pay for such purchase. During the mid–nineteenth century, railroad financing litigation swamped both state and federal courts. Plaintiffs were typically owners of taxable property that would be assessed to raise the necessary funds for this purpose. Those challenging the constitutionality of financing legislation pressed several claims. One common contention was that the construction of a railroad was not a legitimate municipal or county purpose within the meaning of governing statutes. Another favored argument was that the financing schemes represented the use of the taxation power for private advantage.

In a line of decisions during the antebellum era, courts in every section of the country sustained legislation authorizing local governments to subscribe for railroad stock. The initial decision pointing in this direction was *Goddin v. Crump* (1837). At issue in this case was a subscription by the city of Richmond to stock in the James River and Kanawha Company. This corporation was chartered to develop a river-and-rail transportation system linking the Ohio and James Rivers. It was an ambitious venture that initially relied on state funding and private investment. These resources proved inadequate, however, and the Virginia legislature empowered the city to subscribe for shares. When the city raised taxes to cover the loans it had taken to pay for stock, an unhappy taxpayer sued Crump, the city tax collector, to enjoin the enforcement of the ordinance. This suit was grounded on the contention that the legislature could not constitutionally empower a city to use its funds outside municipal boundaries. Rejecting this argument, the Virginia Court of Appeals adopted a generous understanding of municipal authority: "It has been argued that corporate powers must be confined to the limits of the corporations. This I think a most imperfect test. . . . The interest of the corporation is the true test of the corporate character of the act."[86] Observing that improved river transportation would rebound to the benefit of the city, the court concluded that the majority of municipal residents were the best judge of whether the stock subscription was likely to advantage the city.

The *Goddin* case involved city investment in what was essentially a public project, but this decision marked an important step in the evolution of the municipal role in financing railroad construction. A direct precedent for local government financing of railroad projects by private corporations was

established in *City of Bridgeport v. Housatonic Railroad Company* (1843).
Anxious to promote a railroad line with a terminus in Bridgeport, the city
in 1837 subscribed to rail stock and issued bonds to raise the necessary capital. The Connecticut state legislature retroactively confirmed this transac-
tion. Stung by construction delays and unprofitable operations, the city
subsequently instituted a test case in the hope of repudiating the bonds.

The Connecticut Supreme Court of Errors delighted pro-railroad forces
by upholding the validity of the bonds. Emphasizing that cities had long
financed a variety of public improvements, the court declared:

> We know, that much of the commercial prosperity of our cities and other
> business communities, depends upon the extent and facilities of the inter-
> course with the interior country, as well as with distant and foreign
> places. To promote this intercourse, by constructing and improving
> roads, canals, bridges, harbours, wharves, etc., has been a very frequent
> object of the enterprise of the inhabitants of such communities; and
> American cities, in their corporate capacities, have frequently given aid to
> such improvements, without exciting alarm, or of being suspected of thus
> oppressing their citizens, or of invading unjustly any salutary principle
> of the social system.[87]

It was therefore an easy step to conclude that railroads were an appropriate
subject of municipal financing. The court next ruled that purchase of stock
for the purpose of encouraging improved transportation, as distinct from
holding stock for speculation, was a legitimate municipal function. Lastly,
the court pointed out that city taxpayers should not be allowed to evade their
financial obligations by inflicting loss on third persons who purchased bonds
and relied in good faith on the city's credit.

Perhaps the most important decision affirming the local financing of railroads was *Sharpless and Others v. Mayor of Philadelphia* (1853).[88] Certain
Philadelphia taxpayers brought suit to enjoin the mayor from subscribing to
the stock of two railroad companies and from paying for the stock by the
issuance of bonds. They complained that these subscriptions would add to
the municipal debt and lead to an increase of taxes. Noting that the city was
authorized by the state legislature to subscribe for railroad stock, the mayor
argued that the trade and industry of Philadelphia would be strengthened by
advantageous rail connections. The case turned upon the constitutionality
of legislation empowering municipal corporations to purchase stock in railroad companies.

Although the Supreme Court of Pennsylvania divided 3 to 2 and each
judge delivered a separate opinion, Chief Justice Jeremiah S. Black ex-

pounded the court's reasoning most fully. Characterizing this issue as "the most important cause that has ever been in the court since the formation of the government," he revealingly sketched the broad policy implications of the outcome. Black pointed out:

> The fate of many most important public improvements hangs on our decision. If all municipal subscriptions are void, railroads, which are necessary to give the state those advantages to which everything else entitles her, must stand unfinished for years to come, and large sums, already expended on them, must be lost.[89]

In addition to these practical considerations, Chief Justice Black observed that a large number of the bonds had passed into the hands of innocent third parties. A declaration that the bonds were invalid, he continued, would have a devastating impact on the city's credit. As Black explained:

> Besides the deadly blow it would give to our improvements, and the disastrous effect of it on the private fortunes of many honest men, at home and abroad, it would seriously wound the credit and character of the state, and do much to lessen the influence of our institutions on the public mind of the world.

Yet in Black's mind, a decision upholding the financing system had equally unattractive consequences. He pictured dangerous speculations encouraged by individuals seeking personal gain from the issuance of municipal bonds. Black issued a dire warning:

> Under these circumstances it is easy to see where the ultra-enterprising spirit will end. It has carried the state to the verge of financial ruin; it has produced revulsions of trade and currency in every commercial country; it is tending now, and here, to the bankruptcy of cities and counties. In England, no investments have been more disastrous than railway stocks, unless those of the South Sea bubble be an exception. In this country they have not generally been profitable. The dividends of the largest works in the neighboring states, north and south of us, have disappointed the stockholders. Not one of the completed railroads in this state has uniformly paid interest on its cost. If only a few of the roads projected in Pennsylvania should be as unfortunate as all the finished ones, such a burden would be imposed on certain parts of the state as the industry of no people has ever endured without being crushed. Still, this plan of improving the country, if unchecked by this Court, will probably go on until it results in some startling calamity, to rouse the masses of the people.[90]

Chief Justice Black cautioned, however, that these policy issues did not resolve the constitutional challenge to the statute.

Reaching the merits of the case, Black concluded that the legislature could lawfully authorize municipal corporations to subscribe to the stock of railroad companies. He rejected the contention that the law amounted to a taking of private property for either public or private use. Black asserted that a "railroad is a public highway for the public benefit." The chief justice insisted that it was a duty of the state to stimulate commerce. In carrying out this duty, a state was free to make improvements directly at public expense or to assign such an undertaking to private corporations. Accordingly, the legislature could authorize taxation for a public work even if it was being carried out under the direction of a corporation. Nor was Black impressed with the argument that the city could only aid the construction of public works located within the locality. He pointed out that the economic interest of the city did not depend on the location of the railroad but on commercial ties created with other communities. In any event, the chief justice stressed that the elected officials of Philadelphia must assess the municipal interests in such railroad projects.

By the end of the antebellum period, the accumulated mass of judicial decisions established the principle that cities and counties could, by legislative enactment, be empowered to subscribe for railroad stock and to issue negotiable bonds in payment.[91] The federal courts raised no objection to such financial arrangements, and indeed provided a forum for the enforcement of bonded indebtedness. The Supreme Court rebuffed various challenges to the validity of local government assistance, based on irregularity in the issuance of bonds, and adhered to the judgment of state courts that the financing legislation was constitutional. Anticipating a recurrent theme in subsequent litigation, the Supreme Court in 1860 expressed sympathy for the position of good faith bondholders. "It would be inequitable," Justice James M. Wayne stated, "if the city could repudiate them [bonds] at all, and more especially, if that were allowed to be done upon the ground of any fault in the corporation in their issue."[92] In *Loan Association v. Topeka* (1874), the Supreme Court observed that this question of legislative power "has been thoroughly discussed" by the state courts and that "a decided preponderance of authority is to be found" sustaining the right of legislatures to confer the power of stock subscription on local government.[93] Late-nineteenth-century treatises on railroad law regarded this matter as settled.[94]

Encouraged by this supportive judicial attitude, antebellum state legislators enacted hundreds of authorizations for city and county aid to rail companies. The actual amount of public financial contribution to railroads remains a topic of debate among historians, and some have stressed the decisive role of private capital.[95] It is not the purpose of this volume to address that debate. Unquestionably, local governments incurred sizable indebtedness for railroad construction. The city of Baltimore, for instance, invested heavily in the stock of the Baltimore and Ohio Railroad.[96] One authority has estimated that before the Civil War, local governments spent more than $125 million on internal improvements, the largest share of which went for rail projects.[97] Given the stringent limitations on state participation in internal improvements and the lack of a national program, local authorities assumed the primary responsibility for subsidizing railroads. It has been calculated that local aid to railroads exceeded the amount of state assistance, and that by 1870 localities had provided one-fifth of rail construction costs.[98] Cities and counties in western states, such as Wisconsin and Iowa, were especially generous in support of railroads.

There were, to be sure, dissenting voices who questioned both the wisdom and the constitutionality of local government aid to railroad companies. Rebuffed by the courts, opponents of the local investment policy pushed for constitutional amendments to curtail the practice. A number of states adopted such prohibitions. The Ohio Constitution of 1851 not only barred state financial aid but also declared that the legislature could not authorize localities to become stockholders or loan credit to corporations. A similar amendment was added to the Pennsylvania Constitution in 1857. Such language in effect overturned court decisions upholding local government aid schemes. Thereafter, the growth of railroads in these jurisdictions was achieved solely with private capital.

Yet amendments of this character posed additional legal questions. At issue in *Cass v. Dillon* (1853) was the effect of Ohio's 1851 Constitution on an earlier railroad stock subscription by a county. The county contended that its authority to make the subscription and levy the necessary tax was abrogated by the new state constitution. The Supreme Court of Ohio, however, ruled that the constitutional provision was prospective and only banned future subscriptions. It expressed concern that to cut off already authorized subscriptions would cripple incomplete lines. At the same time, a constitutional prohibition could not permanently smother railroad sentiment. In 1872, for instance, Ohio lawmakers authorized local governments to build part of a projected rail line in the name of the locality, and then to lease or sell the enterprise to a private company. The manifest purpose of this act was to evade the constitutional ban and permit localities to aid railroads. In *Taylor v. Commissioners of Ross County* (1872) the Supreme Court of Ohio voided the measure as an attempt to indirectly use tax funds to assist railroads.

In addition to state constitutional provisions, a few state courts denied that railroads were public projects eligible for tax-supported funding. Iowa courts followed a checkered course with respect to local government aid to railroads.[99] Although the Iowa constitution of 1846 forbade the state from becoming a stockholder and placed limits on state indebtedness, the state supreme court in *Dubuque County v. Dubuque and Pacific Railroad Company* (1853) affirmed the authority of counties to issue bonds for railroads. The court reasoned that a statute providing for the building of "any roads" encompassed rail lines. In dissent, Judge John F. Kinney argued that a railroad was not a public highway because "it is owned by private individuals, and is in all respects private property." He expressed concern that "in these times of feverish excitement" and "clamor for public improvements" Iowa counties would soon be heavily indebted for railroad purposes.[100]

During the early 1850s many Iowa counties voted bond aid for railroad projects. Amid disappointment over slow construction progress and allegations of fraud, however, public sentiment for bond propositions gradually cooled. Reflecting this change in attitude, the Iowa Supreme Court in *State v. County of Wapello* (1862) overruled *Dubuque County* and held that the legislature had no power to authorize localities to subscribe for railroad stock. The court in effect ruled that the legislature could not bestow on local governments power to acquire stock in a railroad company that the state did not possess under the constitution. The upshot of this decision was to invalidate county bonds in the hands of bona fide investors. Mindful that the ruling could work an injustice, the court fancifully concluded:

> Nevertheless, we are not insensible that in doing so, at this late day, we are liable to expose ourselves and our people to the charge of insincerity and bad faith, and perhaps that which is still worse, inflict a great wrong upon innocent creditors and bondholders—consequences which we would most gladly have avoided, if we could have done so, and been true to the obligations of conscience and principle. Yet it is one of those unfortunate misadventures which sometimes will happen in the best governed and best intentioned communities.
>
> We know, however, that there is such a thing as a moral sense and a public faith which may be successfully appealed to, when the law is impotent to afford relief. These sentiments, we cannot but believe, still reside in the hearts and consciences of our people, and may be involved to save themselves and their state from seeming bad faith.[101]

Not content with expressions of sympathy, a group of bondholders carried the issue of Iowa railroad financing to the Supreme Court. In the famous case of *Gelpcke v. City of Dubuque* (1864), the Supreme Court ruled that the Iowa courts could not divest the contractual rights of bondholders by a retroactive change in the law.[102] The justices maintained that the bonds were valid when issued, and that no change in judicial decision could impair the obligation to pay. To be sure, the Supreme Court did not question application of Iowa's changed interpretation to future bond issues. But *Gelpcke* made clear that the Supreme Court looked with disfavor upon attempts to repudiate local government debt incurred to aid railroads. Over the ensuing quarter century the Supreme Court heard more than three hundred railroad financing cases, and invariably upheld the validity of local bonds.

Despite Iowa's sour experience in the 1850s and the constitutional barrier to the further issuance of local bonds for railroad purpose, zeal for rail construction reappeared after the Civil War. In 1868 the Iowa legislature sought to circumvent the state supreme court by authorizing local government units to levy taxes and make a gift of the revenue to a railroad company. A number of localities promptly voted for such tax aid. The Iowa Supreme Court in *Hanson v. Vernon* (1869) struck down the tax aid statute on grounds that the legislature's power to tax must be exercised for a public purpose. It asserted that railroads were private corporations organized for profit, and that their activities could not legitimately be promoted by taxation even if the public secured some consequential benefit. Undeterred, the legislature immediately enacted another tax aid measure. This time the state supreme court reversed position and sustained the scheme.[103] In short, neither Iowa's constitution makers nor judges could successfully check the popular desire to hasten rail construction through local government financial assistance.

Local involvement in railroad expansion exploded following the Civil War. Voicing a common sentiment, Governor John W. Geary of Pennsylvania proclaimed in 1867: "All public works, among these a liberal and properly restricted general railroad system, . . . should receive the fostering care and most liberal aid of the government."[104] Between 1866 and 1873, state legislatures passed more than eight hundred statutes empowering local governments to assist railroads.[105] Communities in California now joined in this renewed fervor to subscribe for railroad stock.

Michigan was no exception to this pattern of post–Civil War rail subsidy. In addition to a number of special acts, the general railroad aid law of 1869 authorized local governments to help railroads through stock subscriptions or direct donations.[106] This set the stage for *People v. Salem* (1870), the most significant case to reject municipal assistance to railroads. At issue in *Salem* was an application by a railroad company for a writ of mandamus to compel Salem Township to execute and issue bonds pledged for rail construction. Judge Thomas M. Cooley of the Michigan Supreme Court, a leading constitutional theorist of the Gilded Age, insisted that taxation must be imposed solely for a public purpose. He determined that railroads were private enterprises organized to earn profits and that public benefit was incidental. He then struck down an 1864 Michigan act authorizing several townships to grant railroad aid. Cooley sought to draw a line between private rights and legitimate governmental functions. His larger concern was the tendency of those who controlled government to use its powers for their own benefit. By invoking the public purpose doctrine with respect to taxation, Cooley hoped to forestall continued public subsidy of private corporations. This was a manifestation of Cooley's well-known hostility to class legislation, laws that benefited one group in society at the expense of others.[107]

Although the Supreme Court of Wisconsin reached a similar result,[108] Cooley's opinion in *Salem* did not attract broad support elsewhere. Timing was crucial. Cooley's effort to rely on the public purpose doctrine to halt aid to railroads was a case of too little, too late. Most jurisdictions had already sustained these laws, and at this point judicial invalidation of municipal bonds threatened to destroy public credit.[109] Not surprisingly, most state courts declined to follow Cooley's lead. Since diversity of citizenship was often present, many bond cases were brought in federal court. The Supreme Court in *Township of Pine Grove v. Talcott* (1873) also rejected *Salem* and permitted enforcement of Michigan railroad bonds in federal court. After noting the importance and public character of railroads, the Court took the position that the validity of commercial securities was as a matter of general jurisprudence not state law.

Despite the modest impact of *Salem* on the immediate issue of railroad aid, the decision had some lasting significance. It did stop local government assistance to railroads in Michigan. Future rail growth in that state was accomplished entirely by private capital. The public purpose doctrine, if generally not used to limit railroad aid, was frequently invoked to strike down grants of public revenue to other types of private business.[110] Revulsion against the perceived excesses of railroad subsidy schemes was a key ingredient in the Supreme Court's endorsement of the public purpose doctrine as a limitation on the tax power in *Loan Association v. Topeka* (1874). Further, *Salem* was a vital step in the reconceptualization of railroad companies as primarily private enterprise.

The panic of 1873 helped to galvanize opposition to the local subsidy system. Amid economic hard times and keen disappointment over incomplete lines and rail bankruptcies, public enthusiasm for municipal bonding waned sharply. A number of states, such as New York, Illinois, and Missouri, amended their constitutions to prevent localities from giving property, subscribing to stock, or extending credit to private corporations. This development marked the effective end of direct public financial support for railroads in most jurisdictions.[111] Nonetheless, the policy of local assistance to encourage rail construction persisted in some far western states into the 1880s.

Several lessons can be derived from this history of extensive local government aid to railroads. First, antebellum courts were disinclined to second-guess legislative policy with respect to railroad financing. Judges placed a stamp of approval on various schemes to stimulate construction of a rail network, but played a relatively passive role in the formulation of policy. Indeed, as indicated in *Sharpless*, courts commonly refused to consider the desirability of particular railroad projects. Of course, there is no doubt that many judges shared the prevailing sentiment in favor of a railroad system. But legislators, not courts, determined the range of promotional activities. Not until public backing for railroad financing schemes abated was it possible to close the door on this practice.

Second, the courts were often presented in effect with a fait accompli. Municipal or county stock subscriptions had typically been made and bonds issued before litigation reached the appellate level. There was no easy way to restore the status quo, even if the judges had been so inclined. A decision to strike down governmental financing would have benefited local taxpayers at the expense of those persons who purchased bonds in due course. The fundamental inequity of allowing a local government unit to repudiate its own obligations, notwithstanding ratification at public referendum, was evident to state and federal courts. Hence, courts seemingly adopted the position that subscription to railroad stock by local government was questionable, but disregard for contractual obligations was simply unacceptable.

Third, despite occasional disillusionment during periods of economic crisis, dominant public opinion was eager for local government to foster better transportation. It is neither accurate nor helpful to picture localities as helpless victims of railroad machinations. Rather, as Lawrence M. Friedman has observed, "the great bulk of farmer-settlers had a desperate hunger for transport" and consequently "the subsidies were popular."[112] This was demonstrated by the repeated one-sided votes at local referenda in favor of issuing railroad bonds. Periodic worry about mounting public debt was dispelled by the promise of growth and prosperity. The widespread popular clamor for rail financing was underscored by the fact that in at least two states, Ohio and Wisconsin, individuals mortgaged their land to subscribe for stock in railroad companies. The experience in Wisconsin, where farmers purchased railroad stock in exchange for mortgages on their farms, was particularly dire. During the early 1850s, nearly six thousand farmers subscribed for railroad stock. The railroads offered the mortgages as security for the sale of bonds in eastern capital markets. The panic of 1857 caused massive railroad default and rendered the stock worthless. Wisconsin farmers faced foreclosure at the hands of bondholders. The Supreme Court of Wisconsin upheld the validity of the obligations and struck down a series of statutes designed to prevent foreclosure. Wielding the contract clause and treating the bondholders as bona fide purchasers, the Wisconsin court in effect recognized the need to protect investment capital in an undeveloped region.[113]

Lastly, the pattern of pervasive local financing of railroads calls into question the thesis that antebellum lawmakers preferred to subsidize economic development through changes in legal rules rather than by direct financial outlay. In fact, both states and localities were prepared to amass considerable debt to encourage rail enterprise. No doubt many legislators hoped that dividends on railroad stock would avoid the need for taxation to retire this debt. When that naïve expectation was dashed, however, the burden inevitably fell on the taxpayers.

Railroads in the South

The singular social and economic environment of the antebellum South caused lawmakers to adopt strongly interventionist policies toward railroad building. The root problem was the inadequate amount of private capital for development. "The financial burdensomeness of slaveholding . . . ," Ulrich Bonnell Phillips explained, "is of course largely responsible for the great difficulty experienced in raising stock subscriptions among the planters, and for the scantiness in the total railroad investment."[114] Not only did the capital-intensive nature of slavery diminish available local money, but northern and foreign investors were skeptical about the profitability of southern railroads. Hence, they were skittish about purchasing stock in southern lines. As sectional tension mounted, moreover, many political and business officials in the South were reluctant to have local railroads fall under the control of northern financial interests. It followed that reliance on private enterprise to bring about rapid development of railroads in the South was futile.

Yet the pressing need for improved transportation in the South could not be ignored. Southerners were already worried that their region was falling behind in terms of wealth and population. The *American Railroad Journal* put the issue succinctly in 1855: "The States must come to the aid of the roads, or remain without them."[115] So while northern states amended their constitutions to forbid state support for internal improvements, jurisdictions in the South pursued a different course. Contrary to their conservative and tight-fisted image, many southern state governments embraced a variety of far-reaching programs to promote railroads. Indeed, historians have estimated that as much as 55 percent of the expenditure on railroads in the South was provided by the public. It is particularly apt, therefore, to characterize southern railroading as a form of mixed enterprise.

Several southern states built railroads as publicly owned enterprises, in much the same manner as earlier state-sponsored canals. For instance, Georgia constructed the Western and Atlantic Railroad. Likewise, in several situations the Virginia Board of Public Works assumed the role of entrepreneur and built rail lines itself when private capital was unavailable.[116]

A more common pattern, however, was for state governments to funnel massive subsidies into private railroad corporations. Virginia, North Carolina, and Florida created boards of internal improvements to provide centralized direction for state transportation investments. Virginia appropriated more funds for railroad construction than any other southern state. Starting in 1832, the Board of Public Works was authorized to borrow funds on state credit to purchase railroad stock. State financial support for rail projects grew steadily over the next two decades. In short order Virginia was furnishing a majority of the capital for a number of railroad companies, often purchasing three-fifths of the stock. For all its financial backing, however, the board never engaged in planning for improved transportation, and relied on private individuals to initiate projects.[117]

North Carolina also launched a major program of railroad construction.[118] After a halting start and a disappointing experience with state endorsement of railroad company bonds, lawmakers came to the realization that private enterprise was unlikely to produce a satisfactory rail system. In 1849 the legislature incorporated the North Carolina Railroad, under a plan whereby the state would purchase two-thirds of the stock once the balance was subscribed by private interests.[119] The state system was expanded in 1855, when the legislature chartered two additional railroads with a provision for two-thirds state ownership. North Carolina remained an active investor in rail enterprise until after the Civil War.

Such heavy state involvement with railroads was not without problems. The political necessity to satisfy a multiplicity of local interests led to battles over routes and made public funding uncertain and irrational. In practice, state financial support exacerbated the localism endemic to the South before the twentieth century. Historians have debated the extent to which southern states were able to overcome the deficit of private capital through public support of railroad construction. In contrast to the North, where private managers had begun to supplant local control and to fashion an integrated rail system, state and local jealousy hampered the growth of an efficient rail network in the South. But states of the antebellum South did more than any other region to experiment with publicly owned railroads, and to demonstrate the advantages and pitfalls of such a policy.[120]

In addition to direct state investment, southern lawmakers relied on a variety of other capital-raising techniques. Grants of monopoly status and authorization of municipal stock subscriptions tracked such policies elsewhere. Localities from Virginia to Alabama supplemented state aid by purchasing stock in railroad companies. To stimulate private investment, southern legislators also occasionally gave banking privileges to railroad companies. The hope was that the right to engage in banking would heighten interest in railroad shares. This scheme was first utilized in some northern states to encourage canal building, but was pursued more aggressively in the South. A number of jurisdictions, such as South Carolina and Mississippi, experimented with railroad banks. The most notable examples of this policy came in Georgia, where two railroads were permitted to establish banks. In Georgia, at least, the link between banking and railroading proved successful and helped to finance rail expansion.[121]

Tax Exemption

Despite a willingness by state and local governments to underwrite part of the cost of railroad building, lawmakers everywhere preferred to harness private capital. To this end, legislatures were generous in granting tax exemptions to railroad companies. Fearful that the threat of taxation would discourage private investment in speculative rail ventures, lawmakers in a number of jurisdictions saw exemption from various taxes as a means of encouraging development. The pattern was established early. The 1827 charter of the Baltimore and Ohio Railroad provided that the company's capital stock should be exempt from tax.[122] Several Rhode Island charters granted during the 1830s declared that "the property and stock of this corporation shall be exempted from every species of taxation" for twelve years after the railroad was opened. Similarly, the charter of the New Jersey Railroad provided that no taxes would be levied until five years following completion.[123]

Tax exempt status for railroads was thus common. Nearly every railroad charter issued by South Carolina before the Civil War, for instance, contained such a provision. The typical act specified a term of years from the date of completion as the duration of the exemption. Some charters permitted the state to levy taxes only if annual profits of the railroad exceeded a set amount. Often both the capital stock and the property of the railroad company were immune from taxation. There were, however, many variations and generalization is difficult. Some exemptions contained no fixed duration, and apparently were intended to be perpetual.[124] The scope of the immunity also posed vexing questions.

Grants of tax exempt status were used most aggressively during the formative era of rail development, but the policy was continued in some jurisdictions well after the Civil War. Sparsely settled western states saw immunity from taxation as an inducement for eastern capital. The New Mexico general railroad act of 1878 sweepingly declared: "To aid and encourage the construction of railroads in this Territory, all the property of every kind and description of every corporation formed under this act shall be exempt from taxation of every kind and description" for six years after completion of its line.[125]

Although widely granted, tax exemption provisions became controversial in time. Detractors argued that such immunities constituted favoritism and unfairly burdened other taxpayers. They asserted that the legislature could not relinquish the sovereign authority of taxation. Consequently, the validity and extent of railroad tax exemptions was challenged in several cases.

In *Mayor and City Council of Baltimore v. Baltimore and Ohio Railroad Company* (1848), the city sought to levy taxes on the real and personal property, as well as the capital stock, of the railroad. At issue was the language in the charter exempting the capital shares of the company from the imposition of any tax. Seeking to ascertain legislative intent, the Maryland Court of Appeals recounted the history of the Baltimore and Ohio:

> The Legislature and the people of Maryland regarded the completion of the work as a great State object, tending eminently to promote the future wealth and prosperity of Maryland, and particularly of the City of Baltimore, and to contribute to the permanence of the Union of the United States. They also were duly sensible that this gigantic and patriotic undertaking could not be accomplished but at great expense and hazard of pecuniary loss to its undertakers. As an encouragement to the enterprise they were willing to confer on it every immunity, privilege and exemption which could reasonably be required, and tend to its completion.

The court added that the legislative plan "was to confer a certain substantial, not a nominal benefit, on the stockholders, and to induce capitalists to risk their money in a novel and hazardous enterprise." Noting that the legislature could limit its sovereign authority to tax by express language, the

court expansively held (1) the exemption in the charter covered city as well
as state taxes, and (2) the exemption applied to the property of the company
that gave value to the capital stock.[126]

Similarly, the Supreme Court of Illinois upheld a provision in the 1851
charter of the Illinois Central Railroad limiting the company's tax liability.
Under the charter, the railroad was exempt from taxes for six years, the estimated period of construction. Thereafter, the company was obligated to pay
7 percent of its gross income to the state in lieu of state and local taxes. In
1853 the county of McLean assessed a property tax on the railroad. Abraham Lincoln, arguing on behalf of the Illinois Central, maintained that the
legislature had the constitutional power either to grant tax immunities or to
commute the tax rate for a fixed sum. The Supreme Court of Illinois, in *Illinois Central Railroad Company v. County of McLean* (1855), adopted Lincoln's analysis. It stressed broad legislative power over taxation and pointed
out that lawmakers possessed authority to grant tax concessions for the public benefit.[127] These decisions were particularly important because they
restrained the imposition of local taxes that, in the aggregate, would place a
heavy financial burden on rail enterprise.

When courts generally sustained and generously construed railroad tax
immunities,[128] they were acting to effectuate legislative policy to encourage
rail construction by an indirect subsidy. More remarkable was the position
adopted in a few states that railroads were exempt from taxes because they
were public works, like highways or canals. The leading case for this proposition was *Inhabitants of Worcester v. Western Rail Road Corporation*
(1842), decided in Massachusetts by Chief Justice Shaw. The town of
Worcester attempted to tax the local real estate and buildings of the railroad. Shaw described the railroad as "a great public work, established by
public authority, intended for the public use and benefit." From this premise he reasoned that the company was necessarily exempt from tax on buildings incident to its transportation business. Here Shaw inferred a tax
immunity in the absence of any express language in the charter by stressing
the public dimension of railroading. On the other hand, nothing in the decision intimated that the legislature was not free to levy future taxes. Most
jurisdictions denied this doctrine of implied exemption and required an
express grant of immunity.[129]

All observers agreed that the taxing power was one of the most essential
attributes of sovereignty. For this reason courts usually insisted that any surrender of the authority to tax had to be evidenced by an explicit grant, and
doubtful wording was interpreted in favor of continued governmental power.

But Pennsylvania went a step further. As stated earlier, in the *Mott* case the Supreme Court of Pennsylvania ruled that the legislature could not grant a tax exemption binding on future legislatures. Although this reasoning was echoed in a number of decisions in other jurisdictions,[130] it ran afoul of the Supreme Court's position that grants of tax exemption were contracts within the shelter of the contract clause.[131] States were therefore not at liberty to impose taxes in violation of express immunities. As a result, the tax exempt status of certain railroads persisted well into the twentieth century. Long after the formative era of railroad building, courts wrestled with the interpretation and scope of tax exemptions.

Eminent Domain and the Acquisition of Land

In addition to monopoly status, financial contributions, and tax exemptions, state governments invariably granted railroads the authority to exercise eminent domain. This is one of the most intrusive powers of government because it entails taking property from individuals against their will, albeit upon payment of compensation. Originally spelled out in individual railroad charters, the right of eminent domain to acquire land for the construction of rail lines was typically conferred on all carriers by the general railroad laws.[132] Some acts extended this right to acquire timber, stone, or gravel from adjacent lands for use as building materials.[133] The states had previously delegated eminent domain to canal companies and private industrial interests, but railroads made use of this power on an expanded scale because they required sizable amounts of land for rights-of-way. Lawmakers correctly recognized that railroads must be constructed upon a feasible route and could not detour around the land of persons who refused to sell upon reasonable terms.

The delegation of eminent domain power to railroads compelled courts to give systematic attention to the taking of private property for government-sponsored projects and hastened the development of takings jurisprudence. The large-scale acquisition of land by railroads set the stage for a collision between two classes of property owners, entrepreneurs and landholders. Implicit in the railroad cases were a number of basic issues in takings law. Foremost among these was the question of what constitutes "public use" for which property may constitutionally be taken.

State and federal courts repeatedly sustained acts authorizing railroads to take private property against constitutional challenge.[134] Reluctant to impede the progress of railroading, courts across the country brushed aside arguments that property was being taken for private gain, not public use. Instead, they reasoned that private railroad corporations were carrying out a public purpose by improving transportation. It was deemed immaterial that legislators sought to effectuate this public benefit through a profit-seeking corporate body that charged for its services. Courts stressed that legislators had broad latitude to decide how best to secure improved modes of travel. They further maintained that the notion of public use was not synonymous with ownership by the public. In 1837 the Supreme Court of North Carolina summarized the prevailing position:

> An immense and beneficial revolution has been brought about in modern times, by engaging individual enterprise, industry, and economy, in the execution of public works of internal improvement . . . [the land] is taken to be immediately and directly applied to an established public use, under the control and direction of the public authorities, with only such incidental private interests, as the legislature has thought proper to admit, as the means of effecting the work and insuring a long preservation of it for the public use.[135]

Accepting the notion that railroads were simply another form of public highway, courts upheld the delegation of eminent domain by stressing the public responsibilities of railroad companies. This line of analysis was similar to the reasoning employed to validate public financial aid to railroad companies. Legislators sometimes facilitated this outcome by enacting laws that declared that land taken by railroads was deemed to be for public use.[136]

At least one prominent jurist felt that this conclusion was disingenuous. Writing in *Salem,* Thomas Cooley termed the exercise of eminent domain by railroads "a convenient fiction, which treats a corporation managing its own property for its own profit, as merely a public convenience and agency." He suggested that only "an overriding public necessity" could have induced courts to permit railroads to use eminent domain.[137] But by 1870, even Cooley was disinclined to reopen the question. As Cooley feared, the judicial response to the railroad cases did much to weaken the public use requirement as a restraint on the exercise of eminent domain.

Notwithstanding utilitarian considerations and judicial endorsement, legislatures in some jurisdictions found bothersome the open-ended conferral of eminent domain upon railroad companies. A few states even made abortive attempts to curb the condemnation of land for rail construction. For example, in 1840 the New Hampshire legislature banned the use of eminent domain by new railroads and declared that such enterprises could not acquire land without the consent of the owner. When this step contributed to a halt in railroad building in the state, however, the lawmakers relented. Under an 1844 act, carriers were authorized to petition the board of railroad commissioners for a determination that the proposed route would serve the public interest. If the board concurred, eminent domain could be employed to complete the line.[138] Illinois also experimented with a qualified delegation of eminent domain. Railroads incorporated under the Illinois general railroad act of 1849 needed legislative sanction before they could exercise eminent domain. The purpose of this limitation, as explained by the Supreme Court of Illinois, was for the legislature "to reserve that power until it could judge for itself whether the proposed road would be of sufficient public utility to justify the use of this high prerogative.[139] This restraint, however, proved impracticable and was repealed in 1872.

Inseparable from the exercise of eminent domain by railroads was the acquisition of land by other means. The interest that historians have shown in issues relating to condemnation should not obscure the fact that railroads obtained much of their land for depots and rights-of-way through gifts, voluntary purchase, and prescription.

Both special charters and general laws expressly contemplated that railroads would receive gifts of land. Early New York charters, for example, provided that the companies could take "all such voluntary grants and donations of land and real estate, for the purpose of said road, as shall be made to the said corporation." The Illinois general railroad act of 1849 declared that carriers could receive land "by voluntary grants and donations."[140] Railroads were not slow to take advantage of this opportunity. Given the widespread enthusiasm for rail construction, many individuals willingly gave land to advance such projects. As Harry N. Scheiber has written, "we know with certainty that in other instances individual landowners made generous gifts of property for rights of way."[141] Most of the right-of-way of the Baltimore and Ohio Railroad from Baltimore to the Potomac River, for example, was donated. The same carrier also obtained a good deal of land in Virginia gratuitously.[142] Likewise, rights-of-way were frequently given to Ohio railroads.[143] Landowners in Michigan donated much of the Central Railroad's right-of-way.[144] In 1851 the North Carolina Railroad reported that land for its projected line had been freely given.[145]

Cities and state governments soon followed suit. Starting in the 1830s, a series of South Carolina acts vested unclaimed state lands contiguous to the route in the railroads. An 1853 Iowa statute allowed railroads to pass over any lands owned by the state without payment.[146] Such provisions were a harbinger of extensive state land grants to subsidize rail expansion.

In addition to donations, state law invariably empowered railroads to purchase and hold land.[147] The acts usually required the company to negotiate with owners to purchase the necessary real property. Only in the event that the parties could not agree as to the terms of purchase was the railroad authorized to resort to eminent domain. Courts insisted that an effort to reach agreement with landowners concerning payment for desired land was a prerequisite to an eminent domain proceeding. In *O'Hara and Darlington v. Pennsylvania Railroad* (1855), the company petitioned for the appointment of commissioners to ascertain the compensation for certain land. Objecting to confirmation of the commissioners' report, the landowner charged: "No effort was made by the said company at any time, to agree with [the owners] for compensation for the property entered upon and taken by them." The Supreme Court of Pennsylvania reversed a judgment based on the report, and held that proof of an effort to reach agreement must be made in order to justify the appointment of commissioners.[148]

Several factors discouraged casual reliance on eminent domain. There was always the risk of sizable awards. Moreover, the delays attendant upon eminent domain proceedings were significant in encouraging negotiated settlements.[149] One leading scholar of railroad law concluded: "Most railroad property is acquired by voluntary purchase. Condemnation proceedings are expensive and lengthy. . . . The law does not allow them to condemn until they have first endeavored to buy, and this endeavor is generally an honest one."[150] Much evidence supports this claim. The Baltimore and Ohio commonly purchased rights-of-way if it could not secure donations, and only used eminent domain when owners demanded exorbitant prices.[151] Land agents for the Western Railroad in Massachusetts likewise preferred to negotiate with landowners than turn to legal proceedings.[152] None of this is to deny that eminent domain was an important tool for the rail industry, but only to stress that its use must be viewed in perspective.

As with municipal financing, legislators, not judges, were largely responsible for determining eminent domain policy with respect to railroads. The fundamental decision to delegate eminent domain power to private railroad companies was generally seen as a matter of legislative policy. As one treatise writer explained, "the power of eminent domain is a political power vested in the legislative department, and, in the absence of constitutional restrictions, is to be exercised in its discretion, on such occasions and by such methods as it may see fit."[153] For the most part, the courts simply ratified a legislative judgment that the construction of rail lines by private entrepreneurs served the public interest. "Once eminent domain had been established as a legal doctrine in each state," Sarah H. Gordon pointed out, "the role of the courts consisted in adjusting claims rather than modifying or reversing the doctrine."[154] Judges, however, did play an important role in resolving issues that arose from the actual exercise of eminent domain by railroads. Foremost among these was the question of just compensation, a subject explored in Chapter Eight.

Consolidations and Allied Enterprises

The history of railroading has been characterized by a persistent tendency toward consolidation. Although merger activity has been primarily associated with the late nineteenth and twentieth centuries, the combination of small railroads into larger systems started well before the Civil War. Such mergers were often driven by the need to achieve an economy of scale and upgrade service. Consequently, local railroads gradually fell under the control of trunk lines.

The consolidation movement raised a number of legal issues. It was generally thought that railroads could combine only with legislative permission. This was grounded on the premise that corporate powers were limited to those spelled out in the charter of incorporation.[155] In fact, lawmakers commonly authorized the consolidation of railroad companies. Initially, this took the form of special legislation. The most important rail merger of the antebellum era occurred in 1853 with the formation of the New York Central Railroad. By an act passed that year, the New York legislature empowered a group of short-line railroads between Albany and Buffalo to unite, thus forming a single connection across upstate New York.[156] The decade of the 1850s saw some jurisdictions, such as Michigan and Kentucky, enact laws allowing combination by any railroads.[157] By the 1870s general railroad statutes routinely authorized such consolidation.[158] Despite periodic concerns about concentrated economic power, lawmakers at the state level made little concerted attempt to halt the inevitable rail mergers. Some states did, however, prohibit the consolidation of parallel or competing lines. The implications of such restrictions are considered in Chapter Three.

Aside from formal consolidation, railroads could form various other types of business alliances. One pattern was for one railroad to lease another. There was a division of authority as to whether a railroad could lease its property without legislative approval. Some states adhered to the view that there was no legal obstacle to such a course unless it was prohibited by law.

Yet there was also authority that a railroad could not lease its property absent legislative sanction. This conclusion rested on the notion that a railroad company held its franchise for the public good, and that a transfer of this privilege violated public policy.[159] In practice, however, state legislatures frequently authorized, or subsequently ratified, the lease of rail lines. In *Gratz v. Pennsylvania Railroad Company* (1862), for instance, the Supreme Court of Pennsylvania found that the legislature had empowered two companies to enter a lease arrangement. Moreover, states increasingly enacted general legislation allowing all railroads to lease and operate other lines. It should be noted that the lessee of a railroad was bound by the terms and conditions in the charter of the lessor.[160]

Still another device to unite lines was the purchase by a railroad of stock in another rail company. This action was highlighted as early as 1851, when the New York legislature authorized railroads to subscribe for stock in a Canadian line. A stockholder challenged the validity of the act in *White v. Syracuse and Utica Railroad Company* (1853). Brushing aside an argument based on impairment of contract, the New York Supreme Court pointed out that the Canadian railroad "will furnish additional facilities of travel to a large population, spread over an extensive tract of country, and will probably, and almost necessarily, increase the number of persons who will come to this state, and pass over the road of the defendant."[161] In short, the court emphasized that the purchase of stock was of potential benefit to both the general public and the railroad company. Within a few years several jurisdictions passed statutes allowing all railroads in the state to purchase stock in other lines.[162]

The policy implications of this trend to consolidate, whether by merger, lease, or acquisition of stock, became more apparent by the end of the nineteenth century. Before the 1880s, however, lawmakers placed few barriers in the path of rail combinations.

Besides consolidation with other lines, early railroads acquired property interests in other facilities and types of transportation ancillary to rail traffic. Charter grants in the 1830s often empowered railroads to construct storehouses and wharves, and to operate steamboats.[163] The latter right was especially vital because it permitted companies to link rail and waterborne travel, and to provide through connections. In time, the right to operate affiliated transportation facilities would become commonplace.[164] The Wisconsin general railroad act of 1872 typically declared: "It shall be lawful for such companies to build, construct and run as part of their corporate property, such number of steamboats or vessels as they may deem necessary."[165] Lawmakers thus contemplated that railroads might furnish an integrated scheme of transportation.

New Realities and New Laws

"People will have railroads," the *American Railroad Journal* editorialized in 1850.[166] This pithy comment tells us much about the formulation of early railroad law. Responding to the broad public enthusiasm for improved transportation, legislators scrambled to enact laws that promoted railroad development. Corporate charters and general acts were crafted to achieve this end. Legislators played the central role in shaping the legal environment of railroading and in allocating public resources to underwrite rail enterprise. Railroading, then, was a prime example of the affirmative use of law to bring about, in Willard Hurst's famous phrase, the release of individual creative energy.[167]

With few exceptions, courts endorsed the legislative program of fostering railroads through generous charter provisions, local government financial assistance, and open competition with older modes of transportation. Even the most forceful action by the judiciary—the protection of investors against repudiation of bonded indebtedness incurred to aid railroads—upheld the legislative policy of capital formation in the face of vacillating local opinion.

Until about 1870 railroad law was largely promotive in character. But legislators and judges were not unmindful of the potentially harmful dimensions of railroading on individuals and communities. As discussed in later chapters, from the initial charters lawmakers sought to regulate aspects of railroading. After 1870, moreover, legislators would increasingly turn their attention to controlling the behavior of the iron horse.

2

Civil War and Federal Land Grants

Many areas of American public life were profoundly shaped by the Civil War, and the law of railroading was no exception. "As far as our railroads are concerned," the *American Railroad Journal* lamented in December of 1860, "the effect of the present political agitations is simply disastrous, and to a degree that can hardly be estimated."[1] Although partially accurate, particularly with respect to southern railroads, the impact of the Civil War was more complex than this comment suggests. The outbreak of hostilities in 1861 saw both sides seeking to harness rail service for military needs, and imposing a measure of public control. At the same time the war provided a great impetus for enlarged involvement of the federal government in railroad expansion. Both of these developments set the stage for a host of legal issues.

The strategic use of railroads for military purposes during the Civil War has been examined by a number of historians and is not reviewed here.[2] Rather, our concern is how the conflict affected the legal status and governance of railroads. The legal issues relating to Civil War railroading had a lasting consequence, because they foreshadowed similar concerns during the world wars.

Railroads in the Confederacy

The inadequacy of southern railroads on the eve of the Civil War has been well documented.[3] Although new railroad track in the South grew markedly during the 1850s, the total mileage was only half of that in the states of the Union. Even worse, southerners had not developed trunk lines that served the region. They had instead generally built short, intrastate routes designed to transport staple crops from the interior to coastal ports. This parochial system was in large measure the result of heavy state government financial support. At a number of key points, moreover, railroads entering cities remained unconnected. Freight arriving at such important junctions as Chattanooga, Richmond, Charlotte, and Savannah had to be unloaded and hauled across town. Railroads in Florida were physically isolated, having no connection with other southern carriers. To complicate matters, southern lines were plagued with a number of different track gauges. This prevented the exchange of rolling stock between railroads. The upshot was confusion, delay, and expense in moving troops and military supplies.

Southern railroads also suffered in a number of other ways. Lines in the South were cheaply constructed and poorly equipped. There was an enormous disparity between the Confederacy and the Union in terms of skilled employees, engines, and rolling stock. Lacking sufficient steel mills and engine-building plants, the Southern states found it impossible to maintain track in sound condition or to replace destroyed or worn-out engines So acute was the rapid deterioration of Southern lines that officials feared a complete collapse of service as early as 1862.

Under the circumstances, efficient management of the South's railroads was essential for the Confederate cause. Yet, despite pledges of cooperation by railroad companies and the Herculean efforts of a few government officials, the Confederacy never formulated a coherent policy toward its railroads. A leading historian has aptly concluded that "the Confederates by no means made the best use of what they had."[4] Several factors help to explain this failure by Confederate leaders. It was widely believed at first that any war would be short, and hence there was little attention given to long-range planning. On a more fundamental level, Confederate rail policy was undermined by states' rights ideology, pervasive localism, and disinclination of the Confederate government to forcefully assert control over the railroads.

A glance at the faltering steps taken by the Confederacy and Southern state governments illustrates the extent of the problem. Consider the issue of railroad rates for Confederate military traffic. Stirred by patriotic fervor and contemplating a brief conflict, many railroad companies early in 1861 pledged free transportation for military personnel and materials.[5] Not surprisingly, this generous if unrealistic scheme broke down almost at once. From the outset some states did not rely on corporate patriotism to control rates. Alabama, for example, enacted a statute that promised exemption from all state and local taxes if railroads would agree to carry troops and munitions free of charge.[6] Going a step further, the Florida legislature mandated that railroads transport free the property and troops of the state or the Confederacy.[7] This legislation proved unworkable for the simple reason that railroads could not provide service without revenue.

Such corporate gestures and piecemeal laws fell woefully short of establishing a uniform rate for military traffic or furnishing an adequate return for the carriers. To remedy this situation, the Confederate Postmaster General, John H. Reagan, convened a meeting of rail executives in Montgomery, Alabama, in April 1861. At what proved to be the first of a series of similar conventions, railroad companies approved a plan to carry Confederate troops at two cents per mile and military freight at "half the regular local rates." Equally significant, the railroads were willing to accept payment in Confederate bonds or treasury notes. Since local charges varied considerably, the desired uniformity was not achieved.[8] Another convention, held in Chattanooga, Tennessee, in October, divided military traffic into four classes with uniform rates for each category. Under the stress of war and resulting inflation, this arrangement also fell apart in time. Some railroads successfully petitioned for higher rates. Other carriers unilaterally boosted charges on military freight to commercial levels. The last Confederate railroad convention, in April 1864, agreed upon a new schedule that substantially raised rates on military traffic.[9]

It is important to bear in mind that the Confederate government made no attempt to fix the charges for private traffic. Consequently, the rates for civilian passenger and freight services soared. The Confederate policy of negotiating rate schedules for military transportation, while far from perfect, worked reasonably well under the difficult circumstances. Government freight was carried at rates well below those charged private shippers. On the other hand, the failure to control private rates created a perverse incentive for railroads to favor nongovernment business. Although critics assailed the rapaciousness of railroad companies, it is only fair to emphasize that all parties were caught in an inflationary spiral.

A more pressing issue than railroad rates was the need to close gaps in the existing rail network. New trackage was imperative to link carriers and to expedite shipments. Since private capital was obviously scarce, the Confederate Congress authorized a number of loans to encourage speedy construction of additional track.[10] The most vital proposed connection was between Danville, Virginia, and Greensboro, North Carolina, for which Congress in 1862 approved a $1 million loan to a newly organized company.

This modest rail construction program by the central government sparked a sharp debate in the Confederate Congress. Pointing to a provision in the Constitution against spending "to promote or foster any branch of industry," opponents argued that the measure was unconstitutional. Confederate President Jefferson Davis, however, countered that the project could be justified as a military necessity, and this position carried the day.[11] Much of the opposition to the Virginia–North Carolina link, while couched in constitutional terms, reflected the fear of local economic interests that a new route would divert business.

A number of other rail projects also received Confederate loans. The most important of these was the completion of an unfinished line across central Alabama. The construction of the authorized lines was hampered by shortages of iron, machinery, and labor, as well as by uncooperative state officials and Union army advances. Nonetheless, some of the lines were completed and proved beneficial. State governments also aided the Confederate cause by making loans to railroad companies to complete routes.[12]

As this record indicates, intense localism plagued efforts to formulate a coherent rail policy for the Confederacy. This often found expression in legal barriers to the construction of through routes. The situation in Petersburg, Virginia, is instructive. Concerned about congestion and delay at that point, General Robert E. Lee early called for a connection between railroads entering that city. Yet Petersburg officials steadfastly resisted closing this gap, relying on a Virginia statute that banned rail building on city streets without the permission of municipal authorities. In June 1861 the Virginia state convention dispensed with the state law and approved construction of a temporary rail link. Even so, the convention sought to accommodate local concerns. It prohibited the transportation of private freight over the connection, and mandated removal after the war.[13] Despite these concessions, the Petersburg Railroad Company remained reluctant to build track in the city at corporate expense. A rail officer noted that "a great repugnance is felt by the citizens of Petersburg to any connection between the roads in question."[14] The firm grip of parochialism is manifest in the begrudging attitude of Petersburg officials in the face of wartime exigencies. Only with the direct supervision and financial backing of the Confederate government was the Petersburg gap closed. Petersburg officials, however, continued to protest. In December 1861 the city council adopted a resolution expressing its opposition to "a permanent connection" between Petersburg and Richmond.[15]

Although the Confederate construction program was a qualified success, the inability of the Confederate government to exercise effective control over the existing rail network contributed to military failure. President Davis never developed a systematic railroad policy, and was reluctant to interfere with the operations of private rail companies. State-owned lines proved especially troublesome. Because of its commitment to states' rights, the Confederate government found it awkward to override sometimes obstructionist state officials. Opposition to central governmental control of Southern railroads, then, had deep political and philosophical roots. Yet military necessity could not be entirely ignored. The result was a number of hesitant moves toward governmental supervision of the rail system.

The Confederate Congress initially shared the hands-off approach to railroad operations. An 1861 bill authorizing the president to regulate railroads and seize uncooperative lines died. The following year a more ambitious proposal to impose military control over rail operations failed in the Senate. By early 1863 Southern rail service had markedly deteriorated. Cooperation among railroad companies remained elusive. While professing support for the military effort, rail executives insisted upon corporate autonomy and put private interests first. For instance, most carriers refused to allow their rolling stock to run on the tracks of other lines for fear that the cars would not be returned.

As the importance of rail transportation to the war effort became increasingly evident, President Davis in January 1863 noted "the limited capacity of the railroads" and called for "the control of the roads under some general supervision."[16] In response, Congress enacted legislation giving the executive branch authority to requisition rail service, to impose through schedules, to seize any railroad refusing to comply with government orders, and to allocate rolling stock from one railroad to another. The act further provided that the government could remove the rails or machinery of any railroad in order to maintain other lines. Potentially sweeping, the law was sensitive to constitutional scruples in two respects. First, in a bow to states' rights, those railroads "exclusively owned" by any state were exempted from the seizure and rolling stock removal provisions. Second, where the government exercised its power to impress a railroad or to allocate rolling stock, the payment of just compensation was required.[17] Even during the wartime crisis lawmakers respected the deeply engrained constitutional norm that private property could not be taken without compensation.

Notwithstanding the promise of more efficient transportation, the Confederate government rarely invoked the new legislation. Perhaps Davis saw the act largely as a threat to secure cooperation. Perhaps he ultimately concluded that the private operators could manage the railroads more effectively than the harried government. Despite frequent disputes with local military authority, the day-to-day operations of the railroads therefore remained the responsibility of rail executives.

So the 1863 law did not halt the downward slide of Southern railroads.[18] To be sure, no legislation could overcome the fundamental defects of railroads in the South or arrest the inexorable collapse of their lines under wartime conditions. But the failure of the Confederate government to utilize the 1863 act cost the South any chance to ameliorate the shortcomings of its rail service. Consequently, localism and the private concerns of railroad companies continued to hamper effective usage of railroads. An exasperated Confederate officer declared in April 1864: "That the railroads should come under military control I am becoming every day more satisfied. There seems to be a desire to work for the road's interest rather than sacrifice all convenience for the country's cause."[19]

Finally, in February 1865 the Confederate Congress enacted a broad statute that empowered the secretary of war to take over temporarily any railroad, and to treat the employees as soldiers. Once again, railroad companies were promised compensation for any damages suffered during the period of governmental operation.[20] This measure, of course, came too late to make any difference in the final days of the Confederacy.

A corollary legal issue also warrants attention. Heavy military use caused track and rolling stock to disintegrate. Since it was virtually impossible to obtain supplies from either foreign or domestic sources, the railroads had no means of replacing worn-out equipment. Thus, the Confederate government began to remove track from branch lines or railroads threatened by capture in order to maintain service on trunk lines. In 1862, for instance, military officers took up the track of the Alabama and Florida Railroad in the face of a Union army advance. Not surprisingly, this impressment policy angered railroad executives. They were quick to denounce the cannibalization of their company's assets for the benefit of other carriers. So intense was the opposition that in some cases local military commanders hesitated to seize tracks. In legal terms, the removal of track and equipment was based on the general impressment laws authorizing seizure of private property for military use upon payment of compensation.[21] In the case of one Georgia railroad, claims for removed rails and other equipment were settled after the war by a state guarantee of railroad company bonds.[22] Although in time the Confederates managed to secure a reasonable amount of track, the impressment policy was carried out in a fitful and uncoordinated manner. It directly contributed, moreover, to the sorry state of the Southern railroad network after the war.

There was massive physical destruction of railroads in the South. In addition to often harsh use by the Confederate army, retreating soldiers burned bridges and tore up track. For its part, the Union army also inflicted systematic injury on Southern railroads. General William T. Sherman gave particular attention to destroying railroads on his famous march of 1864–1865. His troops twisted track, burned ties and depots, and seized engines. By the conclusion of the war, more than half of the railroad facilities in the South had been demolished. To add to the chaos, many Southern lines actually lost money during the war. The operating and maintenance expenses of railroading mounted more rapidly than rates for government traffic. Despite paper profits, the carriers were paid in depreciated Confederate bonds and money, which were worthless at the end of hostilities. John F. Stover has aptly pointed out that the "various destructive forces left southern railroads a shambles by the end of the war."[23] The rehabilitation of rail service would become a major policy focus during the post–Civil War era.

Railroads in the Union

By every measure the railroads in the states of the Union were superior to their Southern counterparts.[24] Not only did the Union possess about two-thirds of the nation's trackage, but Northern lines benefited from more sturdy construction. There had been a good deal of double tracking in the North. Additionally, the Union had a marked advantage in the supply of engines and rolling stock, as well as in the availability of skilled labor. Perhaps most important, by virtue of mergers and cooperative arrangements Northern rail companies had begun the process of consolidation into trunk lines. The physical connection between lines, which remained such a point of contention in the South, had been largely achieved. Consequently, the more highly integrated railroad facilities in the North could render efficient wartime service.

Under these favorable circumstances, there was less need for the Union to supervise rail operations. Nonetheless, Congress quickly took steps to assert governmental control if warranted. The centerpiece of this policy was the 1862 act authorizing the president to take possession of any railroad when public safety required.[25] The employees of a seized company were to be placed under military control. Mindful of the taking clause of the Fifth Amendment, Congress provided that commissioners should assess the amount of compensation for such seizure, subject to congressional approval. The act was to remain in force no longer "than is necessary for the suppression of the rebellion."

In practice, President Abraham Lincoln had no desire to take control of the railroads and sparingly exercised this sweeping authority. Both Lincoln and Secretary of War Edwin M. Stanton were prominent railroad attorneys who understood transportation problems. They preferred to keep the lines functioning under private management. The 1862 statute, then, was treated primarily as a weapon to secure the cooperation of railroad companies for the military effort. Government policy, as explained by George Edgar Turner, held that "so long as any railroad in the loyal states operated effectively and without prejudice to the war effort the government would not interfere with its internal affairs."[26] Only when railroads were unable or unwilling to discharge their duties would the executive take action. Lincoln's approach was singularly successful. Railroad companies were supportive and provided efficient service with a minimum of governmental control. Still, Lincoln did not hesitate to take temporary possession of lines in a few situations.[27]

To implement the 1862 act, Secretary Stanton named General Daniel C. McCallum to be the director of railroads. McCallum acted in part as a liaison officer with carriers in the Union states, relying largely upon persuasion. Moreover, his appointment led to the formation of the United States Military Railroads. This department was responsible for administering captured lines in the South and for maintaining rail service in combat areas. Its ability to rapidly repair destroyed track and bridges was legendary. By the end of the war, the United States Military Railroads operated more than 2,000 miles of track and four hundred engines.[28]

The government also had to address the question of establishing a rate schedule for transporting troops and military freight. A meeting of railroad officials in February 1862 adopted a uniform rate schedule of two cents per soldier per mile. Freight rates were calculated on the current level of charges of individual carriers, with the government receiving a 10 percent discount. Although many considered these rates to be generous, some railroads negotiated for higher charges. Separately, the railroads were directed to give priority to government shipping.[29] The government made no effort to curtail the rates for private freight, and with increased business Northern lines generally experienced considerable wartime prosperity. It is noteworthy that the Union, like the Confederacy, sought to fix rates through negotiation and contract rather than regulation. The preference for private economic ordering continued throughout the wartime emergency.

Another issue that emerged from railroading during the Civil War concerned liability for property destroyed in the course of military action. The landmark decision analyzing the obligation of the government to pay compensation for damage caused during wartime was *United States v. Pacific Railroad* (1887). The dispute arose out of a Confederate invasion of Missouri in 1864. During the ensuing struggle, thirteen bridges on the railroad's main line were destroyed, some by Union forces to halt the Confederate advance. The railroad company readily agreed to an army request to rebuild the bridges as soon as possible, but insisted that the government was responsible for the cost of the bridges destroyed by the Union army. General McCallum then ordered the immediate rebuilding of four bridges by the government. Subsequently, the government sought to offset the cost of construction from the amount owed the company for transportation services.

Writing for the Supreme Court, Justice Stephen J. Field ruled that under the rules of war the government was not responsible for destruction of private property in battle. He expressed concern about imposing a potentially huge liability upon the public. It followed that the government had no obligation to indemnify the railroad for bridges destroyed to halt an enemy advance. Field was careful to distinguish liability for property destroyed in military operations from property appropriated for military service. In such cases he recognized that the practice was to provide compensation. Further, Field maintained that military necessity did not compel private parties to pay the cost of roads or bridges rebuilt by the government, even if the works so constructed were afterward used by the landowner. Consequently, the government could not offset the cost of the four bridges against the railroad.

Although the railroad prevailed on the facts presented, Field's opinion in *Pacific Railroad* was instrumental in curtailing application of the just compensation principle to the destruction of property by military operations. This constitutes an important exception to the protection afforded owners under the Fifth Amendment. Despite its later influence, however, the *Pacific Railroad* decision is not without problems. Field fails to consider whether the deliberate demolition of property might persuasively be seen as the functional equivalent of requisition for military purposes.

The Transcontinental Railroad

The Civil War provided the final impetus for construction of the long-discussed railroad to the Pacific. Fueled by dreams of increased commerce and perceived military needs, the push to build a transcontinental rail line began in the 1840s and gained momentum when California became a state. It was widely thought that the federal government would have to assist such a vast undertaking. Private entrepreneurs simply did not possess sufficient resources to finance railroads across undeveloped areas of the country. During the 1850s the government sponsored surveys of possible routes, but sectional rivalry prevented the formulation of any concrete plans. Southern members of Congress insisted upon a railroad running from their region to the Pacific, and promoted the 1853 Gadsden Purchase of territory from Mexico to facilitate such a route. Despite the rivalry, in 1856 all the major political parties favored federal aid for a transcontinental line. Four years later, Lincoln was elected president on a platform that declared: "That a railroad to the Pacific Ocean is imperatively demanded by the interests of the whole country; that the Federal Government ought to render immediate and efficient aid in its construction."

There had been agitation for federal assistance to rail construction since the 1840s. Such a step was not without precedent. Despite lingering Jacksonian sentiment hostile to federal involvement with internal improvement projects, Congress had made land grants to help underwrite the building of canals in several states. Senator Stephen A. Douglas of Illinois was instrumental in winning passage of the initial federal land grant for railroads. He sponsored an 1850 law that, as amended, granted land from the public domain to Illinois, Alabama, and Mississippi to encourage construction of a trunk line from Mobile to Chicago.[30] The state legislatures were given discretion as to how to dispose of the land to achieve the congressional purpose. In 1851, for example, Illinois turned over the federal land to the newly organized Illinois Central Railroad. Several features of the 1850 act warrant emphasis because they became a model for later legislation. The law granted a right-of-way through public land as well as alternative sections of public land along the proposed route for each completed mile of track. This introduced the famous checkerboard pattern that characterized subsequent land grants. The act also imposed conditions that were included in later grants and gave rise to considerable litigation. Land grants were subject to forfeiture unless the projects were completed within a ten-year period. Further, the act provided that the railroad must remain "a public highway for the use of the government, free from any toll or other charge whatever, for any property of the United States, or persons in their service."[31] This ambiguous language established the policy of reduced land grant rates for federal government traffic.

The 1850 act inaugurated the era of generous federal land grants to support railroading. Congress was promptly swamped with requests by other states for similar grants. By a series of laws between 1852 and 1857, Congress gave millions of acres to ten states, including Florida and Michigan. The states in turn were free to sell the land and use the proceeds for railroads or to donate the land to individual lines. After 1857 the growing sectional controversy brought a temporary halt to the land grant program.[32]

Not until the Southern representatives left in 1861 could Congress address the matter of constructing a rail line to the Pacific. The economic prospects for such a venture were uncertain. The route would proceed through unsettled territory and there was little prospect for immediate return on investment. Under the circumstances it was hardly a surprise that the federal government furnished financial backing to encourage the project. Given the vast extent of the public domain, grants of land were the cheapest way for Congress to provide a subsidy. The western land, after all, was of little value until transportation became available. Yet it was hoped that the land grants would make private investment in the enterprise more attractive. Noting the intense political pressures of the Civil War era for building a transcontinental rail connection, the Supreme Court later explained congressional policy:

> The project of building the road was not conceived for private ends; and the prevalent opinion was, that it could not be worked out by private capital alone. It was a national work, originating in national necessities, and requiring national assistance.
>
> The policy of the country, to say nothing of the supposed want of constitutional power, stood in the way of the United States taking the work into its own hands. Even if this were not so, reasons of economy suggested that it were better to enlist private capital and enterprise in the project by offering the requisite inducements. Congress undertook to do this, in order to promote the construction and operation of a work deemed essential to the security of great public interests.[33]

These considerations were reflected in the Pacific Railway Act of July 1862, signed by President Lincoln.[34] Because the provisions of this measure generated both controversy and protracted litigation, its terms require careful attention. Rather than undertake the building of a transcontinental railroad itself, Congress authorized two private companies to carry out this task. The act incorporated the Union Pacific Railroad to construct a route westward from Nebraska. The Central Pacific Railroad, already chartered under California law, was empowered to lay track eastward from California. This was consistent with the antebellum preference for private enterprise as the vehicle for bringing about internal improvements.

A cash-strapped Congress was careful not to advance any money to the railroads. Instead, the act provided for two types of subsidy as an inducement for private investment. The first involved land grants in alternative sections along the route directly to the railroad companies instead of to the states. This manner of disposition became the pattern for most subsequent grants. There was an ample amount of public land in the West, but the actual value of such grants was uncertain. The land was to be conveyed to the companies only on completion of a specified amount of mileage. Because the land was thus not a resource immediately available to finance construction, Congress extended a second subsidy in the form of thirty-year government bonds. The bonds were to be issued to the companies as work progressed. The expectation was that the companies could raise capital by selling the bonds to investors. Hence, the bonds in effect represented a loan to the railroads. At maturity the companies were obligated to repay the principal and interest. To secure repayment, Congress declared that the amount of the bonds constituted a mortgage on railroad property. In fact, the subsidy bonds were generally sold well below par value in the open market.

Besides the conditions attached to the land grants and subsidy bonds, Congress imposed some regulations on the projected transcontinental route. Perhaps foremost was the requirement of a uniform gauge for the entire line. Congress did not, however, mandate a special rate for government traffic. The act merely directed that military and government shipping should enjoy a preference "at fair and reasonable rates of compensation, not to exceed the amounts paid by private parties for the same kind of service." Congress inserted provisions designed to secure repayment of the subsidy bonds. All compensation for services rendered the government was to be applied toward payment of the subsidy bonds. Similarly, once the line was completed, 5 percent of the net earnings of the companies was to be used to retire the debt. In addition, Congress reserved the right to reduce rates whenever the net earnings of the companies should exceed 10 percent upon cost. To encourage prompt completion of the venture, Congress further provided that if the line was not finished by July 1, 1876, "the whole of all of said railroads" should be forfeited to the United States. Congress also explicitly retained the power to alter, amend, or repeal the act "having due regard for the rights of the company." The scope of this qualified reservation clause would be the subject of dispute, but arguably it did not authorize unlimited changes by the government.

Notwithstanding these seemingly generous terms, the promoters of the Union Pacific found it difficult to raise the necessary capital from private sources during wartime for such a speculative scheme. Accordingly, in 1864 Congress amended the act in ways favorable to the railroad companies.[35] The size of the land grants was doubled, and land bearing coal and iron was included in the grants. The lien on railroad property to secure repayment of the subsidy bonds was subordinated to bonds issued by the companies. By in effect taking a second mortgage, the government made it possible for the railroads to raise capital through sale of their own securities. With respect to the compensation paid by the government for rail service, Congress now insisted that only one-half of the amount be applied toward subsidy bond repayment. That change allowed the companies to use the other half of the governmental payments for construction purposes. Finally, the time set for completion of the route was extended for one year. The 1864 amendment enhanced the potential for raising money from private investors.

The colorful story of building the transcontinental railroad has been told by a number of historians.[36] Although construction was marred by shady financial practices, the line was completed in May of 1869, taking much less time than many initially expected. The nation took great pride in this achievement, but was increasingly bothered by the extent of the land grants and allegations of bribery and financial wrongdoing.

These fears came to a head with the Credit Mobilier scandal, which tarnished the Union Pacific's image. In 1864 key officers and stockholders of the Union Pacific organized a separate construction company, known as the Credit Mobilier of America. Through a combination of dubious accounting practices, huge dividends paid to directors and insiders, and gifts of stock to important political figures, the company was engulfed in accusations of financial villainy during the 1872 presidential election. Although some of the charges against Credit Mobilier may have been overblown, the fact remains that the company had been a vehicle to siphon money from the Union Pacific to enrich a small group of insiders while delaying payments for labor and construction expenses. In the meantime, the Union Pacific itself was almost broke.[37]

Some now contended that the aid scheme had been unduly generous and urged that the business affairs of the railroad companies should be carefully reviewed. The companies did not appear to be making preparation to pay their debt to the government. Accordingly, the financial health of the Union Pacific and the Central Pacific became a major worry for Congress during the 1870s. Much of this concern focused on whether the companies would be able to meet their obligation for repayment of the subsidy bonds, due in the mid-1890s.

As a consequence, Congress began to shift priorities with respect to the transcontinental project. Initially, the primary object of Congress was to advance construction of the line and attract private capital to that end. Once this goal was achieved, Congress became increasingly preoccupied with the security of the bonded debt. Not only did both the Union Pacific and the Central Pacific have massive outstanding liabilities, but each company had issued its own bonds, which had a paramount lien to that of the United States. Still, this emerging emphasis on reimbursement laid bare the tension between the underlying purpose of the Pacific Railway Act and the 1864 amendment to promote the transcontinental line and the government's desire for repayment of the loan.

Efforts by the government to adjust the terms of these acts produced frequent litigation over the rights of the parties. Reacting to the Credit Mobilier scandal, Congress in 1873 directed the secretary of the treasury to withhold all payments to the railroads for transportation services as a set-off against bond interest.[38] In *United States v. Union Pacific Railroad Company* (1875), the Supreme Court ruled that the government had no right under the statutes to withhold such payments. Pointing out that the very purpose of the 1862 and 1864 acts was to induce private investment and promote building of the transcontinental line, the Court concluded that Congress had assumed a share of the risk in an experimental venture.

Fear that the existing arrangement would not guarantee repayment persisted, however, and this prompted Congress to pass the Thurman Act of 1878.[39] This measure amended the Pacific Railway Act and created a sinking fund in the Treasury Department. Both the Union Pacific and the Central Pacific were required to deposit half of the compensation received from the government for service into the sinking fund. Recall that the other half was already applied toward liquidation of the bonds under the 1864 act. This sinking fund was to be used to pay the claims of first-mortgage holders and the principal and interest on the subsidy bonds when such obligations matured.[40] The law also extended the lien of the government to subsequently acquired property of the railroad. The Thurman Act represented another attempt to withhold the entire amount payable to the railroads by the government. The gist of the law was to increase the annual payments toward retirement of the debt. It altered the financial scheme in a less favorable direction for the companies and diminished the amount of capital available for improvements or dividends in order to secure the bonds years before they were due. From the perspective of the railroads, Congress was changing the terms of the basic deal halfway through.

Picturing the congressional acts of 1862 and 1864 in contractual terms, the railroads lost no time in challenging the constitutionality of the Thurman Act as a deprivation of property without due process. In the *Sinking Fund Cases* (1879) the Supreme Court, by a vote of 6 to 3, sustained the legislation. Chief Justice Morrison R. Waite, writing for the majority, emphasized that Congress expressly retained the power to amend the original charter, and that this reservation gave notice to the railroads of the possibility of alteration. Invoking the notion that railroads were chartered to effectuate a public purpose, he noted that "railroads are a peculiar species of property, and railroad corporations are in some respects peculiar corporations."[41] Waite pointed out that the United States was in the dual position of a sovereign and a creditor of the railroad companies. While the government was bound by its contracts, the Chief Justice observed, it did not relinquish the sovereign power to enact future regulations. He concluded that legislation, which just required the companies to contribute toward the payment of their bonded indebtedness, did not deprive them of property. Waite asserted that the statute was a reasonable regulation designed to safeguard continued corporate solvency.

Although their reasoning varied somewhat, the three dissenters insisted that the dispute involved the sanctity of contracts, and that Congress could not impair existing arrangements by adding new terms. Justice Field, for instance, recognized that, in the eyes of public sentiment, the Pacific railroad companies were viewed as unduly wealthy and powerful.[42] But he asserted that this view furnished no justification for the repudiation of contracts by the government. By impairing the contract implicit in the 1862 and 1864 acts, Field reasoned, the Thurman Act unconstitutionally deprived the companies of property without due process.

The upshot of the *Sinking Fund Cases* was an early assertion of federal regulatory authority over railroads, even to the extent of changing the original deal. It also underscored the indistinct separation between public and private spheres in railroad law. In time the *Sinking Fund Cases* became a much cited precedent in the field of government contracts. It established the authority of the government, as sovereign, to enact laws affecting its own contractual arrangements, but also set some limits on the scope of reservation clauses.

Creation of a sinking fund did not resolve the tangled financial questions surrounding the Pacific railroads. The Thurman Act proved inadequate, in part because of a decline in railroad income during the late nineteenth century. The act also posed interpretative questions. In *United States v. Central Pacific Railroad Company* (1886), for instance, the Supreme Court ruled that the government could not withhold compensation under the Thurman Act for transportation services over those sections of a railroad constructed without the aid of government bonds. This decision, of course, diminished payments into the sinking fund.

In 1887, amid further allegations of bribery and corruption, Congress authorized the president to appoint three commissioners to investigate the financial management of all railroads that received aid in government bonds.[43] The Pacific Railway Commission conducted extensive hearings, and concluded that the companies were unlikely to be able to repay the debt owed to the government in the 1890s. The majority report urged that the debt be refunded and the time for payment extended. Emphasizing the improper and fraudulent behavior by the aided companies, one commissioner called for steps to forfeit the charters of the railroads, and the appointment of a receiver to sell their assets. In response, President Grover Cleveland made plain his opposition to putting the aided lines under government control.[44] Resisting pressure to foreclose its mortgage on the companies, the government made a series of efforts to achieve a settlement. Various proposals were debated for years. Eventually, the government agreed to refund the debt for another ten years starting in 1899. The obligation was finally paid in the early twentieth century. The protracted struggle over the debt of the Pacific railroads aroused considerable public animosity, and helped to fuel the drive to tame railroad power.[45]

Later Land Grants

Before the completion of the initial transcontinental railroad, Congress made land grants to encourage other routes to the Pacific. The 1864 grant to the Northern Pacific Railway was particularly generous. Several carriers also received sizable land grants from a number of states. Public opinion, however, gradually turned against the land grant policy. Large grants of land to railroads conflicted with the goals of the Homestead Act to make land available to settlers. Land recovered by the government could, of course, be opened for public settlement by homesteaders. In 1870 the House of Representatives urged that the policy of giving land to railroads should be halted. A year later Congress made the last major railroad grant. In the aggregate, railroads actually received title to 131 million acres of federal land, supplemented by 49 million acres contributed by the states. The amount of land granted was larger, but some projects were never completed or otherwise could not qualify to earn title to the land. The vast bulk of the land granted to railroads was located west of the Mississippi River. Fourteen railroads received nearly all of the land grants.[46]

The land grant program has long been a topic of controversy among historians. It has not been easy to achieve agreement even about the monetary value of the grants to the railroads. By and large, historians have tended to present land grants in an unfavorable light. There has been a tendency to exaggerate the amount of public subsidy and overlook societal benefits. The subject deserves a fresh look. Certainly, the land grant policy accelerated the construction of rail connections to the Pacific. This achievement in turn contributed to the economic growth of the nation. Moreover, it is not clear that the railroads in fact reaped great gains from the grants, as sale of this land proceeded slowly and much of it was virtually worthless. With respect to the original transcontinental grant, Stephen E. Ambrose has tellingly observed: "The land grants never brought in enough money to pay the bills of building either railroad, or even to come close."[47] It is not my purpose, however, to resolve the economic issues pertaining to the land grant policy.[48]

Legal questions arising from the land grants vexed courts and legislators until well into the twentieth century. Two sets of issues warrant exploration.

The first related to conditions in the land grant legislation. Enactment of grant legislation did not immediately transfer title to a railroad, nor determine the amount of acreage it was entitled to receive. Rather, the companies might lose the grant benefits if they failed to meet certain conditions. Virtually every act specified a time limit within which the railroad was to complete its line. In effect, carriers had to earn land by actual construction. Once a proposed route was established, land to satisfy the grants was withdrawn from settlement until the railroad was finished. In the event that land along the projected railroad was already sold or otherwise unavailable, the companies were allowed to select other property known as indemnity lands. The companies would then apply for patents to their grants once the conditions were satisfied. A patent secured the right of the party receiving the grant. As public sentiment cooled on grants to railroads, there emerged a movement to forfeit unearned grants. The second group of legal issues pertained to the rate reductions for government traffic contained in most land grant acts.

Efforts to Forfeit Railroad Grants

The desire of settlers to have greater access to western land, fear of land monopoly, and resentment against the failure of many railroads to meet the time limit in grants fueled debates in Congress and a drive to recover land grants that had expired. Yet the Supreme Court early signaled its reluctance to sustain forfeiture. At issue in *Schulenberg v. Harriman* (1874) was the nature of the interest created under an 1856 act conveying land to Wisconsin for the construction of a railroad. The statute stipulated that if the line was not completed within ten years, "the lands unsold shall revert to the United States." Wisconsin transferred its interest in the land to a railroad company, and provided that the carrier could acquire title to portions of the land as the line was completed. Although Congress extended the reversion period for five years, the railroad was never constructed. Then the railroad instituted a suit against Wisconsin for removing timber from the granted lands. Concluding that the act constituted a presently effective grant of title subject to a condition subsequent, the Court ruled that title to both the land and the timber remained in the state until the federal government asserted a forfeiture by judicial proceeding or legislative action. In other words, breach of the condition did not automatically void the land grant. Although the decision rejected the railroad's claim in the immediate case, the rationale was protective of grants. This decision in effect allowed railroads to patent land after the time limits had expired. The onus was on the government to affirmatively enforce its right to recapture the land. As a result, railroads were able to acquire sizable acreage for lines not constructed within original time limits.[49]

Despite this setback, the forfeiture movement gained momentum in the 1880s. Since the Supreme Court saw the recovery of unearned land grants as a legislative matter, Congress became the central battleground. Amid intense public pressure, Congress passed several measures that forfeited a number of grants to certain carriers totaling more than 28 million acres. But Congress for years resisted enactment of a general statute forfeiting all lands not earned within stipulated time periods. Finally, in 1890 Congress passed a moderate general forfeiture law that recovered land from some specified railroads, but left untouched the bulk of the land grants.[50]

Two land grants stirred prolonged controversy and illustrate the legal questions arising from forfeiture efforts. One involved attempts to recapture land from the Oregon and California Railroad Company for the violation of provisions governing land sales.[51] In 1866 and 1869 Congress granted land in Oregon to a company to be designated by the state legislature for the purpose of constructing a railroad. The 1869 amendment contained a settler's provision that required that "the lands granted by the act aforesaid shall be sold to actual settlers only, in quantities not greater than one quarter section to one purchaser, and for a price not exceeding two dollars and fifty cents per acre." Clearly designed to encourage the development of farms, the settler's provision was grounded on faulty assumptions. In the first place, the land at issue was heavily forested and valuable for timber, not agriculture. The logical purchasers of such land were timber companies. Second, the requirement that the land be sold in small tracts at modest prices to settlers clashed with the primary purpose of the land grant policy to encourage rail development.

When the Oregon and California Railroad Company found itself in financial difficulty, it violated the acreage and price terms of the settler's provision by selling land to timber companies at market value. Between 1872 and 1903 the Oregon and California Railroad disposed of substantial acreage on this basis. It should be noted that other railroads ignored similar homestead clauses with impunity, but the actions of the Oregon and California triggered a call for forfeiture. This set in motion a complex series of legal maneuvers.

Influenced by the anti-railroad climate of the Progressive Era, critics of the land grant policy seized upon the settler's provision as a vehicle to force the company to relinquish its remaining grant. In 1907 the Oregon legislature petitioned Congress for relief from violation of the homestead clause. A year later Congress directed the attorney general to institute a lawsuit seeking to recover the granted lands because the railroad violated the terms of the grant.[52] Congress made clear, however, that it was not declaring a forfeiture but simply authorizing the attorney general to present such claim to a court. The attorney general brought a lawsuit seeking alternative relief: (1) a declaration that all unsold lands of the Oregon and California Railroad were forfeit to the United States, or (2) an injunction requiring the railroad to comply with the sale terms of the 1869 act.

The Supreme Court in *Oregon and California Railroad Company v. United States* (1915) ruled that the settler's provision was in the nature of a covenant rather than a condition subsequent. In reaching this conclusion, the Court stressed that forfeiture presented many practical difficulties and was antagonistic to the basic purpose of promoting rail construction. The justices recognized that the land was better suited for timbering than cultivation. Therefore, they held that the government was entitled to an injunction for at least six months against further sales of land or timber "until Congress shall have a reasonable opportunity to provide by legislation for their disposition in accordance with such policy as it may deem fitting under the circumstances and at the same time secure to the defendants all the value the granting acts conferred upon the railroads."[53] Effectively, the Court tossed the matter back to Congress, insisting only that any solution respect the interests of the railroads. This outcome was consistent with earlier cases leaving the question of forfeiture to the legislative branch.

Congress in 1916 enacted compromise legislation to resolve the controversy. The Revestment Act of 1916 forfeited all the unsold land grant of the Oregon and California Railroad, totaling about 2,900,000 acres, to the federal government.[54] It further provided that the railroad should receive a sum equal to the total acreage of the land grant, at $2.50 an acre, less the amount already earned by the railroad for land sold. The company challenged this valuation of its grant, but the Supreme Court sustained the act in 1917.[55] It required several years of negotiation, however, before the government and the railroad agreed on the amount of a final payment.

The Oregon and California Railroad was left to ponder why Congress reclaimed its land grant while overlooking the violation of similar settler's provisions by other carriers. Clearly, the aggressive stance of Oregon officials, timber speculators, and business operators played a crucial role in bringing about forfeiture. Yet the company did not emerge empty-handed. Although the railroad lost the opportunity for speculative gain, it did retain the monetary value of the original grant.

Another long-running land grant dispute concerned governmental efforts to reclaim part of the huge grant of the Northern Pacific Railway Company.[56]

Under an act of 1864, as modified in 1870, Congress made an unusually lavish grant for the purpose of building a line from Lake Superior to Puget Sound. After several extensions, the date for completion of the line was set for 1879. By the late nineteenth century it seemed likely that since mineral sites and tracts already occupied were excluded, not enough land had been set aside to satisfy the company's title claims. Nevertheless, the government removed acreage from the indemnity areas and put the land in a forest reserve. This had the effect of further reducing the land available to the railroad. In 1905 a patent was mistakenly issued to the Northern Pacific for land in a forest reserve. A suit by the government to cancel this patent triggered a Supreme Court decision explicating the nature of land grants. The Court in *United States v. Northern Pacific Railway Company* (1921) ruled that the proposal of a land grant by the government, coupled with acceptance by the company, constituted a contract. It followed that the government could not appropriate indemnity lands for another purpose if there was not enough land to satisfy the government's obligation under the grant.

Although the Northern Pacific prevailed on the forest reserve issue, a new challenge emerged. Congress in 1924 opened an investigation into allegations that the railroad had breached the contract by not finishing its line within the time limit set by the original acts. In 1929 Congress enacted legislation retaining all lands within any forest reservation, providing for compensation to the company for any indemnity lands placed in national forests, and directing the attorney general to bring suit to resolve all claims by the company to federal lands.[57] The 1929 act was not a declaration of forfeiture, but a bid for a judicial determination of the rights of the parties. This maneuver produced additional complex litigation and an inconclusive decision by the Supreme Court.

The government maintained that the railroad breached its contract in a number of respects, and was therefore not entitled to either additional land or compensation. Particular stress was placed on the argument that the railroad had failed to meet the condition of completing the projected line within the fixed time. An equally divided Supreme Court expressed no opinion on the alleged contract violations, in effect upholding the lower court order dismissing these complaints. The Court expressly rejected the government's contention that the Northern Pacific obtained land illegally by adopting an unnecessarily circuitous route. Moreover, the justices affirmed their earlier ruling that the government could not withdraw lands from the indemnity sections when such action frustrated the railroads' right of selection under its grant. The Court, however, remanded for trial a government claim that the railroad was guilty of fraudulent practices in selecting land.[58]

It was now evident that lengthy and piecemeal forfeiture litigation, which often turned on particular facts, was not an ideal vehicle for settling the continued uncertainty over the extent of railroad land grants. Accordingly, in 1940 Congress gave all land grant railroads an opportunity to waive their claims to unpatented land due under their grants.[59] As an inducement, Congress provided that railroads filing such waivers would be entitled to charge full rates on government freight, except for military traffic. This represented a partial abrogation of the land grants rates, a topic considered later in this chapter. The 1940 act also declared that the companies would not be compelled to reconvey any patented lands. The railroads accepted these terms, and the government was able to recover about 8 million acres. While details remained to be negotiated, litigation over the Civil War era land grants finally came to an end.

The drive to recover unearned railroad land grants achieved some success, but fell well short of its goal. As Morton Keller succinctly explained: "The courts blocked any major surrender of railroad lands under the forfeiture laws."[60] It remains to consider why the Supreme Court was so adverse to the forfeiture of railroad land grants. At one time critics pictured the Court's treatment of land grant disputes in the late nineteenth and early twentieth centuries as evidence that the justices were pawns of big business.[61] In recent years, however, revisionist historians have done much to dispel this outmoded perception of the Court's work.

A more compelling explanation for the Court's behavior lies elsewhere. First of all, courts were traditionally reluctant to lend support to forfeitures.[62] Abhorrence of forfeiture was an ancient maxim of equity. Courts had long refused to enforce literally forfeiture provisions in contracts when such relief was deemed inequitable. Consequently, courts preferred to find any limitation on a grant to be a covenant not a condition subsequent.

Furthermore, deep reasons of policy underlay the line of decisions on land grants. While the public temper shifted, the Supreme Court remained mindful of the national purpose behind the original land grants. The justices insisted that governmental aid "was a wise liberality for which the government had received all the advantages for which it bargained, and more than it expected."[63] Stressing the importance of transcontinental rail connections, the Court observed that the land grant policy "was justified by success."[64] Indeed, the justices cautioned against reading history backward. It would be erroneous, they asserted, to conclude "that because the railroad is attained it was from the beginning an assured success."[65] Instead, the justices emphasized the difficulties in constructing lines across mountainous regions and unsettled areas. In sum, the Supreme Court viewed the land grant schemes in a relatively benign light and felt that, under the circumstances, railroad shortcomings did not warrant the harsh penalty of judicially ordered forfeiture. The Court was careful, however, to leave the final word on the recovery of granted land to Congress.

Land Grant Rates

In addition to conditions governing the time of completion of lines and the sale of land in specified manners, virtually all land grants required railroads to transport government traffic, both freight and personnel, at reduced rates. Many historians have pointed to these rate concessions as evidence that the government received tangible economic benefit that equaled or exceeded the value of the land granted. In other words, quite apart from the public advantages of obtaining transcontinental connections and rapid settlement of the western states, the rate reductions arguably represented a kind of quid pro quo for the railroads' share of the public domain.[66] Computation of the savings to the government are tricky, however, and the economic implications of the rate reduction provisions remain a matter of contention. This debate will not be addressed here.

The land grant rate clauses generated a number of legal problems. Foremost was a determination of the amount of the rate reduction. This turned upon an interpretation of the grant language. The rate provisions were not identical,[67] and a few grants, such as the 1862 act creating the Union Pacific, contained no rate concessions. A small number of grants declared that government freight should be carried for free. But most land grants contained language that mandated that "the said railroad . . . shall be and remain a public highway for the use of the government of the United States, free from toll or other charge upon the transportation of any property or troops of the United States."[68]

The initial construction of this language took place during the Civil War. The War Department agreed to pay the "free from toll" carriers reasonable rates for the transport of troops and freight. Despite some criticism, this practice continued after the war. In 1874 Congress halted further payment to such railroads for transportation services. A legal challenge to the government's action ensued. In *Lake Superior and Mississippi Railroad Company v. United States* (1877), a sharply divided Supreme Court declared that the "free from toll" proviso did not entitle the government to transportation without compensation. Rather, the Court drew a distinction between use of the railroad by furnishing one's own vehicles and reliance on transportation by the company. This difference was rooted in the early notion that railroads, like canals and roadways, were open to anyone with the proper equipment. The Court's majority reasoned that the "free from toll" clause meant simply that government could use the line with its own vehicles for free, but did not obligate the company to provide transportation services without charge. The Court also pointed out that this interpretation was consistent with views of the War Department. Although possibly frustrating the intent of Congress, the Court reached a conclusion favorable to the railroads by strictly construing the terms of the grant.

It was still necessary to ascertain the amount that the "free from toll" carriers were to receive for the use of transportation services. In 1879 the Court of Claims developed a formula that the government should pay the railroads 50 percent of the rates charged the public for shipments over land grant mileage. This represented the amount deemed necessary to compensate the lines for the cost of transportation.[69]

Eventually, Congress moved to treat all land grant railroads alike. An 1892 statute provided that the 50 percent formula should apply to both the "free from toll" carriers and those lines over which Congress reserved the right to fix rates for government traffic. By the 1920s subsequent legislation extended the same reduced rate schedule to virtually all land grant lines. The land grant rates also had a significant impact on the charges for government traffic generally. In order to secure government business, many competing lines entered equalization agreements to carry freight at the same reduced rate as land grant carriers.

Calculation of the rate concession for particular shipments was troublesome and gave rise to a number of legal disputes. The government naturally sought to obtain the largest amount of rate reduction, and the Supreme Court generally sustained the government's position. Thus, the justices held that the government was entitled to a land grant concession on any reduced rates offered to the public, and that the government could claim a reduction on the longer land grant mileage of an original route even if an alternative was actually used.[70] Another issue was the practice of the government to compute the lowest possible charges on the basis of impractical circuitous routes. In *Southern Railway Co. v. United States* (1944), the Supreme Court determined that the government could claim a larger deduction based on a longer route with more land grant mileage even if such a route was so uneconomical that it would never in fact be utilized. Picturing the land grants as a form of prepayment for reduced rates, the Supreme Court in the twentieth century tended to resolve rate disputes in favor of the government.

While the judiciary wrestled with the extent of the rate concessions, a movement to repeal the land grant rates gained momentum during the late 1930s.[71] With much of the industry facing bankruptcy, railroads saw repeal as a source of additional revenue. By this time the federal government was the nation's largest shipper. In 1938 a committee of three commissioners of the Interstate Commerce Commission recommended removal of the special rates as a means of providing financial relief to the troubled rail industry. The Transportation Act of 1940 granted the carriers partial relief. As noted earlier, the act provided that railroads that relinquished unpatented land grants could end reductions for nonmilitary government shipments. The railroads and the government continued to quarrel, however, over the amounts payable to the government and what shipments constituted military traffic. There were also concerns that preferential rates for the government unfairly increased the shipping costs of the public and undermined the policy of treating shippers equally.[72] Eventually, the economic distress of the industry, the sense that the federal government had been reimbursed in excess of the value of the granted land, and the desire to avoid continued litigation over computation of rate reductions carried the day. In December 1945 Congress repealed the land grant rates for military traffic, effective in October 1946.[73] Henceforth, the government would pay the standard commercial rates for all its shipments. With this action the nation marked a milestone, effectively bringing closure to the legal issues emanating from the Civil War era land grants.

Railroads in the Reconstruction South

It remains to explore one further impact of the Civil War on railroad law. As discussed earlier, Southern lines suffered extensive damage during the war and were nearly inoperable by 1865. Any move to rebuild railroads in the region necessitated heavy financial outlays. Yet it was widely believed that the economic recovery of the South was dependent upon improved transportation facilities. Accordingly, the rehabilitation of rail service became a major emphasis of the Reconstruction state governments.[74] Since Congress showed no inclination to finance the rebuilding of southern lines and private capital was clearly inadequate, state leaders turned again to public aid schemes. This approach simply represented a continuation of prewar policy. Although such programs were subsequently shrouded by allegations of corruption, there was initially broad postwar enthusiasm for renewed subsidization of rail construction.

Southerners promoted railroads in a number of ways. Legislatures across the region liberally granted railroad charters that conferred generous privileges. Alabama and Florida enacted general railroad incorporation laws to encourage the formation of companies.[75]

More important, Reconstruction lawmakers aggressively promoted railroad building through extensive state aid programs.[76] In contrast to a number of northern states, southern state constitutions generally did not prohibit railroad aid schemes. Where they existed, moreover, constitutional limitations were evaded. Southern courts were generally sympathetic to state schemes to encourage railroading. In *Matter of Executive Communication* (1871), the Florida Supreme Court ruled that railroads were "public works" within the meaning of the state constitution, and that the legislature could assist rail projects. As during the antebellum era, public assistance to rail enterprise took various forms. Some southern states, including North Carolina and Louisiana, subscribed to railroad company stock. A more common technique was to loan the state's credit. Lawmakers endorsed railroad bonds or exchanged state bonds for company securities.[77] Under Alabama legislation of 1867 and 1868, for instance, the state was authorized to guarantee the principal and interest of railroad bonds as sections of track were completed.[78] Moreover, legislatures often granted state lands to companies as an incentive to construct lines. During the 1870s Texas and Florida made open-handed land grants to encourage railroading.

Consistent with the antebellum pattern, local government also provided a considerable subsidy for railroads. An Alabama 1868 law authorized cities and counties to purchase stock in railroad companies and issue bonds to pay for the stock. Under this general legislation, communities enthusiastically pledged sizable amounts to subscribe for railroad stock.[79] Numerous special laws in other jurisdictions empowered localities to extend aid to particular enterprises. Even Virginia, which did not give state financial assistance to railroads after the Civil War, broadly allowed local support.[80] The statutes usually required a public referendum, but rail promoters experienced little difficulty in securing approval.

Another key element in the promotion of economic development by Reconstruction state governments was the grant of tax exemptions or tax incentives to railroads. For legislators, such tax concessions had the advantage of not incurring any immediate expense. Not only did some lines continue to enjoy the benefits of antebellum tax exemptions, but a new round of tax privileges was granted in the hope of encouraging railroad ventures.[81] Over time, however, such concessions served to increase the tax burden on small landowners and fueled popular hostility toward railroad companies.

State assistance to rail enterprise also took the form of the use of convict labor to construct lines.[82] In a number of states, railroad companies leased convicts, usually for a nominal sum. The convicts labored to build roadbeds, often under dreadful conditions. Ready access to the forced labor of convicts for hazardous work represented another kind of subsidy for railroads.

Despite these efforts to utilize law instrumentally, railroad growth in the South lagged. Even with various types of governmental aid, southern railroads experienced financial difficulty. Although the initial problem was rail restoration, a good deal of new mileage was constructed in the decade following the Civil War. Alabama and Georgia added substantially to their rail systems. Yet as a whole the rate of construction in the South was markedly less than in the North. A number of projects floundered, leaving a bitter legacy of unbuilt lines, worthless securities, and higher taxation. Further, even when operating, many southern lines were thinly capitalized and remained unprofitable. Doubtless some carriers were mismanaged, but the fundamental problem was that an impoverished region could not furnish sufficient traffic.[83]

The panic of 1873 drove many southern lines into default and made plain the meager results of the railroad aid policy. Public opinion turned sharply against continued financial support for rail ventures. This was shown in the adoption of state constitutional provisions designed to close the door on railroad subsidies. Thus, the Georgia Constitution of 1877 prohibited the pledge of state credit to any corporation or the acquisition of stock by the state. The constitution further directed that the legislature not authorize units of local government to extend such aid to companies. A similar provision was added to the Florida and Alabama Constitutions in 1875. Judicial decisions also reflected this retreat from a subsidy policy. In 1877 the Supreme Court of Arkansas invalidated an issue of state bonds to encourage rail construction. The court concluded that the public referendum authorizing the bonds was improperly conducted, and that the bonds were void even in the hands of good faith purchasers.[84]

Amid the financial collapse of southern carriers and the dismantling of aid programs, new problems arose. Weakened southern lines increasingly fell under the control of northern investors and were integrated into wider rail networks. State governments furthered this process by selling their holdings in local companies. For example, 1870 and 1871 Virginia laws authorized the sale of the state's interest in various railroads. Not only did these sales at distress prices constitute a loss, but the lines in question passed to outside investors.[85] North Carolina likewise disposed of its stock holding in several rail companies following the Civil War.[86] More important in the extension of northern control was the movement to consolidate southern lines. The 1868 merger of two Virginia lines into the Chesapeake and Ohio Railroad was a harbinger of things to come. Virginia legislators encouraged this move with generous charter provisions for the new company. Subsequently, the Southern Railway Security Company, a syndicate of northern investors, purchased a controlling interest in a number of southern lines. Although the company eventually failed, it gave additional impetus to rail combinations. During the depression period of the 1870s the Louisville and Nashville Railroad expanded through the acquisition of insolvent companies. Many of the southern rail companies that experienced financial difficulties in the 1870s were acquired by northern interests. Having barely recovered from the Civil War, southern railroads were ill prepared to deal with an era of economic distress.[87]

The increasing domination of northern capital over southern railroads aroused concerns among traditionalists. In 1882 the Reverend Robert L. Dabney of Virginia lamented this development in a speech:

> Once the Commonwealth owned all the highways by water and by land. . . . Now the highways are the property of great carrying corporations who command more men as their disciplined *employees* than the government's own standing army, before whose revenues the whole incomes of commonwealths are paltry trifles, to whose will legislatures hasten to bow. Each of these roads points virtually to New York. To that city, yes, to one corner of Wall Street in that city, centre all their debts, their loans, their revenues, their chief management.[88]

Such complaints did not stem the tide toward consolidation. Indeed, there was little viable alternative given the South's lack of investment capital. As railroad companies were no longer identified with the region but viewed as agents of northern domination, popular resentment of rail practices grew. By 1880 southern lawmakers were at the forefront of the drive for more rigorous governmental regulation of the industry.

3

Regulatory Landscape
of the Nineteenth Century

B efore 1870 railroad law was primarily concerned with the encouragement of rail enterprise. After that date lawmakers gradually shifted their
focus toward controlling the behavior of the iron horse. Although questions
of safety and service were important, unhappiness with rates was the principal force behind the push for more vigorous railroad regulation. Controversies over rail charges are commonly associated with the Granger laws of
the 1870s. But this issue was not new in the Gilded Age. Rather, the perceived need to control railroad rates was anticipated in the initial corporate
charters of the antebellum era.

Legislative authority to determine rates can be traced to common-law
roots. As a business that transported goods and passengers from place to
place, railroads were treated as common carriers.[1] To leave no doubt on this
score, a number of early charters declared that railroads were to be regarded
as common carriers.[2] The common law had long placed special obligations
on common carriers. Among these was the duty to provide service for all
shippers at reasonable and nondiscriminatory prices. Thus, state statutes
requiring that all persons must have equal transportation service were
deemed simply declaratory of the common law.[3] This insistence on reasonable and equal terms, however, did not mean that every category of freight
and all individuals had to be transported at the same rate. In other words,
absolute equality of rates was not required. The common law allowed carriers considerable latitude in setting rates. Hence, a common carrier could
charge different prices for the transportation of distinct species of freight or
classes of passengers, provided that no customer paid more than a reasonable charge. For instance, railroads could offer special excursion group fares
or charge more for passengers who paid on the train instead of purchasing
a ticket in advance. Likewise, common carriers were generally free to offer
rate concessions to attract freight business.[4] A railroad company, moreover,
could change the schedule of charges at its convenience without prior public notice. The reasonableness of charges at common law was traditionally

subject to judicial oversight upon the complaint of individual parties. Courts did not determine reasonable rates, but acted to protect shippers against excessive or discriminatory charges. Enforcement of common-law obligations against carriers therefore rested primarily upon the initiative of private complainants.

Early Railroad Charters

From the outset railroads had been subject to a degree of state control. Early corporate charters usually contained provisions establishing rudimentary protections for the public. The chartering process, then, was the first vehicle of rail regulation. Through the charter terms, lawmakers could specify corporate powers and duties.[5] These charters raised a number of regulatory issues and attempted to formulate solutions.

The rate provisions in railroad charters sought to displace traditional judicial supervision with legislative regulation of charges. State courts raised no objection to this assertion of legislative authority. A New York court casually commented in 1831: "The Legislature may also, from time to time, regulate the use of the franchise and limit the amount of toll which it shall be lawful to take, in the same manner as they may regulate the amount of tolls to be taken as a ferry."[6]

Notwithstanding specific rate provisions, the antebellum charters proved ineffective as a vehicle to control railroad prices. As a practical matter, the rail companies continued to exercise a wide discretion in setting charges. The problems with charter-imposed rates become evident when one considers the diverse regulatory schemes. A threshold difficulty was that rate provisions varied widely from charter to charter, not only among the states but even within jurisdictions. Still, there were enough points in common to permit a degree of generalization.

Many early regulations reflected a misperception as to the nature of the railroad business. Lawmakers drew a misleading analogy between railroads and canals and turnpikes. They proceeded on the assumption that rail lines would be like public highways and waterways, and open to anyone who provided his own vehicle and paid a toll. As the Supreme Judicial Court of Massachusetts explained: "The railroad contemplated by our earliest legislation upon the subject was but an iron turnpike, the use of which was to be paid for by tolls collected of persons travelling upon it."[7]

Under this rationale, railroads were incorporated as both roads and transportation companies.[8] It was anticipated that others might put their own cars and motive power on the tracks so long as they observed company rules.[9] An 1832 Rhode Island charter, for instance, authorized a toll "on all passengers and property, of all descriptions, which may be conveyed or transported upon said road, at such rates per mile" as might be set by the company. After empowering the company to set rules for the form of cars and weights of loads, the charter declared that "said road may be used by any person who may comply with such rules and regulations."[10] Similarly, an 1830 Ohio act incorporating a railroad declared that all persons who paid the prescribed toll could "with suitable and proper carriages use and travel upon the said railroad subject to such rules and regulations as the corporations are authorized to make."[11] In 1834 South Carolina lawmakers empowered the Edgefield Rail Road Company to adopt necessary regulations whenever the company "shall deem it expedient to open the said Rail Road, or any part thereof, to public use."[12] These measures clearly contemplated the possibility of open usage of the rail system.

In this regard, the frequent use of the term "toll" in early charters to describe the railroad's right to receive compensation is revealing. The word "toll" was commonly understood as payment for the use of roads or waterways, not for transportation services.[13] As if to underscore this point, many acts empowered railroad companies to erect toll houses and gates along the route to facilitate the collection of tolls.[14]

The notion of open access to rail lines soon proved to be infeasible. In practice, railroads could only be utilized by special vehicles adapted for rails. The expense of constructing such cars and locomotives, and the difficulty of complying with company rules, precluded individuals from taking advantage of the opportunity to use railroads like turnpikes or canals.[15] Moreover, for safety reasons it was impossible to have a number of engines not under single management operating on a line. The law belatedly recognized this reality. An 1845 Massachusetts act abrogated the right of the public to treat railroads like a public highway by declaring that only engines belonging to the company could operate on the lines.[16] By the late 1840s charters routinely provided that railroads had the exclusive right of transporting passengers and goods.[17] Indeed, many charters empowered railroad companies to seize all vehicles and locomotives used on their track without permission.

The unfortunate comparison between railroads and roads and canals, however, had a lingering impact on rate regulation. Legislators were prone to cast rate schedules in terms of mileage. A Tennessee charter of 1835 required that transportation charges "not exceed thirty-five cents per hundred pounds on heavy articles and ten cents per cubic foot on articles of measurement for every hundred miles and five cents a mile for every passenger."[18] A number of

South Carolina, Georgia, and Virginia charters contained similar rate provisions.[19] Likewise, a New York measure in 1836 set a maximum rate of three cents per mile for the transportation of passengers.[20] Even charters that did not specify a definite rate nonetheless adhered to price formulas based on mileage. Thus, Connecticut and Rhode Island granted a series of charters during the 1830s that authorized railroad companies to establish a toll on passengers and property "at such rates per mile." An 1849 amendment to a Connecticut act of incorporation prescribed "a uniform rate per mile shall be charged for the transportation of such passengers and freight."[21] Ohio legislators explicitly invoked the canal model as a basis for determining charges. Several Ohio acts empowered railroads to charge "any sum not exceeding the sums charged for tolls and transportation on the Ohio Canals on the same kinds of property or passengers."[22]

The practice of fixing uniform charges per mile, however, did not readily comport with the realities of the railroad business. In fact, distance was usually not the crucial factor in determining charges because of high fixed costs.[23] The actual operating expenses to the railroad of carrying passengers and freight a greater distance was frequently less than for a shorter trip. Commentators expressed concern that uniform rates based on mileage made little sense, and scattered evidence indicates that the railroads simply ignored the per-mile charter requirements by charging less for long-distance through traffic.[24] But the per-mile charter provisions foreshadowed the bitter long haul–short haul dispute that fueled the clamor for more aggressive rate regulation in the late nineteenth century.

Another group of charters did not contain maximum rate provisions but sought to limit railroad charges by placing a ceiling on the profits to be earned by carriers. Massachusetts, for example, authorized railroad companies to determine their own rates, but reserved power in the legislature to alter or reduce charges so long as such imposed rates should not "be so reduced as to produce, with said profits, less than ten per cent per annum."[25] In like manner, a Florida charter of 1850 allowed the railroad to fix charges upon giving sixty days notice. The charter then provided that once the charges had repaid the cost of building the railroad, the company must adjust rates so "that not more than twenty per cent per annum shall be received upon the whole amount of said stock, and the expenses thereon."[26]

Some jurisdictions adopted a hybrid system of regulation. A Vermont act of 1835 combined the mileage formula with judicial supervision of profit. It declared that upon application of local property owners, the state supreme court could alter transportation charges so long as the carrier should not receive less than 12 percent annually on capital stock for fifty years and not less than 6 percent thereafter.[27] Several Virginia charters in the mid-1830s authorized railroads to receive sums not exceeding set amounts per mile, but added that once net profits equaled the capital stock and 6 percent annual interest, then the charges should be regulated by a public agency to yield to net profit of 6 percent over the amount necessary for repairs. In 1837 this dual formula was enacted as part of a general regulatory regime to govern the incorporation of railroads in Virginia.[28]

This approach linking profits and rate controls had the signal advantage of avoiding inflexible rates that were not readily adjustable to meet varying needs and conditions. On the other hand, regulations based on profit did not have much efficacy in the antebellum era. Railroading was an expensive and speculative venture. Promoters often could not raise sufficient capital to put proposed lines in operation, and therefore a large number of railroad charters proved abortive. Although there were some exceptions, few railroads earned a sizable profit or paid dividends before 1860.[29] Many carriers used their net earnings to reduce outstanding debt and purchase new equipment. The depression of 1839 reduced the value of railroad stock and frightened investors who saw no likelihood of return on their capital. Thus, the underlying problem was securing capital in the face of uncertain return, not putting a lid on huge profits.[30] Under these circumstances, charter provisions governing net income were typically so generous as to represent no real basis for limiting rates. It followed that rate regulations based on the amount of return on investment rarely placed meaningful restraints on rail charges.

Other factors also undercut the early charters as a source of effective rate regulation. First, a number of charters contained no price restrictions. As one authority observed, "most charters empowered the railroads to make such rates as they saw fit."[31] For example, an 1837 South Carolina charter simply authorized the company to fix such passenger and freight rates "as to them shall seem necessary and proper to secure a reasonable and adequate return upon the capital invested."[32] Along the same line, the Supreme Court of Ohio noted: "In the early history of railroads in this state, a few companies obtained from the legislature irrepealable charters without any restriction upon the right to fix the rates for transportation."[33]

Second, early charter provisions were concerned only with establishing a scheme of maximum rates. No charter attempted to control minimum charges or dealt with the question of rate structure. This vital point left railroad agents free to offer competitive rates to attract business from canals and turnpikes so long as they did not transgress the ceiling on maximum prices.[34] Hence, the charters did not address the practice of rate cutting and preferential treatment for certain shippers or localities.

Third, the charters rarely contained an adequate enforcement mechanism. Most states in the antebellum era did not even have a railroad commission. Enforcement of rate regulations was left to the initiative of private shippers through court action to recover the excessive amount paid.[35] Not surprisingly, there were few such suits.[36] Actions for excessive fares turned upon the disputed construction of provisions in corporate charters. The wrongful exaction, moreover, was commonly so small that a shipper would not readily pursue expensive and protracted litigation, and incur the possible enmity of the railroad.[37]

To be sure, a few states moved to strengthen the hand of a complaining shipper. A number of Virginia charters established both a statutory penalty to be recovered by "the injured party" if a railroad demanded more than the lawful rate, and a civil action for damages suffered. These provisions were enforced by judicial proceedings. Such measures were incorporated into Virginia's 1837 act creating general regulations for railroads. In the same vein, New Jersey enacted legislation to impose a statutory penalty on a carrier that charged more than the fare allowed by law. Although providing a degree of financial incentive, these provisions still required private enforcement and did not provide an effective remedy.[38]

Lastly, the economic and political climate was not ripe for vigorous implementation of rate restrictions. The enthusiasm for railroads continued unabated until the 1870s, and many expressed concern that increased controls would discourage investment and greater rail development. In Rhode Island, for instance, the state railroad commission opposed a drive to enforce the per-mile rates specified in various charters on grounds such regulation would be detrimental to the emerging rail industry.[39] In the late 1850s the New York legislature rejected proposals to make rail charges proportionate to transportation distance.[40] It further appears that railroad freight rates were generally lower than for other forms of land transportation, and tended to drop in the decades before the Civil War.[41] This circumstance sapped any sustained push for strict rate controls.

The rate provisions in individual railroad charters posed a number of interpretative questions. Foremost among these was the impact of consolidation on corporate rights and duties under the charter of an acquired company. Courts generally concluded that the purchaser or lessee of a railroad was bound by the limitations and terms contained in the charter of the acquired line. In other words, purchased or leased lines were not operated under the charter of the acquiring company but under their original charter. This principle had important implications for the rate-making process as railroads cojoined. Rate provisions applied only to the company designated in the original charter, and did not extend to the acquiring line.[42]

This review of the rate provisions in early charters underscores the accuracy of George Rogers Taylor's observation: "Limitations on railroad charges were usually so generously drawn as to impose no burden at all."[43] A focus on the seemingly boilerplate restrictions on railroad rates runs the risk of overlooking a more salient truth. Regulation was never as confining as the text of charters would suggest and the railroads were largely able to set rate schedules without regard for legislative interference. The hand of public regulation rested lightly on railroads in the antebellum era. The carriers would naturally come to attach more weight to the skein of events than to seemingly irrelevant charter language. This de facto authority to determine their own charges would in time come to be viewed as the norm by the railroads, and thus helped to set the stage for sharp political and legal battles when states eventually asserted a broad right to supervise rail rates.

State Purchase Clauses

Early railroad charters in a number of jurisdictions, including New York, Vermont, Massachusetts, and Ohio, contained provisions that authorized the state government to purchase the property and franchise of the company after a set time period. The language of an 1832 Ohio charter was typical: "That the State shall have the right at any time after the expiration of twenty years from the completion of said rail road, to purchase and hold the same for the use of the State, at a price not exceeding the original cost of said road, and ten per cent thereon."[44] Similar provisions also appeared in several of the first state general acts governing the formation of railroads.[45] The point at which the legislature could exercise this power varied, extending as long as fifty years from completion of the line in some charters. Another crucial consideration was the statutory purchase price. The purchase clauses commonly utilized the cost of the original construction, together with some allowance for profit on the company's investment, as the formula for the purchase price. If the market value of the railroad increased above the statutory price, as was likely over time, a state stood to make a windfall profit.

State purchase clauses reflected the initial ambiguity about the nature of rail enterprise. Content to rely in the main on private entrepreneurs, lawmakers were nonetheless reluctant to close the door on public ownership. There was, moreover, uncertainty in the antebellum era whether the state could acquire a corporate franchise through eminent domain. The reservation of a right to purchase eliminated any doubt about the state's authority. In any event, state governments made almost no attempt to purchase railroads under these provisions. Given the aversion of most lawmakers to state ownership and management of rail systems, this was hardly a surprise. As a practical matter, state acquisition was not a realistic option. Indeed, charters and general laws enacted after 1850 tended to omit such language. State purchase clauses were, however, from time to time brandished as a threat to further regulatory goals.[46]

Late in the nineteenth century, New Hampshire fleetingly entertained the possibility of purchasing the Concord Railroad under its 1835 charter. In response to a request from state legislators for an advisory opinion, the Supreme Court of New Hampshire addressed some of the legal issues implicit in purchase clauses. Writing for the court, Chief Justice Charles Doe blocked state acquisition of the railroad at the statutory price, thereby frustrating the move for state purchase. He reasoned that the state purchase clause in the original charter had been repealed by subsequent general railroad laws. It followed that the state could only acquire the Concord Railroad under eminent domain, "on payment of its value to the owners, and the property in question cannot be purchased or taken by the state, for less than its value."[47] Although predicated on a reading of railroad statutes, the court's opinion was clearly shaped by constitutional norms protective of property rights. Doe felt that compelling owners to sell a railroad for less than market value was just a form of confiscation. Since no legislators contemplated that the state should pay present value for the line, Doe in effect killed the move for state acquisition.

Regulation by Statute

Building upon the regulatory devices in individual railroad charters, the initial wave of general railroad laws likewise contained provisions regulating charges. As might be expected, these restrictions proved as ineffectual as the charters in curbing railroad rates. There were, of course, numerous variations from state to state. Yet the antebellum legislation was usually so generous and sketchy that it did little to limit the rate-making power of railroad managers.

Consistent with the pattern set by the chartering process, a number of general railroad laws treated distance as the key element in controlling maximum charges. This was particularly true for passenger fares. Thus, acts in New York, Pennsylvania, and Illinois directed that passengers not be charged more than three cents per mile.[48] Such legislation typically allowed the railroads wide discretion in setting freight charges. Laws in many jurisdictions authorized the legislature to alter rates, but only if the reduced charges did not diminish profits below a specified figure, usually 10 or 15 percent a year.[49] As the Supreme Judicial Court of Massachusetts explained in 1850: "No limit . . . is placed by law to the toll which a railroad company may claim, except that when the net income shall be over ten per cent on the capital expended, it may . . . be reduced by the legislature."[50] In practice, of course, railroads rarely exceeded the profit ceiling before the Civil War, and thus lawmakers had no occasion to exercise the reserved power to alter rates. Indeed, some states, such as Missouri, simply authorized railroads to receive compensation and placed no statutory limit on the amount of charges.[51]

As rail connections grew, the interchange of passengers and freight between lines gave rise to a special rate regulation problem. It was necessary to adjust the compensation between the respective carriers. A Massachusetts statute of 1845 directed that if the companies failed to reach an agreement, court-appointed commissioners could fix the rate of compensation. The courts had no difficulty in upholding awards by the commission, and even broadly construed the power of the commissioners to encompass prescribing the time schedule for connecting trains.[52] The exchange of passengers and freight between lines necessitated a regulatory solution if private negotiations proved fruitless, and other jurisdictions adopted this mechanism.

Railroad statutes enacted shortly after the Civil War tended to reflect these antebellum models, with a slightly enhanced emphasis on setting maximum rates. Alabama's general incorporation act of 1868, for example, restricted freight charges to five cents per ton per mile and passenger fares to three cents per mile.[53] During the 1870s Maryland and New Jersey enacted general railroad laws that similarly adopted a mileage formula to limit both freight and passenger charges. Statutes by themselves, of course, do not furnish evidence of meaningful rate regulation. It seems likely that even the modest statutory provisions were infrequently enforced and often ignored.

This outcome may well have reflected the unexpressed realization that the complexity of rate setting did not readily yield to either legislative or judicial supervision, and was best left to the marketplace. Jurists recognized that the notion of a reasonable rate was elusive. The Supreme Judicial Court of Massachusetts in 1859 pointed out that, with respect to rail transportation, "the question of compensation is affected by a vast number of circumstances, and necessarily becomes complicated by the great variety of considerations which bear upon it." Among other relevant factors, the court stressed the amount of invested capital, operational expenses, depreciation of track and rolling stock, population of the territory served, and competition. Rejecting a pro rata formula, the court emphasized that a reasonable compensation "cannot be established by adopting a rule which would make a single and uniform price for the transportation of each class of passengers, or of freight, over equal distances on every part of the road."[54] In 1873 the Supreme Court of Illinois similarly concluded: "What is a reasonable rate of freight over a railroad, is, at best, a mere matter of opinion, depending on a great variety of complicated facts."[55] Sharing the widespread preference for private economic ordering, these judges displayed a healthy skepticism about governmental price-fixing with respect to rail transportation charges.

The continuing demand for railroad expansion, anemic enforcement mechanisms, and the vexing nature of rate making all contributed to the limited character of state rate regulation before the 1870s. The implicit policy was that rate determination should remain in private hands subject only to slack legislative mandates to check abuses of this authority. Yet many lawmakers harbored an ambivalent attitude about the need for public control of rates, and stopped short of a laissez-faire philosophy. They perceived a need to place at least some outer constraints on railroad practices. Although reluctant to be drawn into the business of rate setting, judges raised no insurmountable objections to state oversight of charges. Rate enforcement before the 1870s was more symbolic than substantive, but the early charters and general railroad laws did furnish a precedent for the imposition of more rigorous control once public opinion shifted.

The Granger Laws

The 1870s witnessed the beginning of a sea change in popular opinion regarding the railroads. Calls for more stringent regulation mounted, eclipsing the earlier policy of encouragement and subsidization. This altered political landscape would have profound implications for railroad law.

The roots of anti-railroad sentiment were varied and knotty, and are only sketched briefly here.[56] No longer a fledgling industry, railroads increasingly dominated American economic life. Since manufactured goods and agricultural products moved primarily by rail, merchants and farmers were frequently dependent on rail facilities to reach distant markets. Shippers complained of excessive and discriminatory freight charges. These concerns were heightened as transportation on rivers and canals declined, making competition with waterborne transportation less effective as a regulator of railroad rates.

Much of the impetus for regulation in the late nineteenth century was a response to railroad rate-setting policies for freight. Transportation charges generally declined during the Gilded Age. The chronic complaint against the carriers, therefore, was not exorbitant charges but unequal treatment of shippers and communities. Every shipper was convinced that someone else was getting a better rate. Resentment of alleged rate discrimination was at the heart of the calls for governmental controls.[57]

The rate issue, however, was more complex than critics realized. It bears emphasis that the determination of railroad charges was not an exact science. As a general proposition, railroads charged whatever the traffic would bear, as determined by competition and the value of the commodity shipped. In setting rates, railroad managers were guided largely by the need to attract business. In revealing testimony, William H. Vanderbilt, president of the New York Central, explained the rate-making process to New York's Hepburn committee in 1879:

> Q. Are you consulted when a special rate is made?
> A. No.
> Q. Will you tell this committee what your instructions are?
> A. My instructions are, to do the business, get our share of it as against all competitors, and do the business at the same price that they do . . . The day of high rates has gone by, and the railroad men have come to that conclusion; got to make money now on the volume of business . . . I do think it is perfectly proper for a common carrier to vary his price according to the volume of traffic that he has.[58]

In short, bargaining with shippers over rates was commonplace, and the posted tariff represented little more than the starting place for negotiations. The need to meet competition produced rate cutting and preferential treatment for certain customers.

Rate differentials took several forms. Large shippers obtained special rates and thus enjoyed the advantage of reduced transportation costs. An especially controversial practice was rebating, the grant of an often secret refund to shippers with economic clout. Such special favors to large enterprises were naturally unpopular with small shippers, who viewed these arrangements as invidious price discrimination. Although termed personal discrimination by critics, there is room to doubt that such lower rates were per se discriminatory. To some extent, preferential treatment could simply reflect the economy of scale in transporting a large volume.

Another type of price differential was the result of competitive forces. At location points where competition existed, railroads typically charged low prices, and even carried freight at a loss, in order to win business. In contrast, transportation charges between communities served by a single carrier were higher, in part to offset losses elsewhere. The underlying problem was that railroads faced fierce competition on interstate lines connecting major markets, but had de facto monopoly status in many smaller communities. Shippers in noncompetitive areas felt victimized by the railroads and agitated for laws protecting local interests from monopoly pricing. As Ari and Olive Hoogenboom explained: "The fact that railroads competed in some areas and monopolized other areas made rate rationalization difficult."[59] There was resulting conflict between those who benefited from competitive rates and those dependent on a single railroad. Complaints about the rate structure, therefore, mirrored tension between rival communities and interests as much as between those localities and the railroads.

An allied problem involved the long haul–short haul rate differential. Railroads commonly charged a higher price for short, usually intrastate, hauls than for long hauls, even though the short haul was included within the longer distance. This gave rise to one of the most bitter and misunderstood rate controversies of the late nineteenth century. In fact, there was often a compelling economic justification for long haul–short haul rate differences. Distance was not the determining factor in setting rates. Railroads insisted that competition, not discrimination, was responsible for holding down the cost of long-distance transportation. Moreover, the operating expenses of carrying local freight were proportionally higher than those for long hauls. Short-haul freight was commonly in small quantities, and there was frequently no return traffic, adding to the cost of servicing rural communities.[60]

But economic arguments did not avail in the political arena. It became an idée fixe that long haul–short haul rate differentials were a type of discrimination against merchants and farmers at noncompetitive points. The southern states were particularly irate about the issue because the ready availability of waterborne transportation affected railroad rates at many points in the region.[61] Harking back to the per-mile rate provisions in some antebellum charters, critics urged that rates be based on mileage without regard to competition. Such a proposal, however, was unrealistic and unworkable. To raise all charges to the short-haul level would aid noncompetitive points at the expense of the large urban markets. On the other hand, reducing local charges to long-distance levels threatened the economic health of the rail industry. Any proposed change in the rate system produced a vigorous protest from someone.

While certain shippers and communities were nursing their rate grievances, many railroad companies were experiencing financial difficulties. Railroading was an industry with unusually high fixed costs. Intermittent rate wars, fueled by competition, undermined profitability and drove weak lines into receivership. Another mischief resulting from rate wars was abrupt fluctuation in charges, which disturbed shippers. To curb these destructive tendencies, railroads formed voluntary associations to stabilize prices and to divide traffic and revenue among members.[62] Yet this system of pooling was suspect because it stifled competition, which many still saw as an important check on railroad behavior. Pools, moreover, were widely thought to be invalid and therefore proved unstable.[63] Invariably, some carrier cheated and the pooling arrangement collapsed after a short life. One goal of the rail industry in any regulatory scheme was to legalize pooling.

It appeared that the railroads and their critics were talking past each other. Railroads believed they were subject to uninformed and self-serving complaints. They were blamed for the consequences of competition, and then assailed for attempting cooperation. Historians would do well to look with a critical eye at allegations of rate abuses by the railroads. Although the Progressives tended to accept these complaints at face value, one should bear in mind that merchants and farmers had their own economic agenda, and were quick to invoke the "public interest" as a cloak. Still, rail critics voiced legitimate concerns. Many of the charges flung at the railroads were overstated but not entirely untrue. By the late nineteenth century railroads exercised vast and unchecked power over the economic life of communities along their lines. A deep sense of vulnerability animated allegations of railroad favoritism and demands for some degree of public control.

Another factor in the growing antagonism toward railroads was the changing relationship between rail companies and the communities they served. As mentioned earlier, many railroads were initially created at the behest of local business interests in the hope of securing trade for their particular city. This local focus was inevitably lost when railroads consolidated and became large interstate lines with numerous constituents. Many smaller communities, especially in western and southern states, resented the growing domination of railroads in their region by eastern financial interests. On the other hand, investors were more concerned with profit than with promoting local interests. Such disparate expectations obviously contained the seeds of conflict.[64]

Other problems also contributed to a negative image of railroads as exploitative and greedy monopolies. Allegations of political corruption and stock manipulation, exacerbated by public relations blunders on the part of rail executives, tarnished the industry. The classic battle between Daniel Drew and Cornelius Vanderbilt in 1868 for control of the Erie Railroad was marked by pervasive chicanery. Railroad officers amassed personal fortunes, often through shady business practices. Bitter labor disputes and well-publicized accidents added to the public's discomfort with rail management.

Growing unhappiness with railroads stemmed from political fears as well as economic concerns. Put bluntly, many observers felt that railroads wielded undue political clout and threatened the very basis of republican government. Critics pictured the railroads as political masters of subservient legislators and demanded that these predatory enterprises be brought to heel. This argument was congruent with the long-standing American distrust of concentrated power and fear of monopoly privilege.[65]

Much of the antagonism toward railroads was prompted less by specific complaints than by unease about the sweeping economic and social transformation of American public life in the decade following the Civil War. Rapid industrialization and urbanization caused a good deal of social dislocation. As the nation's first big business, railroads were the most visible symbol of the new industrial order. Consequently, railroads were often treated as a scapegoat for the economic frustrations attendant on the emergence of large-scale enterprise and a national market for goods.

Faced with a clamor to control railroad behavior, Congress inconclusively investigated the matter in the mid-1870s. Many lawmakers adhered to the view that preservation of competition was the best remedy for perceived rate abuses. In 1874 a Senate committee recommended that the federal government construct an east-west canal, supplemented by rail connections, to compete with the private carriers. Rejecting direct governmental control of rates, the committee reasoned that such federal competition by government-owned rail connections would hold down the cost of transportation. Nothing came of this proposal, in part because of its prohibitive cost, but the conviction that competition was preferable to governmental regulation found repeated expression in opposition to rate-control schemes. Only gradually did many observers come to the conclusion that competition itself might be a cause of railroad problems. The 1874 report, however, did prefigure eventual federal supervision of the rail system.[66] Yet it would be another decade before the federal government addressed the legal issues created by railroad practices.

Since state governments had traditionally been the primary locus of economic regulations and railroads were formed under state charters, it was not surprising that enlarged supervision of railroads emerged at the state level. Although historians have long attributed the upsurge in anti-railroad attitudes to aggrieved farmers in the Middle West, the movement for railroad controls had eastern origins.[67] In 1839 Rhode Island created the nation's first railroad commission. Connecticut and Maine established similar agencies during the 1850s. These commissions had limited authority, dealing primarily with safety issues and connections between carriers, and feeble enforcement powers.[68] New York fleetingly experimented with the commission form of regulation in the years before the Civil War. Established in 1855, the New York commission was authorized to gather information and investigate the financial records of railroad companies. The commission, however, could only report violations of law to the legislature and attorney general. At the behest of the rail industry, the legislature abolished its commission in 1857 and returned to a situation in which railroads were, as a practical matter, virtually free of state controls.[69] Proposals for legislation to curb perceived railroad abuses were advanced from time to time in the eastern states during the antebellum era, but produced meager results.

Yet the use of commissions as a regulatory device was potentially attractive. Experience during the antebellum period demonstrated that legislators and judges were simply not in a position to supervise the dynamic and complicated operations of railroad companies. Effective controls required constant attention by an expert body, not occasional legislative interference. Thus, railroads provided much of the impetus for the growth of administrative regulation in the late nineteenth century.

The struggle to achieve meaningful regulation of railroads took a new turn with the creation of a more potent Massachusetts commission in 1869. The commission was broadly vested with "general supervision of all railroads." It was empowered to investigate accidents and ascertain whether railroad companies were complying with their charter obligations. Railroads were required to furnish any information required by the commission. The commissioners could recommend repairs and changes in either operations or rates to companies. Moreover, they were required to file an annual report to the legislature discussing general railroad policy. Significantly, the commission could just make recommendations, not order changes.[70] To achieve reform, the commission relied on persuasion and the force of public opinion. As Charles Francis Adams, Jr., the commission's chairman and most prominent member, later explained: "The board of commissioners was set up as a sort of lens by means of which otherwise scattered rays of public opinion could be concentrated to a focus and brought to bear on a given point."[71] Adams envisioned a close and cooperative relationship between the commission and the railroads. Despite its lack of enforcement authority, the Massachusetts commission was widely seen as a nuanced and promising response to the railroad problem. A number of other jurisdictions, particularly in the East, patterned their railroad commissions after the Massachusetts advisory model.

More radical sentiment toward railroad regulation found expression in the so-called Granger laws passed in several middle-western states. Although the Granger laws are commonly presented as an outgrowth of western agrarianism, in actuality business groups played the decisive role in securing strict governmental controls.[72] The elaborate railroad provision of the Illinois Constitution of 1870 set the stage for this departure. Declaring that railroads constituted "public highways," the constitution mandated that the legislature enact laws establishing "reasonable maximum rates" for passengers and freight and preventing "unjust discrimination and extortion." The Illinois legislature responded in 1871 with a measure setting railroad charges and forbidding any rate discrimination in the transportation of freight over equal distances. A commission, fashioned on the Massachusetts advisory model, was created to oversee the act. In *Chicago and Alton Railroad Company v. People ex rel. Koerner* (1873), the Supreme Court of Illinois invalidated the statute on grounds that the lawmakers could only outlaw unjust discrimination, and could not make a mere rate differential conclusive evidence of a violation. Due process norms dictated that railroads must have an opportunity to offer a defense of their rates. The court, however, was sympathetic to the aims of the law. It emphasized that legislatures clearly had authority to prohibit unreasonable charges and unjust discrimination, and that such power rested on common-law principles governing common carriers.[73]

Abandoning efforts to fix railroad charges through statutes, Illinois lawmakers then took an unprecedented step by establishing a strong railroad commission with power to prescribe maximum rates. Such tariff was to be deemed prima facie evidence in court that the rates fixed were reasonable. The burden of proof in rate disputes was placed on the railroad. Likewise, any railroad charging a higher amount for transportation over a lesser distance was prima facie guilty of unjust discrimination. The act further provided that the existence of competition at points on the line was not a justification for rate discrimination. The commission was empowered to investigate compliance with the act and to institute legal proceedings against violators, thereby relieving private shippers of this burden. In marked contrast with the advisory approach adopted by eastern states, the Illinois commission relied on coercion to achieve regulatory goals. The 1873 act brought about both procedural and substantive innovations, and marked a watershed in the evolution of railroad regulatory machinery.

Other states in the region—Iowa, Minnesota, and Wisconsin—promptly enacted similar Granger laws.[74] The most drastic of these was Wisconsin's Potter law of 1874. The measure classified freight, and set the maximum charges for each class. A commission was created to administer the law, examine railroad records, and take action to enforce the rate provisions. The commissioners were also empowered to reduce but not increase the statutory rates. Appalled by the imposition of low rates on such key items as wheat and flour and the resulting drop in revenue, the railroads openly resisted the Potter rate schedules.[75] Denounced by Adams as "the most ignorant, arbitrary, and wholly unjustified law to be found in the history of railroad legislation," the Potter law became a powerful symbol of western radicalism.[76]

Railroads and eastern investors watched the spread of Granger laws with dismay. Some pictured the growth of tough rate regulation as virtual confiscation of invested capital. Reacting to attacks on railroad interests, Charles Doe voiced concern: "The West & South may favor an unlimited legislative power of confiscating property belonging to Eastern & Middle States or to foreigners."[77] Other commentators questioned the economic assumptions behind the Granger laws, noting that the cost of rail transportation was in fact becoming cheaper, and argued that the real cause of agricultural distress was overproduction, not freight rates. In a blistering critique of the Granger movement as "the organized assault on property in railroads," Adams warned that severe regulation would discourage future investment and undercut improved rail service.[78]

For their part, railroad companies assailed the Granger laws in both the political arena and the courts. Playing upon the fear that rate regulation would retard railroad expansion, the carriers quickly engineered repeal or modification of much of the legislation. Wisconsin, for instance, repealed the Potter law in 1876, and railroads in that state remained largely unregulated until the early twentieth century. Responding to the concern that rate controls would discourage investment, the Iowa legislature replaced the legislatively fixed rate schedule with an advisory commission.[79] The hostility of the railroads, coupled with general suspicion about activist government, undercut strict state regulation by the end of the 1870s.

While the railroads were successfully working toward repeal of the Granger laws, they challenged the constitutionality of state rate regulations in a number of lawsuits. This cluster of cases raised issues that framed the legal debate over railroad regulation for decades. To what extent could states control the operations of interstate carriers? Did rate regulations unconstitutionally impair the obligation of contract by altering provisions in railroad charters? Did rate laws represent confiscation of private property without due process?

The Supreme Court initially rebuffed the constitutional challenge to state rate-setting powers in a group of decisions known as the *Granger Cases* (1877).[80] At issue in the leading case, *Munn v. Illinois,* was an Illinois statute that fixed the rates for storing grain in elevators. The principles articulated by Chief Justice Morrison R. Waite in *Munn*, however, were applied in companion cases to state control of railroad charges. Emphasizing that common carriers had long been subject to regulation, Waite ruled that lawmakers could control the use of private property affected with a public interest. In a parallel case, Waite easily concluded that railroad companies were "engaged in a public employment affecting the public interest and . . . subject to legislative control as to their rates of fare and freight, unless protected by their charters."[81] Moreover, he insisted that legislators had final authority to determine the reasonableness of rates. "For protection against abuses by the legislature," Waite added, "the people must resort to the polls, not the courts."[82] Taking a narrow view of the protection afforded property rights under the Fourteenth Amendment, the Court seemingly closed the door on judicial review of state-imposed rates. Similarly, the justices brushed aside the railroads' argument that, under their charters, they enjoyed the right to fix rates without legislative abridgement. The Court agreed that the charter of a railroad company was protected by the contract clause against state impairment, but found either that the terms of the charters in question did not preclude legislative determination of rates or that the states had expressly reserved the power to amend corporate charters.

Nor did the carriers fare better with the contention that state regulation of railroad charges amounted to an unconstitutional interference with the power of Congress to govern interstate commerce. The Supreme Court reasoned that, absent congressional action, the states were free to control business activity even though such regulation might indirectly affect commerce outside their borders.

Clearly, the railroads suffered a major defeat in the *Granger Cases*. All of the constitutional arguments against rate regulation were rejected, and the decisions seemingly left railroad property subject to the virtually unfettered power of legislators. To be sure, the railroads had already obtained repeal or modification of the original Granger laws. But the danger remained because the Supreme Court had given a green light to state-imposed rate schemes in the future. Reflecting industry sentiment, *Railway World* pictured the *Granger Cases* as "the most important, and, in some respects, the most unfortunate decision ever made by an American court of last resort."[83]

The railroads, however, could find some comfort in the vigorous dissenting opinion by Justice Stephen J. Field. A forceful proponent of the view that the due process clause of the Fourteenth Amendment protected economic liberty from state regulation, Field espoused a dynamic conception of property that encompassed the right to use and to derive income. He warned that by fixing the prices of a business enterprise, the government could effectively deprive the owner of the benefits of such property. "The legislation in question," Field maintained, "is nothing less than a bold assertion of absolute power by the State to control at its discretion the property and business of the citizen, and fix the compensation he shall receive."[84] Although Field did not carry the day, his dissent prefigured heightened judicial scrutiny of railroad rate laws.

Another legacy of the call for public regulation of railroads in the 1870s was the adoption of detailed railroad provisions in state constitutions. Control of railroads was the topic of heated debate in state constitutional conventions. The pioneering Illinois Constitution of 1870 served as a model for other jurisdictions. The Nebraska Constitution of 1875 and the Texas Constitution of 1876, for instance, declared railroads to be public highways and authorized the legislature to set "reasonable maximum rates of charges." Delegates to the Georgia constitutional convention in 1877 discussed railroads at length, and drew up clauses designed to check perceived railroad abuses. Fear that the Southern Pacific Railroad had a stranglehold on economic life produced radical anti-railroad outbursts at the California convention of 1878–1879. The convention adopted provisions to create a popularly elected railroad commission with power to set maximum rates.[85] These railroad clauses were part of a trend toward prolix state constitutions in the late nineteenth century; they also reflected deep concern over the economic power of railroads. Such constitutional provisions created a framework for regulation, but ultimately relied on legislative enforcement to achieve meaningful results.

To be sure, not all state constitutional conventions sought to control railroads. Members of the Colorado convention of 1875–1876 were worried that regulation would discourage further construction of rail mileage in the state. Consequently, all proposals to regulate rates were defeated.[86]

Closely allied to the issue of rate regulation was the controversy over free railroad passes. Railroad companies commonly issued free passes to public officials, friendly journalists, and managers of large businesses. There were repeated allegations that such passes constituted a form of bribe to secure influence for the carriers. But this dark image of free passes was not entirely deserved. In actuality, railroads were often pestered with demands for free transportation by important officials and shippers. The carriers were understandably hesitant to arouse hostility by refusing such requests. Indeed, state legislators more than once hinted at retaliation should railroad companies attempt to curtail free-pass privileges. From this perspective, the practice of granting passes looked more like extortion than bribery. One historian observed that "the roads were victimized by the practice to the point where they felt themselves prisoner to it."[87]

As early as 1855 Rhode Island attempted to curb the issuance of passes.[88] During the 1870s several state constitutions banned free passes on railroads. Thus, the Pennsylvania Constitution of 1873 declared that no railroad could grant passes to any person except company employees. California's constitution even provided that acceptance of a free pass by a public official constituted forfeiture of office. Yet there is room to doubt that these clauses were effective. Consider the experience of Alabama. Although the state constitution of 1875 prohibited free passes for legislators and officials, the legislature failed to establish any penalties for violations. Consequently, the practice continued for decades.[89] There is also evidence from other jurisdictions that railroads ignored or evaded anti-pass laws.

Movement for Federal Regulation

While the states continued to experiment with regulatory schemes, some voices began to insist that federal controls were essential to address the problems of the railroad industry. The states found it difficult to regulate effectively the growing network of interstate carriers. In 1870 Adams perceptively noted that "practically, state lines are done away with by corporations created by States."[90] Isaac F. Redfield, author of a leading treatise on railroad law, was another early advocate of federal government supervision of rail lines.[91] In the wake of the violent railroad strikes of 1877, Thomas A. Scott, president of the Pennsylvania Railroad, called for federal regulation to safeguard interstate rail traffic and prevent forcible interference with rail operations.[92] A number of bills to establish national supervision of railroads were introduced in Congress during the late 1870s.

The movement for federal controls gradually gained momentum in the 1880s. President Chester A. Arthur in 1883 recommended that Congress take action to curb railroad abuses. The Republican national platform in 1884 called public regulation of railroads "a wise and salutary" principle, and endorsed congressional legislation to this end.

Despite this mounting pressure, Congress moved cautiously in tackling what became known as "the railway problem." A major obstacle was that federal regulation was pushed by diverse shipper, farmer, and geographic interests, and there was no agreement on either the nature of their grievances or the desired legislative remedy. Reflecting this underlying confusion, the House of Representatives and the Senate passed quite different bills. The

House favored the Reagan bill, which absolutely banned rebates, pooling, and long haul–short haul differentials. It made no provision for a regulatory agency, and left enforcement to private actions in court. In marked contrast, the Senate preferred the moderate Cullom bill. This measure sought to outlaw rate discrimination and rebates, but did not prohibit pooling and contained an elastic long haul–short haul clause. The Cullom bill also provided for the creation of a commission with discretionary power to enforce the law. Significantly, neither bill attempted to impose maximum rate regulation. Not only were railroads uniformly opposed to rate setting, but the state rate laws were widely seen as failures.

Attempts to adjust the differences between the House and Senate proceeded slowly. It was clear, however, that some type of federal regulation was in the offing. At this juncture, the Supreme Court ruled in *Wabash, St. Louis & Pacific Railway v. Illinois* (1886) that state regulation of interstate railroad rates invaded federal authority under the commerce clause. Reasoning that state rate controls threatened to negatively impact trade among the states, the Court declared that "this species of regulation is one which must be, if established at all, of a general and national character, and cannot be safely and wisely remitted to local rules and local regulations."[93] The *Wabash* decision in effect overturned part of the *Munn* doctrine and greatly restricted the power of states over interstate railroads. Since most freight shipments were interstate, the result of *Wabash* was a regulatory vacuum. The ruling helped to break the legislative deadlock and bring about passage of the Interstate Commerce Act in 1887.

Yet translating the amorphous public desire for railroad regulation into specific legislation was not a simple task. Unsurprisingly, the act represented an untidy compromise between the Reagan and Cullom bills. It created the Interstate Commerce Commission (ICC) with power to conduct hearings and issue orders to halt practices in violation of the statute. If a railroad failed to heed an order, the ICC could petition the federal courts to force compliance. The act declared that charges for interstate rail transportation should be "reasonable and just," but did not define this standard or confer rate-making authority on the ICC. Further, the act outlawed rebates or preferential treatment for any shipper. Much to the consternation of the railroads, pooling of traffic or earnings among carriers was banned. However, the act softened the prohibition of long haul–short haul rate differential by inserting the vague phrase "under similar circumstances and conditions." This language seemingly permitted the railroads to retain the differential when warranted by special circumstances. Lastly, carriers were required to file public rate schedules and to furnish information on financial matters and operations to the ICC.[94]

The act was a patchwork of unclear provisions that rested on inconsistent premises. The fundamental defect was uncertainty about the role of competition in the regulated rail industry. Was "the railroad problem" caused by monopoly power or excessive competition? Was the act intended to enhance competition or to encourage industry stability through cartelization? In its first report the ICC explained that the purpose of Congress was "to preserve to the people the benefits of competition."[95] To this end, the act made pooling illegal. Yet a competitive regime led to the practice of offering special rates to attract business. This, of course, contradicted the provisions in the act designed to eliminate price discrimination. Competition without the ability to offer price differentials, however, was largely meaningless. Anxious above all to satisfy the popular clamor to curb perceived railroad excesses, Congress was content to leave unresolved policy issues and interpretative questions to the ICC and the courts.

Historians have exhaustively studied the legislative history of the Interstate Commerce Act, and there is no need to recount the matter extensively here. Much of this inquiry has focused on two questions: (1) the forces in Congress that pushed for rail regulation, and (2) the role of the railroads themselves in the enactment of federal controls. Reflecting unhappiness that railroads in the South were increasingly under the control of northern investors, southern members of Congress consistently favored stringent regulation. Representatives from the eastern states, on the other hand, overwhelmingly preferred only mild restraints on the industry.[96] Thus, sharp sectional divisions characterized the debate over the Interstate Commerce Act. Sarah H. Gordon has persuasively argued: "In many respects the tension between sections was recast as tension between railroad corporations and their customers or 'public,' mediated by the states."[97] The history of railroad regulation illustrates the force of regional concerns and local interests in shaping important federal laws.

The attitude of railroad leaders toward proposed federal regulation has been the subject of intense scholarly debate. Gabriel Kolko advanced the striking but problematic thesis that the rail industry actively sought federal regulation to stabilize chaotic financial conditions.[98] A number of prominent historians have vigorously challenged Kolko's interpretation, pointing out that the industry did not have monolithic views and opposed many provisions of the Interstate Commerce Act. Further, the leading railroad journals were uniformly hostile to the new law. In fact, most rail executives were skeptical about federal controls but resigned to the inevitability of some type of regulation to placate public sentiment.[99] No doubt some rail executives also hoped that federal regulations would afford a means to escape from aggressive and parochial state controls.[100] But there is no basis for concluding that the railroads were enthusiastic about the Interstate Commerce Act. Instead, it appears that Congress displayed little grasp of railroad economics and harbored no secret desire to assist the industry. Still, the act was less severe than the earlier Granger laws with their rigid rate controls.

Despite many ambiguities and shortcomings, the Interstate Commerce Act marked an important watershed in the relationship between business enterprise and the federal government. It represented the first hesitant move by Congress toward administrative regulation of economic activity. Federal railroad regulation, in the words of Morton Keller, "was a leap in the dark."[101]

A Feeble Commission

The early history of the ICC is a study in frustration. Not only did the commission lack adequate enforcement authority, but the Supreme Court struck down every major ICC initiative in the late nineteenth century.

President Grover Cleveland named Thomas M. Cooley, a prominent judge and author of a leading constitutional law treatise, as the first chairman of the ICC. Cooley has rightly received high marks from historians for his management of the fledgling agency. He organized the commission on a judicial model, handling complaints on a case-by-case basis. Taking his lead from Charles Francis Adams, Cooley preferred to mold public opinion and rely on persuasion rather than to use coercion against the carriers. The commission soon received more than a thousand complaints, many based on the long haul–short haul clause of the act. Although hampered by an inadequate staff, the ICC under Cooley made some early headway in stabilizing rates and eliminating discrimination.[102]

Since the ICC lacked authority to enforce its orders, the efficacy of the agency ultimately depended on the federal courts. A railroad could simply ignore an adverse ICC order to adjust rates, and force the commission to seek judicial enforcement of its mandate. The resulting appeal delayed cases for years. Judicial skepticism about the ICC and the regulatory process appeared almost at once. In *Kentucky and Indiana Bridge Company v. Louisville & Nashville Railway Company* (1889), the first judicial test of an ICC order, the federal circuit court set aside a commission finding and directed that the facts be reexamined de novo, including further evidence introduced by any party. The findings of the ICC were treated, in effect, as a preliminary report, not a conclusive determination. Likewise, judges soon found fault with the ICC's determination of rate discrimination. For instance, in *ICC v. Louisville & Nashville Railway Company* (1896), the circuit court insisted that the agency must consider the lack or existence of competition between shipping points in passing upon alleged price discrimination. The court stressed that mileage was not the most important factor in setting rates. Signaling a continued preference for the workings of the market rather than positive legal controls, the court added: "The public at large are greatly interested in competition,—with the more favorable prices which it brings—and, for that purpose, in keeping open the larger markets of the country to all points of production and supply."[103]

Following the path of the lower courts, the Supreme Court during the late nineteenth century narrowly construed ICC authority. Although the act conferred no express power to fix charges, the commission assumed that its authority to review the reasonableness of existing rates encompassed by implication the power to prescribe rates. The Supreme Court closed the door on this practice in *ICC v. Cincinnati, New Orleans and Texas Pacific Railway Company* (1897). Although recognizing that Congress could delegate rate-setting authority to the commission, the Court held that such a broad power could not be implied. The ICC was forced to drop its attempts to set rates for the carriers.

Perhaps the most significant Supreme Court action involved the long haul–short haul clause of the act. At issue in *ICC v. Alabama Midland Railway Company* (1897) was an ICC order that the railroad cease charging a higher rate for shipments to and from Troy, Alabama, than for the longer distance to Montgomery, Alabama. The differential was caused by the existence of competing rail facilities at Montgomery. The justices ruled that railroad competition must be considered when applying the "under substantially similar circumstances and conditions" proviso. It followed that competition justified the carrier in charging lower prices for shipments to Montgomery because the circumstances were not similar. As a practical matter, the *Alabama Midland* decision rendered the long haul–short haul clause a nullity. It was almost always possible to show that competition at one point created dissimilarities. Although much criticized, *Alabama Midland* was quite sensible. The outcome comported with economic reality and minimized injury to the railroads resulting from a rigid reading of the long haul–short haul provision.[104]

The Supreme Court also initially confined the ICC's investigatory authority. In *Counselman v. Hitchcock* (1892), the justices sustained a shipper who refused to testify before a grand jury whether he had received rebates. Finding that the Fifth Amendment privilege against self-incrimination applied to all official proceedings, they ruled that the shipper could not be compelled to give incriminating evidence of illegal activity. An important victory for civil liberties, the decision nonetheless hampered ICC investigation of business practices. In effect, the commission was limited to voluntary testimony. A year later Congress enacted a comprehensive immunity statute prohibiting criminal prosecution of any persons who testified before the ICC. A divided Supreme Court held in *Brown v. Walker* (1896) that this grant of immunity was sufficiently broad to satisfy the Fifth Amendment. In the same vein, the Court validated the ICC's power to subpoena witnesses and compel the production of documents. Whatever the Supreme Court's misgivings about the substantive provisions of the Interstate Commerce Act, the justices were reluctant to undercut ICC investigatory power as a tool to achieve regulatory goals.[105]

By the end of the nineteenth century, the ICC was largely ineffective and devoted much of its energy to gathering statistics about the rail industry. The ICC acknowledged in 1903: "At present this Commission can investigate and report. It has no power to determine what rate is reasonable, and such orders as it can make have no binding effect."[106] Not content with a toothless commission, some railroad managers continued to fruitlessly urge legalization of pooling arrangements. Other executives sought to eliminate the ICC altogether. Richard S. Olney, subsequently attorney general under Cleveland, counseled against repeal of the act. He cogently argued: "It [the ICC] satisfies the popular clamor for a government supervision of the railroads, at the same time that that supervision is almost entirely nominal." He further observed that the ICC would become in time "a sort of protection against hasty and crude legislation hostile to railroad interests."[107] Olney's predictions about the protective role of the commission were not borne out by later developments, but he accurately depicted the modest role of the ICC in the 1890s.

Much scholarly ink has been spilled assigning blame for the enfeebled condition of the ICC. Influenced by the Progressive school, a number of historians have accused the Supreme Court of emasculating the commission. But this assessment does not bear scrutiny. To be sure, the justices followed a pattern of restrictively interpretating the Interstate Commerce Act. This line of decisions unquestionably reflected the Court's favorable disposition toward private economic ordering and skepticism about business regulations. The basic problems with the act, however, were the responsibility of Congress. As discussed earlier, the act was a jumble of shadowy and contradictory provisions. It is hard to see that the Supreme Court frustrated any unequivocal intent of Congress with respect to the rail industry. On the contrary, Lawrence M. Friedman has aptly noted: "Congress was only half-serious about taming the railroads; it was in deadly earnest only about public opinion."[108] Indeed, Congress was not troubled by the Supreme Court's rulings adverse to the ICC, and took no steps to strengthen the commission. Presidents similarly showed little interest. Not until the early twentieth century, responding to new political currents, would Congress revitalize the ICC.

Persistent State Regulation

The *Wabash* decision, and the subsequent creation of the ICC, limited state jurisdiction over railroads to intrastate traffic. Although partially displaced, state regulation of railroads continued to grow in the last decades of the nineteenth century. A majority of states established railroad commissions, even though a number of jurisdictions, including Pennsylvania, New Jersey, Texas, and Maryland, had no such agency as late as 1890. Eastern states generally followed the Massachusetts advisory model, while western and southern states tended to adopt the Illinois system under which commissions could fix rates. Inevitably tied to local interests, state regulation of intrastate charges exacerbated the rate controversy of the Gilded Age. States had every incentive to impose low rates on railroads for local traffic, and in effect to shift the economic burden of railroading to interstate shippers.[109] The potential for state regulation to undercut efforts by the ICC to stabilize rates was evident early. In 1889 the prescient Cooley unsuccessfully urged Congress to extend ICC authority over intrastate rail transportation.[110] Railroads found themselves simultaneously subject to a tangle of federal and diverse state laws.

Railroad leaders had long battled state regulations, and they responded to increased state controls by fashioning a litigation strategy to secure greater constitutional protection for their economic interests. Much of their legal argument was predicated on the due process clause of the Fourteenth Amendment. Ultimately, the carriers were victorious in overthrowing the *Munn* doctrine and establishing federal judicial review of state rate making. In so doing, the railroads made a pivotal contribution to constitutional law by gaining Supreme Court acceptance of the premise that due process imposed substantive restraints on governmental power over private property.[111]

By the mid-1880s the Supreme Court suggested that it might invalidate state-imposed rates in some situations. In *Stone v. Farmers' Loan and Trust Company* (1886), the Court sustained a Mississippi law that empowered a state commission to regulate railroad charges, but cautioned that such authority was not unlimited. The Court warned that "the State cannot require a railroad corporation to carry persons or property without reward;

neither can it do that which in law amounts to a taking of private property for public use without just compensation, or without due process of law."[112]

Building upon this language in *Stone,* Judge David J. Brewer, later appointed to the Supreme Court, granted a pioneering injunction in 1888 against sharp reductions in freight rates ordered by the Iowa railroad commission. Since *Stone* indicated that railroads were constitutionally entitled to some compensation, Brewer reasoned that the state's power to regulate did not encompass the authority to effectuate confiscation of railroad property through the imposition of unremunerative rates. Courts, therefore, could appropriately inquire into the reasonableness of prescribed rates in order to protect railroad companies against confiscation. The Brewer injunction was a key milestone in establishing judicial review of state-mandated rates, and anticipated the next step by the Supreme Court.[113]

In a line of cases during the 1890s, the Supreme Court circumscribed state regulation of intrastate railroad charges. The decision in *Chicago, Milwaukee & St. Paul Railway Company v. Minnesota* (1890) marked a sea change in the Court's jurisprudence. The justices ruled that a railroad company was entitled to make reasonable charges for use of its property, and that the federal courts could scrutinize the substantive reasonableness of state-imposed rates. This ruling contradicted the premise of *Munn* that rate making was solely a legislative matter. Of more far-reaching significance to constitutional law, *Chicago, Milwaukee* signaled the Court's embrace of the view that due process entailed substantive as well as procedural limits on governmental power. In the ensuing decades railroads and other enterprises would increasingly rely on the due process norm to vindicate their property rights in the face of state controls.[114] Continuing along the same path, the justices served notice in *Reagan v. Farmers' Loan and Trust Company* (1894) that they would examine the reasonableness of rates set either directly by the state legislature or by a commission. Finding that the Texas rates at issue provided an inadequate return on capital invested, the Court enjoined enforcement of the regulations as a deprivation of property without due process.

An unresolved issue was how to distinguish a valid rate regulation from confiscation. The Court came to grips with this issue in *Smyth v. Ames* (1898). In 1893 the Nebraska legislature, controlled by the Populists, enacted a law that mandated an average 30 percent reduction in intrastate freight rates. The railroads maintained that such a steep reduction effectively constituted destruction of their property. Writing for a unanimous Court, Justice John M. Harlan agreed with the railroads and held that the statute was unconstitutional as a deprivation of property without due process. He insisted that the reasonableness of charges for intrastate transportation must be decided without considering the profits earned by railroads on their interstate business within the state. Harlan feared that otherwise states would set low rates for local traffic at the expense of interstate shipping. He then formulated a standard for the judicial review of rates: "the basis of all calculations as to the reasonableness of rates . . . must be the fair value of the property being used by it for the convenience of the public." Under the fair value rule, courts looked primarily at the current or replacement value of a company's assets as the baseline for rate determinations.[115]

There were several noteworthy consequences of the landmark *Smyth* decision. First, the federal courts became deeply involved in rate cases, and were required to make complex assessments of the present value of companies. Since *Smyth* was extended to other regulated industries, it applied to utilities as well as railroads. Second, the upshot of *Smyth* was to greatly restrict state rate-making authority over railroads. Any general downward revision of rates was likely to be viewed as confiscatory. Under the *Smyth* formula, for instance, Alabama found it difficult to exercise meaningful control over intrastate rail charges.[116] As the value of assets steadily rose in the early twentieth century, *Smyth* would increasingly bind state regulatory authority.

Lower federal courts were not slow in exercising their new authority over state-imposed rates. Two examples must suffice. In 1895 a circuit court enjoined enforcement of a schedule by the California railroad commission broadly reducing rates. Similarly, another court concluded that the Texas commission had improperly evaluated railroad property on which the company was entitled to receive profits, and blocked implementation of the commission's rate order.[117]

Scholars have generally had harsh words for both *Smyth* and the federal judicial review of the reasonableness of state rates. Despite the complexities of the fair value rule, however, the Supreme Court was responding to legitimate concerns and acted to protect the integrity of the national rail system. Although no doubt a manifestation of the Supreme Court's long-standing solicitude for the rights of property owners, the rate cases were propelled by utilitarian considerations. The Court recognized the vital importance of investment capital in order to achieve economic growth. There is ample evidence that eastern and European investors were alarmed by calls for stringent railroad regulation, particularly in the western states. Yet railroading required a continuous flow of funds to establish new routes and make improvements. Mary Cornelia Porter has cogently explained "that the Court was less interested in rate regulation per se than in assuring that regulated utilities would continue to attract the investment capital necessary for expanding and improving services to the public."[118] The Court's venture into the rate-making thicket was also caused by a realization that state regulations created severe economic burdens for railroads and threatened to disrupt the national market. Since parochial state rate controls had an adverse impact on interstate railroad operations, the federal courts acted to safeguard the rail system.[119] The application of due process norms to state rate making was designed to fashion a uniform national rule governing rates and to protect the expectation of investors. Far from showing blind devotion to big business, the Supreme Court in the rate cases sought to vindicate its conception of the public interest.

Consolidation and Competition

Starting well before the Civil War, some states enacted laws that banned consolidation of railroads with competing or parallel lines.[120] A New Hampshire judge, analyzing the purpose behind an 1867 state act, declared: "The injurious effect of a consolidation is the prevention of competition, and that wholesome restraint upon exorbitant fares which can only be secured by free competition."[121] In the late nineteenth century a number of constitutions, including those of Texas, Michigan, Kentucky, and South Carolina, were amended to incorporate a prohibition of mergers involving railroads with parallel tracks. Neither the Supreme Court nor state courts had any difficulty in upholding the validity of such measures as a means to prevent railroad monopolies.[122] Clearly, both lawmakers and judges still hoped to control railroad behavior by preserving competition.

This lingering reliance on the competitive model found other forms of expression. In 1903, New York decided to upgrade the Erie Canal, a move designed to promote a rival transportation system in order to hold down railroad charges.

Although deeply rooted in American history, this attachment to the values of competition was in tension with the scheme of administrative controls implicit in the Interstate Commerce Act. These distinct policies clashed after Congress passed the Sherman Anti-Trust Act in 1890. A product of public alarm over the apparent power of large-scale business to control markets and fix prices, the Sherman Act affirmed the ideals of competition and free markets. Among other provisions, the act outlawed contracts and combinations in restraint of trade. It was an open question whether railroads were subject to the Sherman Act. Many believed that the antitrust law did not apply to the rail industry because Congress had already established a special system of governance for railroads.

During the 1890s railroad companies continued to fashion private co-operative arrangements, with the implied approval of the ICC.[123] This took the form of traffic associations among carriers to maintain uniform rates and eliminate price cutting. Not exactly pools, which were banned by the Interstate Commerce Act, those traffic associations nevertheless had certain pooling features. Rail executives took the position that traffic associations were consistent with the goals of the Interstate Commerce Act to establish reasonable and stable rates. Significantly, the ICC made no move to challenge such rate agreements. Commissioner Martin A. Knapp, contending that the duties of railroads as common carriers were inconsistent with competition, championed a policy of cooperation:

> It follows that the principle of competition, which governs the relation of industrial forces, has but limited application to the business of railroad transportation, and that public welfare would be conserved by authorizing rival lines to make enforceable agreements with each other respecting the movement of competitive traffic.[124]

Rail leaders were stunned when a sharply divided Supreme Court in *United States v. Trans-Missouri Freight Association* (1897) struck down an association rate agreement as a violation of the Sherman Act.[125] Writing for a majority of five, Justice Rufus W. Peckham held that railroads were covered by the antitrust laws. He next adopted a literal interpretation of the Sherman Act as invalidating all combinations in restraint of trade. Noting that many looked to competition to secure proper transportation charges, Peckham brushed aside the railroads' argument that the act prohibited only unreasonable restraints of commerce and that the rate agreement served the public interest.

In dissent, Justice Edward D. White articulated what later became known as the rule of reason. The act should be construed, he asserted, in terms of the traditional common-law distinction between reasonable and unreasonable restraints of trade. White insisted that the Interstate Commerce Act was designed to establish stability of rates and to eliminate rate wars. It followed that rate agreements among carriers were reasonable and in accord with the purposes of the act. White's dissenting opinion highlighted the conflict between the antitrust and administrative approaches to railroad regulation. He expressed concern that the majority opinion undercut the Interstate Commerce Act:

To my mind, the judicial declaration that carriers cannot agree among themselves for the purpose of aiding the enforcement of the provisions of the interstate commerce law, will strike a blow at the beneficial results of that act, and will have a tendency to produce the preferences and discriminations which it was one of the main objects of the act to frustrate.[126]

White would be vindicated when Congress eventually exempted the rail industry from antitrust laws.

The Supreme Court's invalidation of rate agreements had ironic consequences. Instead of fostering competition, the Court gave a boost to the consolidation of the rail industry into a few major systems. To be sure, railroading had long been characterized by combinations and mergers. As early as 1871 Adams predicted that consolidation was inevitable. He dismissed state laws against the merger of competing lines as "utterly futile, almost childish," and sagely declared that no legislation could halt this trend.[127] Collis P. Huntington, president of the Southern Pacific Railroad, touted the advantage of rail consolidation to both the public and the industry.[128] In actuality, the Sherman Act was no more successful than state laws in curbing the process of combination.

By the early years of the twentieth century, much of the nation's trackage was under the control of a small number of principal combinations. This merger movement, of course, tended to eliminate competition, and rendered less important the outlawing of pools and rate agreements. Despite periodic expressions of concern, legislators and commissioners largely acquiesced in the merger process.[129] For instance, in 1900 the New York railroad commission reported that the consolidation of railroad interests appeared irresistible, and seemed optimistic that such developments would benefit the public.[130] The consolidation of the rail industry was a response to economic conditions and the unsettling aspects of competition. Doubtless, mergers would have taken place in any event, but the Supreme Court's decision in *Trans-Missouri* hastened the process.

As the consolidation process gained momentum toward the end of the nineteenth century, states gradually downplayed competition as a regulatory tool. Legislators started to restrict the building of new railroads. Recall that the general railroad acts, beginning in the antebellum era, allowed free entry into the rail industry. Any group of persons could secure a railroad charter by application and undertake construction of a line. This laissez-faire attitude was congruent with a policy of encouraging competition, but fit less well with the growth of administrative controls. Encouraged by the existing railroads, the New York commission in 1883 recommended changes in the law to block unnecessary rail construction.[131]

The New York legislature reversed course in 1892, and prohibited the construction of new railroads except when the commission issued a certificate of public convenience and necessity. No longer was the building of a railroad a matter of right. The statute placed the decision about the appropriateness of additional rail lines in the hands of a commission rather than entrepreneurs. Applicants were required to show the need for their proposed construction. A New York court observed that the law "was evidently intended to restrict the building of roads not actually needed, in order to protect not only existing railroads, but also citizens from investing in alluring but profitless enterprises."[132] The court added that, in view of the authority of the railroad commission over rates, allegations of high charges would not make a strong case for another line. Other jurisdictions soon also mandated regulatory approval before the construction of new facilities.[133]

A certificate of public convenience and necessity, unknown at common law, was first developed in connection with railroads and later required for various public utilities. Reflecting concern that in certain industries competition might harm the public interest, the utilization of such a permit curtailed entry into the business. Ostensibly intended to prevent waste, limits on entry obviously benefited current enterprise. In New York, for instance, the established carriers urged entry barriers as a safeguard against competition. Despite vestiges of the competitive model, railroads were increasingly treated as regulated monopolies.

Railroad Service

The rate controversy dominated the public discussion of railroad regulations in the Gilded Age, but issues relating to rail service warrant brief attention. Many customers were more concerned with transit delays, poor stations, and freight congestion than the amount of charges. A good deal of state legislation was thus directed toward remedying inadequate services and facilities. Under an 1849 Illinois statute, for example, carriers were obligated to furnish freight cars for shippers within a reasonable period of time after request. This was a somewhat aspirational requirement, considering that railroads sometimes did not have enough cars. The exchange of passengers and freight between connecting lines was the source of much regulation. A Michigan statute of 1873 provided that railroads must, for compensation, transport the cars of other carriers.[134] By the end of the nineteenth century, state commissions were typically given the power to compel the interchange of traffic.[135] More controversial was the action by state commissions to force railroads to acquire land and extend their tracks to connect with other carriers. Yet the Supreme Court upheld such orders, reasoning that railroads were public highways and that a judgment enforcing track connections was a reasonable accommodation of the public need.[136] The justices may well have been influenced by the fact that the exchange of cars was the general practice in the industry.

Adequate facilities for passengers was also a recurring concern for lawmakers. Rhode Island addressed this issue as early as 1855, directing railroads to provide suitable facilities and accommodations for passengers.[137] During the 1880s legislators and railroad commissions across the nation paid particular attention to passenger depots. Faced with mounting passenger complaints about the poor quality of station facilities, state lawmakers mandated improved accommodations. Despite their preoccupation with freight rate, legislators and commissions played a key role in improving facilities for passenger travel.[138]

Calls for Public Ownership

As discussed in Chapter One, a number of states, particularly in the South, owned and operated railroads in the antebellum era. In several European countries railroads were developed as a government enterprise. It was perhaps not surprising, therefore, that some observers in the late nineteenth century saw public ownership as a solution to the "railroad problem."[139] Starting in the 1870s, there were periodic calls for the government to acquire and operate the rail system. Illinois Grangers in 1873 saw government ownership of selected lines as a vehicle for competition with privately owned carriers. The idea often surfaced after bitter strikes or during periods of economic distress. In 1877 railroad strikers urged nationalization of the industry. Similarly, Eugene V. Debs endorsed public ownership of railroads in the wake of the failed Pullman strike of 1894.[140]

The most strident demands for governmental ownership grew out of the Populist movement of the 1890s. Many Populists were convinced that regulation would not tame the powerful rail industry, and that more radical steps were necessary. The People's Party platform of 1892 warned: "We believe that the time has come when the railroad corporations will either own the people or the people must own the railroads." Declaring that transportation was a public necessity, the platform urged governmental ownership and operation of rail lines. In the same vein, California Populists called for public owner-ship of the Southern Pacific Railroad.[141]

Although a measure of the frustration felt by some segments of society toward the railroads, agitation for public ownership came to nothing. There was never a sustained demand for such a drastic step, and neither of the major political parties showed any interest. Not only would the expense incurred in any governmental acquisition of the nation's largest industry have been staggering, but nationalization clashed with deeply engrained values of private property and free market ordering. Adams was an early skeptic about the wisdom of public ownership. He stressed the unhappy experience of var-ious state governments in the construction of railroads, and argued that pub-lic ownership of such a vast enterprise was basically inconsistent with the very notion of a limited government.[142]

Proposals for a governmental takeover of the railroads continued to be advanced from time to time in the first decades of the twentieth century. As explored in Chapter Eleven, the federal government did operate the rail sys-tem during World War I. Aside from this brief and sobering experiment, the notion of public ownership sparked little interest. For the most part, talk of nationalization largely served as a club to win railroad compliance with reg-ulatory objectives. While the prospects for public ownership faded, the early twentieth century witnessed a renewed push for stringent controls over the industry.

4

Arteries of Commerce

As railroads became the principal avenue of interstate trade, their far-reaching operations raised a multitude of novel questions about the balance between federal and state authority over commerce. Railroads therefore played a key role in the formulation of commerce clause jurisprudence during the nineteenth and early twentieth centuries. Although Congress was granted power to regulate commerce "among the several States," it made little comprehensive effort to do so before 1900. Even the Interstate Commerce Act of 1887, for example, did not address many aspects of railroading. Absent federal legislation, the states continued to take the lead in shaping much of railroad law. Yet increased state legislation raised possible conflicts with congressional acts. As a practical matter, moreover, the burdens imposed by state law had the potential to impede the movement of interstate trade by railroads. Anxious to protect a multistate free market, courts carefully scrutinized the regulatory authority of Congress and the states.

Bridging Navigable Waters

An early challenge to national authority over commerce grew out of the clash between railroads and competing waterborne transportation. Before 1800 bridges were relatively infrequent, and the common law treated obstacles to navigation as a nuisance. Bridges, however, were an essential link in the expanding railroad network. As railroads started to cross navigable rivers and lakes with substantial structures, boat operators claimed that such bridges impeded water transportation. Steamboat interests lobbied against legislative authorization of bridges, and instituted litigation to remove bridges as an obstruction to waterborne commerce.

It was generally recognized that the states could control use of navigable waters, but that this authority was subordinate to congressional power over interstate commerce. Since Congress had not asserted its jurisdiction over navigation, the states assumed the power to allow the erection of bridges even though navigation might be somewhat impaired. Early railroad charters, as well as the general railroad acts, often conferred the right to cross navigable waters. A representative 1833 North Carolina charter declared: "That it shall and may be lawful for the company . . . so to construct all such bridges as it may be necessary for them to erect for the purposes of their rail road."[1] A South Carolina charter of 1849 granted the right to bridge any rivers or watercourses provided that navigation was not impaired.[2] Likewise, the Illinois general railroad law of 1849 authorized carriers to construct lines across any watercourse, but required that they not impair the usefulness of the stream.[3] Still, state statutes also recognized the potential for railroad bridges to block navigation. General railroad laws in New York and Missouri, for instance, prohibited the construction of bridges over streams navigated by steamboats so as to prevent such navigation.[4]

Moreover, it was a matter of dispute how far a state could approve bridges that interfered with interstate commerce. State legislative approval was not conclusive as to whether a particular bridge constituted an interference with navigation. Final determination rested with the federal courts. Particularly contested were bridges that passed between two states.

The development of new bridge designs in the antebellum era, notably suspension wire technology, made it possible to span greater distances. This opened the door for the construction of more ambitious bridges and heightened the conflict between railroads and shipping interests. Railroad bridges generated considerable litigation during the 1840s and 1850s and helped to define the reach of congressional authority over commerce. In the late 1840s, for instance, steamboat operators unsuccessfully battled a proposed railroad bridge across Lake Champlain.[5] The 1856 charter of the Hudson River Bridge Company set the stage for another conflict.[6] River shippers assailed the rail bridge over the Hudson as an obstruction to navigation. Construction of the bridge was temporarily enjoined, but, on appeal, the Supreme Court was equally divided as to whether the federal courts could exercise jurisdiction over the dispute.[7] Consequently, the suit was dismissed and the bridge was completed in 1866.[8]

The bridge controversy first reached the Supreme Court in *Pennsylvania v. Wheeling and Belmont Bridge Company* (1852, 1856), a protracted lawsuit with profound implications for railroading.[9] As authorized by a Virginia statute, the Bridge Company erected a drawbridge across the Ohio River. Pennsylvania brought suit to enjoin the bridge as a public nuisance, alleging that the structure would obstruct navigation on the river. The Wheeling bridge, although not initially planned for railroad use, was subsequently redesigned for this purpose. In any event, the members of the Court clearly saw the bridge as a harbinger of growing railroad demands to cross navigable waters.

Finding that the draws in the Wheeling bridge could not accommodate the larger steamboats without a lowering of their chimneys, the Court majority ruled that the bridge impeded the free navigation of the Ohio River. Lacking a declaration by Congress that the construction of bridges was not an obstruction to navigation, the majority held that it was incumbent on the courts to remedy a public nuisance and uphold the right of navigation. Suggesting a preference for waterborne commerce, the majority warned that if bridges "for the contemplated railroads" multiplied, steamboat traffic would be destroyed and "our beautiful rivers will, in a great measure, be abandoned."[10] The Court directed that the Wheeling bridge be elevated or removed to abate the nuisance.

Justice Peter V. Daniel, writing in dissent, saw the situation quite differently. He maintained that so long as Congress had not acted, the states retained the right to authorize the erection of bridges. Picturing the dispute as one between rival modes of transportation, Daniel stressed the advantages of railroads over river transport. Prohibit bridges, Daniel darkly predicted, and "the rapidly increasing and beneficial system of railroad communication is broken up, and a system of narrow local monopoly and inequality sustained."[11]

Daniel's opinion proved to be the better guide for future developments. No amount of judicial nostalgia for steamboats could halt the advance of rail technology. The *American Railroad Journal* warned that the Supreme Court's ruling "must ever operate as an insurmountable objection to bridging the western rivers." It called upon Congress to proclaim the Wheeling bridge part of a mail route and thus legitimize the structure.[12]

In response to the Court's decision, Congress in 1852 declared the Wheeling bridge a lawful structure, and stated that boats navigating the Ohio River should not interfere with the bridge. The Supreme Court, in an 1856 decision, deferred to congressional authority over interstate commerce. "The regulation of commerce includes intercourse and navigation," the Court explained, "and, of course, the power to determine what shall or shall not be deemed in judgment of law an obstruction to navigation."[13] Congress had in effect overruled the prior Court decision. The Wheeling bridge controversy indicates that Congress was more attuned than the Supreme Court to the need to encourage railroading. More significant, the act validating the Wheeling bridge created a mechanism whereby Congress could regulate the crossing of navigable waters. Over the ensuing decades Congress passed a large number of acts giving sanction for specific bridge projects. Most of these were built by railroad companies.[14]

Other proposed bridges were also the subject of litigation. In 1854 a federal circuit court enjoined construction of a drawbridge over the Schuylkill River, concluding that the bridge would interfere with navigation. The court acknowledged that, at common law, every obstruction to a public waterway might be deemed a nuisance, but perceived that a degree of flexibility was necessary to accommodate rail travel. Short or occasional shipping delays, according to the court, would be weighed against the advantages of the bridge. Recognizing the conflict between modes of transportation, the court observed:

> Intercourse by means of turnpikes, canals, railroads and bridges, is a public necessity. A railroad constructed by the authority of a state, is often many thousand times more beneficial to the interests of commerce than the unlimited freedom of navigation over unimportant inlets, creeks or bays, or remote portions of a harbor.[15]

Even without congressional approval of bridge projects, judges were moving toward a balancing test to determine if a bridge constituted a nuisance.

The most celebrated clash between railroads and steamboat interests involved the first train bridge to span the Mississippi River. In 1853 the Illinois legislature chartered the Railroad Bridge Company, a corporation closely affiliated with two railroads. The Bridge Company was empowered to erect a bridge across the Mississippi River at Rock Island, Illinois, "in such manner as shall not materially obstruct or interfere" with river navigation.[16] From the outset the project was engulfed in what the *American Railroad Journal* termed "a nest of litigation."[17] There were repeated efforts to prevent construction or to compel removal of the bridge. The initial suit was instituted by the secretary of war seeking to halt the crossing of Rock Island on grounds that the island was a military reservation. It was further alleged that the bridge would impede navigation by steamboats. Pointing out that Rock Island had been long abandoned as a military post, the federal circuit court refused an injunction. The court also took the position that until Congress acted to protect river navigation, the federal government lacked authority to obtain judicial redress for supposed obstructions to commerce.[18]

A more famous challenge to the bridge was presented in the *Effie Afton* case. The circumstances of this dispute are shrouded in mystery. Only a few weeks after the bridge opened in April 1856, a steamboat, the *Effie Afton*, seemingly spun out of control after passing the draw span and rammed a pier. The steamboat quickly burst into flames and ignited a span of the bridge. Railroaders were convinced that the *Effie Afton* was loaded with inflammable material and deliberately rammed the bridge. Steamboat interests, on the other hand, maintained that the accident demonstrated the dangers of the Rock Island bridge to river navigation. The owners of the *Effie Afton* brought suit to recover damages sustained by reason of the obstruction of commerce. Represented by Abraham Lincoln, the Bridge Company offered evidence to show the culpability of the steamboat. Lincoln and the Bridge Company prevailed when the jury could not decide whether the bridge was an impediment to navigation, and the suit was eventually dropped.[19]

With the status of the Rock Island bridge still unresolved, a St. Louis steamboat operator brought suit to have the bridge declared a nuisance that imperiled river navigation. Upholding this contention, the trial judge directed that the portion of the bridge located on the Iowa side of the river be dismantled. In the midst of the Civil War, however, the Supreme Court reversed this judgment and dismissed the complaint. The justices did not squarely address whether the bridge amounted to a nuisance, ruling that the federal courts did not have jurisdiction over the Illinois side of the bridge and that elimination of just the Iowa section would not abate the alleged obstruction to river commerce. Of greater significance, the Supreme Court expressed doubt that the bridge was a serious impediment to navigation, and observed that under the plaintiff's argument no lawful bridge could be built over the Mississippi River. "Nor," the Court added, "could the great facilities to commerce, accomplished by the invention of railroads, be made available where great rivers had to be crossed."[20]

The outcome of the Rock Island litigation effectively established the right of railroads to bridge rivers. Soon a number of railroads spanned the Mississippi River, many with express congressional authorization. As Albro Martin sagely observed: "The Rock Island bridge case was a milestone in the vast changes in American law and jurisprudence that the railroads were bringing."[21] States were henceforth able to authorize such construction provided that the structure did not amount to a material impediment to waterborne commerce. Legislators were left to decide which form of transportation best served the public interest, and how to adjust competing interests.[22] As shown earlier, Congress also hastened this process by placing its seal of approval on numerous railroad bridges. The pressing need for railroad bridges as a vital link in the national market for goods convinced courts and legislators to modify the common-law insistence on the free navigation of entire waterways.

Dormant Commerce Power

Well before the Civil War, the Supreme Court established the principle that the commerce clause, by its own force, impliedly restricted the power of the states to interfere with business operations across state lines. Under this interpretation, the very purpose of the commerce clause was to secure a national market for goods.[23] Yet the courts had never taken the position that the states lacked authority to affect interstate commerce in any manner. The states were the center of regulatory activity, and state laws designed to safeguard the public health, safety, or morals often had an incidental impact on the movement of goods or persons from state to state. As with the controversy over bridges, judicial protection of a multistate market presented issues of federalism. The courts had to strike a balance between national free trade and state power to regulate.

The full potential of this negative or dormant aspect of the commerce clause was not realized until the second half of the nineteenth century. State railroad regulations generated a steady stream of cases in which the federal courts were called upon to protect interstate commerce in the face of burdensome state laws. Railroad litigation was therefore a major force in shaping the dormant commerce power. "Railroad and other transport cases," J. Willard Hurst explained, "bulk large in the creation of late-nineteenth century commerce clause law."[24] As the Supreme Court wielded the dormant commerce power with increasing frequency, the justices took special aim at state laws that either discriminated against or unreasonably burdened the flow of interstate trade.[25] The 1886 *Wabash* decision, treated in Chapter Three, was an early example of the new judicial vigor. There the Supreme Court struck down state-imposed controls on the charges for interstate shipments on the ground that this practice interfered with commerce.[26] Numerous other challenges to state regulation of railroads followed. Since the Supreme Court evaluated the factual circumstances of these cases on an individual basis, consistent patterns of decisions are hard to discern.

The Court generally allowed the states broad leeway to ensure the safety of passengers and goods. Laws prescribing the qualifications of the operating employees of a railroad passed constitutional muster. An 1887 Alabama statute required that all locomotive engineers driving a train in the state should be examined for competence and licensed by a state board. Brushing aside the argument that each state might impose a different requirement and in effect burden interstate commerce, the justices in *Smith v. Alabama* (1888) upheld the measure as a safety provision that only incidentally touched commerce. Similarly, the Supreme Court sustained a statute prohibiting persons with color blindness from engaging in train operations. Absent federal legislation governing the qualifications of rail employees, the Court ruled that the states retained authority to guard against accidents within their territory.[27]

State governance of railroad operations and imposition of safety devices also found a sympathetic judicial hearing. As is examined more fully in Chapter Five, states and localities had long controlled the speed of trains. In *Erb v. Morasch* (1900), the Supreme Court sustained the application to interstate trains of a municipal ordinance restricting train speed. The Court likewise upheld a Georgia law that required all trains to blow a whistle and reduce speed at every road crossing despite the delay to interstate traffic.[28] Yet state regulation of train speed was not without constitutional limits. For example, when it was shown that application of the Georgia road crossing law to an interstate train would substantially increase the running time, the Supreme Court concluded that the statute was an unreasonable burden on interstate commerce.[29]

State authority to mandate safety equipment was repeatedly affirmed. The practice of heating passenger cars by means of a stove inside each car raised the perilous hazard of fire if the train crashed or derailed. As was often the case, technological innovation paved the way for new legal requirements. The development of a forced-air heating system rendered the older stoves obsolete. In 1887 New York banned the use of stoves inside passenger cars. A railroad headquartered in Connecticut challenged the law as a burden on interstate commerce, arguing that possible conflicts between differing state laws regarding the heating of passenger cars would be a hardship to rail traffic across state lines. In the important decision of *New York, New Haven and Hartford Railroad Company v. New York* (1897), the Supreme Court stressed the power of states to protect the security of passengers within their territory and ruled that such authority trumped possible inconvenience to interstate trains. Adopting the same mode of analysis, the Court validated a Georgia law prescribing electric lights on all locomotives, including those operating in interstate commerce.

Another group of commerce clause issues related to efforts by the states to compel the stoppage of interstate passenger trains at designated points. By the 1880s railroad companies were introducing express trains that connected major urban areas and made only a limited number of stops at intermediate destinations. Concerned that the needs of local passengers were being neglected, state legislatures and railroad commissions frequently required railroads to stop their trains at communities along the route. Since such directives had the potential to impede directly interstate travel, courts carefully scrutinized stoppage requirements. The results are not easily reconciled, but in general the Supreme Court weighed the seriousness of the impact on commerce against the goals served by the regulation.[30]

From the mid-1890s to the first decade of the twentieth century, the Supreme Court heard a series of challenges to state stoppage laws. Indeed, in 1907 the Court observed that state statutes and commission orders "directing the stoppage of through interstate trains, have frequently, within late years, been before this court."[31] The justices invalidated a number of such laws deemed unduly burdensome to interstate commerce. At issue in *Illinois Central Railroad Company v. Illinois* (1896) was a law requiring all passenger trains to stop at every county seat, even if this entailed a detour out of their routes. Stressing that the effect of this statute was to delay a fast mail train, the Supreme Court pronounced it an unconstitutional hindrance of commerce. In the same vein, the justices voided a 1907 Missouri law mandating that all passenger trains stop at junction points with other carriers. They stressed that the railroad already provided adequate facilities for travelers at these intersections, and that the stopping of through trains was an unreasonable burden on interstate commerce.[32]

Yet not all state stoppage laws were found invalid. In *Lake Shore & Michigan Southern Railway Company v. Ohio* (1899), a sharply divided Supreme Court held that a statute compelling railroads to stop three passenger trains daily each way at villages of more than three thousand inhabitants did not infringe on national power over commerce. The Court noted that the Ohio law merely required that a certain number of trains stop at the designated places, leaving the companies free to operate other trains on a through basis. It viewed this stoppage statute as a police power regulation designed to serve the needs of local passengers. Nor did the commerce clause inhibit a state from directing intrastate passenger trains to stop at every county seat.[33]

The continuing controversy over the stoppage laws tells us much about the growing tension between state regulations and the national economic system. Courts labored to reconcile traditional state regulatory authority with the new realities of a national market. As the Supreme Court explained, stoppage statutes "have been approved or disapproved as they have seemed reasonable or unreasonable, or bore more or less heavily upon the power of railways to regulate their trains in the respective and sometimes conflicting interests of local and through traffic."[34] To resolve this clash, the Supreme Court articulated several factors to be considered in assessing the constitutionality of local regulations. A primary concern was the adequacy of existing rail service. Once local needs were satisfied, the Court reasoned, railroads were free to provide express trains without state-imposed restriction. The size of the community was also important. The justices pointed out that "it is not reasonable to suppose that the same facilities can be given to places of very small population that are supplied to their neighbors who live in much larger communities."[35] Another factor was the existence of competition for passenger business. "We are not obligated to shut our eyes," the Supreme Court emphasized in 1900, "to the fact that competition among railroads for through passenger traffic has become very spirited, and we think they have a right to demand that they shall not be unnecessarily hampered in their efforts to obtain a share of such traffic."[36] As in other areas of law, the Court's attachment to the market economy clearly influenced its treatment of the stoppage issue.

Judicial exercise of the dormant commerce power restrained other state rail regulations as well. A look at attempts to enforce Kentucky's constitutional ban on long haul–short haul rate differentials is instructive. In *Louisville and Nashville Railroad Company v. Kentucky* (1902), the Supreme Court had no difficulty in sustaining application of this regulation to transportation within the state, reasoning that any effect on interstate commerce was too remote to interfere with federal authority. On the other hand, the Court in *Louisville and Nashville Railroad Company v. Eubank* (1902) struck down a move to enforce the Kentucky long haul–short haul provision against shipments across state lines. The Court concluded that the effect of the state ban was to regulate interstate rates.

State laws governing the responsibility of railroads to shippers also ran afoul of the commerce clause. Freight shipped through different states was often transported on two or more carriers. When goods were lost or damaged, shippers found it difficult to ascertain the carrier upon whose line the loss occurred. To assist shippers, a Georgia statute imposed on the initial railroad an obligation to trace the shipment and to report how and by which company the freight was lost or destroyed. Failure to obtain such information rendered the initial carrier liable for the damages suffered. In *Central of Georgia Railway Company v. Murphey* (1905), the Supreme Court ruled that the statute was an unconstitutional burden on interstate commerce because the initial carrier could be held liable for the negligence of a connecting railroad.

Likewise, the Supreme Court voided an order of the Arkansas railroad commission that carriers must, upon written application, furnish freight cars to shippers within five days. The justices pointed out that this requirement hampered the interchange of cars with connecting railroads and, in practice, favored local shippers at the expense of interstate commerce.[37]

Even local flood control projects were found to impinge upon federal authority over commerce between the states. At issue in *Kansas City Southern*

Railway Company v. Kaw Valley Drainage District (1914) was an order to remove railroad bridges over the Kansas River that allegedly contributed to an overflow of the river. The Supreme Court, speaking through Justice Oliver Wendell Holmes, Jr., emphasized that the bridges were "a necessary part of lines of commerce by rail among the states." Such a direct interference with interstate commerce, Holmes reasoned, could not be justified by invoking the police power to alleviate flooding. In short, he maintained that "the dominant requirements of commerce" must prevail over local concerns.[38]

Judicial protection of railroading as an instrument of interstate commerce reached a culmination in the leading case of *Southern Pacific Co. v. Arizona* (1945).[39] Under a 1912 statute, Arizona prohibited the operation of a train of more than fourteen passenger or seventy freight cars. The train limit law was passed at the behest of railroad unions, which sought to ensure employment by eliminating the possibility of longer trains. By the 1920s, however, more powerful locomotives were capable of hauling trains longer than seventy cars, and the Arizona law was increasingly seen as burdensome to transcontinental rail shipments. During the 1930s a handful of other states enacted similar train limit laws. But the Nevada law was promptly invalidated on the grounds that it constituted state interference with interstate commerce.[40]

Arizona defended its law before the Supreme Court as a safety measure to reduce the danger of accidents on long trains. The Court pointed out that the operation of longer trains was standard practice among American railroads, and that the Arizona law added materially to the cost of providing rail service in the state. Finding only a tenuous connection between the law and the supposed safety concerns, the Court determined that the regulation of train length went "too far" and had a serious adverse effect on the maintenance of an efficient rail transportation system. The *Southern Pacific* decision built upon the earlier line of railroad cases to formulate the modern test for applying the dormant commerce power, explicitly weighing the state's interests against the impact on interstate commerce. As a practical matter, moreover, the ruling allowed the carriers to take advantage of improved technology and to operate trains of whatever length they wished.

One should not understand the Supreme Court as championing railroad interests in its handling of dormant commerce clause cases. Instead, the justices harbored a well-founded concern that state regulations increasingly threatened to disrupt the free flow of national commerce. Railroads, as the principal arteries of interstate trade during the late nineteenth and early twentieth centuries, were major beneficiaries of this judicial solicitude for the multistate market. While the railroads certainly did not prevail in every commerce clause challenge to state laws, the commerce clause often had the effect of freeing the rail industry from inconsistent and narrow state controls.

Congressional Preemption

Congress, of course, had unquestioned authority to enact legislation governing interstate transportation. When Congress legislated with respect to a particular subject, the courts early insisted that the paramount federal statute superseded any inconsistent state law. But since Congress rarely used its power to regulate commerce during the nineteenth century, there were relatively few instances in which federal and state laws conflicted. Absent congressional action, the federal courts, as discussed earlier, played the key role as arbiter of competing state and national interests with respect to commerce.

This picture changed markedly as the twentieth century progressed. After 1900 Congress became more active in regulating the economy and in policing state encroachments on interstate trade. The broadening reach of federal statutes left less room for state legislation on the same subjects. As is examined more fully in Chapters Ten and Eleven, Congress in the first two decades of the twentieth century enacted a comprehensive scheme of federal railroad regulation. One consequence was further displacement of state regulatory authority over the rail industry.

A series of Supreme Court cases stressed that once Congress exercised its paramount power over railroads, state regulatory authority ceased. A revealing example of this trend arose from the Hours of Service Act of 1907, in which Congress limited the hours of consecutive work by railroad employees in interstate commerce. The Supreme Court held that Congress had asserted its control over the working schedule of railroad employees and that hence there was no room for any state legislation on the subject.[41] Similarly, in *Southern Railway Company v. Reid* (1912), the Court ruled that Congress, by enacting the Hepburn Act of 1906, had entirely taken control of interstate railroad rate making, and that an inconsistent North Carolina statute was unenforceable. Regulations issued by federal agencies also superseded state laws, as the case of *Pennsylvania Railroad Company v. Public Service Commission* (1919) demonstrated. The Supreme Court was asked to consider whether a state law governing the rear cars of trains could be enforced in the face of elaborate ICC regulations. Writing for the Court, Justice Holmes emphasized the superior authority of Congress and federal agencies, and opined that states could not impose an additional obligation on carriers. "But when the United States has exercised its exclusive powers over interstate commerce so far as to take possession of the field," he observed, "the States no more can supplement its requirements than they can annul them."[42]

Given the long-standing economic nationalism of the Supreme Court, decisions giving a broad reading to federal railroad legislation were hardly a surprise. Indeed, congressional action served to reinforce the Court's position that efficient interstate transportation needed uniform laws, not the inevitable confusion resulting from different state provisions. Although the Court spoke in terms of preserving federal authority, the distributional effect of these decisions was to release the railroads from compliance with state regulations that were often more onerous than the federal requirements. Significantly, it was the carriers who invoked the commerce clause or claimed that congressional measures excluded state regulation.

As the first national industry that touched the economic life of most Americans, railroads were the subject of regulation at both state and federal levels. Inspired by a concern for their own interests, the carriers instituted court challenges that contributed materially to the growth of the commerce clause as a shield against state legislation. The ultimate impact of railroad litigation in this field was to enhance federal court authority and to lay the basis for later developments that redefined the balance between state and federal power over the economy.

5

Law Governing Railroad Operations

A long with improved transportation and the promise of economic growth, railroads brought new hazards to adjacent landowners and persons crossing tracks. Locomotives killed livestock, started fires, and collided with vehicles at highway intersections. Courts early recognized the perilous nature of railroading. "The business of railroads," the Supreme Court of Vermont observed in 1854, "is especially dangerous."[1] Decrying the "appalling disasters that are so frequently occurring," the Supreme Court of Tennessee noted a public expectation that judges should hold railroads "to that care and diligence, which the law prescribes for the safety and protection of all persons who extend to them their patronage."[2]

For all of their enthusiasm for the development of rail enterprise, legislators and judges recognized the need to balance the rights of railroads with the interests of other property owners. They did not confer unqualified privileges on railroads, and insisted that the carriers take care to avoid accidents and injury to others. Acknowledging that "there are none who are not impressed with the importance of railroads," the Supreme Court of Missouri nonetheless pointedly asserted in 1858: "The other interests in the state are not all to be made subservient to the railroad interest."[3] Throughout the nineteenth and early twentieth centuries, states enacted a host of laws governing railroad operations. Many of these regulations imposed substantial compliance costs on railroads, belying the notion that lawmakers invariably preferred railroads over other private interests.

Rail travel also raised a number of legal issues regarding the treatment of passengers. Disputes over the nonpayment of fares were particularly vexing. Here, as well, legislators and judges sought to reconcile competing interests.

Railroad Fence Laws

One of the most troublesome legal issues raised by the spread of railroads was the question of fencing rights-of-way. Resolution of this matter was closely tied to the liability of railroads for injuries to livestock and passengers when locomotives collided with domestic animals. The dangers posed by railroading caused antebellum lawmakers to rethink the traditional rules governing fencing, and to place carriers under a duty to enclose their tracks.

The prolonged controversy over the construction of railroad fences had its roots in the English common law. At common law, owners of livestock were obligated to prevent their animals from trespassing on the land of others. It followed that stock could not lawfully run at large and that owners of farm animals were in effect required to fence their own land.[4] Conversely, absent a charter or statutory provision, railroads had no duty to fence their track against trespassing animals.

A large number of jurisdictions, particularly in the northeast, initially adhered to the common-law rule. A leading case upholding this proposition was *Railroad Company v. Skinner* (1852), decided by the Supreme Court of Pennsylvania. The court developed a utilitarian rationale for the common-law rule. Extolling the advantages of rail travel, the court dismissed the suggestion that the train crew should be concerned with "those loitering or roving cattle by which our railways are infested." The court was also sensitive to the expense involved in erecting fences along extensive routes, adding that "the cost of fencing them would be greater than could be borne."[5] Likewise, the Supreme Court of Michigan took the position that railroads were not required to fence their lines for any reason, and asked rhetorically whether carriers should "be compelled to assume the guardianship of all stray cattle, horses, and swine, usually found strolling along on the track of their railroad?"[6] In short, under common law, owners allowed livestock to wander at their peril and had no recourse if the animals were killed on tracks.

Another group of states, including most southern jurisdictions, rejected the common-law rule as inapposite to local land settlement practices. These states followed the custom that livestock were allowed to run at large and graze on unenclosed land. Access to the open range was treated as a valuable right, and therefore livestock owners were not responsible for damage caused by wandering animals to unenclosed land.[7]

This attitude markedly shaped the law with respect to railroad fencing. For example, in *Vicksburg and Jackson Railroad Company v. Patton* (1856), the Supreme Court of Mississippi found the common law inapplicable to a state with large areas of unenclosed woodlands and prairies. Since animals could lawfully go at large, railroads had to take care not to injure grazing animals on their tracks. Although the railroad was under no legal obligation to fence its track, the court suggested that railroads would be prudent to enclose their rights-of-way in order to avoid liability for accidents. The

Supreme Court of Missouri even asserted that popular attachment to the open range outweighed the desire for railroads:

> The range, as it is called, is a source of wealth to many of our citizens, and nothing would induce them more resolutely to oppose the location of a railroad in the vicinity than the knowledge that it would impose on them the obligation of keeping their cattle and stock in inclosures.[8]

While jurists debated the suitability of the common-law enclosure rules in the age of railroads, legislators began to place carriers under an affirmative duty to fence their lines. As early as 1836 a New York charter required the Schenectada and Troy Railroad to "erect and maintain sufficient fences upon the side of the route of their said road."[9] Massachusetts in 1846 became the first state to enact legislation mandating that every railroad fence both sides of its entire length.[10] Starting in the late 1840s, general railroad acts in many jurisdictions, including New York, Michigan, Illinois, and New Mexico, compelled carriers to construct fences along their track and cattle guards at crossings. Although the details and timing varied from state to state, lawmakers were moving to modify the common law and place the responsibility for fencing on the railroads.[11] The *American Railroad Journal* applauded this trend as the best way to avoid accidents and financial loss. "It hardly seems that it should be necessary," the *Journal* opined, "to compel corporations to fence in such valuable property as a good railroad."[12]

State fencing statutes worked a major change in the law to reflect the new realities of railroading. The reasons for this abandonment of the common law were best explained by the New York Court of Appeals in *Corwin v. New York and Erie Railroad Company* (1855). The court questioned whether the common law was any longer adequate "when applied to the new circumstances and condition of things arising out of the general introduction and use of railroads in the country."[13] It emphasized that a collision with animals on the track often caused derailments and injury to passengers. The most efficacious way to prevent such accidents, the court reasoned, was to fence the track, and this duty was more appropriately placed on the railroads than on thousands of individual landowners along the rights-of-way.

Both state and federal courts uniformly sustained the constitutionality of fencing laws as a police power regulation against a variety of challenges.[14] Recognizing that "the legislature, by its enactment, was looking more to agricultural interests than to the protection of railroad property," the Supreme Court of Indiana insisted that lawmakers had the power to regulate transportation safety.[15] Consistent with its record of upholding the validity of rail safety measures, the Supreme Court, in a line of cases during the late nineteenth century, brushed aside attacks on state fencing laws as deprivations of due process and equal protection in violation of the Fourteenth Amendment. Justice Stephen J. Field, writing for the Court in *Missouri Pacific Railway Company v. Humes* (1885), defended the fencing statutes as an exercise of the state's authority to prevent accidents. He observed:

> In few instances could the power be more wisely or beneficiently exercised than in compelling railroad corporations to inclose their roads with fences. . . . The speed and momentum of the locomotive render such protection against accident in thickly settled portions of the country absolutely essential.[16]

Nor did courts find any constitutional infirmity in applying fence laws to railroads previously organized under special charters that contained no such requirement. All railroads, courts easily concluded, were subject to the police power. As explained by the Supreme Court of Vermont, legislators could "impose new obligations and restrictions on these roads . . . as by not allowing them to run in an unsafe condition."[17]

Widespread passage of railroad fence laws changed the terms of the legal dialogue and raised a number of disputes. Courts were repeatedly called upon to construe the language of the acts. What constituted a sufficient fence for purposes of compliance with the law? Would a barbed wire fence satisfy the statutory requirement? To what extent could railroads discharge their duty by contracting with adjacent landowners to construct and maintain a fence? Statutes in some jurisdictions expressly contemplated this possibility. Was a railroad liable for injury to livestock when the landowner failed to erect the fence as agreed? These and other questions made the fencing laws a fruitful source of controversy.[18]

Injury to Livestock

Liability for farm animals killed or injured by collision with trains was a contentious issue throughout the nineteenth century, pitting farmers against carriers. In 1855 the New York Court of Appeals observed that there was "much litigation growing out of the killing and injuring of cattle along the road, producing irritation and exciting angry and, at times vindictive passions."[19] Lawsuits over injuries inflicted on livestock by railroads were ubiquitous. It is not my plan to treat these cases exhaustively, but just to sketch the shifting parameters of railroad liability for injuring animals.

Before the enactment of fence laws, it was difficult for an owner of live-stock to recover for injury in states adhering to the common-law view. In such jurisdictions the railroad owed no duty of care toward trespassing animals, and owners were deemed negligent for failure to confine their stock.[20] There were even a number of cases in which carriers recovered damages from owners for allowing cattle to get on the track and cause a derailment.[21]

The liability picture was quite different in open-range states. Since cattle were not trespassing upon unenclosed railroad land, the responsibility of carriers for injuring livestock turned upon a showing of negligence. Yet the owner still had to prove that the injury to the animals was the result of railroad negligence. Courts heard a good deal of testimony about alleged excessive speed, failure to sound whistles, and careless lookouts. Although juries were generally sympathetic to farmers, claimants often confronted severe evidentiary problems. The owner usually did not know how or when the stock were injured, and the only witnesses to most livestock accidents were railroad employees.

Several southern states eased the evidentiary burden of stock owners by shifting the burden of proof. In the leading case of *Danner v. South Carolina Railroad Company* (1851), the Supreme Court of South Carolina held that a prima facie presumption of negligence was created upon proof that livestock were injured on tracks. Then the onus was placed on the carrier to prove that the accident occurred without fault on its part. The court warned: "It would give dangerous license and indemnity to the destruction of cattle" if the burden was put on the owner to show the manner in which the livestock were destroyed.[22] As one historian noted, the *Danner* rule "imposed a nascent form of strict liability upon the railroads in livestock death cases."[23] Similarly, legislatures in Georgia and Tennessee enacted statutes that required carriers to rebut a presumption of negligence when a train injured farm animals.[24] An 1852 Alabama act went a step further, making railroads strictly liable for killing livestock with no opportunity to demonstrate due care. But a successor statute was invalidated by the Supreme Court of Alabama as a violation of due process, and thus owners could only recover by proving negligence.[25]

Not all southern states followed the *Danner* precedent. Courts in Florida and Texas, for instance, continued to insist that an owner must prove negligence on the part of the railroad. The Supreme Court of Florida explained that a train "has just as much right to run as cattle have to range" and that mere proof of injury to livestock by a collision did not demonstrate wrongdoing.[26] Also, the Supreme Court of North Carolina narrowly construed a statute raising a presumption of negligence against carriers, and explicitly balanced the advantages of rail travel against injury to livestock:

> The railroad system, traversing the country in all directions, contributes largely to the development of its agricultural, commercial and other resources, and this result is attained mainly by the certainty, regularity and rapidity with which the trains move and transportation is effected . . . and though occasional injury may be done to stock allowed to stray upon the road-bed, this inconvenience is greatly outweighed by the benefits conferred upon the whole country by railway transportation.[27]

This decision clearly placed railroad development ahead of accountability for harm to farm animals.

Despite occasional pro-enterprise language, southern lawmakers were generally more inclined to safeguard agricultural interests than to single-mindedly promote railroading. Owners of injured livestock did not prevail in every case, but southern courts and legislators were sensitive to the concerns of farmers and fashioned legal doctrines that put pressure on railroads to pay for stock injuries. By the late nineteenth century, railroads operating in the South faced many stock claims and preferred to settle with farmers rather than litigate.[28] The special economic arrangements of the South affected the evolution of the law governing the relative rights of railroad companies and owners of livestock.[29]

The spread of fence laws in northern and western states also increased the potential liability of railroad companies for collision with livestock. Such statutes typically provided that carriers were responsible for all damage to farm animals until the required fences were erected. This gave the railroads a strong financial incentive to comply with the law. Once a fence was constructed, moreover, the railroads were not liable for injury to livestock unless negligence was shown.[30] As an additional inducement for compliance, a number of states made railroads liable for double the amount of any loss resulting from an omission to fence their lines.[31]

The statutory duty to fence was an imperative, and the failure to fence rendered the company liable for all ensuing damages. It was unnecessary for the livestock owner to prove negligence by the railroad. As explained by the Supreme Court of Missouri, "the right to recover is made to depend only upon the fact of an injury being done and the omission to build and maintain suitable fences and cattleguards."[32]

In effect, the fence laws made railroads absolutely liable for injury to livestock upon unfenced track. As the nineteenth century progressed, railroads were more likely to be found liable for hurting wandering animals. Indeed, as shown in Chapter Nine, the law generally provided better protection for livestock than for injured employees. But conflict between railroads and farmers over stock continued to occupy the courts, and was resolved on an untidy case-by-case basis with an emphasis on particular sets of facts.[33]

Fire

Fire was another hazard emanating from the growth of railroads. Sparks from locomotives frequently ignited fields, fences, and buildings along rights-of-way. As with the cases involving livestock, lawmakers sought to reconcile the competing interests of railroads and landowners.

At common law, the lighting of a fire on one's own land was treated as an extrahazardous activity, and the person who made it was absolutely liable for any resulting injury caused, regardless of the degree of care employed. Perhaps concerned that absolute liability would retard the fledgling rail industry, American courts early shied away from such a rigorous standard and predicated liability for burning adjacent property upon a showing of negligence. In *Ellis v. Portsmouth and Roanoke Rail Road Company* (1841), a locomotive set fire to a fence running parallel to the track. Rejecting an argument premised on strict liability, the Supreme Court of North Carolina asserted that "no man, unless he has engaged to become insurer . . . against unavoidable accidents, is responsible for damage sustained against his will and without his fault."[34] The court maintained that there could be no liability for the fire on the part of railroad without fault. But the court aided the landowner by finding a prima facie case of negligence, and requiring the railroad to prove its due care to avoid the injury. Other courts also determined that railroads were liable for damages from fire only when the carrier was negligent in its operations. Finding that a railroad was not responsible for fire caused by sparks except on proof of negligence, the Supreme Court of Pennsylvania stressed the negative economic consequences of a strict liability standard: "They would in effect become insurers of every property . . . contiguous to the road, a grievance which might prove destructive to the interests of the company."[35]

A number of jurisdictions enacted statutes that affirmed the negligence principle but shifted the burden of proof to the railroad to show it used reasonable care to prevent injury by fire. For example, an 1838 Maryland act provided that when property was destroyed by fire from a locomotive, the onus was on the carrier to disprove negligence.[36] A Michigan law likewise declared that railroads were liable for all damages caused by fire unless the company could prove that its engines "were in good order" and that "all reasonable precautions had been taken."[37] In other words, absence of negligence was a defense. The defendant railroad could attempt to demonstrate its diligence by offering evidence that the locomotive was properly constructed, equipped with an approved spark arrester, and managed by a competent crew. The question of negligence, however, was generally submitted to a jury, whose sympathies were often with the local landowner.[38] In some jurisdictions, jury sentiment led railroads to settle most fire cases.

Even when railroads took every reasonable precaution, sparks from locomotives still caused fires. The negligence standard was increasingly seen as insufficient to protect adequately the property of adjacent landowners from loss by railroad fires. Starting with Massachusetts in 1840, states began to pass statutes that imposed absolute responsibility on railroads, independent of any fault, for fire originating from locomotives. Such measures also gave railroads "an insurable interest in the property for which it may be so held responsible in damages along its route," and authorized carriers to procedure insurance on their own behalf.[39] This made it possible for carriers, at least in theory, to cushion their heightened risk by obtaining insurance on land along their rights-of-way.[40] Over time similar laws were enacted in many jurisdictions, including Vermont, South Carolina, and Colorado. Given the unique problem of fire spreading from railroads, lawmakers were effectively restoring the common-law rule of strict liability while encouraging the carriers to get insurance.

Federal and state courts uniformly upheld the constitutionality of statutes making railroads absolutely liable for fire damages.[41] The Supreme Court sustained Missouri's strict liability law in *St. Louis and San Francisco Railway Company v. Mathews* (1897). Noting that fire had long been regarded as a dangerous element, the justices held that the statute was a valid exercise of state police power to protect property against loss occasioned by the use of locomotives. "The right of the citizen not to have his property burned without compensation," the Court declared, "is no less to be regarded than the right of the corporation to set it on fire."[42] When both parties were blameless, the Court reasoned, the legislature could properly assign the duty of insuring property to the railroad that created the peril of fire by its use of locomotives.

In some jurisdictions courts created another hurdle to the recovery of fire-related damages by distinguishing between proximate and remote consequences of negligence. As exemplified by the revealing New York case of *Ryan v. New York Central Railroad* (1866), these courts limited railroad liability to the proximate or direct result of the wrongful spread of fire. In *Ryan* a locomotive ignited a fire on railroad property. The fire quickly spread and destroyed the plaintiff's house. The Court of Appeals denied any recovery on grounds that the locomotive was not the proximate cause of the injury to the plaintiff's house. Liability attached only when property was consumed by fire directly communicated from the locomotive. In reaching this remarkable decision, the court was clearly worried about the impact of ruinous liability for accidental fires: "To sustain such a claim . . . would subject [the railroad] to a liability against which no prudence could guard, and to meet which no private fortune would be adequate."[43]

Most courts, however, firmly rejected such a crabbed view of railroad responsibility for careless fires.[44] Instead, they insisted that carriers were liable for all the natural consequences of their negligent actions. The mere fact that a fire spread from its place of origin did not render the injury remote or absolve the railroad. The Supreme Court of Illinois was particularly impatient with the argument that railroads faced bankruptcy if charged with all the damages resulting from fire. Noting that "however useful they may be," railroads were operated for "pecuniary profit," the court observed:

> but we do not see why [railroads] should be exempted from the moral duty of indemnification for injuries committed by the careless or wanton spread of fire along their track, because such indemnity may sometimes amount to so large a sum as to sweep away all their profits.

Better that a railroad company "should be reduced to bankruptcy, and even suspend its operations," the court maintained, than that the carrier should be allowed to escape responsibility for fires and the loss fall on innocent landowners.[45]

As this record makes plain, for the most part neither judges nor legislators let their enthusiasm for railroading keep them from holding railroads accountable for injuries caused by fire. This was not a situation in which legal rules worked largely in favor of railroad interests. On the contrary, legislators in many jurisdictions altered the legal norms to benefit the victims of railroad fires. With some exceptions, courts regularly upheld jury verdicts awarding damages for such fires. There is little to suggest that lawmakers were consciously promoting railroad development at the expense of landowners.

Grade Crossings

Another set of legal issues arose from the frequency of collisions at the places where rail tracks crossed highways. From the first days of railroading until the mid–twentieth century, grade-crossing accidents plagued both rural and urban Americans. This constant danger led states to adopt various preventive measures almost from the advent of the railroad.

One common statutory provision required trains to ring a bell or sound a steam whistle as they approached crossings.[46] Failure to comply with this mandate rendered a railroad company liable for a monetary penalty and for any damages that an injured party suffered by reason of such omission. Likewise, statutes directed that railroads post warning signs at crossings.[47] There is room to doubt the effectiveness of these requirements in reducing accidents, but they proved to be relatively noncontroversial. Courts readily concluded that the bell or whistle requirement was a valid exercise of the police power to protect public safety. Indeed, failure to give the necessary signal was treated as a prima facie case of negligence.[48] Statutes mandating bells or whistles occasionally posed questions of interpretation. New York courts, for instance, considered whether this obligation applied only when the railroad and roadway crossed at the same level. A judicial ruling that the law required ringing a bell or blowing a whistle even when the track was elevated and passed over the highway caused the legislature to change the provision to cover only crossings at grade level.[49]

Discharge of this statutory duty was not always popular with the public. Ringing bells or blowing whistles sometimes frightened livestock and may have exacerbated problems with horse-drawn conveyances. Since railroads were required by law to give signals at crossings, courts found that carriers were not responsible for injuries occasioned when horses were frightened by the noise and ran away.[50]

Following the Civil War, the requirement of warning signals and signs was increasingly seen as inadequate to prevent crossing accidents. There was ample evidence that drivers and pedestrians simply ignored warning signs. As vehicular traffic grew, the number of collisions mounted. Crossing multiple tracks was especially hazardous because trains were often moving in both directions at once.[51]

Judges and legislators therefore debated the imposition of additional safety devices on the carriers. The Supreme Court of Illinois broadly defined railroad responsibility in 1873: "The rights of the company and the public to the use of the crossing are mutual, but it is the duty of the company to provide the proper safeguards, and the degree of diligence must be in proportion to the hazard."[52] Because the operation of railroads made crossings dangerous, the court added, "they may be compelled to bear the expenses of such measures as may be adopted" to secure the lives and property of those using the roadways. It followed that a railroad company could be compelled to provide a flagman at busy crossings. State legislatures also moved to enlarge the obligations on carriers with regard to crossings. A Michigan statute authorized the Commissioner of Railroads, when "the public interests require," to order railroads to maintain a gate or a flagman at crossings."[53] This generous understanding of regulatory authority opened the door for states and localities to mandate automatic safety devices as technology developed.

Rising concern about crossing accidents dovetailed with greater obstruction of highways by railroads. As trains grew longer, they often blocked highways when stopping at stations, inconveniencing roadway users and causing traffic problems. Slow-moving freight trains also caused traffic in urban areas to back up. This obstruction of intersections generated a legislative response. Statutes, beginning in the mid–nineteenth century, prohibited any railroad from obstructing highways for more than a few minutes, and limited any such blockage to the purpose of receiving passengers or fuel.[54] Nor did courts display much sympathy with railroads that blocked city streets, even for the purpose of switching freight cars. "No railroad company," the Supreme Court of Illinois sternly lectured, "can claim the right to obstruct the streets of any town, and if they do, they must abide the consequences."[55]

The move to eliminate grade crossings first appeared in the antebellum period. Several New England states empowered localities to require railroads to erect bridges over their track at places of intersection with roads.[56] By the 1870s, as the speed of trains increased, grade-crossing accidents became more severe. This development, coupled with the continuing problem of highway obstruction, caused many states to adopt a policy of eliminating grade crossings. State regulatory commissions started to compel the separation of track and roads by means of bridges or underpasses. In 1870 the Connecticut Railroad Commission urged enactment of a "law which will tend to abolish all such crossings within a certain number of years upon all railroads."[57] Following the construction of Grand Central Depot, the New York Central Railroad and New York City split the cost of putting the approaching track underground.

Grade removal, of course, was expensive, and the question of who should bear the expense was much contested. In the late 1870s, the City of Rochester, through a combination of regulatory pressure and negotiation, convinced the New York Central to elevate its tracks through the city, with the carrier paying all costs.[58] In 1889 the Connecticut legislature went a step further, enacting a comprehensive scheme that compelled railroads to remove one grade crossing annually for each sixty miles of track. The costs of elimination were allocated between the state and the railroad. The Supreme Court affirmed the validity of this statute in 1894, accepting the notion that grade crossings were in the nature of a nuisance that the state could abate.[59]

This decision set the tone for a series of federal and state cases that allowed states to saddle railroads with all or a substantial share of the expense of eliminating grade crossings. At root the question turned upon whether carriers could be appropriately held responsible for dangerous intersections. The courts paid little heed to railroad arguments that tracks were often laid long before roadways were built, and that the public, not the carriers, benefited from crossing improvements. Nor were courts concerned that heavy expenditures to remove grade crossings might result in bankruptcy for financially pressed carriers.[60]

The imposition of these costs on the railroads was justified as safeguarding the public from dangers incident to rail operations. Not only were railroads seen as causing the peril, but courts proceeded on the assumption that the public's right to use highways was superior to railroad interests. Writing for the Supreme Court in 1921, Justice Oliver Wendell Holmes, Jr., stated:

> Grade crossings call for a necessary adjustment of two competing interests—that of the public using the streets and that of the railroads and the public using them. Generically the streets represent the more important interest of the two. . . . They always are the necessity of the whole public, which the railroads, vital as they are, hardly can be called to the same extent.[61]

From the outset, then, courts were fully supportive of legislative and administrative efforts to spur grade separation.

Despite a receptive legal climate, the task of grade elimination proceeded slowly in the early decades of the twentieth century. Although many carriers in time came to embrace grade removal as a way to avoid tort liability for accidents and to move trains more rapidly, the heavy financial outlay was a major obstacle. Railroad commissions found it difficult to secure compliance from nearly insolvent lines. Localities often balked at paying their allocated share of the expense. The eradication of grade crossings by tunnels and overpasses also produced undesirable changes in urban neighborhoods and frequently aroused intense local opposition.[62]

By the 1930s courts and regulatory bodies began to take a fresh look at the legal issues arising from grade-crossing removals. Two factors were responsible for this reevaluation. The first was the onset of the depression. Absent a compelling public safety need, regulators were reluctant to inflict heavy removal costs during a period of general financial distress.[63] Second, the rapid growth of automobile and truck traffic created a new and potent source of competition with railroads. Statutes requiring carriers to obviate grade crossings now appeared in a new light—as a boost to rail competitors.

In response to the changed economic circumstances, the Supreme Court cast a more skeptical eye on the constitutionality of orders to abolish grade crossings. The first harbinger of change was a 1933 decision striking down a Virginia commission order to construct an overpass made without prior notice to the carrier or a hearing. The Court concluded that such administrative action constituted a deprivation of railroad property without due process.[64] The justices then moved more forcefully to limit state authority in *Nashville, Chattanooga and St. Louis Railway v. Walters* (1935). At issue was a Tennessee order requiring the carrier to bear half the cost of separating a particular grade by constructing an underpass. Stressing "the revolution wrought by motor vehicle transportation," the Supreme Court, in an opinion by Justice Louis D. Brandeis, pointed out that a law valid when enacted might later become unconstitutional by virtue of different circumstances.[65] The Court was clearly troubled by evidence that grade removal primarily benefited commercial highway users in active competition with railroads. It remanded the case for a consideration of whether the order was so unreasonable as to deprive the railroad of property without due process. In *Walters* the Court signaled, however tentatively, that the power to eliminate grade crossings was subject to constitutional limitations.

Allocation of the costs to obviate grade crossings remained a topic of litigation into the mid–twentieth century. Following *Walters*, courts started to insist that grade-removal orders must be for the protection of public safety and not for the promotion of more rapid motor vehicle traffic.[66] Courts continued to uphold a number of commission orders placing at least part of grade-removal costs on railroads regardless of whether the carrier received any direct benefit, but they also found at times that particular improvement projects that substantially assisted truck and bus traffic constituted an undue burden.[67]

One could question whether the courts ever came to grips with shifting patterns of transportation and massive expenditure of federal funds upon highways in their handling of the post–World War II grade-removal cases. Public policy came to markedly favor motor vehicle traffic. It was increasingly less tenable to assert that grade separations were driven solely by safety concerns or that railroads should automatically be assigned the primary blame for dangerous crossings. But, for better or worse, lawmakers and judges were disinclined to revisit this issue.

Although the most common example of state-mandated expenditures involved grade separations, lawmakers also required carriers to change existing structures or construct improvements to serve public convenience in other respects. The Supreme Court of Appeals of Virginia, in a typical case, explained that when a railroad crossed a public highway, it was under a continuing duty to make such alterations as changed conditions required. Hence, a carrier could be compelled, at its expense, to enlarge a bridge over its tracks in order to serve a growing city population.[68] In *Chicago, Burlington and Quincy Railway Company v. Drainage Commissioners* (1906), the Supreme Court likewise held that a state, as part of a drainage project, could compel a railroad to remove an existing bridge and erect a new one with a larger opening for an increased volume of water. Brushing aside an argument that this requirement constituted an unconstitutional taking of railroad property, the Court ruled that the cost of rebuilding was merely an incidental injury resulting from the exercise of the police power. Similarly, the Supreme Court upheld a Chicago ordinance requiring a carrier to lower or remove its tunnel under the Chicago River in order to accommodate river navigation as well as a municipal order directing replacement of an embankment with a bridge.[69] Certainly, the justices made little effort to shield railroads from the imposition of heavy financial burdens. Mechanically invoking the police power, they did not carefully analyze which party should bear the cost of desired improvements.[70]

Other Safety Regulations

During the nineteenth century, the legal system established standards to govern other aspects of rail operations. Many of these regulations were concerned with public safety, and deserve brief attention to indicate the far-ranging nature of public controls over the industry.

Americans were keen enthusiasts for rapid modes of travel. Responding to popular demand, railroad companies ran faster trains. Yet as early as the 1850s the increased speed of trains contributed to a spate of accidents. With the advent of more powerful locomotives following the Civil War, accident rates mounted steadily.[71] Not surprisingly, legislators saw a need to regulate the speed of trains, particularly in urban areas. The New Hampshire Code of 1867 restricted train speed to six miles an hour near towns. Florida's general railroad act of 1874 provided that trains could not exceed four miles per hour through city streets or when crossing drawbridges. Similar measures were enacted in other jurisdictions, and many cities passed ordinances dealing with train speed.[72]

Courts had no hesitancy in enforcing speed regulations. The Supreme Court of Wisconsin stressed that "a strict observance" of speed restrictions was "essential to public welfare."[73] The court even suggested that officials should institute criminal prosecutions against railroad employees who disregarded the speed limit statute. Moreover, the operation of a train faster than allowed by law was treated as negligence by the company.

The operation of steam-powered locomotives in urban areas proved troublesome to city residents. Aside from the risk of fire caused by sparks, locomotives filled the air with smoke and cinders. Public pressure gradually built to eliminate steam engines from city streets. An 1873 City of Richmond ordinance banned steam-powered locomotives from certain locations, a move sustained by the Supreme Court as within municipal power to govern use of the streets.[74] By the late nineteenth century, coal smoke from engines was a major source of air pollution in American cities. A number of communities, such as New York City and Chicago, enacted smoke control ordinances and attempted to pressure rail companies to adopt smoke abatement technologies. Yet progress was slow, in part because early municipal ordinances were ineffectually enforced. The development of electric power gave additional impetus to the removal of steam engines from crowded areas. A number of city ordinances in the first decade of the twentieth century sought to compel electrification of tracks entering terminals.[75] In 1923, moreover, the New York legislature prohibited the use of any motive power by railroads except electricity in New York City.[76] Only gradually, however, did other communities follow this lead.

To safeguard passengers, states also took a hand in the formation and operation of passenger trains. Legislation early proscribed the placing of baggage or freight cars in the rear of passenger cars. Since deadly fire often resulted from wrecks, states commonly made it illegal to illuminate passenger cars with kerosene or other explosive materials. With the hazard of fire in mind, laws in a number of states ended the practice of locking passenger cars while trains were in motion.[77] State railroad commissions were empowered to inspect the construction of tracks and bridges and to recommend adoption of safety devices.[78] Lawmakers clearly asserted the authority to impose detailed regulations on carriers to serve public safety.

The movement to enact safety legislation received the strong endorsement of the *American Railroad Journal*. An 1852 editorial noted: "The introduction of railroads has been so recent, that legislation has by no means kept pace with their development, nor with the necessity of providing for the public safety."[79] The *Journal* urged that railroads be required to use the best materials for track and cars, and that their operations should be subject to safety inspections. Such sentiments underscore the prevalent lack of sympathy with careless rail operations.

Relations with Passengers

A good deal of legislation focused on the relationship between passengers and railroads. Much of this was directed toward the improvement of basic services. But legislators also enlarged the authority of carriers to discipline passengers.

During the early period of railroading, there were chronic complaints about unreliable service and the difficulty of making connections with other lines. In response a number of states, starting in the late 1840s, required railroads to run passenger trains "at regular times to be fixed by public notice" and to "furnish sufficient accommodations for the transportation" of passengers.[80] Such provisions became common after the Civil War, and in theory forced railroads to operate according to a schedule. But a patchwork of state laws could only do so much to bring about orderly train schedules. The goal of improved scheduling was not achieved until most carriers adopted standard time in 1883.

Courts fashioned an additional protection for passengers by holding railroads liable for negligent transportation. These cases involved situations in which trains either carried persons beyond their destination or neglected to pick up passengers at flag stations. Failure to make the proper signal was usually the cause of such mishaps. Emphasizing that railroads were bound to transport passengers to their destination, the Supreme Court of Pennsylvania articulated the general rule in 1854: "if a passenger is negligently carried beyond the station where he intended to stop and where he has a right to be let off, he can recover compensation for the inconvenience, the loss of time, and the labor of traveling back."[81] Similar cases arose in other jurisdictions. Carriers were also responsible when trains omitted to stop at small stations when properly signaled. In one Mississippi case a would-be passenger had to walk ten miles in the rain after a train passed his station without stopping.[82]

At the same time, railroads exercised considerable control over the behavior of passengers. It was generally agreed that railroad companies could prescribe reasonable rules for conducting their business. Passengers were bound to comply with these regulations, and could be removed from trains for violations. Statutes throughout the nineteenth century enlarged the duty of carriers to check the behavior of unruly passengers. As early as 1849 Vermont authorized conductors to put out any passengers who "shall be disorderly, or drunk, or refuse to comply with all the reasonable regulations of the corporation."[83] In the Gilded Age, Wisconsin lawmakers gave conductors the power to arrest passengers using profane language or gambling on trains.[84] New Mexico also empowered railroads to eject disorderly persons and gamblers.

By far the most common exercise of railroad power to remove passengers involved persons who refused to pay the required fare. As Sarah H. Gordon has pointed out, passengers "frequently violated the most fundamental rule— paying for the ride."[85] In 1848 New York empowered conductors to remove without unnecessary force any passenger refusing to pay the required fare. Subsequent railroad legislation in other jurisdictions uniformly contained such provisions.[86] Upholding the right of carriers to eject passengers for nonpayment, courts maintained that persons who did not pay could be treated as trespassers. The rationale for this rule was plain. "To deny to a railroad corporation the power to expel persons from its cars," the Supreme Court of Illinois explained, "would be substantially to destroy its franchise to carry passengers."[87]

States were divided as to whether delinquent passengers could be put off trains between stations. Absent a statutory ban, the general view was that conductors could remove nonpaying passengers at any point and were not obligated to transport them to the next station. The Supreme Court of Ohio voiced the premise behind this rule: "To hold that this could only be done at a railroad depot . . . would deprive a railroad company of its chief safeguard against that kind of fraud or imposition."[88] But the expulsion of persons between stations, especially when dealing with sick, elderly, or female passengers or children, proved troublesome in practice. Consequently, state legislatures gradually limited the power to remove passengers to regular stopping places or near houses.[89] "This was, no doubt, deemed essential, by the legislature, to the safety of the traveling public," the Supreme Court of Illinois stated, "rather than leave it discretionary with every conductor to say arbitrarily what is a safe and proper place to put the passenger off."[90]

Despite general acceptance of the principle that railroads could eject passengers for nonpayment, the exercise of this power often gave rise to controversy. Two types of dispute were common. One concerned lost tickets and bona fide disagreements about the amount of the fare. A second line of inquiry turned upon the alleged use of unreasonable force by railroad employees to accomplish the removal.

It was standard practice, of course, for railroads to issue a ticket when the fare was paid. Courts treated such tickets as evidence that payment had been made. As a consequence, passengers were obligated to keep tickets safe and to exhibit them upon request by the conductor. Failure to comply with this requirement rendered a passenger subject to removal. Courts reasoned that this rule was necessary to protect the carrier and ensure payment of the fare. Conductors could look to the ticket and were not expected to conduct an investigation into the issue of payment.[91]

Carriers regularly sold special tickets limiting the time within which the ticket was to be used or restricting use to certain trains. If these terms were not followed, the ticket ceased to have any validity, and conductors could expel passengers who refused to pay another fare.[92]

Railroads commonly charged more for passengers who did not obtain tickets at a station and paid their fare to the conductor on the train. This was regarded as a reasonable arrangement to compensate the company for the additional inconvenience of handling such payments. But heated disputes arose when stations were closed and passengers unable to procure tickets. Under these circumstances, courts took the position that a conductor could not demand the extra fare and had no right to remove passengers who refused to pay it.[93]

Even when railroads could lawfully remove passengers, exercise of this right was hazardous. Some passengers resisted expulsion and had to be forcibly removed.[94] Allegations of assault and battery against conductors were pressed by expelled passengers. Courts refused to sanction excessive force, as when conductors hit passengers or pushed them from moving trains.[95]

Some legal historians have maintained that American law in the nineteenth century was preoccupied with the encouragement of economic growth, and that legal rules were altered to foster commercial enterprise. No doubt both judges and legislators shared the popular enthusiasm for economic expansion, and especially for railroad development. As shown in earlier chapters, the legal culture certainly did much to facilitate railroading.

Yet one must be cautious in viewing lawmakers as one-dimensional champions of the rail industry. Railroad law was clearly not just a vehicle to aid the carriers. Instead, judges and legislators early recognized the dangers of railroads and sought to impose a degree of public control over the conduct of railroad business. They were particularly sensitive to the rights of adjacent landowners, safety concerns, and relations with passengers. Even acknowledging that enforcement was spotty, the economic effect of regulations was to increase the cost of rail operations. Far from allowing carriers a free hand, lawmakers enacted a host of preventive measures and insisted that railroads must bear the cost of regulations to protect the public.

6

Railroads and Social Conflict

Since railroads touched so many aspects of American life, they were inevitably caught up in a variety of long-standing social concerns and new anxieties. Railroad law was therefore shaped by the worries and attitudes of the polity. Lawmakers and judges were called upon to adjust the interests of railroads with other social and economic practices. The law governing railroads interacted with the legal rules pertaining to such contested matters as slavery, race and gender relations, religious observance, and criminal behavior. The changes unleashed by railroading gave a new dimension to a number of social conflicts.

Slavery

During the antebellum era, southern railroad companies relied heavily on slave labor. Slaves were used primarily for roadbed construction and track repair, but also served as station helpers, brakemen, and firemen.[1]

Railroads owned many slaves outright, but in addition they commonly hired bondsmen from their owners. Such slave hiring constituted a bailment, a legal relationship in which one party takes temporary possession of the personal property of another. Verbal or written contracts frequently provided for the rate of hire, the treatment of the hired slave, and the type of work to be performed. Absent such contractual terms, courts relied on the common law of bailments to resolve conflicts between owners and railroads over the treatment of hired slaves.[2]

Use of hired slaves for dangerous occupations, such as railroading, raised the possibility of injury or death to the owner's human property. Railroads, as bailees, were held liable when the employment of a slave violated a contractual provision. In a case involving the death of a slave railroad worker, the Supreme Court of South Carolina declared that "the use of a thing hired, in any way different from that for which it is hired, makes the person hiring it liable for any injury or loss in such services."[3] Although owners were deemed to accept the risks inherent in hiring their slaves to engage in haz-ardous work, railroads were still responsible for any injury to hired slaves resulting from their mismanagement. For example, in *Tallahassee Rail-Road Company v. Macon* (1859), a slave was engaged in laying track. When the slave became ill and died, the owner alleged neglect of medical attention by the railroad company. Affirming a jury verdict for the slave owner, the Supreme Court of Florida determined that "any failure to bestow that degree of care and attention which a kind and humane master would bestow" con-stituted negligence by the bailee.[4]

Nor were railroads necessarily able to avoid liability for injury to hired slaves by exculpatory language in the bailment contract. At issue in *Memphis and Charleston Railroad Company v. Jones* (1859) was a stipulation providing: "The said railroad company assuming no responsibility for dam-ages from accidents, or any cause whatever."[5] Strictly construing this agree-ment, the Supreme Court of Tennessee ruled that the carrier was not protected against injury occasioned by willful misconduct or gross negligence.

Although courts tended to protect the property rights of slave owners under bailment contracts, the matter of tort liability for injury to slaves caused by rail operations was more complex. At root was the fundamental question of whether slaves were simply property or human beings capable of rational action. This issue, which permeated southern tort and criminal law before the Civil War, was key in allocating the burden of accidents between masters and railroads. Specifically, southern courts had to decide if the doctrine of contributory negligence and the fellow servant rule, both sta-ples of nineteenth-century tort law, applied to slaves.

Liability decisions did not fall into a neat pattern, but courts sometimes treated slaves injured in railroad accidents much as they would free persons in the same circumstances. In a number of cases, for instance, owners sued railroads for killing or injuring slaves who fell asleep on the tracks. Denying recovery, courts readily distinguished between slaves and other chattels, and asserted that slaves were capable of avoiding danger. The Supreme Court of North Carolina explained that "as the negroes were reasonable beings, endowed with intelligence, as well as the instinct of self-preservation and the power of locomotion, it was a natural and reasonable supposition that they would get out of the way." It added that to expect an engineer to stop a train whenever a slave was seen lying on the track would obstruct the railroad and "render it impossible for the company to discharge their duty to the public, as common carriers."[6]

Southern courts, however, almost uniformly refused to equate slave rail-road workers with free employees for purposes of tort liability. Under the fellow servant rule, an employer was not responsible for an employee injured on the job by the negligence of another worker. The rule was premised on the notion that an employee could bargain for increased compensation for dangerous work, or could quit an unsafe job. Obviously, these considerations did not apply to slave labor. Moreover, treating slaves as free workers contradicted the logic of the slave system, which required absolute subordination. As the Kentucky Court of Appeals pointed out: "A slave may not, with impunity, remind and urge a free white person, who is a co-employee, to a discharge of his duties, or reprimand him for his carelessness or neglect."[7] This unwillingness to treat slaves as a fellow servant meant that responsibility for accidents was placed on the carriers.

North Carolina courts alone adhered to the view that slaves should be on the same footing as free labor with respect to accidents. In *Ponton v. Wilmington and Weldon Rail Road Company* (1858), a slave employed as a brakeman was killed when another employee failed to adjust a switch. Applying the fellow servant rule, the Supreme Court of North Carolina maintained that the slave owner should have provided for the responsibility of the railroad in the bailment agreement.

By and large, courts in the South sustained the interests of slave owners against rail enterprise. This outcome underscored the high legal status of slavery, notwithstanding the broad enthusiasm for railroad expansion. Some historians have advanced the thesis that tort law was modified in the nineteenth century to favor commercial growth by shielding business from liability. The implications of this argument for railroading are considered in Chapter Nine, but the judicial treatment of slave workers suggests that this contention should be approached with caution. Where economic interests clashed, the primary concern of southern legislators and jurists was to safeguard the system of human bondage.

Railroads had the potential to destabilize the institution of slavery by facilitating the escape of slaves from their masters. As early as 1837 a Virginia statute prohibited railroads from transporting any slaves without having first obtained the written permission of the owner. Violators were subject to a monetary penalty.[8] Some carriers adopted similar rules as a matter of company policy.[9]

The bitterly contested matter of recapturing fugitive slaves in northern states also affected railroad law. In *Rodney v. Illinois Central Railroad Company* (1857), a Missouri slave owner sued the carrier to recover the value of a runaway slave. He alleged that the railroad transported the fugitive as a passenger to Chicago, thereby aiding the slave's escape. The Supreme Court of Illinois held that enforcement of the federal fugitive slave acts was a question for the federal courts. Stressing that the state constitution prohibited slavery and governed the status of persons within the jurisdiction, the court rejected any common-law claim for the value of a slave.

Racial Segregation

Passenger accommodations were often influenced by local social attitudes. Reflecting strong racial antagonism, some railroad companies in the North before the Civil War adopted a policy of excluding blacks from cars reserved for white passengers and placing them in separate cars. Since common carriers were obligated to transport all persons who paid the fare, the power of railroads to classify passengers on the basis of race proved controversial. Yet the antebellum law of common carriers allowed companies to make distinctions in the availability of accommodations on account of race. Only a handful of lawsuits challenged this practice, and these were generally unsuccessful.[10] In 1857 a New York judge submitted to a jury the question of whether a company regulation mandating race-based seating was reasonable. Instructed to consider "the probable effects upon the business and interest of the company from allowing blacks an equality as passengers with the whites," the jury returned a verdict for the railroad, in effect upholding the company's segregation policy.[11]

The Civil War did not produce an immediate change in judicial deference to the practice of providing separate cars or segregated seating. Courts insisted that black passengers could not be excluded from common carriers, but were reluctant to upset segregation policies that reflected local social attitudes.[12] Hence, in the leading case of *West Chester and Philadelphia Railroad Company v. Miles* (1867), a black woman was removed from a train because she refused to sit in a designated section. Noting the general custom of racial separation, the Supreme Court of Pennsylvania ruled that the company's regulation promoted the comfort and order of passengers.

During the Gilded Age the practice of racial segregation gradually faded on northern rail lines. This development was hastened by the passage of statutes in some states, including Massachusetts and Pennsylvania, which made it illegal for railroads to distinguish among passengers on account of race. Federal and state courts also looked askance at the exclusion of black passengers from first-class cars, at least when equal facilities were not provided.[13] These rulings called into question the common practice of assigning blacks to older and less comfortable cars.

Racial segregation practices on southern lines during the 1870s and 1880s varied widely.[14] Some carriers treated all passengers alike, while others imposed a policy of separate cars or restricted access to first-class accommodations. To complicate matters, segregation regulations were inconsistently enforced.

In the late 1880s several black passengers challenged the segregation rules of southern railroads before the Interstate Commerce Commission. The Interstate Commerce Act of 1887 forbade carriers from giving undue preferences and from subjecting "any particular person . . . to any undue or unreasonable prejudice or discrimination." Claimants saw this provision as a possible tool to ban racial discrimination. The ICC, however, in a series of cases upheld company regulations requiring separate cars. It reasoned that railroads did not act with undue prejudice in recognizing general public sentiment favoring racial separation. But the commission did futilely order that carriers provide equivalent accommodations to those furnished white passengers paying the same fare.[15]

In the late nineteenth century, southern states began to impose formal racial segregation on many aspects of public life. Perhaps emboldened by the ICC decisions, state laws mandated separate facilities for blacks on trains.[16] There was little pretense that in practice segregated facilities were equal to the accommodations afforded white passengers.

Although railroad companies were not all of one mind regarding the separate-car laws, many carriers battled the enactment of such legislation. Opposition was fueled by several concerns. The foremost point of contention was the additional expense of providing separate cars or compartments. In addition, the carriers were saddled with onerous enforcement responsibilities and faced legal penalties for violations. Moreover, the separate-car laws were passed at a time when railroads were engaged in running struggles against state regulation of their operations, and had no enthusiasm for further public controls. Segregation measures were commonly promoted by the same political forces that favored extensive public control of railroads. Rail managers also feared that separate-car laws would chill the interest of northern investors in southern lines.

There is ample evidence that many carriers were not in favor of state-imposed segregation. In South Carolina, for instance, railroads successfully blocked a separate-car law during much of the 1890s. Similarly, North Carolina railroads in 1899 attacked a separate-car bill as unnecessary and costly, pointing out that there was an insufficient number of black first-class passengers to justify separate coaches. The Louisville and Nashville Railroad was bitterly unhappy with segregation laws because of the cost involved.[17] Some lines in Louisiana posted the requisite signs but made no attempt to separate passengers.

Notwithstanding the efforts of these carriers, the rising segregationist tide, coupled with growing anti-railroad sentiment, brought about passage of separate-car laws across the South. Statutes then extended segregation to railroad terminals.

As they feared, railroads were soon embroiled in the messy business of enforcing the separate-car laws. In addition to the requirement that railroad companies provide separate cars or compartments, conductors were obligated to assign passengers to their respective facilities along racial lines. Unsurprisingly, some carriers made little effort to implement the law. There were numerous criminal prosecutions of railroads or conductors for failure to comply with the policy of racial separation, a testament to the resiliency of railroad hostility.[18] Highlighting the economic burden placed on railroads, a Texas court maintained that business considerations did not excuse noncompliance:

> We think the plain requirement of the statute is that railroad companies doing business in this state as common carriers of passengers for hire must provide separate coaches, whether the particular train is actually carrying at the time both white and negro passengers or both.[19]

Railroads, according to this view, needed to run separate cars in anticipation of the possibility that black passengers might request transportation.

Not only were the segregation laws uneconomic for the carriers, but attempts to enforce the separate-car requirement sometimes sparked resistance from blacks. It was often necessary to eject or arrest passengers for failure to comply with orders of the conductor to change seating. In several instances fights resulting in fatalities erupted when conductors sought to remove blacks from white cars.[20]

Yet another legal headache for railroads arose when conductors mistakenly compelled white passengers to ride in a coach for blacks. Courts heard a number of cases in which white passengers sought to recover monetary damages for the mortification of having to ride with blacks.[21] Reasoning that the law imposed a duty on carriers to assign passengers to the proper cars, courts often found railroads liable for such misconduct by their agents. In essence, the wrongful assignment of white passengers was treated as a personal insult. As a Texas court explained, compelling a white passenger to ride in a car for blacks constituted "such a violation of law and breach of duty as to render a common carrier of passengers liable in damages for such discomfort and humiliation as are proximately caused from such breach of duty."[22] In the same vein, the Kentucky Court of Appeals in 1912 upheld an award of punitive damages for the humiliation suffered by a white passenger forced to ride in a black car.[23] This line of cases further illustrates the difficulties experienced by railroads in enforcing the separate-car laws.

To compound the dilemma for the railroads, it was not always an easy task for a busy conductor to ascertain a passenger's racial identity. Thus, a Kentucky court recognized: "What race a person belongs to cannot always be determined infallibly from appearances, and mistakes must inevitably be made."[24] Railroad officials were in the unhappy position of having to make racial classifications at their peril.

Confronted with an economic and administrative headache, railroads early contested the validity of separate-car laws. At issue in *Louisville, New Orleans & Texas Railway Company v. Mississippi* (1890), the first railroad segregation case to reach the Supreme Court, was a statute mandating separate cars or compartments for all rail transportation within Mississippi. The railroad argued that the need to stop and add a separate car at the state line constituted an undue burden on interstate commerce. Noting that the statute applied only to travel within the state, the Supreme Court denied that the law impermissibly controlled travel among the states. The justices, however, expressly reserved judgment as to whether the assignment of interstate passengers by race would burden commerce. The decision thus left open the theoretical prospect that interstate black passengers could escape segregation, but in practice railroads separated interstate passengers as well.[25]

The Supreme Court broadly validated separate-car laws in the landmark case of *Plessy v. Ferguson* (1896). Rejecting challenges based on the Thirteenth Amendment and the equal protection clause of the Fourteenth Amendment, the Court ruled that segregation statutes were a reasonable exercise of state police power. The opinion was predicated on the assumption that equal facilities were available to both whites and blacks. *Plessy* has been the subject of a voluminous literature,[26] and it is not my purpose to treat the decision in detail. But several points bear emphasis with respect to railroading. First, there is evidence that the railroads in Louisiana cooperated in arranging this test case because they disliked the separate-car laws. Second, Justice John Marshall Harlan's eloquent dissent, in which he invoked the ideal of a color-blind constitution, was shaped by the unique duty of common carriers to transport all persons on equal terms. He stressed that "a railroad is a public highway," and noted that the industry was governed by special rules.[27]

As separate-car laws spread, many carriers, for the sake of convenience, adopted their own regulations to segregate interstate as well as intrastate passengers. In *Chiles v. Chesapeake & Ohio Railway Company* (1910), the Supreme Court upheld this segregation policy. Explaining that railroads could adopt reasonable regulations in accord with "the general sentiment of the community," the justices concluded that inaction by Congress amounted to a declaration that lines could by their rules separate white and black passengers in interstate commerce.[28] The *Chiles* ruling allowed railroads to conform to societal dictates, even beyond the letter of state law, without fear of liability from excluded black passengers.

Notwithstanding the nominal requirement of equal facilities, the blunt reality was that the service afforded black passengers was inferior in every respect. Blacks were routinely assigned to antiquated and unclean cars. A particular sticking point was lack of access to first-class and sleeping cars. Anxious to minimize the expense of complying with state laws, railroad companies simply did not provide such accommodations for the relatively few black travelers who could afford them. The ICC made little sustained effort to require equal facilities. In 1914, however, the Supreme Court demonstrated a fleeting interest in examining the "equal" component of separate rail facilities. It took aim at an Oklahoma statute that authorized carriers to furnish sleeping and dining cars for whites while not providing similar accommodations to black passengers. The state sought to justify the law by pointing out that there was insufficient demand to make separate sleeping and dining cars for blacks profitable. Writing for the Court, Justice Charles Evans Hughes rejected the argument based on the volume of traffic. Instead, he insisted that constitutional rights were personal and that black passengers were entitled to equal treatment.[29] Although the decision had limited immediate impact, it pointed toward the eventual demise of segregated rail travel. Given the economic realities, railroads could not in actuality provide equal facilities.

The Supreme Court delivered a further blow to segregated rail travel in *Mitchell v. United States* (1941). It ruled that under the nondiscrimination provision of the Interstate Commerce Act, blacks purchasing first-class or sleeping car tickets must be furnished accommodations equal to those afforded white passengers. The justices again declared that negligible demand for such services by blacks did not excuse the failure to offer equal first-class facilities. Although the decision did not end racial segregation, it put teeth in the mandate of equal treatment for all passengers. Left with the difficult task of complying with the *Mitchell* mandate in the face of state separate-car laws, railroads in the South typically modified segregation practices to allow interstate black passengers limited access to dining and sleeping cars. The entry of the United States into World War II caused a huge increase in passenger travel and hastened the trend toward abandoning racial segregation in first-class facilities.[30]

Segregated transit collapsed during the 1950s. In practice a number of carriers allowed segregation to quietly lapse for first-class passengers. Some lines even abandoned entirely segregation on interstate trains. The Supreme Court contributed to this process in *Henderson v. United States* (1950), holding that the denial of dining service to a black passenger when seats were available at tables reserved for whites violated the Interstate Commerce Act. This decision marked the effective end of segregated dining cars. Moreover, in 1951 Maryland repealed its separate-car law. Congress debated proposals to outlaw racial discrimination in interstate travel. Following the Supreme Court's watershed decision in *Brown v. Board of Education* (1954) invalidating school segregation, the ICC banned separate treatment of interstate railroad passengers in trains or stations. In 1956 the Court extended the *Brown* principle to public transportation, effectively overruling the separate but equal doctrine.[31]

The rise and fall of separate-car laws illustrates how railroading became entangled in larger social struggles not of its own making.

Race and Railroad Employment

Racial antagonism similarly impacted railroad employment practices. After the Civil War large numbers of blacks continued to serve as firemen and brakemen on southern lines. Only whites, however, held the more prestigious positions of engineer and conductor. The emergence of rail unions in the late nineteenth century led to increased pressure to exclude blacks from railroad jobs. The major operating unions—brotherhoods for engineers, conductors, and firemen—restricted membership to whites. Not only did unions adamantly block promotions of blacks to the post of engineer or conductor, but they also pressured employers to limit the number of black workers. To this end, unions championed separate seniority systems based on race and employment quotas for blacks.[32] They also lobbied legislative bodies to enact literacy tests or impose licensing requirements in an effort to eliminate black firemen.[33]

This racial antipathy, coupled with the fear that black workers depressed the wages of whites and hampered union effectiveness, sparked several strikes by southern rail unions in the early twentieth century seeking to achieve their exclusionary goals. Perhaps the most famous was the Georgia "race strike" by white firemen in 1909.[34] Unhappy that the Georgia Railroad was hiring large numbers of black firemen, the white firemen went on strike and demanded the elimination of all black firemen. White mobs attacked trains and beat black firemen. With rail service virtually halted, the union and the company accepted arbitration under the auspices of the federal government. Rejecting most union demands, the arbitrators ruled that the Georgia Railroad could continue its practice of employing black firemen provided that the line pay blacks and whites the same wages. Although the union hoped that the equal pay requirement would cause the railroad to eliminate gradually black firemen, the carrier continued to employ many black fireman and other workers into the 1920s.

The desire to curtail black rail employment precipitated other strikes as well. In 1911 a move by the Cincinnati, New Orleans and Texas Pacific Railroad to assign black firemen to a desirable route in Tennessee triggered a three-week strike. The upshot was a compromise of sorts. The carrier agreed to limit the number of black firemen, but retained the authority to assign black workers to some preferred runs.[35]

As discussed more fully in Chapter Eleven, World War I brought a temporary federal government takeover of the rail industry. This development had significant implications for black railroad workers.[36] In 1918 the Federal Railroad Administration issued General Order 27 mandating equal wages and treatment without regard to race for workers who performed the same tasks. Generally speaking, however, government operations of the railroads strengthened union power. Confronting yet another series of racial strikes, the Railroad Administration imposed new regulations that forced blacks out of various positions and further restricted their employment opportunities.

The plight of black railroad workers worsened after World War I. The Railway Labor Act of 1926 compelled carriers to negotiate with the bargaining representative of their employees. The 1934 amendment to the act gave a union selected by a majority of any class of employees the exclusive right to bargain for all employees in that category. As Richard A. Epstein has pointed out, the effect of this legislation was "to change the balance of power by giving the white majority total control over the choices of both black workers and the railroads."[37] Black workers were now represented by all-white unions bent upon restricting black railroad employment. The courts upheld the certification of unions that formally barred black members as the exclusive bargaining representative. Flexing its new power, the firemen's union in the 1930s and 1940s negotiated a series of discriminatory contracts with railroads that sharply curtailed the use of black firemen.[38]

In *Steele v. Louisville and Nashville Railroad Company* (1944), the Supreme Court made a modest attempt to protect black employees from discriminatory union actions. At issue were contracts negotiated by the firemen's union to reduce the number of black firemen on carriers in the southeast. The blacks were given no notice or opportunity to be heard with respect to these agreements. The Supreme Court ruled that a union representing a craft under the Railway Labor Act was obligated to protect equally all members of the craft without discrimination.[39] However, the duty of impartial representation imposed in *Steele* fell short of safeguarding the interests of black workers. *Steele* did not compel the rail unions to admit black members, nor did it prevent unions from making many small decisions that covertly disadvantaged blacks. The major operating unions did not remove their formal race bar until the 1960s, by which time black employment on the railroads had been largely eliminated.

The long history of racial discrimination by rail unions was encouraged in part by laws and administrative rulings. One scholar has observed that "in no other industry has collective bargaining had such disastrous results for Negroes."[40]

Ladies' Cars

The advent of passenger trains meant that travelers from all stations of life could mingle in the cars. This was potentially upsetting to mid-nineteenth-century sensibilities, particularly with respect to women passengers traveling alone. As a result, many railroads set aside special ladies' cars. Access to these first-class cars was limited to women and men traveling with female passengers. The ladies' cars were often cleaner and more comfortable than the standard coaches, and smoking was typically forbidden. No law or judicial order mandated special accommodations for female passengers. Rather, the railroads themselves sought to impose a degree of social ordering consistent with the mores of the age.[41]

Ladies' cars were generally accepted because they reflected the social attitudes of nineteenth-century Americans in which gender distinctions were taken for granted. Courts and commentators agreed that railroad companies had the authority to designate certain cars exclusively for women and the men accompanying them.[42] As the Interstate Commerce Commission explained in 1887:

> It is both the right and the duty of railroad companies to make such reasonable regulations as will secure order and promote the comfort of their passengers. In the exercise of this right and the performance of this duty, carriers have established rules providing separate cars for ladies, and for

gentlemen accompanied by ladies; and their right to make such rules as
to sexes is nowhere questioned. A man, white or colored, excluded from
the ladies' car by such a rule, could hardly claim successfully under the
Act to Regulate Commerce that he had been subjected to unjust discrimination and unreasonable prejudice or disadvantage.[43]

Indirectly, however, the existence of the ladies' car gave rise to a number of
legal issues. The widespread acceptance of segregation by gender provided
a potent analogy to justify racial distinctions in rail service.[44] Moreover, many
of the cases attacking racial segregation on railroads were instituted by black
women who were denied entry to the ladies' car. Their complaints fused
racial, gender, and status concerns.[45]

The most comprehensive judicial examination of the reasonableness of
providing a separate car for female passengers occurred in *Bass v. Chicago
& Northwestern Railway Company* (1874). A male passenger, unhappy with
standing in a smoking car without a seat, attempted to enter the ladies' car.
He was forcibly removed by railroad employees, and brought suit to recover
for injuries and indignity. The Supreme Court of Wisconsin had no difficulty
in upholding the validity of a separate car for women:

> The use of railroads for the common carriage of passengers has not only
> vastly increased travel generally, but has also specially led women to
> travel without male companions. To such, the protection which is a nat-
> ural instinct of manhood towards their sex, is specially due by common
> carriers. And, in view of the crowds of men of all sorts and conditions
> and habits constantly traveling by railroad, it appears to us to be not
> only a reasonable regulation, but almost if not quite a humane duty, for
> railroad companies to appropriate a car of each passenger train primarily
> for women and men accompanying them; from which men unaccompa-
> nied by women should be excluded, and even women or men accompa-
> nying women of offensive character or habits; so as to group women of
> good character on the train together, sheltered as far as practicable from
> annoyance and insult. It is a severe comment on our civilization that such
> a regulation should be necessary; but the necessity is patent to all expe-
> rience and intelligence.[46]

But the court also insisted that the regulation must be enforced in a reasonable manner. If there were no seats available elsewhere, the court reasoned, it would be appropriate to admit male passengers into the ladies' car.
It was additionally bothered by the forcible nature of plaintiff's removal
from the ladies' car. In effect, the court recognized a qualified right of male
passengers to peacefully enter the ladies' car when they could not find seats
elsewhere.

Indian Land Titles

Railroads impacted on the Plains Indians in many ways. They hastened settlement of the West and the growth of cities, which developments in turn steadily diminished the geographic domain of Indian nations. Railroading also interfered with buffalo hunting. During the 1860s some tribes struck back with futile attacks on the construction sites of the Union Pacific Railroad.[47]

By far the most important legal question regarding Indians raised by the western railroads was the ownership of land occupied by Native Americans. Consequently, railroads played a key role in shaping governmental policy affecting the land rights of Indians. The building of transcontinental railroad lines necessitated the acquisition of rights-of-way through territories reserved for use by Indians. Congress repeatedly granted railroad companies permission to construct lines across these lands. In the Pacific Railway Act of 1862, which became a model for later legislation, the federal government agreed to "extinguish as rapidly as may be the Indian titles to all lands falling under the operation of this act and required for the said right of way and grants hereinafter made."[48] One of the objectives of the Indian Peace Commission, established by Congress in 1867, was to secure the safe building of railroads.[49] Congress also approved treaties that guaranteed rights-of-way for routes through Indian lands. For instance, the Fort Laramie Treaty of 1868 with the Sioux contained a number of provisions to safeguard the building of railroads:

> 1st. That they will withdraw all opposition to the construction of the railroads, now being built on the plains.
>
> 2d. That they will permit the peaceful construction of any railroad not passing over their reservation as herein defined. . . .
>
> 6th. They withdraw all pretence of opposition to the construction of the railroad now being built along the Platte river and westward to the Pacific ocean, and they will not in future object to the construction of railroads . . . but should such roads or other works be constructed on the land of their reservation, the government will pay the tribe whatever amount of damage may be assessed.[50]

The extent to which Indian nations were sovereign and held rights in land were long-standing issues in the American polity. Chief Justice John Marshall had early ruled that ultimate title to land was in the United States, and that Indians had merely usufructuary or occupancy rights that were under the control of Congress.[51] Hence the government always held title to Indian lands, even that land reserved to particular tribes. The expression "Indian title" was therefore something of a misnomer. It imparted only the notion that Indians had a right to live on the land, subject to disposition by Congress. The appearance of the railroad presented these questions of sovereignty and ownership in a new context and with fresh urgency.

In a line of decisions the Supreme Court adhered to the view that the United States owned the reserved land occupied by Native Americans, and could transfer this land subject to their right of occupancy. The Court further held the government could extinguish this right of occupancy whenever and however it saw fit. For example, the justices in *Buttz v. Northern Pacific Railroad* (1886) stressed that a land grant to a railroad conveyed the fee simple title to the company. This grant was subject to the right of occupancy by Indians, but in this case such limited rights had been subsequently extinguished by agreement. Thereafter, the Court in *Missouri, Kansas and Texas Railway Company v. Roberts* (1894) enlarged governmental authority over land occupied by Indians. At issue was an 1866 act that granted a right-of-way to the railroad but contained no language extinguishing the Indians' right of occupancy. Nonetheless, the Court concluded that the railroad must necessarily take possession of the right-of-way and that therefore the act impliedly abolished Indian occupancy rights. In other words, the grant to the railroad conveyed both fee simple title and possession. Under *Roberts*, virtually every right-of-way provision had the effect of eliminating possessory rights.

Railroads were even able to acquire rights-of-way across land owned by an Indian nation in fee simple. In 1884 Congress granted a right-of-way through the Indian Territory, now Oklahoma, to the Southern Kansas Railway Company. The act required the company to pay compensation for any property taken and established a procedure to determine the amount of compensation. Pointing to various treaties, the Cherokee Nation maintained that it owned these lands in fee simple. Moreover, the Cherokee Nation argued it was a sovereign state and retained the exclusive right to exercise eminent domain within its territory. The Cherokees sought to enjoin the railroad company from building a line across their land. Brushing aside these arguments, the Supreme Court in *Cherokee Nation v. Southern Kansas Railway Company* (1890) emphasized that the Cherokees were not a sovereign or independent people, and were under the control of the United States. It followed that Congress could exercise the power of eminent domain over lands held in fee simple in Cherokee territory, and could delegate this authority to railroads.

As discussed earlier, Congress abandoned the policy of making land grants to railroads in 1871. In the ensuing decades, however, Congress enacted two general right-of-way acts conferring broad power on any railroad company to acquire routes through Indian lands. The 1899 measure authorized companies, with the approval of the secretary of the interior, to build lines upon payment of compensation for land taken. Three years later, another act expanded the power of the carriers to condemn rights-of-way without the secretary's approval.[52]

The ready disposition of Indian lands for railroad lines was part and parcel of the late-nineteenth-century policy of breaking up the large reservations and settling individual Indians on their own parcels. By 1930 this policy was widely seen as a failure, and there was a move to restore tribal autonomy. One result was a sea change in attitudes toward Indian land rights. A more skeptical assessment of railroad claims was evident in *Great Northern Railway Company v. United States* (1942). In that case the railroad was drilling for oil and gas on its right-of-way. Influenced by the change in government policy, the Supreme Court determined that the carrier had obtained just an easement rather than a fee simple title. Hence, the subsurface oil and gas remained the property of the government and the railroad could not continue its drilling.

The willingness of Congress in the nineteenth century to favor railroad rights-of-way at the expense of Indian occupancy rights highlights legislative determination to foster rail construction to the Pacific. Judicial rulings were fully congruent with this policy. To be sure, the need of railroads to acquire routes was only one aspect of the larger drive to transfer vast tracts of Indian-occupied land to white settlers. But the railroad companies were clearly a major force in reinforcing a legal culture in which Indian land claims were subordinated to the economic development of the western states.

Operations on Sunday

Yet another example of how railroads were caught up in broader social questions was the controversy over running trains on Sunday. The emergence of rail travel produced a clash between the need to accommodate economic change and the desire of many to reaffirm the religious dimension of American life. Since the colonial era, lawmakers had proscribed labor, selling, and amusements on Sundays. Despite their obvious religious base, such measures were routinely upheld in the nineteenth century as exercise of the police power to provide a day of rest.[53]

Sabbatarians lobbied throughout the nineteenth century to curb railroad operations on Sunday. Stressing both the need of railroad employees for a day of rest and moral imperatives for observing Sunday, the *American Rail-road Journal* before the Civil War called for railroads to halt Sunday trains.[54] Despite the steady growth of Sunday service, sabbatarian agitation did not cease. One prominent author proclaimed that "the railroad is often one of the most dangerous foes of the Sabbath."[55] At the end of the nineteenth century, critics urged federal legislation to restrict the transportation of freight on Sundays and circulated petitions in opposition to Sunday trains. "The running of Sunday trains," the *Railroad and Engineering Journal* declared in 1889, "has been a subject of some discussion and considerable agitation lately." Although expressing doubt that complete stoppage of trains on Sunday was feasible, the *Journal* editorialized that the "railroad man ought to have his day of rest as well as any other American citizen."[56] In the face of these pressures, railroad officials insisted that they were responding to competitive pressure from rival lines, demands of shippers for speedy transportation, and the desire of passengers to travel on Sunday.

Most Sunday laws were originally silent with respect to the running of trains. Courts consequently struggled to reconcile the prohibition of commercial activity on Sunday with the perceived need for transportation on that day. In *Sparhawk v. Union Passenger Railway Company* (1867), a group of Philadelphia citizens sought an injunction to prevent the carrier from operating passenger trains over city streets on Sunday. Concluding that the movement of trains on Sunday violated a 1794 act, the Supreme Court of Pennsylvania nonetheless determined that such service was not a nuisance and could not be enjoined. Railroads were in effect allowed to continue their Sunday passenger operations despite being in technical violation of the law.

Other courts reached a similar result by pointing to exceptions in the Sunday laws. Typically, these statutes contained an exemption for works of "charity" or "necessity" on Sunday. Courts were frequently called upon to resolve whether the operation of a train constituted a "necessity" within the meaning of the law. A number of courts concluded that running passenger trains on Sunday was a necessity, reasoning in part that some people used trains to attend religious services and care for the sick. During the late nineteenth century some state legislatures expressly exempted passenger trains from the Sunday statutes.[57] Connecticut and Vermont authorized their state railroad commissions to permit the running of Sunday trains as public necessity required. In 1902 the New Jersey Court of Chancery declared: "People travel about on Sunday, and, of late, railroad trains are permitted to run on Sunday."[58]

An allied question concerned the operation of excursion trains on Sunday. Unlike regular passenger service, excursion trains were usually arranged for the purpose of enjoying recreational trips to places of interest at special fares. In an age before automobiles, excursions provided a Sunday outing and were very popular. Although such trains did not easily fit the common understanding of necessity, courts in the late nineteenth century readily found that the running of excursion trains was not in violation of the Sunday laws.[59]

As might be expected, freight trains proved to be the most contentious issue in applying Sunday laws to rail operations. State regulations varied widely. Some jurisdictions, such as New Jersey and Georgia, statutorily prohibited the running of freight trains or the unloading of goods on Sunday. Other states, including Texas and West Virginia, amended their laws to expressly permit Sunday freight service. Still other jurisdictions made an exception for the shipment of livestock, perishables, and mail.[60] South Carolina law, for instance, authorized the Sunday shipment of vegetables and fruit during harvest months. Laws that restricted the operation of freight trains on Sunday were anathema to railroad companies, and they successfully opposed enactment of these regulations in some states.[61] As was the case with other state regulations, the increasingly interstate character of the railroad business was hampered by a bewildering assortment of conflicting state Sunday laws.

Inevitably, the application of Sunday laws to rail shipments across state lines was challenged as a violation of the commerce clause of the Constitution. State courts were divided on this point. In *Norfolk & Western Railroad Company v. Commonwealth* (1891), the Supreme Court of Virginia determined that a state law prohibiting the movement of interstate freight trains on Sunday unconstitutionally obstructed interstate commerce. Other courts upheld restrictions on Sunday rail traffic between states. The Supreme Court in *Hennington v. Georgia* (1896) approved the enforcement of state Sunday laws against freight trains running from state to state. The majority concluded that the Sunday law was a police power regulation to fix a day of rest that had only a limited effect on interstate commerce. Dissenting, Chief Justice Melville W. Fuller stressed that rail transportation was national in character, and asserted that "requiring the suspension of interstate commerce for one day in the week amounts to a regulation of this commerce, and is invalid because the power of Congress in that regard is exclusive."[62]

Although *Hennington* resolved the constitutionality of halting the Sunday operation of interstate freight trains, Fuller's dissent more accurately pointed to the future. Railroads were eventually able to run Sunday trains with little difficulty. As the public, especially in urban areas, became more dependent on the benefits of daily rail service, the number of exceptions to the ban on Sunday service multiplied. Courts tended to construe the "necessity" provision broadly, and every exception undermined the policy behind the law. Enforcement of the laws was spotty, and the carriers were able to circumvent the remaining restrictions.

During the twentieth century, public sentiment gradually turned against strict enforcement of Sunday laws. The reasons for this change were varied, and reflected in part the growing secularization of American society. Railroads were an important catalyst in bringing about this shift in attitude. Over time, people came to rely on railroads for Sunday newspapers, mail, and excursion trips, and to accept rail operations on that day as an integral part of life. Although Sunday laws were occasionally enforced against the operation of freight trains into the 1920s,[63] railroads contributed to the eventual downfall of Sunday closing provisions.

Crime

The advent of railroading influenced criminal law in a number of ways. State laws and railroad charters contained numerous provisions designed to protect rail enterprise and passenger safety by imposing penal sanctions. These measures were part of a larger pattern of utilizing criminal justice to achieve economic and regulatory goals. As early as 1831, for instance, a Rhode Island charter declared that any person who should willfully obstruct passage on a railroad or "in any way spoil, injure, or destroy said railroad" was liable for treble damages and imprisonment.[64] General railroad acts similarly made it a crime to place impediments on tracks or to destroy railroad property. The Missouri general railroad law of 1853 was typical:

§ 49. If any person or persons shall wilfully do or cause to be done, any act or acts whatever whereby any building, construction or work of any railroad corporation, or any engine, machine or structure, or any matter or thing appertaining to the same, shall be stopped, obstructed, impaired, weakened, injured or destroyed, the person or persons so offending shall be guilty of a misdemeanor, and shall forfeit and pay to the said corporation treble the amount of damages by means of such offence.[65]

Concerned about the safety of employees and passengers, the Michigan act provided that any person attempting to cause a derailment was subject to life imprisonment.[66]

The list of railroad-related crimes expanded throughout the nineteenth century. In 1872 Wisconsin made it unlawful for any person other than a railroad employee to walk along the tracks. Such trespass laws were prompted by safety concerns, since trespassers walking on tracks or stealing rides were a recurring cause of fatal accidents. The Illinois Code of 1874 provided that any person "who shall throw any stone or other hard substance at any railroad car, train or locomotive, shall be deemed guilty of a misdemeanor." New Mexico made it a criminal offense for miners to excavate or build tunnels under railroad land without permission.[67]

It is difficult to determine the effectiveness of these laws in safeguarding rail property and public safety. There is evidence, however, that such provisions were enforced from time to time. In an 1851 Ohio trial a man was convicted of second-degree murder for placing an obstruction on the tracks of the Cleveland and Pittsburgh Railroad. Apparently motivated by ill will toward the company, this action caused an accident resulting in loss of life.[68] Later cases also resulted in conviction for obstructing tracks.[69] Trespassers on railroad lines were on occasion arrested,[70] and some carriers enforce a strict no-trespass policy to the present.

Another category of railroad crimes was aimed at wrongdoing by railroad officials, particularly conduct that jeopardized the safety of travelers. Railroad acts, for instance, commonly made it a crime for an engineer or conductor to be intoxicated while operating a train.[71] Statutes also prohibited locking the doors of passenger cars to prevent free exit, and the use of kerosene oil for lighting passenger cars. Any engineer or conductor violating these provisions was deemed guilty of a misdemeanor.[72] Here, too, lawmakers relied on criminal penalties to ensure public safety. Congress even made any willful violation of the Interstate Commerce Act a misdemeanor. Such resort to the criminal law made sense as a regulatory device in an era before the emergence of powerful administrative agencies.

The most dramatic impact of railroading on criminal justice involved train robberies. During the late nineteenth and early twentieth centuries, the United States experienced an epidemic of train holdups.[73] No section of the country was immune, but such robberies were most frequent in western and southern states. Notwithstanding a tendency by some contemporaries to romanticize railroad robbers,[74] train robbery was often brutal and posed a high degree of danger for passengers and crew. Robbers commonly stopped trains by dismantling the tracks or turning switches, thereby causing a derailment. In one particularly grisly incident in 1896, the derailment caused a bridge to collapse, plunging the train into a river. More than twenty passengers and crew were killed.[75] Once the robbers stopped a train, they often stole jewelry and other valuables from the passengers.[76] Moreover, a frequent target was the express car, which carried a safe. Robbers typically used dynamite to wreck the express car and open the safe. Armed express-car messengers forcibly resisted robbery attempts, and there were numerous gunfights between robbers and messengers. Occasionally crew members and passengers were shot.[77]

As the incidence of train robberies mounted, railroad companies feared both economic loss and legal liability to passengers. They worried that frequent holdups would discourage shippers and foreign investors. Also troublesome was the number of lawsuits brought by passengers against carriers for failure to protect their valuables or personal safety. Courts in several states upheld jury verdicts awarding damages for stolen items or personal injuries sustained during robberies. Although judges recognized that railroads were not guarantors of passenger safety, they insisted that carriers must take appropriate steps to prevent robbery. Neglect of this duty to exercise vigilance constituted negligence on the part of the railroads.[78]

In response, railroad companies devised a number of strategies to curb train robberies. They posed sizeable rewards for the capture of robbers and increased the number of armed guards on trains.[79] Additionally, industry leaders urged the imposition of the death penalty for train robbery. Thus, *Railway Age* predicted in 1893 that should lawmakers "make certain death the penalty of train robbery whether the crime happens to result in murder or not . . . the avocation will be speedily abandoned."[80] At least twenty-five states heeded this argument and enacted train-robbery death penalty statutes. In 1891, for instance, California passed a measure, revealingly known as the "Train Wrecking Act," making it a capital offense to obstruct or rob trains.[81]

Since armed robbery was not generally treated as a capital crime, imposition of the death penalty for train robbery sparked a debate over whether such punishment was unconstitutional. Critics maintained that the death penalty was disproportionate to the crime, and thus constituted cruel and unusual punishment. Pointing to the inherent dangers of train robbery and the need for effective deterrence, courts, however, routinely sustained the death penalty statutes. In the leading case of *Territory v. Ketchum* (1901), the Supreme Court of New Mexico stressed the uniquely severe nature of train robbery, and observed that such robbers "display their utter disregard of human life and property, and show that they are outlaws of the most desperate and dangerous character."[82] Executions for train robbery were carried out with some regularity.[83] In contrast, states in the northeast did not pass train robbery death penalty laws, and Congress punished train robbery in the federal territories by imprisonment.[84]

The frequency of train robbery declined markedly after 1910. Although the death penalty statutes may have played a role, several other developments contributed to the drop in train holdups. The increased speed of trains, the adoption of steel express cars, and improved law enforcement made train robbing more difficult. Execution for train robbery virtually ceased by 1920, and thereafter states gradually began to repeal their death penalty laws. Nonetheless, these capital offense statutes stand as a reminder that train robbery was once not only common but endangered the lives of passengers and crew. They also underscore how the criminal law was crafted to protect railroading.

Railroad Police

With facilities strung out over miles of track, valuable cargo sitting in freight yards, and often turbulent labor relations, railroads were highly vulnerable to crime. To meet this challenge, railroad companies formed private police departments. The Baltimore and Ohio Railroad was a leader in the development of railroad police. In 1834 the company employed a city police officer to make an undercover investigation of murders at a construction site. By 1850 it was regularly employing armed guards to maintain order among unruly work crews.[85] Several Illinois carriers turned to Allan Pinkerton to secure police protection through a private agency.

By the mid–nineteenth century, state legislatures began to expressly authorize railroad companies to engage their own police force. A pioneering 1865 Pennsylvania statute empowered the governor, upon request by any railroad in the state, to appoint persons to act as company police. These police officers, whose compensation was paid by the company, could exercise all the powers of municipal law enforcement officers. Specifically, they could arrest offenders for crimes upon or along railroad property.[86] Similar laws were soon enacted in Ohio and Tennessee, and gradually spread elsewhere. They remain in effect to the present.

These police officers typically arrested persons for stealing from railroad cars and expelled trespassers from railroad property or cars. The hybrid nature of railroad police gave rise to some confusion when persons wrongfully assaulted or arrested by railroad police sought to hold the company responsible. Liability turned in part on whether the railroad police officer was considered a public official acting in performance of his duty. One line of authority emphasized that railroad police were public law enforcement officials, notwithstanding their appointment by the company, and that the carrier was not liable for any wrongful acts that occurred in the performance of their public duties.[87] But some courts took the position that, on the facts presented, a railroad police officer was acting within the scope of his employment but not in the line of public duty.[88] The role of railroad police, therefore, denied a tidy solution.

MOTHERS LOOK OUT FOR YOUR CHILDREN!

ARTISANS, MECHANICS, CITIZENS!

When you leave your family in health, must you be hurried home to mourn a

DREADFUL CASUALITY!

PHILADELPHIANS, your **RIGHTS** are being invaded! regardless of your interests, or the **LIVES** OF YOUR LITTLE ONES. THE CAMDEN AND AMBOY, with the assistance of other companies without a Charter, and in **VIOLATION OF LAW,** as decreed by your Courts, are laying a

LOCOMOTIVE RAIL ROAD!

Through your most Beautiful Streets, to the RUIN of your TRADE, annihilation of your RIGHTS, and regardless of your PROSPERITY and COMFORT. **Will you permit this?** or do you consent to be a

SUBURB OF NEW YORK!!

Rails are now being laid on **BROAD STREET** to **CONNECT** the **TRENTON RAIL ROAD** with the **WILMING**TON and BALTIMORE ROAD, under the pretence of constructing a City Passenger Railway from the Navy Yard to Fairmount!!! This is done under the auspices of the **CAMDEN AND AMBOY MONOPOLY!**

RALLY PEOPLE in the Majesty of your Strength and forbid THIS

OUTRAGE!

This 1839 poster, circulated in Philadelphia, reflects both fear of railroad operation on city streets and distrust of out-of-state enterprise. (Union Pacific Historical Collection)

Spanning the Mississippi River in 1856, the famous Rock Island bridge triggered litigation that effectively established the right of railroads to cross rivers. (Rock Island County Historical Society)

Slave labor was widely used to construct railroads in the antebellum South. (North Carolina Division of Archives and History)

The Civil War produced massive destruction of southern railroads, as demonstrated by this scene of an Atlanta roundhouse in 1864. (Association of American Railroads Photographic Collection, Virginia Museum of Transportation)

The construction of the transcontinental railroad, finished in 1869, raised a host of legal issues relating to land grants and payment of debts owed the federal government. (Association of American Railroads Photographic Collection, Virginia Museum of Transportation)

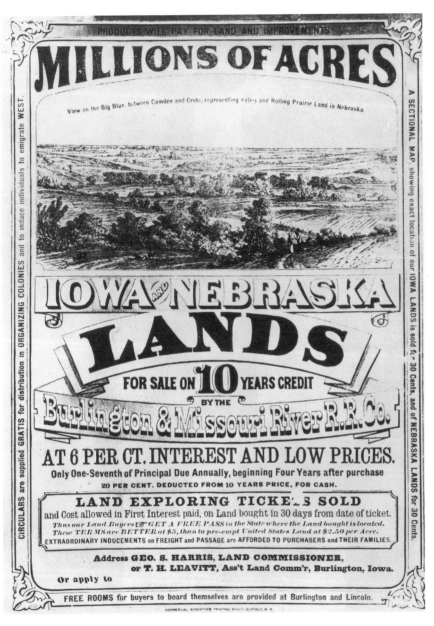

As illustrated by this 1873 poster, western railroads sought to lure emigrants to settle on their land grants by offering generous sale terms. (Association of American Railroads Photographic Collection, Virginia Museum of Transportation)

This train crossing a canal about 1875 is a reminder of the prolonged struggle in the nineteenth century between canals and railroads. (Association of American Railroads Photographic Collection, Virginia Museum of Transportation)

"The Farmer and the Railroad Monster—Which Will Win?" As shown in this 1873 cartoon, anti-railroad sentiment grew after the Civil War and fueled calls for increased governmental regulation. (Prints and Photographs Division, Library of Congress)

"THE MODERN LAOCOON." Characterizing railroads as a monopoly was a popular theme among railroad critics in the 1870s. (Prints and Photographs Division, Library of Congress)

"West Virginia.–The Baltimore and Ohio Railroad Strike–the Disaffected Workmen Dragging Firemen and Engineers from a Baltimore Freight Train." In 1877 a national strike halted rail traffic in much of the nation and led to widespread violence and destruction of railroad property. (Prints and Photographs Division, Library of Congress)

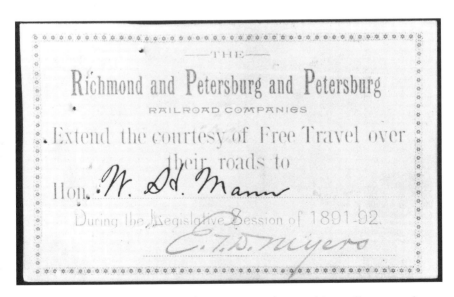

The practice of issuing free passes to legislators, judges, and journalists aroused controversy in the nineteenth century, and was curtailed by the Hepburn Act in 1906. (Virginia Historical Society)

The coupling of train cars by the link and pin method was a common cause of employee accidents until Congress mandated automatic couplers in 1893. (Association of American Railroads Photographic Collection, Virginia Museum of Transportation)

"KING DEBS." Picturing Eugene V. Debs as an obstruction to interstate commerce, this cartoon reflects the national tensions aroused by the Pullman strike of 1894. (Prints and Photographs Division, Library of Congress)

Following the Civil War, convict labor was frequently employed on southern railroads. (North Carolina Division of Archives and History)

"THE FIRST MEAT TRAIN LEAVING THE CHICAGO STOCK-YARDS UNDER ESCORT OF U.S. CAVALRY." The use of federal troops during the 1894 Pullman strike was bitterly controversial. (Prints and Photographs Division, Library of Congress)

Railroad crossings at street level were a cause of both accidents and intersection obstruction, and led to a movement to eliminate grade crossings. (Prints and Photographs Division, Library of Congress)

The scope of judicial review of Interstate Commerce Commission orders was a topic of intense debate before enactment of the Hepburn Act in 1906. (Prints and Photographs Division, Library of Congress)

The advent of the automobile in the early twentieth century gave new intensity to the problem of intersection accidents, and caused courts to place some duty of care on highway travelers. (Prints and Photographs Division, Library of Congress)

The hazards of rail travel, as illustrated by this fatal 1911 derailment on the Lehigh Valley Railroad, markedly shaped the law governing liability for accidents. (Albert R. Stone Negative Collection, Rochester Museum and Science Center, Rochester, N.Y.)

"And in the Meantime—

Uncle Sam.—Why don't you throw him that life-preserver? He may be drowning! The Inter-State Commerce Commission.—Plenty of time! Let's first make sure that he can't swim." Taking a sympathetic view of the railroads, this 1913 cartoon calls upon the Interstate Commerce Commission to approve a rate increase to preserve the industry's financial health. (*Puck*, June 25, 1913)

[Copyright: 1917: By John T. McCutcheon.]

The takeover of railroads by the federal government during World War I was highlighted in this 1917 cartoon. (John McCutcheon. Copyrighted 1917, Chicago Tribune Company. All rights reserved, used with permission)

New Wig Wag Signal near Salem, Virginia, ca. 1930. Frequent accidents at railroad crossings caused lawmakers to require carriers to enact warning signs and safety devices. (Association of American Railroads Photographic Collection, Virginia Museum of Transportation)

7

Insolvency, Receiverships, and Commercial Practices

R ailroading was a major force in shaping important aspects of bank-ruptcy and commercial law. The need to keep financially distressed carriers operating led to innovative uses of equity receiverships and even-tually to the corporate reorganization provisions of the bankruptcy act. Sim-ilarly, railroads influenced the growth of the law governing the duties and liabilities of common carriers in the shipment of goods. As with other facets of railroad law, resolution of these issues was complicated by considerations of federalism. Since railroading was increasingly seen as a national business, federal law gradually displaced state power over the commercial dimensions of the industry.

Insolvency

Throughout the nineteenth century many railroads experienced insolvency. Heavy fixed costs, periods of unduly rapid expansion, competition for busi-ness, the burden of governmental regulations, and mismanagement were among the factors that produced chronic financial distress. The plight of the carriers was aggravated by serious economic downturns in the 1870s and 1890s, which inevitably reduced revenue. Starting with the panic of 1873, railroad insolvencies became commonplace.[1] Indeed, bankruptcy helped to fuel the steady movement toward the consolidation of different lines.

The law controlling the right of creditors to reach the assets of troubled railroads was markedly influenced by two factors: absence of a permanent national bankruptcy law until 1898, and recognition of the unique impor-tance of railroads as an essential avenue of commerce. By the late nineteenth century, the financing of railroads typically involved a complex array of mortgages and debt instruments, and much of the investment capital was provided by eastern or European capitalists. States could enact legislation allowing creditors to levy upon the property of insolvent carriers, but lacked

power to reorganize an interstate enterprise, reach rail property in other jurisdictions, or keep troubled lines functioning. Moreover, not only was the continued operation of lines deemed vital for the public interest, but railroads
were worth more as going concerns than if they were liquidated piecemeal.
Traditional remedies giving individual creditors the power to levy upon and
sell the property of insolvent debtors consequently failed to preserve the value
of rail assets and threatened disruption of railroad service to the public.

During the antebellum era, state court judges were alert to the dangers
inherent in granting relief to particular claimants. In *Dunn v. North Missouri
Railroad* (1857), for instance, the Supreme Court of Missouri ruled that a
mechanic could not obtain a lien for work performed on the bridges of a rail
line. It expressed concern that enforcement of a lien against a portion of the
line would deprive the public of the benefit of the railroad. Similarly, the Kentucky Court of Appeals held that the rolling stock of a railroad could not be
subjected to an execution sale. The result of such a sale, the court reasoned,
would render the railroad useless and impair the rights of other creditors.[2]

After the Civil War, federal courts also adopted a view hostile to foreclosure on portions of a railroad. In 1879 Justice Joseph P. Bradley, in a circuit
court, stressed that a railroad was a public highway and denied that the state
legislature "ever intended that execution creditors might levy upon parcels of
it, and cut it up into sections, and destroy it as a great public thoroughfare."[3]

One increasingly common remedy for railroad creditors was to seek court
appointment of a receiver for an insolvent carrier. Historically, the receiver
of a bankrupt business was a disinterested party who took possession of the
property, sold the assets, paid creditors, and wound up the affairs of the company. But the novel nature of rail enterprise required a new method of handling insolvency. Hence, courts of equity began to give receivers the power
to continue the operations of the line, to borrow additional capital by issuing
certificates that created priority liens on the property, and to manage the line
until an orderly disposition could be arranged. The effect, a critic charged,
was to make the receiver "a sort of partner in the business" with the court
in "performing the function of a common carrier of goods and passengers."[4]
Further, in order to protect railroad property in the hands of the receiver, the
appointing court commonly provided that a receiver was not subject to lawsuits without leave of the court. A receiver could not be sued, even for personal injury claims, on the same basis as a private party. Observing that the
"new and changed condition of things" presented by the insolvency of railroad companies "has rendered necessary the exercise of large and modified
forms of control" over their property, the Supreme Court in *Barton v. Barbour* (1881) upheld the authority of receivers to carry on the business of

bankrupt railroads. In reaching this decision, the Court emphasized the public interest in railroad operations, and declared that "the cessation of business for a day would be a public injury."[5]

Although useful in some situations, even this enlarged understanding of receivership did not provide an adequate response to the problem of railroad bankruptcy. It did stop conflicting claims from consuming the assets and prevent disruption of rail service, but it often only covered a part of the railroad system and was not designed to bring about corporate reorganization. As one commentator explained, "legal machinery was needed which would extend the receivership to the entire system of the debtor and permit its centralized operation pending the development of a plan of reorganization."[6]

Receivership and Reorganization

The law of equity receivership was transformed by the pioneering Wabash receivership of 1884. Contrary to the usual practice in which creditors sought the appointment of a receiver, the Wabash, St. Louis and Pacific Railroad Company requested ex parte the designation of a receiver for its entire line. There was no suit pending against the carrier, and the Wabash was not yet in default on its financial obligations. No notice of the application was given to bondholders. The purpose behind the request was to delay an expected wave of mortgage foreclosure suits until a reorganization plan for the company could be devised. Even more startling, the Wabash asked that its current managers, instead of an outside individual, be named as receivers. In granting the Wabash's application, the federal circuit court was likely influenced by the need for expert managers who could run the line while seeking to organize it on a financially viable basis.[7]

Although the unprecedented Wabash receivership broke new ground in several respects, it rested on important policy considerations. The interests of creditors were no longer the primary consideration in the appointment of receivers. The contractual rights of creditors and bondholders were now subordinated to the public interest that transportation services be preserved if possible. A unanimous Supreme Court, in an opinion by Chief Justice Melville W. Fuller, had no difficulty in validating this novel type of receivership. Fuller declared that the relief sought "was obviously framed upon the theory that an insolvent railroad corporation has a standing in a court of equity to surrender its property into the custody of the court, to be preserved and disposed of according to the rights of its various creditors, and, in the meantime, operated in the public interest."[8] The Wabash model was frequently followed during the depression decade of the 1890s. The standard practice was for carriers in financial straits to seek receivership protection. This new type of receivership pulled the federal courts heavily into the business of supervising troubled railroads.[9]

Several aspects of equity railroad receiverships warrant attention. As we have seen, the general rule was that a receiver, being an officer of the court, could not be sued without leave of the appointing court. Such permission was rarely granted. The result was that litigation arising out of the operation of a railroad in receivership was concentrated in the appointing court, often a considerable distance from where the plaintiff resided. The expense involved discouraged those with small claims. Further, suits against a receiver were heard in equity proceedings without a jury trial. This rule was justified as necessary to prevent interference with the receiver's ability to operate the railroad effectively. But instead of acting simply as a custodian of property, railroad receivers were managing an extensive business, often for years. Since receivers were functioning as common carriers, many argued that the rule compromised the rights of legitimate claimants by restricting their ability to bring suit against lines in receivership. In 1887 Congress abrogated the rule that a receiver could not be sued without permission of the appointing court, and authorized such suits in other forums.[10] The Supreme Court broadly construed this statute in *Gableman v. Peoria, Decatur and Evansville Railway Company* (1900), holding that a receiver appointed by a federal court could not evade the act by removing a pending state court action into federal court.

Another issue arising out of the new railroad receiverships was the relationship between the receivership court and state laws. A number of receivers operated their railroads without regard for state law. In addition, many receivers were slow to pay state and county taxes on rail property, and often challenged the legality of assessments. Congress addressed this issue with an 1887 statute that required receivers to manage property according to state law.[11] But the controversy over compliance with state laws did not fade with this measure.

The problem was highlighted by a bitter dispute that erupted in South Carolina in 1891. The immediate question was the authority of receivers of several railroads in South Carolina to refuse the payment of state taxes, but the larger concerns involved the jurisdiction of the federal courts and the unease of southerners over northern financial control of southern railroads. The receivers declined to pay state taxes because they felt the assessments were excessive. A sheriff was found in contempt of court and imprisoned when he attempted to levy upon freight cars and other property to collect taxes from the South Carolina Railroad. Writing for a unanimous Supreme Court, Chief Justice Fuller upheld the contempt finding and insisted that even the collection of taxes did not justify physical interference with property in the possession of a receiver.[12]

Driven in part by the South Carolina imbroglio, the issue of federal receiverships blossomed into a major political issue. In 1894 the South Carolina legislature petitioned Congress in angry terms, calling for legislation to rein in the power of receivers. Characterizing a receiver as "a Federal proconsul, lording it over a subject province," lawmakers cast the issue in terms of states' rights. They charged that receivers "now . . . defy and deride the powers and prerogatives of sovereign States." Further, the legislature expressed concern that the receiver of the South Carolina Railroad was a representative of northern capital who operated the line with little regard for local needs.[13]

The South Carolina memorial underscored the sectional dimensions of the receivership debate. It was an especially heated topic in southern states because a high percentage of southern carriers went into receivership in the late nineteenth century. In practice, receivership tended to strengthen northern domination of southern lines. Hence, as Harry N. Scheiber explained, the receivership controversy linked "the issues of economic colonialism and federal judicial power."[14]

Although southerners were especially unhappy with court-appointed railroad managers, the controversy was not limited to one region. The scope of the resort to receivership bears emphasis. Hundreds of lines went into receivership during the 1880s and 1890s. It has been estimated that 20 percent of the total mileage in the United States was in the hands of receivers in 1894.[15] As late as 1916, on the eve of American entry into World War I, one-sixth of national trackage was operated by receivers. Many lines, moreover, remained under the control of receivers for lengthy periods of time.

By the start of the twentieth century, railroad receiverships were the subject of frequent complaint. Critics alleged a litany of abuses—that courts appointed receivers too readily and then failed to supervise them adequately; that receivers gave short shrift to the rights of creditors, mortgage holders, and parties contracting with carriers; that it was inappropriate to name as receivers the very managers of insolvent lines; that receiverships continued too long; and that railroads in receivership gained a competitive advantage over other carriers.[16] Moreover, as explained more fully in Chapter Twelve, federal judges began to enjoin strikes against railroads in receivership on grounds such activity interfered with the receiver's ability to manage the line. Consequently, federal courts, receivers, and railroad companies tended to merge in popular perception into a kind of alliance. Critics saw this development as further evidence of federal court partiality toward business enterprise, particularly railroads.[17]

But viewed in economic terms, the equity receivership was a highly successful legal mechanism. It helped many carriers weather the depression of the 1890s. Notwithstanding persistent criticism and the fact that equity receivership was largely fashioned by federal judges absent a bankruptcy law, the core concept of railroad reorganization proved enduring. "The Wabash idea," Albro Martin cogently observed, "swept all before it, and remains the basis of modern railroad bankruptcy law to this day."[18] With the onset of the Great Depression, many carriers teetered on the edge of financial collapse. Congress responded by incorporating principles derived from railroad receiverships into the bankruptcy act. In 1933 Congress adopted Chapter 77, which authorized insolvent railroads to seek reorganization. In a move to eliminate a perceived abuse of the equity receiverships, the railroad might be left in the hands of management or turned over to trustees in bankruptcy selected from a panel designated by the Interstate Commerce Commission. Any reorganization plan required approval by the ICC.[19] The Supreme Court, in *Continental Illinois National Bank v. Chicago, Rock Island and Pacific Railway Company* (1935), upheld the constitutionality of the railroad reorganization provision as within the bankruptcy power of Congress. Significantly, in 1934 Congress extended the reorganization principle to other business enterprises.

The reorganization provisions of modern bankruptcy law can be traced directly to the evolution of equity receiverships to handle insolvent railroads in the late nineteenth century. Given the importance of railroads to the national economy and the complex capital structure of such enterprises, courts could not simply treat railroads as other types of business. Equity receiverships were a bold innovation that, on the whole, served the nation well and preserved rail service during troubled times. Railroads were responsible for the modification of traditional receiverships to meet the novel problems of the industrial age.[20]

Common Carriers

Public transportation services were characterized as common carriers under English common law long before the advent of railroads. The law imposed special obligations on common carriers. Among other duties, common carriers were required to (1) serve all who applied for carriage, (2) charge reasonable rates, and (3) strictly warrant the safe delivery of goods entrusted to them. My focus in this section is on the varied legal issues arising out of the strict standard of liability placed on railroads for the loss of or injury to freight in transit.

It was generally accepted that railroads had impliedly assumed the responsibilities of common carriers. For instance, in 1857 the Supreme Court of Illinois simply asserted: "That railroad companies are common carriers cannot be disputed, and, being so, they are bound and controlled, as a general principle, by all the common law rules applicable to such a position—they becoming, in fact, insurers."[21] Some jurisdictions enacted statutes that confirmed the status of railroads as common carriers.[22] The Michigan general railroad act of 1855 provided: "Any railroad company receiving freight for transportation, shall be entitled to the same rights, and subject to the same liabilities as common carriers."[23] During the late nineteenth century a number of states, including California, Pennsylvania, Montana, and Arkansas, even put in their constitutions a declaration that railroads were common carriers.

It was settled that common carriers were strictly liable without regard to negligence on their part for loss of or injury to goods, unless the loss was caused by acts of God or the public enemy. This meant that railroads were, in effect, insurers of goods shipped on their lines. This strict rule was grounded on the principle that carriers must be vigilant to safeguard goods entrusted to them for transportation. Moreover, since the railroad had complete control over the goods in transit, the shipper was not realistically in a position to prove fault on the part of the carrier. In sum, the rule gave common carriers an incentive to take every care to prevent damage to goods. As the Supreme Court of Indiana explained: "The law against common carriers, where the goods are lost, seems severe, but its severity is necessary to the security of property, and the protection of commerce, and is founded in experience and the deepest wisdom."[24]

There was a good deal of litigation as to what constituted an act of God. Generally, extraordinary storms operated to exonerate a railroad from liability. In *Smith & Co. v. Western Railway of Alabama* (1891), for instance, the Supreme Court of Alabama found that a carrier was not liable for injury caused by an unprecedented flood that overflowed the track and entered freight cars.

A railroad's responsibility as common carrier began when it received freight from a shipper. The deposit of goods at a place where a carrier regularly received property for transportation was treated as a constructive acceptance of delivery without any express notice of the deposit. There was greater dispute over the time when the railroad's liability as common carrier ended. Common carriers were bound to deliver the goods to the consignee. What constituted such delivery was a material inquiry because goods might be damaged between arrival at the place of destination and actual receipt by the consignee.

At common law, land carriers, like wagoneers, were expected to make an actual delivery of goods to consignees on their own premises. Courts early recognized that it was impractical for railroads, with fixed points of termination, to make personal delivery of shipments. At the same time, without notice of arrival, consignees could not be expected at the depot when freight cars were unloaded. Judges, therefore, wrestled with the task of modifying the common-law duties of carriers to meet the situation created by new technology.

There was a division of opinion as to what action by a railroad was required, in lieu of personal delivery, to terminate its liability as a common carrier. One line of authority was exemplified by the leading case of *Norway Plains Company v. Boston and Maine Railroad* (1854). In that case the Supreme Judicial Court of Massachusetts concluded that if the consignee was not ready to receive goods, the railroad was obligated to provide temporary storage. But once the goods had arrived at their destination, the railroad was no longer a common carrier but assumed a different role as warehouse keeper. As warehouse operators, railroads were not insurers and were liable only for losses occasioned by their negligence. Nor, the court reasoned, were railroads required to give notice to the consignee in order to terminate their duties as common carriers. Noting that "the new, and important class of carriers, rail-roads have a peculiarity which renders some of the rules of law . . . touching the delivery of goods carried, inapplicable," the Supreme Court of North Carolina reached a similar result in 1857.[25] It held that usually the railroad's liability as carrier ended when goods were unloaded and stored in a warehouse. Any recovery against the railroad as warehouse operator necessitated proof of fault.

Other courts, however, insisted that railroad responsibility as a common carrier continued until notice was given and the consignee had a reasonable opportunity to remove the goods. They maintained that this rule was more protective of the consignee and effectuated the policy behind the common-law liability of common carriers.[26]

Another much debated question was the extent to which railroads, as common carriers, could limit their strict common-law liability for damage to goods in transit. Railroads frequently sought to restrict their liability by language in bills of lading. These attempts produced constant litigation, which can only be summarized here. The general rule was that common carriers could limit their liability as insurers either by contract or by notice brought home to shippers.[27] This proposition, however, was subject to many qualifications, and courts were not uniform in determining under what circumstances and how far railroads could restrict their liability.[28]

There was a conflict among jurisdictions as to whether a railroad could exempt itself from loss caused by its own negligence.[29] Most courts took the position that carriers could obtain release only for loss not caused by their fault. In other words, a railroad could modify its liability as insurer but not for loss resulting from lack of care. Courts reasoned that to allow railroads to contract against negligence would defeat the policy governing common carriers. Under this analysis, a railroad could secure a discharge only for losses that occurred without its negligence. A few states, however, permitted railroads to contract for exemptions of liability for negligence, at least where the contractual language was unequivocal.[30] Moreover, courts generally ruled that contractual stipulations as to the value of goods fixed the amount of any recovery even if the railroad was guilty of negligence.[31]

A number of states closed the door on railroad efforts to restrict their liability as common carriers. Texas and Iowa, for instance, passed statutes that prohibited railroads from limiting their common-carrier liability. Finding that the Iowa measure was not an unconstitutional state regulation of interstate commerce, the Supreme Court explained in 1898: "Its whole object and effect are to make it more sure that railroad companies shall perform the duty, resting upon them by virtue of their employment as common carriers, to use the utmost care and diligence in the transportation of passengers and goods."[32] In addition, at least two states, Nebraska and Kentucky, inserted in their constitutions language that banned contracts by railroads to restrict common-carrier liability. Reflecting concern that the public suffered from relaxation of the strict common-law rule, these measures in effect restored that norm.

Livestock were frequently transported upon railroads in the nineteenth and early twentieth centuries, and the shipment of animals raised some special issues. The Supreme Court recognized in 1887 that the safe transportation of animals imposed "duties in many respects widely different from those devolving upon a mere carrier of goods."[33] Likewise, the Supreme Court of Illinois pointed out that the shipment of livestock "in railroad cars, in their rapid motion, is attended with great hazard."[34] Not surprisingly, injury to livestock in transit was a fertile source of litigation.

Generally, the same rules that applied to the delivery of goods also governed livestock. Nonetheless, courts realized that the strict liability of common carriers did not always fit comfortably with the transportation of livestock. Several exceptions developed. First, a railroad was not responsible for injuries resulting from the nature and propensity of animals; for instance, animals might kill each other or refuse to eat.[35] Second, some courts were more willing to uphold contracts limiting liability with respect to livestock.[36]

Still, railroads that agreed to carry livestock had to take all reasonable steps for their safe transport and delivery. This entailed the furnishing of appropriate vehicles, loading and unloading animals, and caring for stock during transportation. Many states enacted regulations defining the duty of carriers to feed and water livestock.[37] In 1873 Congress likewise provided that no railroad company that conveyed animals from state to state could confine them in cars for more than twenty-eight consecutive hours without unloading such stock for rest and feeding. Violation of the statute rendered the company liable for monetary penalties and constituted negligence per se.[38] These measures highlight the determination of lawmakers to protect shippers of livestock by clarifying the responsibility of carriers.

In addition to safe carriage, common carriers were obligated to transport and deliver goods within a reasonable period of time. But carriers were not insurers against the occurrence of any delay. They were liable for unreasonable delay on their part, but not for delays occurring without fault. Although railroads were bound to use reasonable care to avoid delay, some delays were deemed excusable.[39]

There were numerous decisions holding railroads accountable for injury to goods caused by unreasonable delay. Livestock and perishable items were especially vulnerable to delay. Thus, in *Illinois Central Railroad Company v. Hays* (1857), the Supreme Court of Illinois upheld a jury verdict awarding damages for delay in the transport of hogs, which resulted in the death of many animals.

There was, however, no fixed rule as to what constituted an unreasonable delay, and the determination depended on the circumstances of each case. For instance, the New York Court of Appeals exonerated a railroad when a shipment of butter was delayed owing to an unusually heavy demand for transportation. Satisfied that the carrier provided as many freight trains as possible, the court observed: "If under such circumstances a railroad company would be liable on account of a tardy delivery, the business would be quite too hazardous to be followed by prudent men."[40] In the same vein, delays caused by unavoidable accidents or storms that prevented the operation of trains excused late delivery.

A vexing issue was the extent to which disturbances and work stoppages arising out of labor disputes allowed a railroad to avoid liability for loss caused by delay. At issue in *Blackstock v. New York and Erie Railroad Company* (1859) was liability for delay in delivering a shipment of potatoes. The delay was caused by a strike of engineers who were protesting new work rules. The New York Court of Appeals ruled that the company was responsible for the actions of its employees, and that a strike did not constitute a legal excuse. It recognized that a "railroad corporation is no doubt peculiarly exposed to loss from the misconduct of its engineers," but nonetheless insisted that the carrier was liable for the damages.[41]

As rail strikes became more frequent in the late nineteenth century, courts began to reconsider the scope of carrier liability for loss caused by work stoppages. They distinguished between strikes by employees—for which companies remained responsible—and violence instigated by crowds of discharged employees and outsiders.[42] Where strikes led to violence and mob action that halted rail traffic, courts tended to relieve railroads from loss resulting from delay. Hence, railroads were generally exonerated when mob violence arising out of the widespread rail strikes of 1877 prevented the timely operation of trains.[43]

Claims for Loss

As the interstate rail network grew steadily, goods were often shipped over several connecting lines to distant points. In case of loss, it was uncertain which carrier was responsible to the shipper. The liability of railroads for injury to goods beyond their own lines was much contested. At common law, a carrier was responsible only for safe carriage over its line, and had no liability for injuries occurring after the goods had been transferred to the custody of another. However, the initial carrier could by express agreement assume responsibility for the safe delivery of goods over intersecting lines. What constituted such a contract was a topic of considerable dispute.[44] Accordingly, state legislators in the antebellum era began to assist shippers by enlarging the common-law duty of carriers for goods transported over connecting lines. An 1847 New York statute made any railroad receiving freight for transport over connecting lines liable as common carrier for the delivery of such freight at the place of destination. The company that had to pay damages because of the fault of a connecting carrier could recover an indemnity from the negligent concern.[45] This law made it much easier for an aggrieved shipper to recover from the initial carrier, while forcing the various lines involved to sort out ultimate responsibility for the loss.

Notwithstanding the strict common-law duties imposed on common carriers, claimants often had difficulty in recovering from railroads for injury to freight or livestock. Experience suggested that railroads were accustomed to resist the payment of legitimate claims in the hope of discouraging claimants faced with the prospect of litigation. To assist claimants, state legislators, starting as early as 1855 in Rhode Island, authorized the award of attorney fees in successful suits against railroads. In the years following the Civil War, state courts were sharply divided as to the constitutionality of such measures. In *Gulf, Colorado and Santa Fe Railway Company v. Ellis* (1897), the Supreme Court invalidated a Texas statute allowing a person with a bona fide small claim against a railroad to recover attorneys' fees. The Court held that the law arbitrarily singled out railroads for a special burden not imposed on other corporations, and violated the equal protection clause of the Fourteenth Amendment.

Other legislative efforts to aid claimants fared better. A number of states enacted laws mandating that common carriers promptly settle meritorious claims for loss or injury to property, and providing a monetary penalty for failure to comply. In 1907 the Supreme Court upheld such statutes as applied to intrastate shipments. Stressing that the law was designed to help claimants recover modest amounts promptly, the Court observed that the purpose of the legislation was "to compel the performance of duties which the carrier assumes when it enters upon the discharge of its public function."[46]

Toward a National Policy

By the early twentieth century, diverse state laws governing carrier liability for property loss, particularly with respect to contractual limits on liability, were causing confusion for railroads and shippers alike. Contracts for interstate transportation were subject to conflicting state policies. This difficulty was highlighted in *Pennsylvania Railroad Company v. Hughes* (1903), which involved injury to a horse shipped from New York to Pennsylvania. Although the contract contained a provision, valid in New York, limiting liability for the horse, the Supreme Court held that, absent congressional legislation, Pennsylvania courts could apply local law that denied the validity of such provisions. The Court pointedly declared, however, that Congress could regulate the interstate carriage of goods, and seemingly invited Congress to take that step.

Three years later, Congress adopted the Carmack Amendment as part of the Hepburn Act. Following the pattern in other areas of railroad law, the evident purpose of the Carmack Amendment was to establish a national uniform policy of carrier liability for injured goods. The amendment mandated that for any interstate shipment a carrier must issue a receipt or bill of lading. The initial carrier was made liable to the receipt holder for loss or damage either caused by it or by any connecting carrier. Further, the amendment declared that no contract could exempt the carrier from the liability imposed by the act. Congress in effect codified the common-law rule that carriers were insurers of goods in transit, and placed liability on the carrier issuing the bill of lading for injury occurring anywhere on the route.

The Supreme Court decided in 1914 that by the Carmack Amendment Congress preempted "the subject" and superseded all state regulations.[47] States were not free to either enlarge or restrict the responsibility of carriers for property entrusted to them. The extent of the displacement of state law, however, was uncertain. For example, the Court found that a statute imposing a penalty on carriers for failure to pay legitimate claims promptly conflicted with the recovery scheme of the Carmack Amendment.[48] More recently, the amendment has been held to preclude the award of punitive damages or suits against carriers based on state consumer laws. Courts have emphasized the importance of uniformity in the law governing interstate shipments. In these situations the amendment has been a shield for carriers.

Nonetheless, the Carmack Amendment retains considerable bite. At issue in *Missouri Pacific Railroad Company v. Elmore & Stahl* (1964) was the liability of a railroad for the spoilage of melons in transit. The Supreme Court took the position that a shipper establishes a prima facie case when he demonstrates that goods delivered to the carrier in good condition were damaged upon arrival. The burden is then placed on the carrier to show that the damage resulted from an act of God or other exceptions to liability. Declining to treat perishables differently than nonperishable freight, the justices affirmed an award of damages.

Legislators and courts, both state and federal, sought to adjust the traditional doctrine of common carriers to meet the new conditions presented by the growth of railroads. They refashioned the principles of common carriers, devised with older forms of transportation in mind, to meet the needs of railroading. Anxious to facilitate commerce by encouraging railroad development, lawmakers and judges balanced the concerns of the industry with the importance of encouraging the safe and timely carriage of goods. They therefore retained the core principle of broad liability for the loss of property in transit.[49]

Finally, it is instructive to note how the railroads' duty as common carriers of goods differed from their responsibility to passengers. As discussed, railroads were to an extent insurers of the safe delivery of goods. In contrast, railroads did not warrant the safety of passengers and were responsible only for accidents caused by their negligence. The liability of railroads for personal injury is explored in Chapter Nine.

8

Property and Taxation

Railroads significantly influenced the law governing real property. In particular, the growth of railroading did much to define the parameters of eminent domain, nuisance, and easements. Rail assets, of course, were subject to state and local taxation. Yet state efforts to tax railroad property had an impact on interstate commerce. Courts were thus called upon to determine the scope of tax exemptions granted to carriers, and to fashion constitutional limits on state power to tax instruments of interstate commerce.

Eminent Domain

As discussed earlier, state legislatures uniformly granted the power of eminent domain to railroad companies. The courts, however, policed the actual exercise of eminent domain and adjusted the competing interests of railroads and landowners. Throughout the nineteenth century, courts heard a steady stream of cases that involved the condemnation of land by railroads. Railroads provided much of the impetus for judges to fashion takings jurisprudence.

At root, these eminent-domain cases involved a clash of values. The delegation of eminent-domain authority to railroads attested to the importance of improved transportation to society at large. Yet the right of owners to enjoy their property free from intrusion was safeguarded by the Constitution and could not be casually disregarded.[1]

Historians have begun to study the realities of railroad takings of property. Much of this interest has centered on the constitutional requirement that "just compensation" be paid. Drawing on state constitutional provisions or natural-law principles, jurists generally agreed that private property could not be taken for public projects without the payment of just compensation.[2] Accordingly, every railroad charter and general act required the company to pay for land or materials acquired to build its lines. Courts agreed that just compensation entailed the payment of market value for property taken.[3] There was, of course, considerable difference of opinion as to how market value should be ascertained. This calculation was complicated by the fact that railroads usually acquired a strip of land through a larger tract. Railroads were clearly obligated to pay for the land actually taken, but there was a dispute as to railroad liability for incidental injury to the adjacent land not physically acquired.

Scholars have debated the extent to which legislators and judges in the early nineteenth century sought to encourage enterprise by limiting the amount of compensation awarded in eminent-domain proceedings.[4] This dialogue has focused on two devices—the offset of supposed benefits and the denial of recovery for consequential damages—that diminished the amount of compensation.

Early railroad charters in many states, including Rhode Island, Ohio, Georgia, South Carolina, and Virginia, expressly adopted the practice of offsetting the imputed benefits of a project against the loss suffered by individual property owners whose land was taken. An 1835 Georgia act, for instance, required that in awarding compensation, the appraisers must consider "the benefit and advantage" that a landowner received "from the erection and establishment of the railroad or works."[5] A series of Virginia charters directed the appraisers to weigh both the injuries to the landowner and "a just regard to the advantages which the owner of the land will derive from the construction of the rail-road."[6] The appraisers were only to award a sum for damages sustained beyond the amount of the benefits received. Similarly, the Missouri general railroad act of 1853 mandated "due allowance or deduction of any advantages or benefits" that parties "will derive from the construction of the proposed railroad."[7]

The statutes themselves, of course, do not shed light on how aggressively the offset policy was pursued. Undoubtedly, the offset provisions opened the door to potential undercompensation of landowners.[8] For example, in 1848 the Supreme Court of Pennsylvania asserted that a landowner benefited by rail construction was not entitled to recover any compensation for land taken. It also expressed concern that "the damages will be swelled to such an amount as greatly to embarrass, if not seriously to endanger, the ultimate success of a work destined at no distant day to increase the prosperity of the commonwealth to an extent beyond the most sanguine calculation."[9] Likewise, the Supreme Court of Illinois insisted in *Alton and Sangamon Railroad Company v. Carpenter* (1852) that increased value to an owner's remaining land resulting from railroad construction might satisfy the constitutional requirement of just compensation. The owner would receive no monetary compensation if the benefit was deemed sufficient to offset the loss. Clearly, the overriding goal of these courts was rail development, and they consequently gave a crabbed reading to the right of landowners to receive just compensation.

Yet despite charters and statutes authorizing the offset of presumed benefits, appraisers in some jurisdictions gave little heed to offsets in determining compensation for land taken. One study points out that in antebellum Virginia landowners were the dominant influence on public policy, and that eminent-domain law was construed to favor property owners over railroads. Offset provisions were not consistently effective in holding down eminent-domain costs to railroads in that state.[10]

Furthermore, there were good reasons to question the equity of offsetting alleged benefits against the loss suffered by individual landowners. The anticipated benefits that could result from a rail project were highly speculative and might never in fact be realized given the uncertain success of many new ventures. The offset of general benefits accruing to the public posed additional problems. Neighboring owners would likely also enjoy land value increase from railroad building, but they did not have to bear the cost by having a portion of their property taken. Thus, offset of general benefits tended to single out individuals to suffer a loss that would advantage the community at large. A delegate explained to the Ohio constitutional convention of 1850–51:

> As a farmer, I am not willing that a Railroad Company should take off a strip from my farm, and pay me for it in "supposed benefits," while my neighbor by the side of whose farm the road runs, without touching it, receives equal "benefits" with me, and yet loses none of his land.[11]

Despite widespread use of the offset notion, it was never universal. A good many charters and general laws required the appraisers to assess damages and made no mention of offsetting benefits.[12] In Connecticut, rail charters in the early 1830s called for the offset of benefits and contemplated that the appraisers might consequently make no award. Subsequent acts, however, dropped the offset requirement.[13] At least one jurisdiction moved early to expressly repudiate the offset of alleged advantages. Several 1836 New York acts mandated the valuation of land taken "without any deduction on account of any real or supposed benefit or advantage which such owners of such lands may derive by the construction of such road." This ban of the practice of offsetting was adopted as part of the New York general railroad law in 1848.[14] These developments suggest that the offset of benefits was falling gradually into disfavor. Indeed, starting with Ohio in 1851, several states amended their constitutions to exclude the consideration of benefits in calculating just compensation.[15]

Even where not expressly prohibited by constitutional or statutory provisions, a deduction for supposed benefits called into question the meaning of
just compensation as a constitutional norm. At least two state courts invalidated awards where the offset of benefits reduced the amount of compensation, and insisted that the constitutional principle of just compensation
must prevail over charter offset provisions. In *Woodfolk v. Nashville & Chattanooga Railroad Co.* (1852), the railroad constructed its line across the
claimant's farm, separating the tract. The Supreme Court of Tennessee held
that the claimant was entitled to receive the value of the land actually taken
in money, and that the amount could not be diminished by any incidental
benefits in the appreciation of his remaining land. On the other hand, the
court permitted the offset of advantages in enhanced value against the damages to the remainder of claimant's land. The Supreme Court of Mississippi
went a step further and voided a charter provision that authorized the offset of benefits. The court reasoned that a landowner must receive the cash
value of both the land taken for the right-of-way and an indemnification for
consequential injury to his adjacent land. Stressing the importance of the just
compensation principle, the judges concluded:

> It was clearly as incompetent for the legislature to prescribe in what he
> should be paid, as to prescribe how much or how little he should receive.
> Manifestly, a party whose property has been taken and appropriated to
> public use in the construction of a railroad, cannot be compelled to
> receive as compensation the estimated enhancement in the value of his
> remaining property.[16]

Other courts modified the offset of benefits in ways that strengthened the
rights of landowners. They distinguished between the offset of general benefits for the community at large and special benefits that increased the value
of a particular tract.[17] As early as 1849 the Supreme Judicial Court of Massachusetts rejected the practice of charging a landowner "for all the incidental benefits, which he receives from the location of the railroad . . . while his
neighbor, who is equally benefited, is exempt from any contribution to this
object." The court then insisted that any offset should be limited to the "direct
benefit, or increase of value of the remaining part of the tract," and excluded
"the most uncertain and fanciful estimation of anticipated advantages to other
parcels."[18] Following suit, the Supreme Court of North Carolina in *Freedle v.
North Carolina Rail Road Company* (1856) confined any deduction to those
advantages peculiar to a particular tract. In short, judges grew increasingly
skeptical about the invocation of general prosperity or improved transportation as a basis for reducing eminent-domain awards. Legislators also began

to tighten the requirements for offsetting alleged benefits. In 1852 Illinois lawmakers banned the consideration of general advantages in eminent-domain proceedings for transportation facilities.[19] The Florida general railroad act of 1874 only authorized the deduction of "any real benefits" the landowners derived from the project. This practice of distinguishing between general advantages to the public and special benefits to particular land continued in some jurisdictions into the twentieth century.[20]

Historians still have much to do to illuminate the frequency and extent to which awards were reduced by offsets in eminent-domain proceedings. Yet two conclusions seem warranted. First, there was a good deal of diversity among jurisdictions and even between charter provisions in a single state with respect to offsetting. The law within states vacillated over time. For a period in the late nineteenth century, North Carolina banned the offset of any benefits, but then restored the former practice of allowing the offset of special benefits.[21] This gave rise to considerable confusion as to when a deduction could be made for supposed advantages. A leading commentator on railroad law, Issac F. Redfield, aptly observed in 1888: "But in consequence of numerous ingenious speculations in regard to possible advantages and disadvantages arising from the public works for which lands are taken, the whole subject has become, in this country especially, involved in more or less uncertainty."[22] Second, the practice grew increasingly controversial during the nineteenth century, and states moved to stop or curtail benefit offset as a factor in the exercise of eminent domain by railroads. Railroads did much to bring about the modern rule in most states under which a setoff of benefits against the value of land taken is prohibited, and only special benefits may be considered with respect to damages to land retained by the owner.

Offsetting of benefits was not the only device to protect railroads from large condemnation awards. They could sometimes escape liability in eminent-domain proceedings by invoking the concept of consequential damages. Narrowly construing the definition of a taking, numerous antebellum courts ruled that compensation was only constitutionally mandated when property was physically acquired and did not encompass indirect or consequential injuries. As the Supreme Judicial Court of Massachusetts explained in 1852: "The law does not propose to grant indemnity for all losses occasioned by the laying of a railroad."[23] Courts repeatedly held, for example, that use of city streets by railroads did not constitute a taking of property when owners of adjacent lots suffered a diminution of land value.[24] Another instructive decision is *New York and Erie Railroad v. Young* (1859), in which a mill owner sought to recover for damage caused when railroad construction along a river partially blocked the river and diverted water from his mill. The Supreme Court of

Pennsylvania rejected a claim for damage to the mill operations on grounds that any injury was merely consequential.

But the legislative and judicial response to the infliction of consequential damages by railroads was complex and contradictory.[25] On occasion lawmakers adopted positions that favored landowners. The Pennsylvania general railroad act of 1849, for example, provided that railroads should compensate owners of city lots damaged by any excavation on public streets.[26] Moreover, some charters required railroads to pay both for the value of land acquired and for any injury caused. In *Bradley v. New York and New Haven Railroad* (1851), the plaintiff asserted that the foundation of his building was weakened by excavation for an adjacent railroad embankment. The defendant maintained that under both the state constitution and the carrier's charter, the railroad was liable only for property physically appropriated. Pointing to language in the charter that stated that when taking land "said company shall be holden to pay all damages that may arise to any person or persons," the Supreme Court of Connecticut determined that the legislature intended to impose liability for incidental as well as direct injuries. Noting that the action of the railroad did not amount to "a technical taking" of property, the court nonetheless concluded that the right of eminent domain was conferred on the railroad "only on condition that they should pay all damages occasioned by other persons, by their exercise."[27] Construing a statute that made railroads "liable to pay all damages" occasioned by the construction of lines, the Supreme Judicial Court of Massachusetts ruled that the provision was sufficiently broad to make a rail company responsible for an excavation that rendered a well useless.[28]

More significant, railroad building provided the catalyst for some courts in the late nineteenth century to redefine what constitutes a taking of property for constitutional purposes, and in so doing to reject the concept of consequential injury. At issue in *Eaton v. Boston, Concord & Montreal Railroad* (1872) was the removal of a ridge of land by a carrier, causing a river to sometimes flood plaintiff's land. Stressing that property ownership encompassed use and enjoyment, the Supreme Court of New Hampshire ruled that a physical interference with these rights was a taking of property. "The framers of the constitution," the court maintained, "intended to protect rights which are worth protecting; not mere empty titles, or barren insignia of ownership, which are of no substantial value."[29] The court added that if a railroad was an important project, then the traveling public should pay for it and not put the burden on individual landowners. *Eaton* was a harbinger of a more sophisticated understanding of ownership in which property represented beneficial interests, not just title to a physical object. The extent of liability for consequential damages remains a knotty issue today.

Railroad construction helped to bring about other constitutional changes that strengthened the rights of property owners. Starting with Illinois in 1870, most states amended their constitutions to mandate compensation when property was either taken or "damaged."[30] Driven in large part by unhappiness with the inadequate protection afforded landowners hurt by railroad projects, the purpose of these provisions was to give greater security from the incidental damages caused by improvements. In essence, these clauses enlarged the concept of a taking of property and restrained the exercise of eminent domain. "Such provision," the Supreme Court explained, "is eminently just, and is intended for the protection of the citizen, the value of whose property may be as effectually destroyed as if it were in fact taken and occupied."[31]

In sum, the judicial handling of railroad eminent-domain cases was checkered, and one must be careful about generalizations that rail companies exploited individual owners and obtained land at little cost.[32] Despite doctrines that minimized recovery in certain situations, not all courts followed these rules. Indeed, over the course of the nineteenth century the legal system grew more protective of the rights of property owners. Railroad liability was increasingly extended even to indirect injury caused by the construction of lines. In fact, courts upheld a number of sizeable awards against carriers. Eminent-domain payments were a major expense item for railroads, and the cost and delay of such proceedings were a prime reason why companies preferred to negotiate for voluntary purchase of routes when possible.[33] The record calls into question the contention by some scholars that eminent domain constituted a subsidy for rail enterprise.

Aside from questions of just compensation, railroad exercise of eminent domain raised a number of other issues. The mode of assessing the value of property taken was also the subject of controversy. Typically, rail charters and general statutes established an assessment procedure available to both carriers and landowners. Upon petition, a local court was authorized to appoint a panel of commissioners to view the premises and determine the value of the property taken.[34] Some jurisdictions allowed a trial by jury if an aggrieved party appealed from an award by the commissioners.[35] However, there was no constitutional right to a trial by jury in eminent-domain cases.[36] Hence, the legislature in its discretion could decide the manner for ascertaining just compensation. Some scholars have argued that the mode of assessment by commissioners generally aided railroads by ascertaining low property values.[37] But the commissioners were local property owners whose decisions reflected a number of factors, including sympathy with their neighbors. As a practical matter, these assessment procedures did not systematically disadvantage individual owners or result in consistently inadequate awards.

Another concern emanating from the exercise of eminent domain was whether payment was required before the company could take possession of the property. Given the financially risky nature of railroad projects and the precarious solvency of many carriers, owners were understandably concerned that they receive compensation before surrendering possession. Otherwise owners might wind up with no payment and an abandoned line across their property. Courts and legislators once again grappled with how best to adjust the interests of carriers and landowners.

A number of states, including New York, Pennsylvania, and Vermont, enacted statutes that required the payment of compensation before a railroad could enter land.[38] Many individual charters of incorporation contained a similar provision.[39] Courts in several states construed corporate charters or general laws as making the payment of compensation a condition precedent to the appropriation of property by eminent domain.[40] During the 1850s, some jurisdictions, such as Ohio and Kansas, incorporated the principle of prior payment into their constitutions. During the nineteenth century, New Jersey courts repeatedly enjoined railroad construction until the landowner received compensation.[41]

Nonetheless, the right to obtain payment before a railroad took possession of property was not universally recognized and was qualified in several ways. In *Raleigh and Gaston Rail Road v. Davis* (1837), for instance, the Supreme Court of North Carolina insisted that payment need not proceed the taking of property, and that the amount of compensation could be determined subsequently. Suggesting that public exigencies might mandate that property be acquired at once, the court ruled that the constitutional norm was satisfied by legislative creation of a reasonable means for ascertaining just compensation. This view was adopted in some state statutes. Moreover, judicial review of compensation awards by commissioners had the potential to delay rail construction indefinitely. Nearly all states therefore provided that if carriers deposited the amount of any award, an appeal of an aggrieved owner did not prevent the companies from taking possession of the land.

A number of states took the position that the just compensation obligation meant that a railroad must either make or guarantee payment before taking property. Recognizing that the acquisition of property and payment of compensation could not always be concurrent, the Supreme Court of Texas ruled that companies must guarantee future payments "by something more certain than the continuing solvency of a railroad company."[42] The

Supreme Court endorsed this view in the late nineteenth century. Congress authorized a railroad to construct a line across Cherokee territory but did not require payment of compensation before the carrier entered the land. The Court declared that an owner "is entitled to reasonable, certain and adequate provision for obtaining compensation before his occupancy is disturbed."[43] Admitting that this posed a sometimes difficult question, the justices upheld the congressional scheme because the railroad was obligated to deposit twice the amount of the initial award pending final determination of the compensation on appeal. They brushed aside the possibility that the company might be financially unable to pay compensation in excess of the deposited amount as too remote to invalidate the just compensation mechanism. The upshot was that under the federal Constitution, there was no right to receive payment prior to surrendering possession of land provided that compensation was secured.

Nature of Interest Acquired

Another consideration that bears on the exercise of eminent domain is the nature of the property interest acquired by railroads. The basic question was whether the carrier acquired a fee simple title or just an easement for railroad purposes. This important distinction was determinative of the rights of the parties when, for example, a railroad discontinued use of the land or sought to remove timber or minerals from the premises.

There was authority that state legislatures had the power to authorize condemnation of a fee simple.[44] Early railroad charters in many states, including South Carolina and Florida, expressly provided that upon payment of the award, the land vested in the company in fee simple. Likewise, the Illinois general railroad act of 1849 declared that the company "shall become seized in fee of all the lands and real estate" specified in the eminent-domain order. In contrast, the New York railroad law of 1850 provided that railroads could take possession of land and "use the same for the purpose of said road." Such language indicated acquisition of an easement because use was limited to railroad purposes.[45]

But charters and railroad statutes in many jurisdictions employed imprecise wording to describe the property interest acquired by eminent domain. Thus, a Virginia law of 1837 declared that the company "shall be vested . . . in the same manner as if the proprietor has sold and conveyed it to them."[46] Such uncertain language created a fertile field for judicial interpretation of the interests obtained by carriers. Prominent experts took the position that, absent statutory provisions expressly authorizing the taking of a fee simple, railroads should receive just an easement in land condemned for their use.[47] "It is certain, in this country, upon general principles," Redfield declared, "that a railway company, by virtue of their compulsory powers, in taking lands, could acquire no absolute fee-simple, but only the right to use the land for their purposes."[48] Judicial decisions tended to adopt this line of analysis. The Supreme Court of Vermont in 1851 intimated that a legislative delegation of eminent domain was constitutionally restricted to meeting the needs of the railroad for a right-of-way. Hence, the judges ruled that the charter language "seized and possessed of the land" permitted simply acquisition of an easement because such an interest was sufficient for the railroad's purposes.[49] In *Blake v. Rich* (1856), moreover, the Supreme Court of New Hampshire drew an analogy between taking land for public highways and for railroads. It was settled in most jurisdictions that the public acquired an easement in land taken for highways. The court then readily concluded that the railroad obtained only an easement, and that the original landowner retained the rights to trees and minerals on the land.

This trend to construe strictly the authority of railroads to acquire land through eminent domain accelerated in the decades following the Civil War. In 1868 the South Carolina legislature limited a railroad's power of eminent domain to the acquisition of easements. Courts likewise interpreted eminent-domain statutes or read state constitutional provisions to mean that railroads could only acquire an easement by condemnation.[50] As resentment against perceived railroad domination mounted, lawmakers in some states, such as Indiana and North Carolina, also took steps to constrain the condemnation powers of railroads. In 1905 both jurisdictions enacted statutes providing that railroads could obtain an easement only in rights-of-way.[51] This was part of the broader move, discussed earlier, by which the legal system became more protective of the rights of landowners by tightening the use of eminent domain by railroads.

Whether railroads in the nineteenth century took fee simple title or easements in land is a matter of continuing importance and dispute. The railroad network reached a peak of mileage in 1917, and then began a steady decline. Although carriers occasionally utilized eminent-domain procedures in the early twentieth century, the heyday of such acquisitions was over and railroads started to abandon unprofitable lines. Yet the land on which abandoned tracks ran was often still valuable. Consequently, the question of what interest in the land was originally acquired by the railroad remains a lively topic of litigation.[52]

Takings of Railroad Property

In addition to formal exercise of eminent domain, railroads contributed significantly to the evolution of takings jurisprudence by defining which governmental actions, short of outright acquisition of title or possession, effectuate a taking for which compensation must be paid. A contested question was whether legislation compelling owners to bear the cost of compliance with regulations for public safety and welfare constituted a taking. States were prone to place heavy burden in this regard on railroads.

Courts looked skeptically at laws that compelled railroads to transfer the ownership or possession of rail property. At issue in the prominent case of *Missouri Pacific Railway Company v. Nebraska* (1896) was a Nebraska statute that authorized a state agency to order railroads to grant part of their land to private individuals for the purpose of establishing a grain elevator. The law was a response to agitation by farm organizations seeking to control grain-elevator charges by erecting competitive facilities. The Supreme Court, however, ruled that taking property from one person for the private use of another was prohibited by the due process clause of the Fourteenth Amendment, even though compensation was paid. In effect, the Court affirmed the principle that property could be taken only for public use. In 1910 the justices struck down a similar statute that required railroads, upon application, to build at their expense a sidetrack to reach the applicant's grain elevator. Declaring that "railroads after all are property protected by the Constitution," Justice Oliver Wendell Holmes, Jr., writing for the Court, questioned why carriers should be expected to pay for essentially private connections.[53] The Supreme Court determined that requiring a railroad to spend money for private facilities might represent as much a taking of property as an obligation to part with land.

Even more important, the use of eminent domain by Chicago to open a street across railroad land led to the extension of the just compensation principle to the states. In the landmark case of *Chicago, Burlington and Quincy Railroad Company v. Chicago* (1897), the Supreme Court ruled that compensation for private property taken for public use was an essential element of due process as guaranteed by the Fourteenth Amendment. Accordingly, the just compensation norm became the first provision of the federal Bill of Rights to be applied against the states.

Nonetheless, courts generally gave lawmakers broad latitude to compel carriers to construct new facilities required for public safety and convenience. The special issues arising from grade-crossing elimination were considered in Chapter Five. In addition, courts sustained regulations that mandated the removal of existing bridges, the alteration of tunnels, and the building of overpasses. These expensive changes were imposed on railroads even though the rail facilities had long been in place, and the change was intended to accommodate subsequent improvements in transportation or other public works. In this line of cases, courts showed no particular favoritism to railroads and allowed states, under the police power, to place the burden of paying for desired improvements on the rail industry.[54]

In a related development, a state railroad land grant gave rise to the first appearance of the public trust doctrine in American law. In 1869 Illinois gave a large area of submerged land along the Chicago waterfront to the Illinois Central Railroad. The legislators subsequently repealed this law and sought to reclaim the land. A divided Supreme Court held in 1892 that a state could not irrevocably convey land under navigable waters. The Court reasoned that such lands were held by the state in trust for the public and could be alienated only to the limited extent that their disposition was consistent with the public interest in navigation and commerce. It followed that the state could recover the possession of waterfront land from the railroad.[55] Although the notion of public trust had little application for decades, some courts and commentators in the late twentieth century argued that the malleable public trust doctrine might be extended from its traditional submerged land application and used to secure public recreational access easements to beaches and streams.

Law of Nuisance

The appearance of the railroad also contributed to the evolution of nuisance law. The premise of common-law nuisance was that one could not utilize one's own property, regardless of the degree of care, in ways that interfered with a neighbor's land. Liability was predicated on the existence of an injurious use, not upon negligence. William Blackstone gave a classic formulation of this doctrine: "If one does any act, in itself lawful, which yet being done in that place necessarily tends to the damage of another's property, it is a nuisance; for it is incumbent on him to find some other place to do that act, where it will be less offensive."[56] This view expressed a static understanding of property that afforded owners the power to prevent the actions of others that invaded their quiet enjoyment. There is some room to doubt that nuisance doctrine was rigidly applied in England, given the rapid industrialization that occurred there in the late eighteenth and early nineteenth centuries. Yet the potential of nuisance law to retard economic development, through injunctions and damage awards, was clear.

As the most visible aspect of the emerging industrial order, railroads were a prime target for nuisance actions. Further, railroad operations, which extended for miles through city and country, touched a wide range of possible plaintiffs. But courts were reluctant to issue injunctions that would halt transportation projects. Accordingly, antebellum courts relied on both traditional equitable maxims and adjustments in the substantive nuisance law in order to accommodate technological innovation. In time they adopted a balancing test that weighed the economic and social value of the alleged nuisance against the rights of the private property owners. This interjected utilitarian considerations into the determination of a nuisance and usually produced a decision favorable to entrepreneurs.[57]

The construction of railroad tracks over city streets gave rise to numerous complaints. Although the city council typically granted permission for such use, the owners of land fronting on the designated streets often sought to enjoin railroad operations. Pointing to the danger of crossing tracks, the risk of accidents, the obstruction of other vehicles on the street, and the expected decline in business activity, the plaintiffs argued that the value of their property was diminished. Courts universally rejected such contentions, holding that railroads were not of such a noxious quality as to constitute a per se nuisance.

The leading case was *Lexington and Ohio Railroad v. Applegate* (1839). At the behest of local property owners, the chancellor enjoined the defendant railroad from operating its cars along the streets of Louisville. The Kentucky Court of Appeals dissolved the injunction, concluding that use of the streets as authorized by city council did not constitute a per se nuisance. The court noted that the newly completed railroad transported about 550 passengers daily at favorable rates. Stressing that the city officials were not complaining and retained the power to revoke the use of public streets, the court declared that private injury "must be expected from other agents of transportation in a populous and prospering country." In often-quoted language, the court insisted that nuisance law must take account of economic growth:

> The onward spirit of the age must, to a reasonable extent, have its way. The law is made for the times, and will be made or modified by them. The expanded and still expanding genius of the common law should adapt it here, as elsewhere, to the improved and improving condition of our country and our countrymen. And therefore, rail roads and locomotive steam cars—the offspring, as they will also be the parents, of progressive

improvement—should not, in themselves, be considered as nuisances, although, in ages that are gone, they might have been so held, because they would have been comparatively useless, and therefore more mischievous.[58]

Other jurisdictions followed suit. In *Drake v. Hudson River Railroad Co.* (1849), Judge Samuel Jones noted the "great and acknowledged advantages" of rail travel and refused to enjoin the construction of tracks on the streets of New York City. Rejecting a claim of nuisance, he declared that "beneficial inventions of general interest, are not to be rejected, suppressed or arrested, simply because they may in their operations and practical effect occasion to property in their vicinity . . . some contingent or consequential damage."[59] However, Judge Jones held open the possibility that the actual operations of the railroad might become a nuisance at some future point. Concurring, Judge Henry P. Edwards stressed that the city council had the power to permit use of the streets for railroad purposes. He maintained that the use of streets for a railroad simply represented the accommodation of a new mode of conveyance.

Similarly, in *Hertz v. Long Island Railroad Company* (1852), the court vacated an injunction against running a steam-powered train through a village. The plaintiff, an adjacent landowner, alleged that smoke from the engine filled his house, and he expressed fear of accidents. The court was not impressed. Conceding that the smoke was annoying, the court pointed out that it was not continuous or worse than the disagreeable features of other lawful businesses. The court made explicit the weight given to the utility of railroads, observing that they "cannot be prevented without an entire suspension of one of the greatest improvements of modern times."[60] Private rights, it appeared, must yield to the public interest in improved transportation.

The same reluctance to enjoin railroad operations can be found elsewhere during the antebellum period. In *Grey v. Ohio and Pennsylvania Railroad Company* (1856), a railroad was authorized by the council of the City of Allegheny to construct its track through a reserved common pasture. Alleging that the erection of railroad facilities on the commons destroyed use of the area for pasturage and diminished the value of lots fronting on the commons, an adjacent landowner sought an injunction on grounds that the railroad constituted a nuisance. The Supreme Court of Pennsylvania noted that the plaintiff was not actively using the commons for pasturing and that "the property taken in this case has scarcely any appreciable value." An equally divided bench refused the requested injunction, holding that the "rule in equity requires the court to balance the inconveniences likely to be incurred by the respective parties."[61]

By the eve of the Civil War, it was settled that, absent special circumstances, courts would not enjoin the building of railroads as a nuisance. In *Geiger v. Filor* (1859), the Supreme Court of Florida dissolved an injunction blocking railroad track in Key West and observed:

> Railroads in cities or towns cannot with propriety be termed nuisances. They are decided not to be such in numerous cases, both by English and American Courts. They are in use in the principal cities of Europe and this country, and, when regulated by proper restrictions, are valuable aids to commerce. Nor could it well be otherwise. A road of this kind presents but a smoother surface for a wagon or carriage than that which prevails in the adjacent part of a street, thus giving facility instead of raising obstruction to the movement of produce or the transfer of passengers.[62]

Likewise, in *New Albany and Salem Railroad Company v. O'Daily* (1859), the Supreme Court of Indiana flatly stated: "A railroad in a city is not, necessarily, a nuisance, and the injunction cannot be sustained on that ground."[63]

The transformation of nuisance doctrine during the nineteenth century remains a subject of contention among legal historians.[64] My goal is to demonstrate that in nuisance actions courts consistently declined to issue injunctions halting railroad operations. In reaching this result, courts employed a variety of legal devices. Some emphasized the discretionary nature of equitable relief. In *Drake,* for instance, the court declared that "a stronger case must be presented, and the impending danger more imminent and more impressive than this complaint . . . to justify us in the application of these severe and coercive measures."[65] Other courts generally revamped the substance of nuisance law to incorporate balancing tests that gave primary weight to public goods provided by railroads and other entrepreneurs. Furthermore, railroads were particularly successful in relying on statutory justification. Courts often pointed to legislative authorization of railroad construction as a defense to actions that might otherwise be treated as a common-law nuisance.[66] A revealing decision is *Williams v. New York Central Railroad* (1854), in which a New York court observed: "That which is authorized by an act of the legislature cannot be a nuisance."[67] The Blackstonian notion that landowners should be protected against activities that caused injury was supplanted by the view that lawmakers could prefer entrepreneurial activity. Railroads were a major factor in bringing about this new understanding of nuisance law.

Although courts devised ways to avoid granting equitable relief against nuisances arising from economic development, they continued to award damages in at least some situations. In so doing, courts in damage suits cited the common-law definition of nuisance and began to blur the distinction between nuisance and a compensable taking of property.[68] Thus, in *Fletcher v. Auburn and Syracuse Railroad* (1841), the court ruled that legislative authorization to use a highway protected the railroad against claims of a public nuisance, but not from claims of private damages for consequential injuries to adjacent landowners. The court viewed such injury as a claim for taking property without compensation.[69] Similarly, in *Brown v. Cayuga and Susquehanna Railroad* (1855), the New York Court of Appeals affirmed a jury verdict against the railroad for obstructing a stream and causing flooding of plaintiff's land. The court held that legislative permission to cross watercourses did not justify injury to adjoining owners. Concurring, Judge Hiram Denio treated the suit as an action in nuisance and observed: "Every one is bound so to use his own property that it shall not be the means of injury to his neighbors."[70]

Although courts moved away from strict liability for nuisance and were wary of enjoining railroad projects, they partially vindicated the rights of aggrieved property owners by awarding damages. Two leading decisions by the Supreme Court illustrate this inclination. In *Baltimore & Potomac Railroad Company v. Fifth Baptist Church* (1883), the church complained that noise, odors, and smoke emanating from an adjacent engine repair shop interfered with religious services and depreciated the value of its building. Upholding a monetary judgment against the railroad, the Supreme Court was unimpressed with the carrier's defense of congressional authorization to operate a line. The Court observed that "such authority would not justify an invasion of others' property, to an extent which would amount to an entire deprivation of its use and enjoyment without compensation to the owner."[71]

This thought was developed further in *Richards v. Washington Terminal Company* (1914), a decision that fused takings jurisprudence with nuisance law. The Supreme Court asserted:

> We deem the true rule, under the Fifth Amendment, as under state constitutions containing a similar prohibition, to be that while the legislature may legalize what otherwise would be a public nuisance, it may not confer immunity from action for a private nuisance of such a character as to amount in effect to a taking of private property for public use.[72]

It pointed out that the noise and vibration incident to running trains were shared generally by property owners and did not amount to a taking of property. On the other hand, the smoke and gas forced out of a rail tunnel by a fanning system imposed a particular burden on plaintiff's nearby property.

The owner was therefore entitled to compensation for the private nuisance that constituted a taking of property.

Careful not to enjoin improved transportation facilities, nineteenth-century judges implicitly restricted application of common-law nuisance to damages actions. While hardly insignificant, damage awards did not block railroad construction. Moreover, railroads could spread the expense among shippers and investors. In effect, courts permitted entrepreneurs to pay compensation rather than abate a nuisance. Because of the high value assigned by American society to completion of a railroad system, the railroads were at once a driving force for changing nuisance law and a major beneficiary of the new and more flexible approach.

Taxation of Railroads

The history of railroad taxation is complicated and contested. During the antebellum era railroads enjoyed a favorable tax status designed to encourage railroading. As discussed earlier, many states granted tax exemptions to railroad companies. In addition, it was widely felt that railroads escaped taxation by underreporting the value of their property. Many states during the antebellum era even empowered railroad companies to submit evaluations of their property, and treated such reports as prima facie evidence of taxable value. As state revenue needs mounted, in part as a result of the Civil War, the advantageous tax treatment of carriers was seen as undue favoritism to corporate enterprise and the cause of increased property taxes on small owners. In this altered political climate, legislators sought to raise railroad taxes. Any meaningful steps in this direction necessitated both a challenge to tax exemptions and a mechanism to establish the actual value of railroad property.

But railroads had legitimate concerns about state tax policies. Their lines ran through numerous localities, each of which was inclined to collect a disproportionate share of revenue from railroad property. Moreover, rail assets were immobile and were thus a vulnerable target for taxation. Unlike other enterprises, railroads could not restrain state or local taxation by threatening to leave the jurisdiction. As Lawrence M. Friedman aptly stated, "Railroad tracks once laid could not run away, and the temptation was to get all one could from a captive giant."[73] Not only did state and local taxation of interstate railroads have implications for national commerce, but railroads could claim constitutional sanction for tax immunity grants under the contract clause. Legislators and judges wrestled with the problem of railroad taxation throughout the nineteenth and twentieth centuries.

Reflecting popular resentment at the perceived tax inequity, state legislatures after the Civil War sought to revoke antebellum and Reconstruction
tax immunity grants to railroad companies. Where an exemption was clearly
expressed in a corporate charter, however, the Supreme Court and state
courts ruled that the exemption was protected against subsequent repeal by
the contract clause.[74] But courts insisted that claims of tax immunity must
be clearly demonstrated, and ambiguity was resolved in favor of the state's
sovereign authority to levy taxes. Decisions tended to turn upon the wording of different grants.

Courts also distinguished between tax exemptions contained in corporate charters and general schemes of taxation intended to encourage railroad
building. Courts were reluctant to find a contract where the legislature was
not making a specific promise of tax immunity but rather enacting a policy
that was subject to change.[75] At least one state, on the other hand, took the
position that construction of rail lines, in reliance on a general tax exemption measure, constituted consideration for a binding contract. Emphasizing
the need for improved transportation, the Supreme Court of New Mexico in
1884 saw utilitarian reasons for this outcome: "To expend millions in constructing long lines of railway to and through this remote region was a hazardous undertaking—an experiment—a venture—which any but the boldest
minds would readily shrink from."[76]

Another lively issue was the transfer of tax immunities to successor companies. As the pace of railroad mergers quickened in the late nineteenth century, courts were repeatedly called upon to decide whether the consolidated
enterprise could enjoy the exemption granted in the original charters. Resolution of this question was especially difficult when some of the carriers entering into the consolidation had tax immunity while others did not. In general,
the courts were skeptical about the transfer of special tax status and ruled
that the exemption was lost if the merger produced a distinct new corporation.[77] Thus consolidation helped to eliminate a number of tax exemptions.

The prolonged litigation over the 1833 tax exemption granted to the
Georgia Railroad Company illustrates both the potential longevity of such
immunities and the problem of ascertaining their scope. In 1874 the Georgia legislature, reflecting a hardened attitude toward railroad taxation, passed
a law taxing rail property on the same footing as other property. Yet repeated
attempts to collect taxes on the property of the railroad were rebuffed well
into the twentieth century. In 1947, however, the Supreme Court gave a
restrictive reading to the exemption, holding that the levy of a corporate
income tax was not covered by the immunity. This decision, of course, diminished the value of the exemption to the carrier.[78]

Railroad tax exemptions became a heated political and legal issue in New Jersey by the 1880s. Despite judicial rulings upholding the validity of tax exempt status for certain carriers, legislators were determined to force them to relinquish their immunities. They imposed conditions that railroads seeking an extension of time to complete construction plans or to merge must waive any tax exemption arising from contracts with the state. They also threatened to exercise the option in the original charters to purchase the lines at cost. Not surprisingly, in the mid-1890s the remaining exempt railroads abandoned their claims.[79] Political pressure triumphed over the supposed sanctity of contracts.

With charter grants of tax immunity under attack, states experimented with a wide range of levies on railroads. During the antebellum era, New Jersey, Maryland, and Delaware charged transit taxes on passengers and/or goods transported in the state. To help cover expenses associated with the Civil War, New Jersey in 1862 imposed a new transit tax on foreign corporations, but provided that no tax was required for goods and passengers carried within the state. The levy was obviously designed to fall upon interstate transportation, and the New Jersey Court of Appeals and Errors invalidated the tax as a discriminatory burden on interstate commerce.[80] The Delaware transit tax met a similar fate in 1870.[81] Likewise, the Supreme Court in 1872 found that a Pennsylvania tax on freight carried into or from the state was an unconstitutional interference with interstate commerce. It likened the tax to custom houses placed on the state line to collect duties. "Merchandise is the subject of commerce," the Court observed. "Transportation is essential to commerce; and every burden laid upon it is *pro tanto* a restriction."[82]

With the demise of the Civil War–era transit taxes, states sought to collect revenue from railroads by devising a host of different taxes. They enacted levies upon the real and personal property, the franchise, the capital stock, and the gross receipts of companies. State legislatures also created special boards of assessment to ascertain the true value of railroad property. Throughout the late nineteenth and early twentieth centuries, state and federal courts heard a steady stream of cases challenging the validity of railroad taxes. Courts endeavored to balance respect for state taxing authority with the need to protect interstate commerce from discriminatory tax burdens. Courts generally allowed lawmakers broad latitude to tax carriers, but they fashioned constitutional limits to curtail excessive levies. This complex litigation can only be summarized here.

Carriers repeatedly attacked the practice of valuing railroad property on a different basis than other species of property. In some states this mode of assessment ran afoul of constitutional requirements that taxation should be equal and uniform.[83] Other schemes in which railroad property was singled out for special treatment were assailed as violations of equal protection as guaranteed by the Fourteenth Amendment. It was in one such case, *Santa Clara County v. Southern Pacific Railroad Company* (1886), that the Supreme Court declared that the equal protection clause applied to corporations as well as natural persons. However, the Court separately ruled in a later case that treating rail property differently was not a denial of equal protection. "The right to classify railroad property, as a separate class, for purposes of taxation," the Court explained, "grows out of the inherent nature of the property."[84]

A number of states in the nineteenth century levied taxes based on the gross receipts of rail companies. The states would typically apportion the tax in relation to the amount of the carrier's track in the taxing state. Such gross receipts taxes were repeatedly sustained.[85] During periods of depression, of course, the gross receipts, and consequently the tax liability, of carriers were reduced. This loss of revenue caused Michigan to abandon gross receipts taxation in 1901 in favor of a state property tax on railroads.[86] Other states also shifted to an ad valorem property tax on railroads early in the twentieth century. Assessment of rail property, however, remained tricky because market price was not a practical test, and because the value of a carrier was in its operation as a system.

Taxation of railroads remained a sensitive and complicated issue in the twentieth century. In the early decades of the century the Supreme Court continued to police state taxation of carriers and to look skeptically at discriminatory burdens. For instance, in *Southern Railway Company v. Greene* (1910), the Court struck down an Alabama franchise tax that imposed a tax on foreign corporations doing business in the state, but not on domestic corporations, as a deprivation of equal protection. In reaching this conclusion, the Court emphasized that railroads have a large amount of fixed property that cannot be removed and taken elsewhere. The justices also held in *Great Northern Railway Company v. Weeks* (1936) that a North Dakota tax assessment was arbitrary and resulted in an excessive tax burden. They pointed out that the state failed to give adequate weight to the sharp loss of rail traffic and income suffered by the company as a result of the Great Depression. But with the political and constitutional triumph of the New Deal, courts became more supportive of state taxing power and less concerned with railroad claims.

Notwithstanding occasional judicial oversight, the state and local tax burden on carriers steadily mounted. As early as 1896 the *Railroad Gazette* decried heavy and discriminatory taxation of railroads.[87] By the mid–twentieth century

New York and New Jersey were notorious for high rail taxes.[88] Moreover, for many small communities, the railroad was the principal source of property taxes. Congress joined in the race for rail revenue by placing a federal excise tax on passenger tickets and freight shipments during World War II. These levies were not repealed until more than a decade after the war.

Following World War II the rail industry entered a period of sharp decline. Anxious to rehabilitate the nation's railroad system, Congress identified state overtaxation as a problem. Accordingly, in the Railroad Revitalization and Regulatory Reform Act of 1976 Congress prohibited discriminatory state taxation and authorized carriers to obtain injunctive relief from such levies. The federal courts have again become actively involved in reviewing assessments of rail property and invalidating discriminatory treatment.[89]

9

Liability for Personal Injury

M odern tort law developed rapidly in the nineteenth century, in large measure as the result of railroading. The leading tort cases invariably involved railroad accidents. Collapsed bridges, derailments, collisions, and coupling train cars produced a steadily mounting toll of deaths and personal injuries. By 1890 approximately six thousand people died annually in rail accidents, and another forty thousand were injured.[1] Safety issues, and the potential of new technology to reduce injuries, were matters of popular concern. Judges and legislators sought to fashion liability rules to protect public safety without crippling economic development. To these ends, liability was usually predicated on a showing of fault or negligence.

From the outset, courts recognized the hazards of railroad travel. In 1853 the Supreme Court of Tennessee observed: "The appalling disasters that are so frequently occurring excite a general desire and expectation that the courts will hold [railroads] to that care and diligence which the law prescribes." The New York Court of Appeals similarly declared in 1862 that "railroad accidents were of frequent occurrence; that railroad travel was subject constantly to perils resulting from the carelessness and negligence" of company employees.[2] Not surprisingly, rail accidents generated a flood of lawsuits and claimed the attention of legislators and regulatory commissions.

Courts were certainly not blind to the need to devise tort doctrines that took account of the unique features of railroading. In 1852 the Supreme Court, for instance, ruled that doctrine of *respondeat superior,* holding a company responsible for the negligent actions of its employees, was applicable to railroads. "When carriers undertake to convey persons by the powerful but dangerous agency of steam," the Court lectured, "public policy and safety require that they be held to the greatest possible care and diligence."[3] Later in the nineteenth century the Supreme Court of North Carolina stressed remote corporate governance of railroads as a reason to require a high standard of care:

Ordinarily owned by great syndicates out of the state in which they operate, and their management at all events removed from subjection to that sound public opinion which is so great a check upon the conduct of individuals and of government itself, the sole protection left to the traveller and the employee alike is the application of that law which is administered impartially, and which can lay its hand fearlessly upon the most powerful combination and protect with its care the humblest individual in the land.[4]

Nor were legislators oblivious to safety issues. By the late nineteenth century, legislation increasingly modified common-law norms and extended greater protection to injured parties.

Historical investigation of railroad liability for accidents has been caught up in the larger scholarly debate over whether tort law in the nineteenth century was molded to foster entrepreneurial activity. One influential thesis holds that judges limited liability for personal injury in order to preserve the capital needed by fledgling enterprise. Generous liability rules, it was feared, would raise operating costs. This approach thus amounted to a subsidization of business at the expense of injured parties. Railroads, according to this view, were a prime beneficiary of legal doctrines that shielded enterprise from tort liability.[5] The subsidy thesis has been challenged by a number of scholars who contend that courts often placed a higher value on safety concerns than on economic development. They maintain that tort law was used to reduce injuries and safeguard community standards.[6] Yet another interpretation insists that tort law was guided less by economic considerations than by a widely shared belief that individuals were responsible for the consequences of their behavior and that fault was the only legitimate basis for imposing liability.[7]

This is not the appropriate place to address these contending views. Rather, I suggest that the knotty history of railroad tort liability does not fully support any unifying theory.[8] At no time were railroads able to escape any responsibility for accidents. Although some judges occasionally employed pro-enterprise rhetoric, in other cases courts readily found carriers liable and chastised rail behavior. As in other areas of railroad law, one must be wary about broad conclusions.

Both judges and lawmakers attempted to strike a balance between economic development and railroad responsibility for personal injuries. While courts readily perceived the importance of railroading, they were also mindful of the dangers posed to life and limb. The Tennessee Supreme Court captured this attitude by insisting that "the most perfect safety should be secured" for passengers, while noting that "the rules of accountability should be reasonable, that men may not be deterred from devoting their time, capital, and energies to these very useful, and now almost indispensable, enterprises."[9] It is difficult to demonstrate systematic judicial bias in favor of carriers in personal injury cases. Although an imperfect guide, it is worth stressing that railroads lost as many tort cases as they won in appellate courts.[10] The fact that some results, particularly those limiting recovery by injured rail employees, seem harsh to modern eyes does not establish that carriers were immune from responsibility for accidents or enjoyed undue judicial solicitude.

An assessment of railroad liability for personal injury is further complicated by the interplay between state and national authority. Following the Civil War, railroads frequently invoked federal court diversity jurisdiction to remove cases from state tribunals. Moreover, starting with the Safety Appliance Act of 1893, Congress began to enact rail workplace safety regulations and to create federal remedies for injured employees. By the late twentieth century, courts were wrestling with the preemptive impact of federal legislation on state tort law. As in so many other areas, a national law governing railroad safety and related liability issues slowly emerged.

In order to analyze railroad personal injury cases, it is useful to examine distinct sets of claimants. Carriers were held to different standards of care with respect to employees, passengers, and members of the general public.

Injuries to Employees

Work on railroads in the nineteenth century was extremely perilous. Rail workers ran a high risk of death or loss of limbs.[11] Yet the legal system made it difficult for injured employees or their dependents to recover against railroads. An injured worker had to prove negligence on the part of the company, a task made onerous by the railroad's control of the evidence behind most accidents.

One important issue was the role of custom in determining tort liability. The common law often looked to conformity with industry practice as a factor in ascertaining whether particular actions were negligent. Some courts went so far as to assert that such compliance established that the defendant was not negligent as a matter of law. The Supreme Court of Pennsylvania, for instance, declared in 1890 that "no jury can be permitted to say that the usual and ordinary way, commonly adopted by those in the same business, is a negligent way for which liability shall be imposed."[12] In the leading case of *Texas and Pacific Railway Company v. Behymer* (1903), however, the Supreme Court rejected this view and upheld a finding of negligence against a railroad when a brakeman was thrown from the top of an ice-covered freight car. "What usually is done may be evidence of what ought to be done," the Court observed, "but what ought to be done is fixed by a standard of reasonable prudence, whether it usually is complied with or not."[13] Put another way, an injured party could show negligence despite the carrier's adherence to an industry custom.

Even when company negligence could be shown, the injured claimant still faced a potent battery of common-law defenses that often operated to prevent any recovery. The most important of these was the fellow servant rule, which held that an employer was not responsible for injuries to an employee occasioned by the negligence of a fellow employee engaged in common employment. The first American case to apply the fellow servant rule was *Murray v. South Carolina Railroad Company* (1841), in which the South Carolina court denied any recovery to a fireman who was badly injured by the negligence of the engineer. Dissenting, Judge John Belton O'Neall argued that the railroad should be liable for the negligence of its employees. With respect to the underlying policy considerations, he added that "the more liability imposed on the railroad company, the more care and prudence would be thereby elicited. This result is what the community desires."[14]

Notwithstanding O'Neall's reservations, the fellow servant rule rapidly gained widespread acceptance. The most famous articulation of this rule was *Farwell v. Boston and Worcester Railroad Company* (1842). Writing for the Supreme Judicial Court of Massachusetts, Chief Justice Lemuel Shaw rejected the doctrine of *respondeat superior* in the employment context and ruled that a worker who accepted a dangerous employment had assumed the risks incident to such work, including the carelessness of co-employees. Shaw speculated that wages were adjusted to reflect the increased peril of the job. Since railroad accidents were often caused by the carelessness of other employees, and rarely by the personal negligence of the railroad managers, many injured workers had no recourse against their employer. A suit against a negligent fellow servant, of course, was unlikely to produce any recovery. Although some judges occasionally expressed misgivings, the fellow servant rule was adopted by the majority of jurisdictions.[15]

Application of the fellow servant rule, however, was not mechanical, and judges limited operation of the doctrine by looking closely at what constituted common service. This inquiry was especially vexing with respect to large-scale rail enterprise in which the workforce was divided into different departments that had little contact with one another. This departmentalization reduced the chance to check for careless behavior by other workers. Under these circumstances, some courts concluded that workers in different units were not fellow servants and the employer was liable for injuries caused by negligence.[16] Further, courts formulated the vice-principal exception, which provided that a supervisor represented the company as a vice-principal and was not a fellow servant with subordinate employees. There was a good deal of litigation over what degree of management function made a supervisor a vice-principal rather than a fellow servant, and the results were not uniform.[17] Still, both the different department and vice-principal exceptions undercut the rigor of the fellow servant rule.[18]

Moreover, railroads were under a duty to provide a safe workplace and tools. "The general rule," Chief Justice Melville W. Fuller observed in 1896, "undoubtedly is that a railroad company is bound to provide suitable and safe materials and structures in the construction of its roads and appurtenances."[19] Courts regularly found railroads liable for injuries arising from faulty roadbeds or defective machinery. The fellow servant rule did not excuse lack of care by the company in supplying proper equipment.[20] An allied question was the extent of railroad liability for failure to adopt new safety devices. Courts generally did not require carriers to promptly apply every improvement, but found that neglect of safe appliances once they had come into general use constituted negligence per se.[21]

Companies were also responsible for hiring skillful employees. Where accidents resulted from the employment of incompetent or intoxicated workers, courts held railroads responsible notwithstanding the fellow servant rule.[22]

There were enough exceptions to at least partially temper the fellow servant rule and allow injured workers to recover in some situations. In practice, the rule was not as harsh and one-sided as it is usually pictured. Nonetheless, the experience with frequent railroad accidents did much to spark the reconsideration and eventual elimination of the fellow servant doctrine. The rule was initially fashioned with a small preindustrial workshop in mind. With dangerous equipment and a complex and compartmentalized workforce, railroading made it clear that the fellow servant rule rested on unrealistic assumptions and was not a suitable vehicle to address workplace injuries in a modern industrial society.[23]

In the mid–nineteenth century, states began to enact laws abolishing or curtailing the fellow servant rule for railroad accidents. Georgia took the lead in 1856. Later in the century, a number of states, including Kansas, Iowa, and Indiana, also eliminated the fellow servant rule for rail employees. In 1895 South Carolina placed a provision severely limiting the rule in its constitution. Both federal and state courts upheld the constitutionality of laws abolishing the fellow servant rule against a variety of challenges. Rejecting an equal protection argument that the statutes imposed different liability on railroads than on other enterprises, the Supreme Court pointed out that "the hazardous character of the business of operating a railway would seem to call for special legislation with respect to railroad corporations, having for its object the protection of the employees as well as the safety of the public."[24] As with statutes enlarging railroad responsibility for fire, courts showed no inclination to forestall legislation that increased tort liability for personal injury.

Still, by 1900 most jurisdictions and the federal courts in diversity cases continued to adhere to the fellow servant doctrine. In a series of cases the Supreme Court narrowly construed the vice-principal and department exceptions, and vigorously wielded the fellow servant rule to deny recovery to injured or killed rail employees.[25] These results contributed to the popular perception of a federal judicial forum that favored corporate interests over injured workers. But the Supreme Court's decisions rested on the implicit premise that tort rules had an impact on interstate commerce and that carriers should be governed by uniform rules. This need for uniformity, coupled with mounting dissatisfaction over the fellow servant rule, set the stage for the Federal Employer's Liability Act (FELA) in 1908, a measure discussed on pages 218–219.

Although the fellow servant rule has received the bulk of scholarly attention, railroads had other defenses in employee injury cases. Workers were deemed to assume the ordinary risks incidental to their employment or arising out of the condition of the workplace.[26] In *Vaughn v. California Central Railway Company* (1890), for instance, the Supreme Court of California ruled that an employee engaged for the purpose of repairing track assumed the risk inherent in track washouts caused by a storm. Further, the doctrine of contributory negligence might bar employee suits. If a worker's conduct contributed to his injury, there could be no recovery. Thus, when employees violated work rules or engaged in unsafe behavior, courts denied their claims. The effect was that injured workers had to prove both negligence by the carrier and their freedom from fault.[27]

Despite this array of defenses, railroads were vulnerable in personal injury litigation. They faced a wave of expensive lawsuits and juries sympathetic to injured claimants.[28] Not surprisingly, railroads preferred to settle personal injury claims. Moreover, some railroads created relief associations funded largely by employee contributions. Members received medical attention and financial assistance in case of accidents. A few railroads required relief association membership as a condition of employment, but participation in most schemes was voluntary. Such employee-financed relief plans did provide a substantial amount of help to injured and disabled workers, but they minimized the cost of accidents to the railroad companies.[29]

Relief associations also operated to prevent personal injury lawsuits by employees. A member who accepted benefits from the relief association was required to release any legal claim against the railroad. Hence, an injured worker had to decide whether to sue the company for damages or to accept benefits from the relief fund. Given the uncertainty of any recovery in court, employees must have been tempted to take the payments and thus forfeit the right to bring suit. Courts repeatedly upheld this waiver provision in relief association contracts as beneficial and not contrary to public policy. Some states, however, enacted laws declaring that acceptance of benefits from relief departments should not bar lawsuits for injury or death caused by railroad negligence. Such statutes were invalidated as an interference with the liberty of contract between an employee and the company.[30] Resolution of the release of the right to sue caused by the acceptance of benefits was not achieved until the practice was curtailed by the FELA.

The development of new technologies also impacted the law governing rail accidents. Concerned about defective railroad equipment, state legislatures and commissions sought to compel carriers to adopt various safety devices. Michigan and Wisconsin passed statutes in the 1880s requiring that switches be adjusted or blocked by protective devices to prevent the feet of employees from being caught.[31]

Invention of air brakes and automatic couplers after the Civil War promised enhanced safety for employees and passengers alike. Air brakes eliminated the necessity for a brakeman to climb to the top of moving train cars to manually operate the brakes. Automatic couplers replaced the hand-operated link-and-pin method of connecting cars, and ended the need for workers to go between cars for this purpose. The coupling and uncoupling of cars was one of the most common sources of accidents, resulting in loss of limbs. Although railroad companies gradually adopted these safety appliances for passenger trains, they resisted air brakes and automatic couplers on freight cars. No doubt motivated in part by the expense of converting to the new technology, companies were also bothered by fear of inconsistent couplers that would complicate the interchange of freight cars between lines. But the persistent opposition of railroads to safety device legislation fueled the popular perception that they were indifferent to safety concerns. State safety laws proved ineffective in the face of resistance by interstate carriers.[32]

In 1893 Congress enacted the Safety Appliance Act, which required the use of air brakes and automatic couplers by 1898 on carriers engaged in interstate commerce. Congress did not specify any particular type of coupler, leaving selection of a uniform device to the railroads. The Interstate Commerce Commission was authorized to extend the compliance deadline. In addition, the measure abolished the assumption of the risk defense for injuries arising from a violation of the act. Pointing to financial distress as a result of the depression in the early 1890s, the railroads won two extensions from the ICC, delaying the date for compliance until August 1900. Even then the companies continued to drag their feet.[33]

The railroads, however, received no comfort from the Supreme Court. Instead, the Court broadly construed and vigorously enforced the Safety Appliance Act to carry out the congressional design "to promote the public welfare by securing the safety of employés and travelers."[34] It repeatedly held the carriers liable for injuries to workers that occurred when trains were not equipped with safety devices. In 1907 the justices held that the provision eliminating the assumption of the risk defense encompassed contributory negligence as well, strengthening the protection afforded rail employees.[35] A year later the Supreme Court underscored its determination to enforce the act strictly. Declaring that use of railroad cars without the mandated brakes and couplers gave rise to tort liability, the Court noted:

> It is quite conceivable that Congress, contemplating the inevitable hardship of such injuries, and hoping to diminish the economic loss to the community resulting from them, should deem it wise to impose their burdens upon those who could measurably control their causes, instead of upon those who are in the main helpless in that regard.[36]

Despite judicial prodding, installation of safety devices proceeded at a slow pace. Moreover, the new equipment often did not work well and needed constant maintenance. Nor was there an immediate reduction in accident rates. Indeed, the use of air brakes encouraged companies to increase the length and speed of trains, increasing accident risks. But the history of the Safety Appliance Act was a significant episode in the evolution of railroad law. It opened the door for a series of acts in the early twentieth century that set workplace safety standards and increased employer liability. The Ashpan Law of 1908, for instance, directed that new engines must be so equipped that they could be cleaned from the outside rather than by emptying the ash pan underneath. Further, the judicial response to the Safety Appliance Act dispels the notion that courts invariably interpreted statutes in ways to aid railroads at the expense of weaker parties.

Moving beyond safety appliances, Congress in 1908 overhauled the law of liability for rail accidents with passage of the FELA.[37] Covering railroad employees engaged in interstate commerce, the act abolished the fellow servant and contributory negligence defenses, limited the applicability of assumption of the risk, and invalidated any contractual release of liability when employees accepted benefits from relief associations. In effect, the FELA created a federal statutory negligence action. Congress hoped not only to better protect railroad workers and their dependents but also to encourage companies to become more safety-conscious by raising the cost of accidents. Although hailed as a great improvement, the FELA was not a panacea to the problem of liability for railroad injuries and produced a huge volume of litigation.

The FELA posed a number of vexing interpretative questions. First, it was necessary to decide whether a particular activity by an employee took place within the scope of interstate commerce.[38] This was a fertile source of dispute until the notion of interstate commerce was broadened in the late 1930s. Second, Congress did not establish a no-fault scheme or make carriers the insurers of worker safety. Railroad liability was still predicated on a showing of negligence. This entailed a case-by-case resolution of whether the railroad had failed to act with reasonable care. There were cases in which railroad negligence could not be shown and injured employees received no recovery. Third, courts found that the assumption of the risk defense remained effective under the FELA, except for violation of safety statutes.[39] This much-criticized exception weakened the protection for rail workers. Not until 1939 did Congress eliminate the assumption of the risk defense.

A product of the physical dangers of railroading in the early twentieth century, the FELA has proved an enduring remedy despite periodic calls to replace the act with a workers' compensation plan.[40] Railroad workers continue to be treated differently than employees of other industries for purposes of personal injury liability. Since the FELA superseded state law, rail workers could not take advantage of legal developments at the state level establishing new compensation arrangements. Since World War II, however, the Supreme Court has endeavored to apply the FELA broadly, and has determined that the act covers claims for negligent infliction of emotional distress.[41]

Injuries to Passengers

Train accidents killed or injured many more workers than passengers, but public attention largely focused on disasters involving travelers. The legal system, moreover, was more protective of passengers than of employees. Although carriers were not insurers of passenger safety, they were held to a high standard of care.[42] "As passenger carriers," the Supreme Judicial Court of Massachusetts explained in 1849, the company was "bound to the most exact care and diligence, not only in the management of the trains and cars, but also in the structure and care of the track."[43] Railroads were obligated to carry passengers safely, and were bound to provide suitable equipment and skillful employees. Liability for injury to passengers was based on negligence, but the happening of an accident raised a prima facie presumption of fault by the carrier. The burden of proof was then placed on the company to demonstrate its freedom from blame.[44] In passenger suits, railroads were often held liable for defects in equipment[45] or for the carelessness of employees.[46] Companies were also bound to keep their station platforms in safe condition.[47]

Sometimes lawmakers imposed a statutory duty on railroads to safeguard passengers. An 1850 Florida charter provided that the company "shall be bound and held responsible for any damages to said passengers" as a result of negligence or "bad condition" of the railroad.[48] The Georgia Code of 1861 mandated that a carrier use "extraordinary diligence . . . to protect the lives and persons of his passengers."[49] Likewise, carriers were often required by statute to provide station facilities, and were liable for any injury resulting from failure to perform this duty.[50]

Injured passengers could also take advantage of railroad violation of statutes primarily intended to protect other interests. As discussed earlier, railroads were under a statutory obligation in many jurisdictions to erect fences along their track. The immediate legislative concern, of course, was to protect cattle and other animals on adjoining farms. But courts early took the position that the fence laws were also intended to secure the safety of persons riding on trains. The Supreme Court of Missouri concluded in 1858: "The motive of the law in requiring railroads to be fenced is not the security of cattle only, but chiefly the preservation of the persons and lives of passengers which would be greatly endangered if cattle were not restrained from wandering upon them."[51] If an animal got on the track because the carrier failed to maintain a fence and thus caused a derailment, the company was liable to passengers for any injuries.

Although sympathetic to passenger claims, courts stopped short of making carriers guarantors of travel safety. The New York Court of Appeals pointed out the rationale behind this rule in 1871:

> Railroads are great public improvements, beneficial to the owners, and highly useful to the public. There is a certain amount of risk incident to railroad travel, which the traveler knowingly assumes; and public policy is fully satisfied, when railroad companies are held to the most rigid responsibility for the utmost care and vigilance for the safety of travelers.[52]

It bears emphasis that judicial adherence to a negligence standard with respect to passengers differed markedly from the strict liability rule that governed the carriage of goods.

Consequently, rash or careless behavior by a passenger that contributed to an injury barred any recovery. There were a number of cases in which passengers were deemed guilty of contributory negligence. Two common situations involved passengers jumping on or leaving moving trains,[53] and placing limbs outside the car window while the train was in motion.[54] Statutes codified the conduct expected of passengers. The New Mexico general railroad act of 1878, for example, provided that passengers injured while riding on freight cars or while limbs were projected outside of windows in violation of company regulations were contributorily negligent.[55] Still, one study found that railroad passengers "were only rarely denied a recovery on account of contributory negligence."[56] On the whole, passengers received solicitous treatment from judges and legislators, a fact that seemingly contradicts the contention that the negligence standard was employed to hold down the operating costs of railroads.

Injuries to General Public

Aside from death or injury to employees and passengers, railroad operations resulted in accidents involving members of the general public. A large number of persons, exceeding employee fatalities, were regularly killed while walking along or crossing tracks. Decrying this slaughter, the *American Railroad Journal* in 1856 called for legislation to make trespassing on railroad property a penal offense.[57] Since the only duty owed by a railroad to a trespasser was to refrain from wantonly or intentionally inflicting harm, trespassers or their next of kin found it difficult to secure a recovery. Moreover, persons walking on tracks were easily charged with contributory negligence.[58] Similarly, persons who became drunk and lay down on tracks were unable to prevail.[59]

Children playing on the track or with railroad equipment, however, were a serious problem for railroads. Not only were juries notoriously sympathetic to injured or killed children, but it was hard to establish contributory negligence. Carriers sought to settle such cases when possible.[60]

Railroads regularly collided with pedestrians and vehicles at road crossings. Throughout the nineteenth and twentieth centuries there was a flood of cases arising out of accidents at intersections. Both the roadway traveler and the railroad, of course, were entitled to use the intersection. Courts therefore had to fashion rules that would take into account the interests of the parties while promoting public safety. Railroads were bound to exercise reasonable care to avoid collisions at crossings, and not to interfere with the equal rights of road travelers.[61] Thus, a railroad company might be guilty of negligence for running its train at an excessive rate of speed at a crossing of a public street in populated areas.[62]

Highway users, however, were also under a duty to remain vigilant when approaching railroad tracks. Numerous cases raised the question of whether travelers exercised care when crossing tracks. Courts wielded the doctrine of contributory negligence forcefully to deny recovery to claimants hurt or killed in crossing accidents. To be sure, some travelers acted recklessly. In the leading case of *Harding v. New York and Erie Railroad Company* (1852), the deceased drove a sleigh across tracks without looking for an oncoming train. Finding the deceased to have been contributorily negligent, the New York court warned against allowing compassion to influence jury deliberations. It declared in a revealing comment:

> We can not shut our eyes to the fact that in certain controversies between the weak and the strong—between a humble individual and a gigantic corporation, the sympathies of the human mind naturally, honestly and generously, run to the assistance and support of the feeble.[63]

By the end of the nineteenth century, the duty on highway travelers was articulated in terms of the stop, look, and listen rule. Travelers were expected to stop and look and listen for trains before crossing tracks, especially where there was an obstruction to sight.[64] Some state courts, as in Pennsylvania, imposed an absolute duty on travelers to stop, look, and listen in all situations, and treated failure to do so as contributory negligence.[65]

The stop, look, and listen rule was originally devised to deal with pedestrians and horse-drawn vehicles. The appearance of the automobile in the early twentieth century gave a new intensity to the problem of intersection accidents. Some courts responded by insisting on fixed standards to govern crossing accidents. Writing for the Supreme Court in *Baltimore and Ohio Railroad Company v. Goodman* (1927), Justice Oliver Wendell Holmes, Jr., suggested that a traveler might need to both stop and get out of the car in order to ascertain the approach of a train. He found that the traveler in that case was responsible for his own death. But courts began to make exceptions to the stop, look, and listen rule, and to hold that each case must be decided on its own facts.[66] The Supreme Court gave support to this trend in 1934, declaring that the standard of care of a reasonable traveler depended on the circumstances and that there was no absolute duty to stop at tracks. Indeed, the Court stated: "To get out of a vehicle and reconnoitre is an uncommon precaution, as everyday experience informs us. Besides being uncommon, it is very likely to be futile, and sometimes even dangerous."[67] Increasingly, the question of driver negligence was left for the jury to resolve.

The application of the doctrine of contributory negligence to intersection accidents was not without criticism. As early as 1886 a Florida judge protested the "unjust and unequitable" operation of the rule. He added that "there is no present incentive of personal safety on the train hands to use caution, nor a fear of being compelled to make pecuniary compensation when they can rely upon being absolved from their admitted negligence by some careless act of the plaintiff."[68] Part of the solution to the problem of crossing accidents was found not in tort law but in the move to require grade separations at busy intersections. Moreover, federal safety legislation, such as the Safety Appliance Act, was construed to protect highway travelers at rail crossings. Thus, failure to equip a train with air brakes as required by law eliminated any defense of contributory negligence.[69]

Federal Preemption

The increase in other types of industrial accidents and the ubiquitous automobile mishaps in the twentieth century have reduced the historic focus on railroads as the prime force in shaping tort law. Still, FELA suits and collisions at crossings continue to present challenging issues. The growing web of federal safety laws in the twentieth century has raised the question of federal preemption of state tort laws. The railroad industry has been a major testing ground for such preemption claims.

In 1970 Congress created the Federal Railroad Administration (FRA) to reduce rail-related accidents. The secretary of transportation was given broad authority to prescribe rules relating to railroad safety. Congress directed that such safety orders should be nationally uniform to the extent practicable. There has been considerable litigation as to whether federal regulations under the FRA preempt state tort law claims against railroads. In *CSX Transportation, Inc. v. Easterwood* (1993), growing out of a fatal collision at an intersection, the Supreme Court determined that federal rules governing the speed of trains preempted certain state common-law claims concerning excessive speed. Likewise, the Court concluded in another case that the federal rail safety program, which provided funding for warning signs at crossings, prevented state tort actions seeking to hold carriers responsible for the adequacy of the signs.[70] These results diminish the prospect of recovery against railroads, but are consistent with the persistent trend toward national standards for the interstate rail industry.

The historical literature has commonly pictured railroads as the beneficiary of a harsh tort law regime that favored enterprise at the expense of individual injured parties. Review of the judicial and legislative record suggests that a more balanced portrait is in order. Courts and legislators struggled to adjust deeply ingrained notions of personal responsibility, desire for economic development, concern for accident victims, and considerations of federalism. Notwithstanding general enthusiasm for railroads, there are enough decisions imposing liability on railroads to cast doubt on generalizations about tort law as a sort of subsidy. As Kermit L. Hall has aptly pointed out, "the courts seem to have maintained something of a middle ground in tort law."[71]

10

Railroads in the Progressive Era

A broad-based reform movement, known as Progressivism, emerged in the early years of the twentieth century. Although the political objectives of this coalition were diverse, a paramount goal of Progressivism was to redress the imbalance of economic power associated with the new industrial order. To this end, Progressives urged a more active role for state and federal governments in regulating the economy.

By 1900 railroads occupied a central place in the economic life of the country. Railroad capital represented one-seventh of national wealth, and railroad companies controlled allied businesses such as coal mines, steamships, and hotels. There was also a persistent trend toward the consolidation of lines, which reduced competition and aroused latent fears of monopoly conditions. It was widely believed that the carriers exercised undue political influence, and that rail managers were greedy and dishonest. Reflecting public sentiment, the Progressives took particular aim at railroads and demanded greater public accountability.[1] Prominent political figures associated with the Progressive movement, such as Robert M. LaFollette of Wisconsin and Hiram Johnson of California, fanned antagonism toward railroads.

The feeble Interstate Commerce Commission, created by Congress in 1887, had brought about no basic change in the operations of railroads. Accordingly, President Theodore Roosevelt championed laws to strengthen the ICC. The Elkins Act of 1903 tightened the prohibition of rebates, a step many railroads welcomed. Not everyone, of course, applauded the renewed interest in regulation. The *Commercial and Financial Chronicle* complained: "The whole movement against the railroads is predicated . . . on the idea that they are extremely prosperous and that some of their profits might as well be taken from them and appropriated for the benefit of shippers and the general public."[2] But such protests went unheard in the clamor for closer controls.

New Regulatory Structure

After several years of prodding by Roosevelt, Congress enacted the Hepburn Act in 1906, a development that marked a watershed in railroad regulatory policy. Briefly stated, the Hepburn Act increased the size of the ICC to seven members and extended the agency's authority to certain other common carriers such as pipelines and terminal facilities. It prohibited the issuance of most free passes and gave the ICC power to prescribe uniform accounting methods. The commodities clause of the act sought to divorce transportation from production and manufacturing. With the exception of timber products, railroads were barred from carrying in interstate commerce any materials produced by companies controlled by the carriers. Most important, the Hepburn Act empowered the ICC, upon receipt of a complaint, to review railroad charges and to determine "the just and reasonable rate." Railroads, however, were still free to set rates, and the ICC could not initiate a new rate on its own. The act also limited the scope of judicial review and provided that ICC orders were binding when issued. So strong was anti-railroad sentiment by 1906 that the Hepburn Act passed both houses of Congress by overwhelming margins. Enactment of the Hepburn Act sparked an upsurge in shipper complaints to the ICC.[3] It also marked the first step in the railroad industry's loss of control of the rate-making process.

The Hepburn Act has been at the center of an historical debate over the impetus for railroad regulation and the nature of Progressivism. Gabriel Kolko has asserted that "the railroads, not the farmers and shippers, were the most important single advocates of federal regulation from 1877 to 1916."[4] He posits that railroads sought to escape chaotic market conditions. A more compelling explanation, however, is that smaller merchants who felt that they were disadvantaged under the existing rate structure were the primary advocates of rate regulation. Railroad companies, in fact, were adamantly opposed to giving the ICC rate-making authority.[5] At the state level as well, it was shippers and consumers who pushed for greater control of railroads.[6]

Passage of the Hepburn Act did not stem the tide of anti-railroad sentiment. In 1908 the platforms of both major political parties called for additional regulatory measures. The Democrats in particular asserted that the ICC should be empowered to investigate and fix rates on its own initiative. At the recommendation of President William Howard Taft, Congress in 1910 adopted the Mann-Elkins Act. The law gave the ICC authority to alter rates without waiting for shipper complaints, and to suspend new rates proposed by carriers for as much as ten months in order to assess their reasonableness. The burden of proof of the reasonableness of both proposed and exiting rates was placed on the railroads. Moreover, the act strengthened the ban against long haul–short haul differential by deleting the "under substantially similar circumstances and conditions" clause. As a consequence, railroads no longer had the power to meet competitive conditions by charging lower rates without ICC permission.[7] The Mann-Elkins Act put railroads in a regulatory straitjacket. Not only were they unable to adjust rates to deal with changing economic factors, but control of rate making was given to an agency solicitous of shipper interests and under political pressure to block any rate increases.[8]

The third major piece of Progressive railroad legislation was the Valuation Act of 1913. Under the rule of *Smyth v. Ames* (1898), railroads were entitled to a fair return on the value of their property, but the ascertainment of that value rested on a broad inquiry into a number of factors. To many Progressives, it was an article of faith, however dubious in fact, that railroads were earning exorbitant profits on inflated property values. They insisted that a determination of a fair return for carriers necessitated a physical valuation of railroad property. Concerned that rail assets were overvalued, a number of states at the turn of the twentieth century, including Texas, Michigan, and Wisconsin, engaged in an assessment of rail assets. The theory behind the move for railroad valuation was that it would provide a sound and "scientific" basis on which to calculate reasonable rates. Leading Progressives, such as Robert M. LaFollette, were convinced that a valuation would lead to a cut in transportation charges.[9]

Accepting this premise, Congress in the Valuation Act required the ICC to ascertain the value of all railroad property, taking into account such factors as financial history, original cost, and reproduction cost. A Bureau of Valuation was created, and the work on this complex task lasted well into the 1920s. Railroad companies were obligated to furnish extensive data and often hired their own evaluators to work with the ICC. After the expenditure of millions of dollars by both taxpayers and railroads, the ICC largely confirmed the value of railroad assets and concluded that they were not overcapitalized.[10] The valuation project never served as a basis for rate making. State valuation studies came to much the same result.[11] The valuation exercise did put the quietus to the myth that railroads exaggerated the worth of their assets. This misguided and wasteful project only served to highlight the cost of excessive regulation. It was, in the words of Morton Keller, "a decades-long exercise in futility."[12]

Judicial Response

Since Congress had now unequivocally expressed its intent to regulate rail-road rates, the Supreme Court generally deferred to the legislative program and sustained the enhanced power of the ICC. The justices adopted a narrow approach to judicial review of ICC orders, holding in 1907 that the reasonableness of rates was a factual question and that the findings of the ICC were prima facie valid.[13] In *ICC v. Illinois Central Railroad Company* (1910), the Court ruled that the agency had power to deal with preferential treatment in furnishing freight cars as well as in setting rates. The Court added that it would not "under the guise of exerting judicial power, usurp merely administrative functions by setting aside a lawful administrative order upon our conception as to whether the administrative power has been wisely exercised."[14] Upholding a number of ICC orders that reduced freight charges, the Supreme Court signaled a reduced role for the judiciary in the rate-setting process.[15] It also validated the constitutionality of the 1910 amendment tightening the long haul–short haul clause.[16]

The Supreme Court even upheld the power of the ICC to control intrastate railroad charges that adversely affected interstate commerce. At issue in the famous *Shreveport Rate Case* (1914) was a conflict between federal and state rates for transporting freight to places in east Texas. The charges for shipments from Shreveport, Louisiana, were higher than the rates for shipping the same distance within Texas. In setting the lower intrastate rate, the Texas Railroad Commission made no secret of its desire to protect shippers in Texas from outside competition. To alleviate this discrimination against interstate commerce, the ICC directed the railroads to adjust their rates and to disregard the Texas rate order. Affirming this decision, the Supreme Court maintained: "Wherever the interstate and intrastate transactions of carriers are so related that the government of one involves the control of the other, it is Congress, and not the State, that is entitled to prescribe the final and dominant rule."[17] The *Shreveport Rate Case* strengthened the hand of the ICC and portended a more expansive reading of the federal commerce power. It also aided the railroads in their running battle to escape cumbersome and parochial state regulations.[18]

During the early decades of the twentieth century, the Supreme Court in the main bolstered the ICC's authority and largely retreated from review of railroad rates. Still, the justices never entirely surrendered the field. They set aside ICC rate-reduction orders that were unsupported by evidence,[19] and periodically cautioned against confiscatory rates. In 1908 the Supreme Court observed that "railroads are the private property of their owners" and "in no proper sense is the public a general manager."[20] Moreover, in some respects, the Court construed narrowly the railroad regulatory statutes. It denied, for instance, that the ICC had the power to require carriers to provide freight cars to shippers upon request. The Court expressed concern that such a mandate would, in effect, compel railroads to incur the expense of acquiring additional cars.[21]

Reflecting lingering distrust of the administrative process, the justices also restrained the investigatory powers of the ICC. The case of *Harriman v. ICC* (1908) grew out of an investigation into purchases and sales of stocks in various railroad companies by Edward H. Harriman, a leading figure in the rail industry.[22] Writing for the Supreme Court, Justice Oliver Wendell Holmes, Jr., vindicated Harriman's refusal to answer the commission's questions. He reasoned that the Interstate Commerce Act empowered the ICC to compel the testimony of witnesses only when it was investigating a specific breach of law, not for the purpose of proposing new legislation. Holmes decried "the enormous scope of the power asserted for the commission," and asserted that "no such unlimited command over the liberty of all citizens ever was given, so far as we know, in constitutional times, to any commission or court."[23] In short, where Congress had not spoken clearly, the Court continued to look skeptically at ICC moves.

The Commodities Clause

Recall that the commodities clause of the Hepburn Act made it unlawful for a railroad to transport in interstate commerce any commodity produced by it or in which the carrier had "any interest, direct or indirect." This provision was directed primarily at the ownership or control of anthracite coal mines in Pennsylvania by several railroads. During the Civil War era, carriers, including the Delaware, Lackawanna and Western Railroad and the Lehigh Valley Railroad, began to acquire substantial coal lands, in part to secure a regular supply of coal for their own use. An 1869 Pennsylvania statute encouraged this practice by authorizing railroad companies to purchase the stock of coal enterprises. Five railroad companies rapidly gained dominance in the mining and transportation of anthracite. Mounting concern over the combination of mining and carriage in single entities found expression in the 1874 Pennsylvania Constitution, which declared that no common carrier could directly or indirectly engage in mining or acquire land except for transportation. But this prohibition proved ineffective. It was not deemed retroactive, and railroad companies continued to obtain coal lands through subsidiaries.[24] Courts occasionally voiced apprehension that the anthracite lines acting in combination could diminish competition and artificially raise the price of coal. Thus, the New Jersey Court of Chancery in 1892 invalidated a lease of one coal carrier to another on grounds such arrangement tended to create a monopoly in the coal trade.[25]

By the early twentieth century, the anthracite railroads and their subsidiary coal companies controlled most of the anthracite production in the United States. Critics charged that they were discriminating against independent coal producers and were suppressing competition in the transportation of coal. They argued that these supposed abuses produced high prices for coal, and that the remedy was to restore competition by separating railroad companies from mining activities.

Although much of the controversy over the close ties between railroading and mining was focused on Pennsylvania, it is noteworthy that similar conditions prevailed in the southern bituminous coal regions. The Chesapeake and Ohio and Norfolk and Western Railroads owned much of the mining land in West Virginia. In 1887 the Virginia Farmers' Assembly complained that "the system now practiced by certain railroad companies of buying up, as to monopolize, the coal and other mineral lands of the country is pregnant with the greatest evil."[26] Several states in the bituminous region sought to separate transportation and mining. West Virginia legislators in 1895 enacted a law to prohibit a railroad from engaging in the business of buying or selling coal.[27] The Kentucky Constitution of 1890 declared that no common carrier could own or acquire mines or factories. But the import of these measures was unclear, and any meaningful remedy required relief at the national level.

The agitation against railroad operation of mines culminated in the commodities clause. Obviously, it would be costly for railroads to comply. In addition, it was widely believed that the clause would be found unconstitutional as a deprivation of property without due process. Therefore, the railroad companies took no steps to dispose of their mining property during the two-year period before the effective date of the clause.[28] This set the stage for protracted litigation between 1908 and 1920 as the government tried to break up the anthracite coal combinations.

To the disappointment of the anthracite lines, the Supreme Court in *United States v. Delaware and Hudson Company* (1909) upheld the constitutionality of the commodities clause as within the power of Congress to regulate commerce. The Court, however, gave the law a narrow interpretation, ruling that it only prevented railroads from carrying commodities owned by them at the time of transportation. The clause did not prohibit railroads from transporting coal belonging to corporations in which they held stock. This decision seemingly opened an avenue of escape for railroads to carry the coal owned by affiliated companies. Little, it would appear, had changed because of the commodities clause. Several carriers promptly organized ostensibly independent enterprises that contracted to purchase all the coal produced in railroad-controlled mines. By this maneuver the railroad companies maintained that they had disassociated themselves from any interest in the coal before transportation, thereby evading the ban of the commodities clause.

The Supreme Court, however, looked with disfavor upon such contractual arrangements. Asserting that there was "no intent on the part of Congress to confiscate property or to destroy the interest of stockholders," the Court insisted in the leading case of *United States v. Delaware, Lackawanna and Western Railroad Company* (1915) upon a genuine disposition of the coal mined by carriers before transportation.[29] It concluded that the coal-purchasing company in that case was not an independent buyer but merely the agent of the railroad. Finding a violation of both the commodities clause and the Sherman Anti-Trust Act, the Court enjoined further transportation of coal under the illegal contract. In a series of subsequent cases, which lasted until 1920, the Court made it clear that railroads could no longer carry coal in which they had an ownership interest or resort to nominally separate companies that were in fact just instruments of the railroad.[30] Over the next few years the anthracite lines devised plans to separate coal properties from rail operations.[31]

As with much of the Progressive legislation directed at railroads, there is room to doubt whether the commodities clause achieved its underlying objectives. The loss of control over anthracite mining by the railroad companies coincided with the decline of the anthracite industry in the 1920s. Oil and natural gas production burgeoned as these products began to replace coal. Studies indicate that the divorce of railroads and mining did not reintroduce competition into the anthracite region. As one commentator noted, the separation "has done little to change the state of affairs in the coal business."[32] Worry about railroad domination vanished, and the commodities clause was rarely the subject of subsequent litigation. Finally, in 1995 Congress repealed the clause as part of its decision to abolish the ICC.

Continued State Regulation

Notwithstanding the growth in federal regulations, the states in the early twentieth century enacted hundreds of railroad laws. Many states created or strengthened railroad commissions, giving such agencies the power to set intrastate rates.[33] In 1906, Ohio, for example, passed a comprehensive rail regulatory measure.[34] A year later, New York established a powerful Public Service Commission, with jurisdiction over railroads and utilities. Arguing that stringent controls would discourage investments, railroads in New York were the chief opponents of the law.[35] Still other state legislatures mandated reductions in passenger fares. This outpouring of often contradictory state laws added to the regulatory burden of railroads. A dense jungle of state and federal controls existed side by side in a complex and uncertain manner. It amounted, one historian has concluded, to "a new regulatory chaos" rather than the sound national rail policy fondly envisioned by Progressives.[36]

Although increasingly inclined to support ICC rulings, the Supreme Court persisted in supervising state rate making and service orders for intrastate traffic. In so doing, the Court sought to delineate state and federal spheres and generally upheld national authority. These cases implicated both issues of federalism and the constitutional right of railroads to receive just compensation for the value of their property used by the public. The Supreme Court wrestled with these related questions in the *Minnesota Rate Cases* (1913). Orders of the state commission setting maximum freight rates for traffic within the state were challenged as a burden on interstate commerce and as so low as to be confiscatory. The Court first ruled that states could fix reasonable intrastate rates, but stressed the paramount power of Congress to displace local laws that obstructed national commerce. If the operations of railroads were so blended that adequate regulation of interstate rates could not be achieved without control of local charges, the Court noted that Congress was free to adopt a more comprehensive scheme of regulation. This decision opened the door for subsequent federal legislation that virtually eliminated state rate making.

Turning to the definition of confiscatory rates, the Supreme Court trimmed state power to fix intrastate charges. It was admittedly difficult to segregate intrastate business for the purpose of determining whether state-imposed rates allowed companies a fair return on investments devoted to local traffic. However, the Court insisted that a state could not require low rates on intrastate transportation because the carrier was earning a profit on interstate business. But to separate the value of railroad property used for local traffic necessitated intricate calculations. Adhering to the fair value rule established in *Smyth v. Ames* (1898), the Court set aside one of the challenged rates in Minnesota as confiscatory and unconstitutional.

Following this lead, the federal courts during the Progressive Era repeatedly invalidated rates set under state law as a deprivation of property without due process. The Supreme Court, for instance, struck down a North

Dakota law which required carriers to transport coal at a loss even though the return from the railroad's entire intrastate business was adequate. A state, the Court reasoned, could not segregate one commodity and impose on it an arbitrary rate.[37] Likewise, the Court voided a West Virginia statute that forced railroads to carry passengers at fares that provided just a nominal return.[38] In 1907 the circuit court in Alabama enjoined enforcement of state rate laws, triggering a political struggle that lasted for years.[39] But the states persevered in their efforts to reduce intrastate charges despite the federal courts, creating a climate of regulatory confusion.

A number of state legislatures grew so angry at federal judicial review of intrastate rates that they sought to deter railroads from seeking relief in federal courts. At issue in the landmark case of *Ex Parte Young* (1908) was a Minnesota law that mandated reductions in passenger and freight rates. It also imposed enormous fines and severe criminal penalties on carriers and their agents for violation of the act. The evident purpose of the penalties was to intimidate the railroads and their officers from resorting to the courts to test the validity of the law. Asserting that the reduced rates were confiscatory, railroad stockholders obtained a temporary injunction from the federal circuit court prohibiting Edward T. Young, the Minnesota attorney general, from enforcing the act. Young violated the injunction by seeking to enforce the new rates in state court. Found guilty of contempt, Young was fined, ordered to dismiss the state court proceeding, and jailed until he complied. Young petitioned the Supreme Court for a writ of habeas corpus, arguing that the suit was in reality against the state in contravention of the Eleventh Amendment.

Writing for the Court, Justice Rufus W. Peckham found the penalty provisions unconstitutional because they effectively denied resort to the federal courts to ascertain the sufficiency of rates. Rejecting the Eleventh Amendment defense, he maintained that when a state officer sought to enforce an unconstitutional act, "he is in that case stripped of his official or representative character and is subjected in his person to the consequences of his individual conduct."[40] This distinction between suits against states and suits against state officers alleged to be acting unconstitutionally rested on a convenient legal fiction that facilitated circumvention of the Eleventh Amendment. Thus, *Young* became a foundational decision for Eleventh Amendment jurisprudence.[41]

For my purpose, *Young* is important as the jurisdictional counterpart to federal court oversight of state rate regulations. Clearly, the justices were influenced by their suspicion of state railroad regulations and their desire to safeguard the property rights of carriers. Peckham declared that a company should not be required to risk heavy penal sanctions in order to obtain judicial review of state-imposed rates. He also stressed protection of investment capital, a theme often articulated in rate cases. "Over eleven thousand millions of dollars, it is estimated, are invested in railroad property, owned by many thousands of people who are scattered over the whole country from ocean to ocean," Peckham observed, "and they are entitled to equal protection from the laws and the courts, with the owners of all other kinds of property, no more, no less."[42]

In a line of decisions following *Young*, the federal courts underscored their determination to protect railroad access to a federal forum. Other schemes designed to prevent carriers from appealing to the federal courts were also struck down. A number of states enacted laws under which a foreign railroad company forfeited the right to do business in the jurisdiction should it institute a suit in or remove a suit to federal court. Courts voided these "outlaw" provisions on grounds that resort to federal courts was protected by the Constitution.[43] Similarly, a state law imposing high liquidated damages out of proportion to actual damages for any carriage charge in excess of rates set by the legislature was held to indirectly curtail the right of appeal.[44]

Although historians have focused on the controversy over state rate making during the Progressive Era, state commissions and lawmakers were equally concerned with improving railroad service. They issued numerous orders requiring carriers to upgrade passenger facilities, to alleviate freight congestion, and to adjust the schedule of passenger trains. The New York Public Service Commission, for instance, saw the main issue as quality of service not charges.[45]

The Supreme Court generally allowed the states considerable latitude to impose service requirements to benefit the public interest, even if the effect was to compel a railroad to incur substantial expense. Thus, in *Atlantic Coast Line Railroad Company v. North Carolina Corporation Commission* (1907), the Court sustained an order requiring a railroad to operate an additional local train in order to make a reasonable connection with a through passenger train. It was unimpressed with the argument that this additional train would operate at a loss, so long as the overall rate scheme did not amount to a confiscation of property. Separately, the Court upheld the validity of an order requiring a carrier to interchange freight and passenger cars in intrastate traffic with other lines.[46]

Yet the Supreme Court drew the line at orders that obligated companies to maintain unprofitable enterprises. Justice Holmes flatly declared in 1920: "A carrier cannot be compelled to carry on even a branch of business at a loss, much less the whole business of carriage."[47] This analysis foreshadowed the conflict over railroad efforts to abandon unprofitable routes, which started in the 1920s and accelerated after World War II.

Antitrust Laws

As discussed earlier, Americans have traditionally relied on competition to police most economic activities and determine prices. With respect to the rail industry, competition tended to produce rate differentials as companies sought to attract business. But different rate structures were popularly seen as a form of price discrimination. This in turn provided the impetus for regulations to impose stable and uniform rates, thus curtailing competition. It was absurd to expect much economic competition in a legal environment of controlled rates, but policy makers in the Progressive Era were slow to perceive the inherent inconsistency. They continued to talk in terms of restoring competition even as they built a regulatory apparatus that reduced competition.[48] In addition to strengthening the ICC, therefore, government officials turned to the embryonic antitrust laws to check the growing rail consolidation. Attacks on the concentration of railroad control helped to shape early antitrust doctrine.

The enduring commitment to competition, at least in theory, was evident in vigorous application of the antitrust laws to railroads in the early twentieth century. Courts viewed the consolidation of competing lines with particular suspicion. Since agreements between competing carriers to fix rates had already been condemned, railroad managers developed other legal devices. The famous *Northern Securities* case involved an effort to bring three major railroad lines operating in the Pacific Northwest under joint control. To this end, the principals formed a holding company to manage the railroads and control transportation in the region. A sharply fragmented Supreme Court ruled in 1904 that the holding company was a combination in restraint of trade and violated the Sherman Act. Finding that a holding company was engaged in commerce, a plurality insisted that the act prohibited all restraints of trade, and was not limited to just unreasonable restraints. The dissenters, including Holmes and Justice Edward D. White, maintained that the formation of a holding company did not amount to a restraint of trade.[49]

Despite the symbolic importance of *Northern Securities* as a showcase in President Theodore Roosevelt's trust-busting campaign, it was not a harbinger of the future. Although the ruling temporarily halted merger activity, the Supreme Court soon moved away from a literal understanding of the Sherman Act in favor of a fact-based rule of reasonableness.[50] Even the specific holding was overtaken by events. Dissolution of the holding company did not stop informal collaboration among the three railroads. Finally, in 1970 the railroads once controlled by the Northern Securities Company were merged, suggesting that economic forces eventually triumphed.[51]

The Supreme Court also looked askance at the acquisition of a controlling stock interest by one railroad in a competing line. Declaring that such a step created a dominant entity and tended to restrict competition, the Court held that the 1901 purchase by the Union Pacific Railroad Company of stock in the Southern Pacific Company effected a restraint of trade within the meaning of the Sherman Act. It stressed that the purpose of Congress was to preserve competition in interstate trade. The Court observed that the consolidation of competing railroad systems resulted in "destroying or greatly abridging the free operation of competition theretofore existing" and "tends to higher rates."[52] This latter point was more assumed than demonstrated because the Court offered no evidence about the effect of rail combinations on the level of transportation charges. In the leading railroad antitrust cases of the Progressive Era, the Supreme Court was not sympathetic to the industry's desire to combine.

Antitrust concerns prompted legislation requiring railroads to relinquish ownership of other forms of transportation. By the early twentieth century, railroad companies often operated extensive steamboat lines to supplement rail connections. In 1912 Congress enacted the Panama Canal Act, which prohibited after 1914 railroad ownership of any waterborne common carrier when the railroad might compete for traffic with the water carrier. The ICC was authorized to ascertain whether such competition existed. It was felt that a connection between railroad companies and steamboat lines was inimical to competition and fostered monopoly. In a manner reminiscent of the commodities clause, this measure brought about a divorce of water carriers and railroads.[53]

In 1914 Congress attempted to put more teeth into antitrust policy with passage of the Clayton Anti-Trust Act. This act specifically prohibited a corporation from acquiring the stock of another corporation where the effect "may be substantially to lessen competition." The ICC was empowered to enforce the Clayton Act against common carriers.[54]

Legislative action and judicial decisions applying antitrust doctrine to railroads were intended to foster competition between lines. Since price differences were curtailed by rate regulation, there was an air of unreality about this emphasis on competition. Critics maintained that cooperation among carriers should be promoted, and that the Sherman Act should not be applied to railroads.[55] Nonetheless, the antitrust laws created additional legal complications for the rail industry. Among other consequences, the laws hampered financially strong companies in the acquisition of weak lines. "A natural and wholesome economic process which would be to the advantage of the people of the whole country," one commentator lamented in 1918, "has been balked and practically brought to an end by the application to the railroads of what is popularly known as the Sherman Act."[56] As discussed in Chapter Eleven, Congress in 1920 altered railroad policy, and encouraged the consolidation of lines rather than competition.

Vagaries of Railroad Regulation

The outpouring of railroad laws in the Progressive Era, although modified to some extent in 1920, set regulatory policy for decades. Historians, many of whom reflect the anti-railroad sentiment of the Progressives, have long been prone to hail increased regulation of the industry as a suitable response to supposed abuses. However, they have not scrutinized closely whether these controls served either the public or the carriers. The story of Progressive railroad regulations as an unalloyed triumph is not without problems. It therefore remains to evaluate briefly Progressive regulatory initiatives in the early twentieth century.

The first point is that neither Congress nor the ICC could escape the contradictory view that both competition and consolidation were deleterious. Occasional bursts of antitrust rhetoric aside, legislation was directed largely toward preventing competitive pricing and protecting existing lines. In fact, lawmakers increasingly relied on commissions, not competition, to achieve regulatory goals. State commissions, for example, tended to oppose new railroad enterprises that would duplicate services.[57] This approach, of course, confirmed the privileged position of already established lines against possible competitors and worked at cross-purposes with antitrust doctrine.

In addition to the unresolved tension between competition and regulation, Progressive legislation, in effect, transferred rate-making power from the railroads to agencies. This spawned a number of problems. Although the Progressives sought efficient and scientific solutions to major issues, there was no objective basis on which to judge whether a particular railroad charge was reasonable. The complexity of rate making did not easily yield to administrative resolution. Inevitably, the ICC and state agencies faced political pressure from shippers to hold down rates. Moreover, it was necessary to revise rates frequently in order to meet changing business conditions. But the carriers no longer had the flexibility to adjust charges quickly, and the ICC early proved dilatory in handling rate requests.

One measure of the success of Progressive railroad policy is to examine the workings of the newly strengthened ICC after the Hepburn Act. For several years the ICC heard complaints on a case-by-case basis, focusing on the reasonableness of individual rates and allegations of discrimination. Overall rates remained basically fixed at the 1906 level, despite increased wages and operating expenses. So in 1910 railroads proposed a general rate increase. The ICC, however, repeatedly rejected requests for general rate increases between 1911 and 1916. Part of the difficulty was that commission members could not agree on the criteria for determining reasonable rates. A particular sticking point was whether the poor financial condition of railroads was a consideration that warranted a price hike. The refusal by the ICC to advance rates during a period of general prosperity and rising prices depressed the earnings of rail companies. Such action contributed to the inability of carriers to attract new investment capital. Lack of capital in turn hampered the efforts of railroads to upgrade service and obtain new equipment to handle growing traffic.[58] After decades of railroad expansion, the construction of new track markedly declined.

The link between investment and rate making was emphasized in 1913 by William F. Herrin, chief counsel of the Southern Pacific:

> In order to equip our railroads to meet the demands upon them, and to keep pace with the development of the country, large amounts of private capital must be provided. . . . During recent years the railroads, because of the difficulty of securing the necessary capital, have not been able to make the extensions and improvements required to meet extraordinary conditions . . . such as . . . traffic movements required in case of war.

Noting the recent rejection of applications for a rate increase, Herrin pointedly observed: "The fact remains that the Interstate Commerce Commission, and the State railroad commissions with the power vested in them to fix rates, may make it difficult, if not impossible, for the railroads to obtain the money needed."[59]

Against this background, we should consider the controversial thesis of Gabriel Kolko that the ICC "was aligned, for the most part, with the railroads."[60] He would have us believe that the commission was, as a practical matter, a tool of the industry. This account is highly problematic.[61] As discussed earlier, railroads generally opposed government involvement in the rate-making process. It would indeed be remarkable for any industry to cheerfully relinquish control of fundamental economic questions to a politicized agency. The actions of the ICC during the Progressive Era amply justified the foreboding of the carriers. Rather than formulate a coherent national rail policy, the commission seemed to view its function as holding down transportation charge regardless of economic circumstances or the solvency of railroad companies. Its disregard for the financial needs of the carriers and repeated refusal to advance rates can scarcely be seen as backing Kolko's thesis.[62] Shippers, not railroads, were the beneficiaries of congressional policy and dominated the ICC. A study of the commission cogently concluded: "Clearly in 1911 the ICC was not the captive of railroads; indeed it was hostile to them and friendly to shippers."[63] To be sure, some railroad executives hoped that federal supervision would limit the reach of onerous and inconsistent state laws. But this does not demonstrate that they favored Progressive regulatory policy or influenced the decisions of the ICC.

The conventional interpretation picturing Progressive-Era railroad legislation as the embodiment of enlightened reform needs reappraisal. A more accurate portrayal of the regulatory regime erected by the Progressives points toward failure. Sweeping federal controls did not assure an adequate railroad service, and ultimately benefited neither the carriers nor the public. Heavy-handed rate regulations, administered by a sluggish ICC, contributed to the financial decline of the industry. In 1916 companies operating one-sixth of the nation's track were in receivership. In a final ironic twist, comprehensive regulations were imposed just as the need for them was diminishing. Railroads would soon face competition from motor vehicles, and lose their dominant position in the national economy. But as a legal history of railroading makes clear, legislators are often addressing yesterday's problems.

11

World War I and the Expansion of Federal Regulatory Authority

Facing a hostile political environment, and caught between rising costs and taxes on one hand and a rate structure that remained virtually unchanged on the other, the railroads experienced a difficult period just before World War I. Control of railroad charges prevented the carriers from raising the capital necessary for maintenance or improvements. To add to the industry's woes, there was labor unrest and pressure for higher wages. Passage of the Adamson Act in 1916, instituting an eight-hour workday for railroad-operating employees, substantially increased labor cost. "By the time America entered World War I in 1917," Morton Keller aptly stated, "the condition of the railroads was as unsatisfactory as their regulatory milieu."[1]

The entry of the United States into the world conflict in April of 1917 exacerbated the existing problems of the railroads and presented new challenges. The war generated a flood of freight heading to Atlantic ports. Traffic congestion in these terminals caused a freight car shortage elsewhere. Despite efforts at cooperation, railroad companies found it difficult to coordinate their lines or provide efficient service. Not only were individual carriers reluctant to relinquish competitive advantages, but threatened enforcement of the antitrust laws hampered the ability of the railroads to work together. The result was increasing confusion and a virtual collapse of the rail system during the late fall of 1917.[2] On December 1, the Interstate Commerce Commission suggested that the president take control and operate the nation's railroads. Railroads faulted the ICC's parsimonious rate policy for the breakdown. But the carriers cannot escape any responsibility. Harold U. Faulkner has observed: "The blame in varying degrees had to be shared: neither federal legislators nor railroad management had handled the railroad problem wisely for the benefit of the nation."[3] However one assigns blame, few disputed that the rail system was ill prepared to handle the unprecedented demands of wartime transportation.

Anticipating a possible emergency, Congress had empowered the president in the Army Appropriation Act of 1916 to assume control of the transportation system in the event of war. Invoking this statutory authority, President Woodrow Wilson issued a proclamation on December 26, 1917, placing railroads under government control. He named William G. McAdoo, the secretary of the treasury, as Director General of Railroads. The president commended rail managers for their efforts to meet the nation's wartime transportation needs, but explained that he acted to organize and coordinate railroads under a common authority.[4]

Federal Control

Government operation of the railroads raised several legal questions. Foremost among them was protection of the property rights of the carriers. Wilson stated in his proclamation that the governmental action would not impair the rights of stockholders or creditors "to receive just and adequate compensation for the use and control . . . of their property." Since, as the Supreme Court later pointed out, the government was acting under a right in the nature of eminent domain, compensation for the taking of property was required under the Fifth Amendment.[5] Ratifying the president's seizure, Congress in the Federal Control Act of 1917 addressed a number of issues pertaining to the property rights of the parties. The act provided that (1) railroads should receive as compensation an income equal to their average net operating income for the three years ending June 30, 1917; (2) that railroad property would be returned to the carriers "in substantially as good repair and in substantially as complete equipment" as at the beginning of federal control; (3) that the government should be reimbursed for improvements "not justly chargeable to the United States"; (4) that any income earned during the period of federal control belonged to the government; and (5) that federal control would expire twenty-one months after the end of the war.[6] To implement these guarantees, the government entered into contracts with most railroad companies detailing their rights.

After the carriers were returned to private management in 1920, the government and railroads wrestled for years to adjust claims for compensation. Since the government was making payment for temporary use of the property, the appropriate measure of compensation was a knotty question. There was no precedent involving the temporary taking of such complex properties. The government was not acquiring the carriers outright, and it was in a sense a compulsory tenant paying rent. In such a situation, just compensation was the value of the use of the property. While not perfect, the three-year base period set in the Federal Control Act appeared reasonably equitable. Utilizing this formula, the government paid more than \$2 billion in compensation for the temporary taking of the railroads.[7]

Claims for inadequate maintenance by the government were not so substantial but were more hotly contested. Many railroads suffered physically from the heavy wartime traffic and alleged that their property was returned in inferior condition.[8] Problems abounded in determining the scope of the government's maintenance obligation. The sudden imposition of government control had precluded any precontrol assessment of the physical condition of individual railroads. Hence, there was no convenient standard of reference regarding physical deterioration of rail property under government management. For its part, the government sought to charge the railroads for new equipment purchased and structures built to expedite the movement of traffic. The carriers objected to many of these items on grounds they were of no value upon the return to private control.[9]

Following lengthy investigations, the various claims for compensation were resolved by negotiation, not litigation. All parties desired to avoid protracted and unpredictable lawsuits. The railroads were also anxious to receive a prompt infusion of capital. As then Director General James C. Davis explained:

> The carriers, in the midst of the reorganization period incident to the disorganizing effect of Federal control, were surely in need of ready money, and the Government was anxious to dispose of the just claims incident to the war. . . . It was a situation that called for the exercise of a decent spirit of adjustment by both parties, and in the end this attitude prevailed.[10]

Eventually, the claims for undermaintenance by the government were settled, with the government paying more than \$200 million for wear and tear and loss of equipment.[11]

The record suggests that Congress and governmental officials conscientiously wrestled with the novel and vexing issues of just compensation arising from the temporary takeover of the nation's railroads. They sought to fashion rules that would fairly vindicate the constitutional right of private property and the principle of just compensation in unique wartime circumstances.

In addition to raising questions of property rights and just compensation, the period of federal control had important implications for the ratemaking process. The Federal Control Act authorized the president to initiate rate changes. The ICC could review these rates upon complaint, but could not suspend them pending a final determination as to their reasonableness. Congress also directed the ICC to "give due consideration to the fact that the transportation systems are being operated under a unified and coordinated national control and not in competition." Faced with rapidly escalating costs and generally rising prices, McAdoo ordered a sizeable across-the-board rate increase for freight and passengers in May 1918. Yet another increase would be mandated before federal control ended. Although these steps were in marked contrast to the ICC's stand-pat refusal to advance rates for years, the agency did not review the new rates. Despite the protest of shippers, the government largely bypassed the ICC during the period of federal control. This action by the government tended to substantiate the railroad's prewar contention that they needed additional revenue to maintain efficient service.[12]

Federal control also eroded state regulatory authority over railroads. At issue in *Northern Pacific Railway Corporation v. North Dakota* (1919) was an attempt by the state to compel a carrier to follow the lower state-imposed rate for intrastate shipments rather than the charges fixed by the Director General. In sweeping language the Supreme Court adjudged that the Federal Control Act marked a fundamental change in rail governance and gave the president power to set both interstate and intrastate rates. Stressing the need for unified control of railroad operations, the Court held that the president could supersede state regulations. This decision was a harbinger of further displacement of state power over railroad charges in the Transportation Act of 1920.

One of the most controversial aspects of federal control was the labor policy.[13] The law governing labor relations in the rail industry is treated in Chapter Twelve, but it would be profitable to sketch McAdoo's approach to labor issues here. The Director General faced a shortage of railroad employees, due in part to the military draft and the higher wages paid by other war-related industries. Above all, McAdoo was determined to maintain labor peace and avoid disruptive strikes.

McAdoo responded to this situation with a series of far-reaching concessions that transformed labor conditions on the nation's railroads. He ordered a substantial wage increase in April 1918. Other wage hikes followed. The Adamson Act had already established the eight-hour workday for operating employees, such as engineers, firemen, and conductors. McAdoo extended the eight-hour day to all rail employees, and standardized wages across the country. He also encouraged collective bargaining by banning discrimination against union members. This inspired additional groups of rail employees to organize. The Director General mandated equal pay for black and women workers.

In a more questionable move, McAdoo established an elaborate system of defining and classifying jobs.[14] He prohibited employees from performing the work assigned to another class. In some situations railroads were required to divide jobs among employees. The job classification system inevitably added to labor cost and reduced flexibility in the workplace. Further, the work rules instituted by the Director General would lead in time to a bitter dispute over featherbedding. As technology rendered certain jobs obsolete, the overly precise classification of rail work generated conflict when employers moved to eliminate antiquated positions.

All told, the generous wage advances and encouragement of union growth caused labor costs to rise dramatically during the period of federal control. Adoption of the eight-hour day generated a marked increase in the number of railroad employees. The exigencies of war and the need for uninterrupted rail service greatly augmented union power. Consequently, railroad managers were unhappy to inherit a more unionized and costly labor force from the period of federal control. Escalating wages also contributed to the government's deficit in operating the railroads and explain McAdoo's willingness to raise rates.

The government compiled a mixed record in its management of railroads during World War I. Viewed from an operational perspective, federal control successfully served the nation's wartime needs. McAdoo eliminated traffic congestion, streamlined service, and upgraded equipment and rolling stock. It is doubtful that private managers could have handled the difficult situation more effectively. Nonetheless, between the money paid to the railroads for use of their property and huge operating losses, governmental control proved an expensive endeavor. Even recognizing that the government did not take over the railroads to earn a profit, the financial dimensions of federal control were sobering. Despite much-touted efficiencies of common direction, railroads under government management failed to pay their way.[15]

Once the war ended, there was a wide-ranging public debate over the future of the railroads. McAdoo urged that federal control be extended until 1924 in order to stabilize the industry during a period of reconstruction. More radical were calls for nationalization. Labor unions, which had prospered under federal control, promoted government ownership of railroads. They rallied behind a plan prepared by Glenn E. Plumb, a union attorney. He recommended that the federal government issue bonds, purchase railroads with the proceeds, and lease the lines to a public corporation to run. Similarly, ICC Commissioner Joseph B. Eastman felt that government ownership would provide a long-term solution to railroad problems.[16]

However, Congress and much of the public had become increasingly disenchanted with federal administration of the carriers. Shippers fretted that government control had produced higher rates. A shopmen's strike in 1919 convinced many that rail unions were too powerful. Moreover, government ownership ran counter to the deep-seated American preference for private enterprise. Reflecting this attitude, lawmakers showed no interest in nationalization. As early as December 1918, President Wilson indicated that the railroads were to be returned to their owners, a course of action strongly favored by the rail companies. The president asked Congress to carefully evaluate policy alternatives with respect to railroads. Wilson pointedly remarked that "it would be a disservice alike to the country and to the owners of the railroads to return to the old conditions unmodified."[17] A year later, Wilson issued a proclamation under the Federal Control Act that federal management would end March 1, 1920. The timing of the transfer of the carriers back to private hands was set to coincide with a comprehensive overhaul of rail regulations by Congress. After months of debate Congress made yet another effort to formulate national railroad policy by passing the Transportation Act of 1920.

Transportation Act of 1920

The culmination of the prolonged debate over federal railroad regulations, the Transportation Act of 1920 was a curious Janus-faced measure. It contained a mixture of backward-looking and innovative features. Like the Interstate Commerce Act of 1887, the Transportation Act was a compromise between quite different House and Senate bills.[18] One historian asserted that the act "involved no fundamental changes in the regulatory system,"[19] and certainly the ICC retained its rate-regulation function. Still, the act was less focused on perceived railroad abuses and contained a number of provisions designed to help carriers attain financial stability. Congress seemed to implicitly recognize that the Progressive-Era legislation had not worked well, but the remedy was to impose heightened regulations. Surprisingly, no thought was evidently given to deregulation.

In contrast to earlier railroad legislation, the Transportation Act marked a dramatic departure from the policy of fostering competition. Instead, as Maury Klein observed, "the act sought to create a protected cartel under tight regulation."[20] Congress authorized railroads to enter pooling agreements if the ICC determined that service would be improved and competition would not be "unduly" curtailed. The commission was empowered to set minimum as well as maximum charges. Intended to protect weak lines from price competition, this provision hampered the railroads in competing for business with the emerging trucking industry. Influenced by the wartime experience, the act sought to encourage the consolidation of carriers into a limited number of systems. It was hoped that consolidation would alleviate the problem of financially troubled lines and promote efficiency. Congress directed the ICC to formulate a consolidation plan, but did not give the agency power to compel mergers. Further, the act required ICC approval for the construction of new trackage. According to the Supreme Court, Congress acknowledged that "the building of unnecessary lines involves a waste of resources and that the burden of this waste may fall upon the public."[21] The ICC could thus restrict entry into the rail industry and prevent competition with existing carriers.

Another legislative change from prior practice involved the ICC's rate-making authority. Congress mandated that the commission consider the revenue needs of the carriers in setting rates. The ICC was compelled to set rates at a level that would provide "a fair return on the aggregate value" of railroad property. Moreover, the act gave the commission greater flexibility in applying the long haul–short haul clause. Equally important, the act reduced the power of the states over railroad charges by authorizing the ICC to review and override intrastate rates that discriminated against interstate commerce. This provision was based on the premise that intrastate commerce should contribute fairly to the cost of maintaining the rail system. Noting that low intrastate rates increased the burden on interstate traffic, the Supreme Court in *Railroad Commission of Wisconsin v. Chicago, Burlington & Quincy Railroad Company* (1922) upheld the power of the ICC to order increases in state rates and stressed the paramount authority of Congress to protect and develop national commerce. Consequently, the long-running battle between the states and railroads over rate regulation came to an effective end. State controls ceased to be an important element and rarely produced litigation.[22]

The most disputed provision of the Transportation Act was the recapture clause. Allied to the statutory emphasis on consolidation, the recapture clause represented a kind of relief fund for financially distressed lines. The ICC was ordered to recapture half of the net earnings of any carrier earning more than 6 percent on its investment. An individual carrier receiving such excess was deemed to hold it as a trustee for the United States. The recaptured money was to be placed in a trust fund and loaned to weak lines for the purpose of making improvements. To this extent, the act treated railroads as a group.

Although relatively few railroads were so profitable as to be subject to the recapture clause, the provision raised a host of issues. The obvious purpose was to compel the more profitable lines to subsidize their weaker counterparts. In 1924 the Supreme Court, however, brushed aside the argument that the clause constituted an unconstitutional taking of property. Writing for the Court, Chief Justice William Howard Taft asserted that railroads were only entitled to a fair return on their investment and that hence they did not have title to the excess. Congress, he maintained, could devote this money to the better development of national transportation.[23] Despite judicial validation, the recapture clause proved difficult to administer and engendered lawsuits. In order to calculate recapturable excess income, the ICC first had to ascertain the property value of railroad companies. Profitable lines contested valuation decisions and sought ways to secret income. The recapture clause also made no provision to average the income in good and bad years. Relatively little income was actually recaptured for the trust fund. Historians have universally viewed the recapture clause as a failure. In 1930 the ICC urged repeal of the clause, and Congress took this step in 1933.[24]

A central feature of the Transportation Act was the enhanced power of the ICC. The act, the Supreme Court declared, "seeks affirmatively to build up a system of railways prepared to handle promptly all the interstate traffic of the nation." Unlike some decisions in the late nineteenth and early twentieth centuries that had adopted a narrow reading of ICC authority, the Court now stressed the vast responsibility of the commission. "To achieve this great purpose," the Court explained in 1924, the act "puts the railroad systems of the country more completely than ever under the fostering guardianship and control of the Commission."[25] Nearly every aspect of railroad policy was subject to ICC review. In addition to the duties already discussed, the ICC was empowered to supervise the abandonment of lines, to mandate that carriers provide adequate service, to approve mergers, and to regulate railroad securities. On its face, therefore, the act gave the ICC almost plenary authority over the rail industry. By the 1920s courts were favorably disposed toward the regulation of carriers by an administrative agency. How well the ICC discharged its enlarged responsibilities is considered in Chapter Thirteen.

Concerned as much with fostering the rail industry as with redressing shipper complaints, the Transportation Act was more balanced and evenhanded than the laws of the Progressive Era. Although opposed by some old Progressives, such as Robert M. LaFollette, the measure easily passed Congress. Declaring that "adequate transportation service both for the present and the future can be furnished more certainly, economically and efficiently through private ownership," the Republican national platform of 1920 endorsed the act "as a most constructive legislative achievement." Despite the additional curtailment of private management by the act, many railroad executives were also guardedly upbeat about the measure. The president of the Louisville and Nashville Railroad declared in 1926 that the act "represents a tremendous advance in the scientific regulation of the railroads."[26]

World War I deepened the involvement of the federal government in the economy and boosted confidence in administrative agencies. Railroads were, as usual, in the forefront of these developments, and to some extent victims of them. Despite the disappointing results of the Progressive-Era legislation, Congress remained convinced about the efficacy of regulation. With the Transportation Act, Congress proceeded on the theory that railroads constituted a de facto transportation monopoly that warranted close public control. But the assumptions behind the act were soon undermined as other forms of transportation grew rapidly during the 1920s. In this new and more competitive world, the restrictive features of the Transportation Act badly hurt the very industry it was intended to assist.[27] As is so often the case, legislators and regulators were preoccupied with yesterday's issues, and displayed no clairvoyant grasp of the future.

12

Tangled Labor Relations

A s with so many areas of law, railroads were instrumental in the development of national labor policy. Given the unique importance of railroading to the national economy, the public clearly had a strong interest in
preventing disruptions in service caused by labor disputes. Consequently,
much of the early law governing unions, strikes, and labor injunctions was
fashioned with railroads in mind. Starting in the late nineteenth century, the
federal government was increasingly drawn into railroad strikes that threatened the flow of traffic in interstate commerce.

Labor law evolved slowly in the nineteenth century, and was at first
largely the province of state courts and legislatures. Even after the famous
decision of *Commonwealth v. Hunt* (1842), in which the Supreme Judicial
Court of Massachusetts rejected the doctrine that combinations of workers
constituted a criminal conspiracy, neither the mood of the nation nor the
legal system was supportive of organized labor. Industrialization, however,
brought about fundamental changes in the workplace. Employees worked in
an impersonal and often dangerous environment, and had little bargaining
power to shape the conditions of employment.

Consistent with the experience in a wide range of other industries, the
more skilled railroad employees were the first to organize. In the 1860s and
1870s the operating employees—engineers, firemen, and conductors—created
brotherhoods. Initially formed for benevolent purposes, these essentially craft
organizations preferred to avoid outright conflict with rail management. But
they eventually functioned as a type of nascent labor union. Most railroad
employees, however, were not members of any organization.

Era of Turbulent Strikes

The depression of the 1870s set in motion events that helped to establish an
unhappy pattern of confrontational labor relations. Faced with declining traffic and revenue, carriers instituted a policy of cutting wages to hold down

costs. Wage reductions increased labor militancy. There were several brief work stoppages in the mid-1870s.[1] State lawmakers responded with laws designed to suppress railroad strikes. A number of states, including Pennsylvania and Michigan, enacted measures punishing the obstruction of train operations.[2] As indicated by these statutes, governments in the late nineteenth century relied on the coercive power of law to prevent the interruption of rail service.

This policy would be tested by the great strikes of 1877, a violent conflict of unprecedented magnitude.[3] In May 1877 the Pennsylvania Railroad announced a second 10 percent wage reduction. Other eastern carriers soon followed suit. A spontaneous strike began on the Baltimore and Ohio Railroad in July and soon engulfed much of the rail network. Although the national leaders of the brotherhoods publicly took no part, the strikers successfully halted rail traffic in much of the nation. Tensions mounted, and the governors of several states summoned the militia. The strikes in some cities quickly assumed the character of riots and there was massive destruction of railroad property. Pittsburgh was the scene of a pitched battle between the militia and rioters, and there was widespread looting and burning of railroad cars and buildings. In some communities the crowds were swelled by persons who were not strikers but who harbored a deep resentment at railroad operations on city streets.[4]

Unable or unwilling to control the riots with the militia, the governors of West Virginia, Pennsylvania, and other states called upon President Rutherford B. Hayes to dispatch federal troops to restore order. Hayes acted cautiously and did not assert any general authority to safeguard interstate commerce. He scrutinized the applications for federal assistance carefully and insisted that governors certify that they could not suppress a domestic insurrection. That done, Hayes sent federal troops to several states. In most instances, however, the federal soldiers did not arrive until after the rioting had subsided. The president was in an unenviable spot. Railroad executives grumbled that Hayes should have acted more swiftly, while strike sympathizers charged that he was partial to the railroad companies. Federal troops had been utilized previously to protect property and restore order, but Hayes's trailblazing action was the first time federal soldiers had been sent to halt disturbances growing out of a labor conflict.[5]

Another significant legal development involved federal court sanctions against strikes directed at railroads in receivership. Federal judges in Illinois and Indiana ruled that any action that interfered with the operation of lines in receivership was contempt of court. They reasoned that a strike represented a wrongful disturbance of property held by a receiver, and thus obstructed the administration of justice. A number of strikers were found guilty of contempt and imprisoned. Under this doctrine, as a practical matter, strikes against lines in judicial custody were banned.[6] One historian aptly stated that these decisions "had turned all receivership orders into standing injunctions against strikes."[7] Since numerous railroads were operated by receivers in the late nineteenth century, this doctrine was a potentially broad check to work stoppages. Moreover, the use of the contempt penalty against strikers laid the basis for the future grant of labor injunctions.

By the end of July, the wave of strikes and riots began to lose steam and the carriers resumed operation. The toll exacted by the strike was staggering. More than one hundred persons were dead. Property damage in Baltimore, Chicago, St. Louis, Reading, and other communities was estimated at millions of dollars. The outcome of the strike could be seen as inconclusive. Some strikers were fired, but the practice of wage-cutting was stopped. The great strikes of 1877 sparked calls for the federal government to protect interstate commerce, but there was no agreement as to an appropriate course of action. Neither President Hayes nor Congress showed an inclination to investigate the strikes or fashion a federal labor policy.[8]

Still, the legal ramifications of the great strikes were significant. It established a precedent for the deployment of the federal military in labor disputes. It saw federal judges interject themselves as a key influence in labor relations. It dramatically underscored the fact that railroad labor disputes would typically present problems with a national dimension.

Many carriers in the Gilded Age adopted tactics designed to check the growth of unions—maintenance of blacklists and the use of contracts that made it a condition of employment that workers not belong to any union. Suspected union members or organizers, except for the brotherhoods, were commonly discharged and their names placed on a blacklist. Such lists were circulated to other lines, and had the effect of preventing blacklisted persons from finding employment elsewhere in the rail industry. The blacklist was a means of controlling the workforce. It deserves mention, however, that striking or union activity was only one cause of blacklisting. Most blacklisted employees were proscribed for disciplinary infractions, such as drunkenness on the job or neglect of duty.[9] Employees who signed so-called yellow-dog contracts forbidding union membership could be discharged for violating their terms of employment. It was a common practice for carriers to engage in a wholesale dismissal of strikers.

The nation continued to experience labor unrest on the railways during the 1880s. There was a series of strikes in 1885 and 1886 orchestrated by the Knights of Labor against several carriers in the Southwest controlled by financier Jay Gould. The most important legal consequence was a ringing affirmation of the willingness of federal judges to safeguard railroads in receivership from strike activity. Finding a group of strikers to be in contempt for obstructing receivers in their management of a carrier, Judge David J. Brewer (later named to the Supreme Court) explained: "It is not the mere stopping of work themselves, but it is preventing the owners of the road from managing their own engines and running their own cars. That is where the wrong comes in."[10]

A new chapter in the evolution of railroad labor law began with a strike over wage rates against the Chicago, Burlington & Quincy Railroad. As the strike appeared to flounder, the engineers union asked its members elsewhere to decline to move Burlington cars. This secondary boycott threatened to expand the strike to any lines that handled Burlington traffic. The Burlington, however, obtained federal court orders enjoining other carriers from refusing to exchange cars with the struck line. Judges stressed the duty of common carriers to transport goods and passengers, and expressed determination to protect the public from interruptions of rail service. These injunctions deepened the involvement of the federal courts in railroad labor conflicts. Courts were prepared to act whether or not the lines were in the hands of a receiver. Moreover, they made clear that injunctive power would be used to guard railroads, as instruments of interstate commerce, against secondary boycotts.[11]

In addition to strengthening the role of the federal courts as protectors of carriers against work stoppages, the Burlington strike produced the first timid step by Congress to address railway labor problems. The Arbitration Act of 1888 provided for voluntary arbitration and authorized the president to appoint a commission to investigate the causes of labor controversies. Rarely invoked, the act proved entirely ineffective.[12] Since Congress had neglected to create any machinery to resolve labor problems, the initiative in determining policy remained with the federal courts and the executive branch. They were concerned above all with preventing strikes and boycotts from obstructing commerce.

The famous Pullman strike of 1894 looms large in American labor history. It marked the culmination of nearly two decades of increasingly bitter conflicts between railroads and workers. There is a sizeable literature examining different aspects of this complex saga,[13] but our concern is primarily with the legal dimensions of the Pullman strike. Trends already noted—the growing use of injunctions against railroad strikes and the commitment of federal troops in labor disputes—would mesh to crush the Pullman strikers and shape the environment for the emergence of modern railroad labor law in the early twentieth century.

Angered by an imposed wage reduction, the employees of the Pullman Palace Car Company went on strike. The newly organized American Railway Union, under the leadership of Eugene V. Debs, supported the strikers by engaging in a secondary boycott and refusing to handle trains with Pullman cars. To make the work stoppage effective, strikers and sympathizers forcibly blocked railroad transportation and the passage of mail through Chicago. This action in late June paralyzed much of the national rail transportation network. President Grover Cleveland ordered federal troops into Chicago, although no rioting had yet occurred, in order to ensure that trains moved. This triggered mob disturbances and destruction of hundreds of rail cars. Matters rapidly spun out of control. As violence spread from Chicago westward to California,[14] the Cleveland administration obtained a sweeping injunction from the federal circuit court in Chicago. The court ordered union officials and all persons conspiring with them to cease hindering any train operating in interstate commerce or carrying the mail. This injunction, coupled with the military intervention, broke the strike by late July. The strikers returned to work. Debs and other union leaders were subsequently found guilty of contempt of court for disregarding the injunction and were imprisoned. They applied to the Supreme Court for a writ of habeas corpus.

Speaking for a unanimous Court in the case of *In re Debs* (1895), Justice Brewer denied the writ and forcefully asserted federal authority "to brush away all obstructions to the freedom of interstate commerce or the transportation of the mails."[15] Invoking the public nuisance doctrine, he declared that the government could summon military force to compel obedience to law. Brewer broadly upheld the equitable jurisdiction of the federal courts to prevent unlawful interference with commerce. He sustained injunctive relief on the basis of both the government's property interest in the mails and the sovereign power to protect the general welfare. Rendered long after the Pullman strike had ended, the *Debs* opinion was most significant for placing the Supreme Court's imprimatur on the growing use of labor injunctions.[16]

Toward Railroad Labor Legislation

Although the Supreme Court vindicated the extraordinary efforts of the president and federal judges to halt the Pullman boycott, the turmoil aroused interest in devising a better structure for resolving railroad strikes. "The only question," Herbert Hovenkamp observed "was whether to use a carrot or a stick."[17] A commission appointed by President Cleveland to investigate the strike made a number of recommendations to handle future labor disputes.

After years of debate, Congress passed the Erdman Act in 1898.[18] Covering only "train service" employees, the act authorized the chairman of the Interstate Commerce Commission and the commissioner of labor to mediate labor disputes upon the request of either party. If mediation failed, they could recommend arbitration by a special commission. Arbitration decisions were enforceable in court and binding for one year. The Erdman Act also outlawed the use of yellow-dog contracts and blacklists by employers, implicitly recognizing the right of operating rail employees to join unions. It further prohibited railroads from requiring workers to contribute to health insurance funds.

Enacted in reaction to the Pullman strike and designed to prevent a recurrence of such a disturbance, the Erdman Act was far from perfect. The arbitration mechanism was voluntary, and was virtually ignored until 1906. Thereafter a number of disputes were settled by mediation or arbitration under the act.[19] In *Adair v. United States* (1908), the Supreme Court struck down the portion of the Erdman Act that made it a crime for a railroad to discharge an employee because of his membership in a union. Finding no connection between interstate commerce and union membership, the Court reasoned that the provision infringed the liberty of contract as guaranteed by the Fifth Amendment. Dissenting, Justice Oliver Wendell Holmes, Jr., argued that Congress might reasonably conclude that fostering unions would help prevent strikes. The *Adair* ruling weakened the protection accorded organized labor by the act. For all its limitations, however, the Erdman Act did represent a turning point of sorts. It recognized that injunctions and military force to suppress strikes were not sound answers in the long term to resolve railroad labor problems. "In many ways," Shelton Stromquist stated, "the Erdman Act symbolized the emergence of a new framework for railroad labor relations, at least for the Big Four brotherhoods of operating employees."[20]

Legislative efforts to head off rail strikes intensified in the early twentieth century. The Newlands Act of 1913 established permanent mediation and arbitration boards, but continued to rely on voluntary agreements to accept arbitration. Mediation and arbitration under the Newlands Act were successful in a number of instances.[21] But the arbitration procedures failed to resolve the major controversy in 1916 over the demands by the operating brotherhoods for an eight-hour day instead of the ten-hour standard. The companies strongly resisted a payroll increase at the very time when the ICC was holding down rates. Thus, the carriers could not adjust their prices to reflect the rising cost of labor. The rail unions rejected arbitration and threatened a strike to gain their objectives. With World War I raging in Europe, President Woodrow Wilson sought to forestall the strike by asking Congress to mandate an eight-hour day for those employees who operated trains. Congress passed the Adamson Act embodying the president's proposal. The effect was that overtime compensation would now be computed after eight, rather than ten, hours of work a day for those workers who ran trains, already the best compensated of rail labor.[22]

As Congress and the president became more involved in railroad labor disputes, the federal courts had correspondingly less opportunity to shape policy. The Adamson Act inaugurated a pattern of preventing strikes by enacting new railroad labor legislation. A sharply divided Supreme Court upheld the validity of the measure in *Wilson v. New* (1917). The majority concluded that Congress, under the commerce clause, was empowered in an emergency arising from a nationwide dispute over wages "to compulsorily arbitrate the dispute between the parties by establishing . . . a legislative standard of wages . . . binding as a matter of law upon the parties."[23] This was the first in a series of Supreme Court decisions sanctioning the authority of Congress to regulate labor relations in the rail industry. It was in sharp contrast to the Court's reluctance to acknowledge congressional power over other aspects of the economy.

After World War I, Congress moved to encourage the growth of rail unions and to curtail strikes. Title III of the Transportation Act of 1920, which covered all interstate railroad workers, provided that unresolved disputes over wages and working conditions should be decided by the newly created Railroad Labor Board. Composed of employer, labor, and public representatives, the board heard several thousand cases by 1925. But, as the Supreme Court made clear, the board had no enforcement authority. Rather, Congress expected that the board's decisions would be sustained by the force of public opinion directed against the party at fault in the dispute. Nor did Title III require a railroad company to deal with a union of its employees.[24]

A decision by the Railroad Labor Board precipitated the first nationwide rail strike since 1894. Recall that the private managers inherited from the period of federal control an enlarged and expensive workforce as well as restrictive work rules. Weathering a recession in 1921, the railroads persuaded the Labor Board to order a wage reduction, effective in July 1922, for shopmen. There were more than 400,000 shopmen, including mechanics, boilermakers, and electricians, who repaired and maintained locomotives and rolling stock. The wage cut triggered a strike by shopmen. To ensure continued rail service in the face of the walkout, carriers hired replacement workers and augmented their force of guards. The strike was accompanied by widespread violence and sabotage. As railroad operations deteriorated and fuel shortages developed, President Warren Harding attempted unsuccessfully to broker a negotiated settlement.[25]

Meanwhile, the railroads turned to the federal courts for assistance. They obtained numerous injunctions that prohibited strikers from trespassing on rail property or engaging in violent conduct. Anxious to end the strike, the Harding administration eventually decided to use the stick. In September it obtained from Judge James H. Wilkinson "one of the most sweeping federal injunctions in U.S. history."[26] Wilkinson found that the strikers were engaged in a conspiracy to interrupt commerce, to disregard the decision of the Railroad Labor Board, and to harass replacement workers in violation of the Sherman Anti-Trust Act. Accordingly, he enjoined the strikers from hindering the railroads from repairing equipment, and from acts of intimidation or picketing near railroad property. In addition, Wilkinson sought to undercut the strike by ordering strikers not to ask other workers to cease work and by ordering unions not to spend money in support of the strike. Reminiscent of the earlier *Debs* injunction, the Wilkinson order was more expansive in its scope and even seemed to curtail freedom of speech.[27] The Wilkinson injunction was instrumental in breaking the strike. Fearful of losing their jobs, shopmen gradually began to return to work.

Following the 1922 strike, there was widespread appreciation that Title III was inadequate to handle railroad labor disputes and to prevent disruption of commerce. The political platforms of both major parties in 1924 expressed dissatisfaction with the existing law. "Collective bargaining, voluntary mediation and arbitration," the Republicans declared, "are the most important steps in maintaining peaceful labor relations." They added that "public opinion must be the final arbiter" in any crisis involving the suspension of transportation. President Calvin Coolidge invited rail management and unions to recommend legislation that would improve labor relations. The product of prolonged negotiations, the Railway Labor Act of 1926 (RLA) passed Congress by wide margins in both houses. Despite frequent complaints that the RLA is ineffective and outdated, it has proven remarkably resilient.

Railway Labor Act

The Railway Labor Act was the culmination of decades of experimentation with laws designed to promote the peaceful resolution of rail labor conflicts. To this end, Congress in the RLA fashioned a detailed framework to settle disputes.[28] The act was premised on the notion that the negotiation of collective bargaining agreements was the key to stable labor relations. It was the first federal law to guarantee the right of workers to organize without employer interference. In 1930 the Supreme Court upheld the power of Congress to protect the right of employees to select their own representatives, holding that "Congress may facilitate the amicable settlement of disputes that threaten the service of the necessary agencies of interstate transportation."[29]

The RLA did not undertake to regulate wages or working conditions. Rather, it placed upon carriers and employees the duty of making reasonable efforts to reach agreement. Controversies arising out of the formation or alteration of collective bargaining agreements—termed "major disputes"—are governed by one set of procedures. If a panoply of negotiation and mediation mechanisms fail, the act provides for a series of thirty-day cooling-off periods during which the parties must maintain the status quo. The hope, as the Supreme Court explained, was that such delay "helps to create an atmosphere in which rational bargaining can occur, and permits the forces of public opinion to be mobilized in favor of a settlement without a strike or lockout." Once these procedures are exhausted, both unions and railroads are free to resort to self-help. Disputes relating to the interpretation of existing contracts—"minor disputes"—are handled quite differently. Unsettled minor disputes are subject to compulsory arbitration under the auspices of the National Railway Adjustment Board and strikes over such issues are prohibited.[30]

At the behest of unions, the RLA was amended in 1934. The changes established procedures to resolve representation disputes. The amendment also made more explicit employer actions that interfered with the employees' right to organize, and again outlawed the practice of requiring workers to promise not to join unions. It further mandated that rail companies negotiate only with the selected representative of the employees. The Supreme Court had no difficulty in upholding the constitutionality of the 1934 amendments as within the power of Congress to curb strikes on interstate railroads.[31]

Another issue presented by the RLA was the role of state law in labor disputes. Since railroad controversies typically present national problems, courts construed the RLA to restrict the application of state law. For example, the arbitration procedures of the act have been deemed to preempt state tort claims for wrongful discharge. Similarly, the right of employees to strike and picket is protected by the RLA from state restrictions.[32]

Whatever its shortcomings, the RLA was a pioneering measure. It established collective bargaining and the right of employees to organize in the rail industry a decade before such rights were generally recognized. It also attested to the belief that the rail system occupied a unique position in the national economy and required special labor laws.

Later Labor Disputes

Between the late 1920s and World War II there were no major rail strikes, while other industries were experiencing considerable labor unrest. In this era the RLA briefly enjoyed a deceptive reputation as a "model" labor law. But renewed strife during and after World War II made plain the limitations of the act. Increasingly, threatened strikes were not resolved within the framework of the RLA but by presidential or congressional action.

This interventionist pattern emerged during World War II. The federal government adopted the policy of taking temporary possession of business enterprises to forestall work stoppages. These "seizures" were more technical than substantive because in most cases the private managers continued to operate under governmental supervision. Seizures were initially based on the president's authority as commander-in-chief, but the War Disputes Act of 1943 empowered the president to take possession of any facility necessary for the war effort.[33] In December 1943 President Franklin D. Roosevelt seized the rail system to prevent a strike. He relinquished federal control a few weeks later, once agreements were reached.[34] This reliance on seizures to deal with labor disputes continued after the war. For example, in May 1946 President Harry S. Truman seized the nation's railroads to block an announced walkout. It was in this context that Truman made his controversial proposal to draft striking rail workers into the armed forces. There was yet another government takeover in 1950. Seizures by the federal government preserved uninterrupted rail service, but shifted the responsibility for settlements away from the mechanism of the RLA and to the political branches. Negotiations between rail companies and unions became perfunctory, as all parties awaited executive or legislative intervention.[35] Maury Klein aptly noted that "by 1949 it was manifest that the Act was an inadequate piece of legislation to mediate the escalating strife between management and labor."[36]

In the 1950s a prolonged dispute over fossilized work rules and featherbedding came to the fore. As the industry entered a period of sharp decline, rail companies were determined to reduce high labor costs. Automation rendered certain jobs, especially that of firemen on diesel engines, archaic. But lengthy negotiations were unable to make any headway in breaking the deadlock over this issue. In 1963 Congress averted a strike over work rules by imposing the first peacetime compulsory arbitration. Over the next three decades Congress repeatedly intervened with special legislation in the case of threatened rail strikes. There has been a trend toward imposing arbitration on an ad hoc basis. Thus, in 1991 and 1992 Congress utilized compulsory arbitration of unresolved issues to head off nationwide strikes. This scenario underscored congressional determination to prevent an interruption of rail service, but also bypassed the RLA and collective bargaining.

Full-Crew Laws

Closely allied to the prolonged dispute over featherbedding and work rules was the union-driven campaign to enact state full-crew laws. As the Supreme Court observed in 1966: "the problem of manning trains has presented an issue of constant dispute between the railroads and the unions."[37] This issue again pitted advancing technology against job security, a conflict that was particularly acute in the rail industry. The first law mandating the size of a train crew was passed in Arkansas in 1907.[38] Ostensibly justified as a safety regulation, this statute required three brakemen on all freight trains. The railroads countered that such legislation was unnecessary and expensive, particularly in view of the adoption of air brakes and automatic couplers. In *Chicago, Rock Island and Pacific Railway Company v. Arkansas* (1911), however, the Supreme Court sustained the full-crew law as an exercise of state police power to promote public and employee safety. It brushed aside the argument that the statute burdened interstate commerce.

During the early twentieth century a number of states, including New York, Massachusetts, California, and Wisconsin, enacted similar laws.[39] Most of this type of legislation was passed before 1920. The carriers renewed their challenge to the constitutionality of full-crew provisions in *Missouri Pacific Railroad Company v. Norwood* (1931). Emphasizing changed conditions and improved equipment, they insisted that the law imposed needless expense and was so arbitrary as to violate the due process clause. Although acknowledging that the cost of complying with state safety requirements could be considered in determining due process violations, the Court adhered to its prior decision and once more upheld the statute. These rulings in favor of such a dubious law belie the casual notion that the Supreme Court was a kind of handmaiden for the rail industry.

The shift to diesel locomotives after World War II eliminated most of the functions performed by firemen on steam engines. In the 1950s and 1960s financially hard-pressed carriers launched a campaign to eliminate the firemen from diesel trains.[40] In this connection they took special aim at the full-crew laws, which mandated the employment of a fireman on trains. Many states repealed these measures, and by 1968 only seven jurisdictions retained some sort of full-crew laws for freight trains. The railroads also mounted another round of legal attacks, but obtained scant relief from the courts. The

Supreme Court ruled that the 1963 act imposing binding arbitration over the use of firemen was not intended to supersede state laws on the subject.[41] This result, of course, frustrated attempts to achieve a nationwide solution of the issue.

Lower federal and state courts compiled a mixed record in evaluating full-crew laws. Courts in Indiana, Wisconsin, and New York generally sustained the validity of the statutes, as reasonably related to safety, and rejected the argument that technological advances were sufficient to render the statutes arbitrary and unconstitutional. Perhaps the carriers derived some comfort from the dissenting opinion in the New York Court of Appeals that asserted that "the sole purpose of the full crew law today" was to legislate featherbedding, not to promote safety.[42]

There was clearly a make-work dimension to the full-crew laws. As numerous studies pointed out, these laws did not envision modern rail operations and placed a heavy financial burden on an industry that was facing competitive pressure from other modes of transportation.[43] Congress belatedly perceived that the employment of excess employees was a major financial drain for carriers in difficult circumstances, and granted some relief. The Northeast Rail Service Act of 1981 preempted state crew laws.[44] Few other industries were hindered by such dogged adherence to outmoded laws despite new technologies.

Displacement Compensation

With the Transportation Act of 1920 Congress established a policy of encouraging consolidation of the nation's railroads in the interests of economy and efficiency. But it was readily apparent that unification of lines would result in wholesale dismissals of rail employees. This would obviously affect worker morale and give rise to labor disputes that threatened to frustrate the congressional policy of consolidation.

The depression of the 1930s sparked renewed interest in consolidation as a means of reducing expenses for distressed carriers, but also heightened concern about the loss of jobs during a time of massive unemployment. Railroads steadfastly maintained that they should have the same right as other industries to achieve economy by reducing their workforce. But the Emergency Railroad Transportation Act of 1933, written to foster cooperative action by carriers and elimination of duplicate services, contained provisions to protect rail workers. The act stated that no employee could be dismissed because of any coordination moves. Since any substantial economy necessitated labor displacement, the labor protection sections of the act were a major factor in frustrating the coordination policy.[45]

Confronted with threatened congressional action to legislate compensation for displaced employees, most carriers negotiated the "Washington Agreement" with unions in 1936 covering jobs lost by mergers or coordination programs. Instead of a job freeze, this pact provided financial benefits for workers hurt by mergers. Subsequently, the ICC began to impose similar terms as a condition for approving proposed consolidations. Upholding the authority of the commission to require labor protections, the Supreme Court declared:

> One must disregard the entire history of railroad labor relations in the United States to be able to say that the just and reasonable treatment of railroad employees in mitigation of the hardship imposed on them in carrying out the national policy of railroad consolidation, has no bearing on the successful prosecution of that policy and no relationship to the maintenance of an adequate and efficient transportation system.[46]

Congress in the Transportation Act of 1940 did not adopt a job freeze but directed the ICC to include compensatory wage payments for four years in any merger approvals. This measure went far toward recognizing a property right in a job. In 1942 the Supreme Court ruled that the ICC must also consider the interests of employees in cases involving requests to abandon rail facilities. Thereafter, the ICC included labor protection clauses in abandonment orders.[47]

The rail industry thus became the only business obligated by law to provide income guarantees to displaced workers. The labor protection requirement underscored the confusion that permeated so much regulatory policy. The requirement that carriers make payments to displaced employees worked at cross-purposes with the desire to achieve efficient service by consolidation.

A Path to the Future

Because of their historic role as America's first large-scale enterprise and their vital place in the national economy, railroads became the testing ground for the growth of modern labor law. From the great strikes of 1877 to the present, two themes predominate in railroad labor law. First, lawmakers were invariably reacting to work stoppages or strike threats. Often executive, legislative, and judicial decisions were made in a crisis atmosphere not conducive to careful analysis. Second, lawmakers were preoccupied above all to

prevent disruption to essential rail service. This mind-set frequently mani-
fested itself in one-sided interventions calculated to make the weaker party
yield. The use of injunctions, reliance on the military, encouragement of collective bargaining, and compulsory arbitration were all designed to halt railway strikes.

By the early twentieth century, lawmakers gradually recognized that they
might best achieve industrial peace by fashioning lawful channels through
which rail employees could seek to improve their working conditions. The
trailblazing Railway Labor Act marked a new era in national labor law by
improving the position of unions. Although many principles first developed
for railroad labor were carried over into general labor legislation, Congress
continues to treat transportation labor disputes as a special problem. Sadly,
for all the legal experimentation, rail labor laws failed to find a formula that
encouraged settlements. By the mid–twentieth century both unions and carriers seemed trapped in a mutually destructive relationship. "Half a century
of conflict," Klein pointed out, "had not produced a single constructive
approach on either side for dealing with the real problems that plagued the
industry and threatened the very existence of railroaders."[48] Calls to overhaul or repeal the RLA went unheeded.[49] In a roundabout way the tangled
state of labor relations in the rail industry was a testament to the persistent
significance of rail service to American life.

13

Legal Problems of Railroad Decline

The central subject of this chapter is the response of the legal system to the decline of railroading in the twentieth century. After World War I, the rail industry entered a prolonged period of contraction and stagnation. The causes for this deterioration were many and complex, and are treated only briefly here.

Certainly, a prime factor in the falling off of railroad traffic was the emergence of new modes of transportation.[1] Public interest and congressional favor shifted to motor vehicles. In 1916 Congress enacted the first federal highway program, a step foreshadowing more ambitious federal and state road construction initiatives. Following World War II, federal expenditures for highways skyrocketed. The Interstate and Defense Highway Act of 1956, creating the interstate highway system, aided the intercity trucking business and caused a sharp drop in railroad passengers. Indeed, the trucking industry grew rapidly after 1920 and captured traffic from the railroads. As early as 1935 the Supreme Court commented upon "the revolutionary changes incident to transportation wrought in recent years by the widespread introduction of motor vehicles," and pointed to "the resulting depletion of rail revenues."[2]

Competition from airlines expanded swiftly after 1945. Not only did air travel have the advantage of speed, but the government provided generous funding for the construction of air facilities. Similarly, the government embarked upon an extensive scheme of inland waterway improvements. The St. Lawrence Seaway, for example, was opened in 1959 and carried a large amount of bulk freight.[3]

Such governmental largesse constituted an indirect subsidy to the trucking, airline, and barge industries, and helped to divert traffic from railroads. To be sure, railroad companies in the nineteenth century had received considerable public aid. But the situations are not entirely analogous. Recall that the federal land grants required carriers to transport government freight at reduced rates. There was no equivalent obligation for the twentieth-century projects.

Other problems also buffeted the rail industry. As pointed out earlier, competitive pressures were exacerbated by heavy local taxation and difficult labor relations. The New York Central Railroad had the largest single tax bill in New York City. In addition, railroads were saddled with a rigid regulatory regime that took no account of radically changed circumstances. Thus, truckers could bargain directly with shippers over rates, but railroads had lost that privilege and had to request regulatory approval to offer competitive rates. Stultifying rail regulations worked to the advantage of more flexible truckers.

The symptoms of malaise were widespread and accelerated as the twentieth century progressed. Starting in the 1920s, railroads began to abandon unprofitable routes and curtail service. Abandoned trackage exceeded new construction for the first time. Railroads steadily lost both freight and passenger business, and their share of intercity transportation dropped sharply. In 1958 an ICC examiner, with uncanny accuracy, predicted that rail passenger service would cease within a decade. Experiencing low profitability, and sometimes skirting bankruptcy, rail companies could no longer attract needed investment capital for improvements. Consequently, many carriers suffered physical deterioration of freight cars and roadbeds. Not surprisingly, employment in the rail industry also declined.

Regulatory Policy in the 1920s

Although armed with enlarged authority by the Transportation Act of 1920, the Interstate Commerce Commission was reluctant to take the lead in fashioning a far-reaching railroad policy. Instead, the commission was largely reactive and concerned with rate regulation.[4] The federal courts generally deferred to the ICC on rate issues, and the agency in turn adhered to a status quo policy on rates. It usually denied requests to increase or lower charges. As previously discussed, efforts by the ICC to implement the recapture clause were unsuccessful. Since the recapture clause and the rate provisions of the Transportation Act evidenced a congressional intent to treat the railroad system as a whole, the ICC after 1920 largely dealt with proposed general rate changes rather than particular charges.

The complexity of rate making and the political pressures on the ICC were vividly illustrated by the Hoch-Smith Resolution, passed by Congress in 1925. Agriculture was depressed during the 1920s, notwithstanding general national prosperity. As was so often the case, agricultural interests looked to lower transportation charges as a panacea for their economic distress. Echoing this theme, the Democratic Party platform of 1924 urged that freight rates should be adjusted to give low-priced commodities, such as farm products, lower rates, while placing higher rates on more valuable shipments. A product of this agitation, the Hoch-Smith Resolution directed the ICC to investigate to what extent the existing rate structure imposed undue burdens as between sections of the country and between classes of freight. More specifically, the resolution referred to "the existing depression in agriculture" and called on the commission to make "such lawful changes" in rates as would promote the shipment of agricultural products "at the lowest possible lawful rates compatible with the maintenance of adequate transportation service."[5]

Even though its meaning was not readily ascertainable, the Hoch-Smith Resolution raised a number of troublesome issues. It mandated no definite course of action for the ICC, and could have been seen as just a symbolic gesture by Congress. Still, Congress, in effect, asked the commission to change freight rates to take account of depressed agricultural conditions. Viewed in this light, the resolution was a troublesome example of political pressure on a supposedly expert administrative agency. Moreover, the resolution called into question the entire railroad rate structure. It raised the question of whether favorable rates should be fixed to assist ailing segments of the economy. Such a command was difficult to reconcile with the statutory prohibition of rates giving an undue preference to any locality or type of traffic. The resolution further intimidated that lower charges for agricultural products should be made up by higher rates on other goods, a scheme reminiscent of the recapture clause's attempt to force the more prosperous lines to contribute to weaker carriers. Lastly, the resolution opened the door for every shipper group to seek improved rates at the expense of the carriers or other shippers. Coal interests, for instance, also claimed the sanction of the resolution in a bid for rate relief.

The Hoch-Smith Resolution laid bare the political considerations behind agency rate making. Distressed groups of shippers were simply demanding rate discrimination in their favor. The ICC construed the resolution as stating an additional test for determining rates on agricultural products, but was reluctant to reduce charges.[6] Overruling the commission, the Supreme Court in *Ann Arbor Railroad Company v. United States* (1930) concluded that the resolution did not change the existing standards relating to transportation charges or place agricultural products in a favored class. The Court treated the resolution as merely precatory in nature, and pointedly observed that any reduction of rates below a reasonable return to the carriers would raise constitutional questions.

There was also a historical irony implicit in the Hoch-Smith Resolution. Agricultural interests in the West and South had long complained of the treatment accorded them by railroads and worked to curb rate making by the carriers. Yet, despite the fact that control over rates was transferred to the ICC, farm groups remained unhappy. But now their ire was directed against the commission. Public supervision of transportation charges had not proved a magic solution to agricultural problems.

Another major concern for the ICC during the 1920s was to carry out the congressional policy of improving rail operations through the consolidation of lines. The Transportation Act of 1920 put emphasis on combination, not competition, and required the ICC to prepare consolidation plans for the nation's railroads. Accordingly, the commission formulated a tentative plan in 1921 that combined railroads into nineteen systems.[7] This proposal aroused strong opposition, especially from stronger lines who disliked being yoked with unprofitable carriers. In general, railroads showed little enthusiasm for government-sponsored consolidation schemes. After years of hearings and delays, a reluctant ICC adopted a final plan in 1929. The commission had no power to compel railroad companies to accept its plan, and took no steps to push the carriers toward consolidation. No mergers were based on the ICC plan and the commission preferred to allow railroads to agree upon consolidation by themselves. The onset of the depression ended any hope of planned consolidations, and in 1940 Congress relieved the ICC of the responsibility to prepare merger plans.[8]

Although indifferent to planned consolidations, the ICC approved many mergers proposed by the carriers. This represented a shift from the Progressive-Era invocation of antitrust laws to block mergers and force competition. The Transportation Act gave the ICC sweeping authority to approve acquisition of one railroad by another if the public interest was served. In effect, the commission was empowered to validate consolidations that would otherwise run afoul of antitrust laws. This was illustrated by the Southern Pacific–Central Pacific combine. In 1922 the Supreme Court ruled that the acquisition by the Southern Pacific Company of a controlling interest in the Central Pacific Railway violated the Sherman Act.[9] A year later, however, the ICC determined that the stock acquisition was in the public interest. Hence, the consolidation could proceed, a move that highlighted the diminished application of antitrust policy to railroads.[10]

Under the Transportation Act the ICC also exercised broad control over track abandonments and extensions of service. Unlike other types of enterprise, railroads were under a legal obligation to serve the public and could not discontinue operations without governmental approval. Prior to 1920, the law governing railroad abandonments was not well developed and varied widely from state to state. The enlarged federal authority over abandonments substantially displaced the regulatory power of the states, but states retained a measure of control over intrastate service on operated trackage.[11] During the 1920s the commission approved a number of applications to abandon unprofitable routes, usually in rural areas with light traffic.[12] Influenced largely by financial considerations, the ICC was concerned that forcing carriers to operate service at a loss was inconsistent with the policy of fostering a strong and efficient rail system.

At the same time, the commission was disinclined to order extensions of rail service. Its only attempt at a compelled extension of trackage was checked by the Supreme Court. In 1929 the ICC ordered a carrier to build a line into a territory that the carrier had not previously served. The railroad refused on grounds the venture would be unprofitable. Expressing concern that a required extension of track to serve a new area might constitute an unconstitutional taking of property, the Supreme Court held that the Transportation Act did not empower the commission to compel the construction of lines into new regions.[13]

Although the ICC in the 1920s was often sympathetic to the rail industry, it showed little initiative and generally pursued a hands-off policy. The commission never fulfilled the high hopes of the framers of the Transportation Act. Railroads as a whole enjoyed modest prosperity in the 1920s, but were never as robust as other segments of the industrial economy. In part because of increasingly obsolete regulations, they were especially ill prepared for the depression decade ahead.

New Deal and World War II

With their heavy fixed costs, railroads were severely hurt by the Great Depression. By 1933 they were in desperate shape, having suffered a sharp loss of income. This decline in revenue impaired their credit. Many lines were in receivership or bankruptcy and others were heading in that direction. The ICC was unable to do much to help. The Reconstruction Finance Corporation made substantial loans to carriers, but could not provide a long-term solution to the problems of the rail industry.[14]

The distressed condition of the industry sparked a far-ranging debate over the future direction of railroad policy. A number of New Dealers, such as ICC Commissioner Joseph B. Eastman, pressed the case for government operation of the railroads. In the mid-1930s several bills that proposed public ownership of the carriers were introduced in Congress. But, as before in American history, such proposals died for lack of support.[15]

Instead of public ownership, the New Deal put its faith in a revamped regulatory regime. "Once again," Morton Keller observed, "the regulatory mill groaned and groaned."[16] The first New Deal legislation, the Emergency Transportation Act of 1933, failed to provide any effective remedy for the distressed industry. Harking back to the hope of consolidation in the Transportation Act, the 1933 law created a temporary office of Federal Emergency Coordinator and sought to promote voluntary cooperation among carriers to reduce waste and duplication in rail service. The act was consistent with the early New Deal policy of fostering industry self-regulation. Named Federal Coordinator, Eastman made suggestions to improve service and achieve economies. But he was loath to order changes, and found his efforts at coordination frustrated by the indifference of the carriers and the hostility of the labor unions.[17] As discussed above, the act protected rail workers against job loss by reason of any coordination actions. This job security provision was at odds with the basic purpose of the act to reduce industry expense. "The whole effort," John F. Stover explained, "was rendered largely ineffectual by a provision in the original act which prohibited any economy involving a reduction in rail employment."[18] Few tears were shed when Congress failed to renew the coordination act in 1936.

Another piece of New Deal railroad legislation was an important milestone in the evolution of a social insurance system in the United States. In the face of massive job losses in the early 1930s, rail unions pushed for a law that would offer security for the aged and persuade older employees to retire, thus creating job opportunities for younger workers. The result was the first national pension law, the Railroad Retirement Act of 1934. Enacted at a time when there was no general retirement benefit system, the legislation established the practice of a separate social security scheme for railroad workers. Both carriers and employees were obligated to contribute to a pension fund. Workers were required to retire at the age of sixty-five, and were then eligible for pensions. Unions hoped that this measure would help to alleviate unemployment in the industry.[19]

Perhaps unsurprisingly, the Supreme Court took a skeptical look at this first compulsory retirement and pension system. In *Railroad Retirement Board v. Alton Railroad Company* (1935), a sharply divided Court found several constitutional infirmities with the statute. A number of provisions—such as those awarding pensions to persons who had worked for railroads within the past year but were no longer employed, and those requiring solvent lines to pay into a common fund that would support employees from bankrupt lines—were held to deny due process by taking property from one person and transferring it to another. The second and more serious objection related to congressional authority over interstate commerce. Rejecting the argument that a pension scheme promoted efficiency and employee morale, Justice Owen Roberts, speaking for the Court, ruled that pension laws were not within the scope of the commerce clause.[20]

The *Railroad Retirement* decision was the first major judicial invalidation of New Deal legislation. It cast a long shadow over the constitutionality of the social security system then being considered by Congress. It also set the stage for a bruising showdown between the Supreme Court and the New Deal over the role of the federal government in managing the economy and promoting social welfare.[21] The rail industry, however, avoided further litigation over pension plans. Following intense negotiations, rail companies and unions agreed upon a compromise system embodied in the Railroad Retirement Act of 1937. The validity of this measure was never challenged, and to this day railroad workers have a special social security arrangement.[22]

Congress took yet another stab at formulating rail policy with the Transportation Act of 1940.[23] Reflecting the New Deal preference for governmental supervision rather than competition, the act defined national policy as "the fair and impartial regulation of all modes of transportation . . . , so administered as to recognize and preserve the inherent advantages of each." This ambiguous language raised a number of difficulties. It was not clear how to determine the "inherent advantages" of different types of transportation. Moreover, the act seemingly directed the ICC to prevent destructive competition between rail, motor, and water carriers. As might be expected, the ICC sought to fulfill this uncertain mandate by generally preserving the status quo and blocking price reductions that threatened to reduce the traffic of other modes. Yet the playing field was not level because motor and water transportation were not regulated as tightly as railroads, and thus enjoyed competitive advantages.

Spurred by the industry's economic distress, applications to the ICC for track abandonments markedly accelerated after 1930. World War II produced a new wave of requests to abandon mileage as the conflict required carriers to reallocate equipment from light-traffic lines. These applications pitted local interests against the national policy of maintaining an economically viable rail system. Proceeding on a case-by-case basis, the ICC never developed a coherent strategy regarding abandonments, but nonetheless granted a large number of applications.[24]

The ICC, however, did not have authority over the discontinuance of passenger trains. State courts and regulatory bodies were often influenced by local interests and notoriously reluctant to allow discontinuance of service. Yet, even at the state level, economic hardship was a factor in deciding whether to allow a railroad to curtail operations. In 1931, for example, the Ohio Public

Utilities Commission rejected an application to discontinue passenger service on a branch line between two cities. Although finding that passenger service on the line was unlikely to ever be profitable, the commission insisted that passenger trains be continued for the time being. Still, the agency declared that "we recognize that the road cannot continue this operation for many years unless there is an increase in the use of passenger service," and admonished the involved communities that unless there was greater patronage of the trains it would grant a future request.[25]

The impact of World War II on the rail industry was entirely different than the unhappy experience during World War I. Traffic and revenue increased sharply, and the wartime years were a brief period of prosperity after years of depression. Anxious to avoid another government takeover, the railroads made every effort to cooperate and serve wartime transportation needs. President Franklin D. Roosevelt, instead of turning to federal control, created the Office of Defense Transportation to coordinate war traffic and to provide guidance to carriers. Under private management the railroads did an impressive job during World War II.[26] As was the case in World War I, however, the president bypassed the ICC in setting wartime transportation policy.

Regional Discrimination

As discussed earlier, the clamor for rate regulation in the late nineteenth and early twentieth centuries was fueled in part by sectional tension. Southerners and westerners had long complained about rate differentials that caused them to pay higher shipping costs. A number of economic factors, including light volume and seasonal business, shaped a distinctive rate structure in the South. The ICC, which divided the country into five rate territories, was little concerned with disparities between regions, and sanctioned these rate differentials. It accepted existing regional rate differences as part of the rate-making process.[27] In the 1930s many southern political figures charged that discriminatory rates were a major cause of economic stagnation in the region. Specifically, they alleged a conspiracy among railroad companies to fix rates so as to benefit northern manufacturers and restrict the southern economy to agricultural products. These critics argued that rate differentials kept the South in a colonial status dominated by northern business interests.[28]

There is room to doubt that discriminatory freight rates were a fundamental cause of southern economic stagnation, and indeed the controversy may have diverted attention from more pressing concerns. But southern leaders devoted considerable energy in the 1930s and 1940s to attacking the rate differentials on a number of fronts.[29] Southern governors complained to the ICC, which began an extensive investigation of the rate system. In the meantime, southern congressmen secured language in the Transportation Act of 1940 banning rate discrimination against a region.

While the ICC was deliberating, Georgia Governor Ellis Arnall circumvented the agency and attacked the role of railroad rate associations in a suit invoking the original jurisdiction of the Supreme Court. The suit alleged that private rate associations conspired to fix transportation charges that discriminated against Georgia in violation of the antitrust laws. A sharply divided Court in 1945 granted Georgia leave to file its complaint.[30] The dissenters persuasively pointed out that the ICC was empowered to ascertain lawful rates, and that consequently any judicial decree would be ineffective to establish a new rate schedule. Aside from garnering public attention for the South's grievances, the litigation instituted by Georgia did not contribute to resolving the regional rate issue. In fact, the suit was ultimately dismissed.[31]

The lawsuit by Georgia, however, called into question the legality of rate associations. Such private rate bureaus maintained by railroads had long been tacitly accepted by the ICC. Most carriers, north or south, did not want to have rate-setting groups prohibited. They persuaded Congress to enact, over President Truman's veto, the Reed-Bullwinkle Act in 1948. This measure exempted rate bureaus from the Sherman Anti-Trust Act, and authorized railroads to operate rate associations with ICC approval. The effect was to validate concerted action by railroads to agree on rate schedules presented to the ICC. This in turn undercut Georgia's legal position in the pending Supreme Court action.[32]

In 1945 the ICC found that the rate structure discriminated against the South and ordered a gradual adjustment of rates to obtain regional parity.[33] The Supreme Court sustained this ruling in *New York v. United States* (1947), and regional rate differentials were phased out in 1952. Obviously, both political maneuvers and legal challenges were utilized to bring about the demise of regional rate discrimination.

Regulatory Policy in the 1950s and 1960s

The health of the rail industry continued to decline after World War II. The railroad share of freight and passenger traffic dropped sharply. The deficits resulting from passenger service mounted steadily in the 1950s, and the carriers regularly sought to curtail passenger operations. Commuter traffic was an especially heavy financial drain. Regulatory decisions contributed to weakening railroads in a variety of ways. Resistant to competitive pricing, the ICC generally refused to let railroads reduce rates to attract business from water and motor carriers. ICC rate decisions were wildly inconsistent, and the rate system, covering thousands of items, was a hodgepodge. At the same time, the commission delayed or limited rate increases designed to take account of inflation. In short, the ICC was increasingly viewed as an obstacle to sound transportation policy rather than a useful regulatory agency.

A harbinger of change was the Weeks Committee report of 1955. Concerned about the deteriorating condition of the nation's railroads, President Dwight D. Eisenhower appointed an advisory committee, headed by Secretary of Commerce Sinclair Weeks, to study the situation. In a break with the past, the committee concluded that the rail industry was overregulated. It recommended that carriers be permitted more freedom in setting competitive charges, and that the ICC no longer be allowed to disapprove a rate just because it might hurt other modes of transportation. It also urged an end to state control over discontinuing passenger trains.[34]

Congress was disinclined to act on the Weeks report, but some of its recommendations were incorporated into the Transportation Act of 1958.[35] The act sought to facilitate the discontinuance of unprofitable interstate and intrastate passenger trains by enlarging ICC jurisdiction over curtailment of service and allowing such discontinuances on short notice. Many trains were dropped as a result. Unfortunately, the act failed to resolve the minimum rate quandary. It declared that the "rates of a carrier shall not be held up to a particular level to protect the traffic of any other mode of transportation," but qualified this directive by adding "giving due consideration to the objectives of the national transportation policy." This opaque language only heightened the confusion surrounding competitive rates. In the last analysis, the act did little to assist the struggling railroads.

Criticism of the ICC as a standpat and dilatory agency steadily grew in the late 1950s and the 1960s. A number of academic studies faulted railroad regulation as benefiting neither carriers nor consumers, and called for a reduction of governmental controls. Yet, as demonstrated by the disappointing Transportation Act of 1958, Congress must bear much of the responsibility for maintaining a destructive regulatory regime. It remains to consider why Congress was so disinterested in the decline of the rail industry, and so averse to tackling the problem in a serious way. Several factors explain the years of legislative neglect. The public was enamored with air and motor transportation and increasingly saw railroads as a relic of another era. Trucking interests were now more powerful than railroads in legislative circles. Consequently, railroads received little attention from lawmakers except as a source of local tax revenue.[36] Many in Congress were also reluctant to have their constituents lose the de facto subsidies implicit in rate regulation. Further, legislators in the Progressive and New Deal tradition were closely identified with regulatory regimes and slow to recognize the dubious results of railroad controls.

Merger Movement

From the start of railroading there had been a trend toward consolidation. Initially, this took the form of joining short lines to create a trunk carrier. By the late nineteenth century, mergers began to take place between competing rail companies. Although temporarily halted by periods of antitrust enforcement, the merger movement received additional impetus from the Transportation Act of 1920. As discussed earlier, this statute encouraged railroad consolidation in order to create a strong rail system. ICC approval was required for rail mergers, and such approval conferred immunity from antitrust laws. The Supreme Court made clear in *Minneapolis & St. Louis Railway Company v. United States* (1959) that the commission must consider the effect that a merger would have on competition, but was not bound by antitrust laws and could determine that an acquisition would serve the public interest.[37]

Beset with economic problems, railroad companies in the late 1950s inaugurated a wave of mergers.[38] They hoped to restore their financial health by more efficient operations, implementation of technological improvements, reduction in the number of employees, and elimination of duplicate facilities. In effect, railroads now embraced the consolidation objectives of the 1920 Transportation Act. These proposed mergers, of course, aroused opposition. Worried about the impact on their members, rail unions predictably challenged consolidation schemes. The Department of Justice raised concerns that some proposed mergers might have anti-competitive effects. In addition, competing lines and affected communities sometimes objected to aspects of merger plans and sought modifications.

The ICC, however, shared the enthusiasm of the railroad companies for mergers as a cure for the industry's troubles. Between 1955 and 1968 the commission approved thirty-three out of thirty-eight merger applications.[39] A key decision, which established the pattern of rulings favorable to consolidation, was the 1960 ICC order upholding the merger of the Erie Railroad and the Delaware, Lackawanna and Western Railroad. Brushing aside union objections based on the benefits accorded displaced employees, the Supreme Court in *Brotherhood of Maintenance of Way Employees v. United States* (1961) sustained the merger. This victory signaled a receptive judicial climate for subsequent mergers.[40]

Rail mergers proceeded apace during the 1960s. Two warrant attention here. In 1967 the ICC approved the merger of the Great Northern Railway Company, the Northern Pacific Railway Company, and several subsidiaries.[41] The effect was to undo the 1904 decision of the Supreme Court in the *Northern Securities* case, which had blocked the same combination as a violation of the antitrust laws. The commission found that the advantages of the proposed consolidation to the public outweighed the diminution of competition between rail lines. Stressing that the ICC, not the courts, was to determine whether mergers satisfied the public interest, the Supreme Court upheld the consolidation order in *United States v. ICC* (1970). It took nine years from the initial application to the ICC until the plan received final approval, another indication of the sluggish pace at which railroad regulatory decisions were made even in the face of rapidly shifting transportation needs. Railroad historians have tended to picture the merger of the northern lines as a belated vindication of the wisdom of the original consolidation scheme, and have speculated that railroads might have evolved differently in the twentieth century had the Northern Securities Company been allowed to stand.[42]

If the consolidation of the northern lines has been a success story, the mega-merger of the New York Central Railroad and the Pennsylvania Railroad, the dominant carriers in the northeast, was a disaster. Albro Martin described the Penn Central combination as "the *Titanic* of the railroad merger era."[43] The ICC authorized the merger of the two financially ailing giants in 1967. The agency, however, imposed several conditions that threatened to undercut the viability of the consolidation. First, the commission insisted that the bankrupt New York, New Haven & Hartford Railroad be included in the merged system. This caused a serious cash drain for the Penn Central. Second, the ICC mandated expensive provisions to protect employees from layoffs resulting from the merger.[44] Despite considerable opposition, the Supreme Court sustained the merger in *Penn-Central Merger Cases* (1968). The problems created by the ICC conditions were compounded by inadequate advance planning, chaotic management, and deteriorating service. In 1970 the Penn Central filed for bankruptcy, the largest business failure in the history of the United States to that point.[45] A number of smaller eastern lines dependent on the Penn Central also soon failed.

Toward Deregulation

The collapse of the Penn Central marked a watershed in railroad regulatory law. It made vividly clear that mergers alone were no panacea to the deep-seated problems afflicting the industry. Anticipated savings often failed to materialize. The Erie Lackawanna, for example, experienced increasing financial losses following consolidation and sought bankruptcy protection in 1972.[46] The nation faced an impending railroad catastrophe in the 1970s. Other carriers, such as the Chicago, Rock Island and Pacific, were pushed into bankruptcy. A fundamental change of policy was urgently required if the United States was to keep privately owned rail service.

Having given little attention to the plight of railroads for decades, Congress was spurred to pass a series of laws that recast regulatory policy and substantially limited governmental supervision. In particular, Congress steadily reduced the powers of the ICC, and eventually abolished the agency. Lawmakers first addressed the virtual collapse of rail passenger service by establishing in 1970 the National Railroad Passenger Corporation, popularly known as Amtrak.[47] This quasi-public corporation assumed responsibility for intercity passenger operations. Railroads turning over passenger trains were required to make a payment to Amtrak in order to relieve themselves of passenger obligations. Most carriers followed this course, and thus eliminated the huge deficits associated with passenger travel. Significantly, the ICC was not given jurisdiction over Amtrak.

Congress sought to remedy the plight of the bankrupt eastern railroads with the Regional Rail Reorganization Act of 1973 (the 3R Act).[48] It was apparent that these lines could not be salvaged without federal financial aid. Liquidation of these enterprises was deemed unacceptable because of its disruptive impact on the economy. Accordingly, the 3R Act established a framework for the creation of a new northeastern rail system. In the meantime, federal grants were made to keep these distressed railroads operating.

Calls for deregulation dovetailed with the legislative search for a solution for the eastern rail crisis in the Railroad Revitalization and Regulatory Reform Act of 1976 (the 4R Act).[49] This important measure created the Consolidated Rail Corporation (Conrail) to take over and rehabilitate portions of the bankrupt eastern lines. It also provided substantial federal aid to launch Conrail. Although the goal was for Conrail to eventually operate without a federal subsidy, the new system incurred heavy losses between 1976 and 1980.[50] Of greater significance, the 4R Act reversed seventy years of regulatory policy and granted the railroads greater authority over rate making. Among other provisions, it empowered the ICC to exempt types of rail service from regulation. Further, the commission was directed to decide merger applications within two years.

By the late 1970s the clamor for railroad deregulation was widespread. Pointing to the malaise of the industry, critics blamed the regulatory apparatus for stifling innovation, hampering rail competition with other modes of transportation, and adding to transit costs. At the urging of President Jimmy Carter, Congress passed the landmark Staggers Act in 1980. In this measure, Congress, signaling a fundamental change in philosophy, asserted that "many of the Government regulations affecting railroads have been unnecessary and inefficient" and that "modernization of economic regulation for the railroad industry with a greater reliance on the marketplace is essential in order to achieve maximum utilization of railroads." Lawmakers expressed concern that failure of the rail industry to achieve increased earnings would "result in either further deterioration of the rail system or the necessity for additional Federal subsidy."[51] Accordingly, the Staggers Act focused on rehabilitation of the nation's railroads by improving their financial health. To this end, it embraced deregulation as a means to enhance railroad profitability.[52]

The Staggers Act substantially reduced rate regulation, allowing railroads the flexibility to cut rates to meet competition and to raise rates in most situations. Carriers were additionally authorized to negotiate contract rates with shippers, and as a result goods could be transported at a contract rate rather than at a common-carrier tariff. The burden of proof in most rate disputes was shifted from rail companies to shippers. For the first time since the Hepburn Act of 1906, the freedom to set rates was largely returned to rail managers.

Other provisions of the Staggers Act deserve mention as well. It established expedited procedures for handling abandonment requests. It further restricted state control of intrastate services to prevent the states from undermining national rail policy. It eased the entry requirements to facilitate the establishment of new railroads. It authorized the ICC to exempt sales and spin-offs of rail lines from statutory labor protection provisions.

As a consequence of the Staggers Act, railroads enjoyed considerable freedom to make business decisions without governmental oversight. Conversely, the ICC lost many of its traditional functions. After 1980 the commission primarily focused on mergers and abandonments. This prompted a debate over whether the ICC was any longer necessary. In 1986 President Ronald Reagan advocated the abolishment of the agency. After years of hesitation, Congress in 1995 eliminated the ICC, the nation's oldest regulatory commission. To replace the ICC, Congress created the three-member Surface Transportation Board (STB) within the Department of Transportation. The STB is concerned largely with mergers between carriers, and track construction and abandonment.

The congressional determination to restore a self-sustaining railroad system in the northeast produced additional legislation in the early 1980s. Unhappy that Conrail was still costing the taxpayers vast sums, Congress passed the Northeastern Rail Service Act of 1981 in order to eliminate the need for continued federal funding.[53] To reduce the flow of red ink, Congress (1) eliminated the obligation of Conrail to operate commuter service at the end of 1982, (2) reduced the amount and duration of severance payments for displaced employees, and (3) preempted state full-crew laws with respect to Conrail and any railroad in the northeast region. These cost-cutting measures helped Conrail achieve profitability. Thereafter, consistent with the long-standing American preference for privately operated railroads, Congress in 1986 directed that the government's ownership interest be sold at a public offering of stock.[54] Conrail thus became a private venture.

Regulatory reform also brought about a major overhaul of rail commuter lines. By the 1950s, states such as New York and New Jersey began to provide financial subsidies to rail companies to help defray the cost of commuter service. It has been estimated that the value of the commuter aid given by New York exceeded the amount of public assistance in that state to railroads in the nineteenth century.[55] In a bow to the future, New York purchased the Long Island Railroad in 1965.[56] Gradually, states began to take over and operate commuter routes that were dropped by the privately owned railroads. As a practical matter, substantial public funding is necessary to preserve commuter lines. Today most commuter service is furnished by state transportation agencies, a dim echo of the experiments with state-owned railroads before the Civil War.

Deregulation opened a new era for America's railroad industry. Rail carriers regained a degree of prosperity and competed more effectively with other modes of transportation. Deregulation also created legal issues that await resolution in the twenty-first century.

Epilogue

R ailroading and law intersected in complicated and sometimes contradictory ways. The growth of railroads presented old legal issues in a new
light and forced lawmakers to confront a host of novel problems. Railroads
were a major factor in molding legal norms for the industrial age and in defining the parameters of the federal system. They impacted both public and private law. They highlighted tensions between the emerging national market
and the persistence of localism. They brought about the creation of the first
modern administrative agency, the Interstate Commerce Commission, to provide continuous oversight of economic activity. The ICC became the basis on
which the administrative state was built during the twentieth century. Railroad labor laws, fashioned in the early twentieth century, foreshadowed the
evolution of modern labor policy and collective bargaining. Railroads were
also instrumental in transforming our understanding of private property to
encompass not merely title to physical objects but a cluster of rights to enjoy
and derive profit from ownership. This change in turn helped to expand the
scope of constitutional protection afforded property owners.

No other industry captured the hopes and fears of Americans in the nineteenth and early twentieth centuries to the same extent as railroads. The emergence of interstate railroads aroused latent anti-monopoly sentiment. The
ambivalence of many Americans toward large-scale enterprise was embedded
in railroad law. While eager for rail service, many at the same time loosely
blamed railroads for compounding economic distress and social ills. Shippers
and localities decried rate discrimination, and then sought special advantages
for themselves. The desire to promote the spread of railroads (and later to
maintain a viable rail system) was at odds with efforts to assert public control
of charges and to supervise virtually every aspect of rail enterprise. Further,
regulatory policy underwent kaleidoscopic changes. At one point railroads
were expected to compete while being treated as quasi-public utilities under
increasingly tight regulation that precluded competition. Mergers were blocked
as anti-competitive and then encouraged. Deregulation, starting in the 1970s,
was yet another policy initiative that moved in a very different direction. Legal

developments in railroad history were driven by the perceived needs of rail-roaders, shippers, workers, landowners, injured parties, and the public at particular moments. A quest for consistency is futile.

Several themes stand out in the history of railroad law. First, the legal system was closely involved with railroads from the outset and did much to foster the industry. Railroads at the same time never operated free of any legal restraints. Even the early charters attempted to impose some regulations. There was no era of total laissez-faire. Second, there was a marked political dimension to railroad law. Albro Martin has noted "the essential political nature of transportation laws."[1] At the heart of rate regulation, for instance, was the transfer of the final decision over economic matters from private enterprise to political actors. Notwithstanding the trappings of an independent agency, the Interstate Commerce Commission was subject to enormous political and regional pressure. Third, legislators played the key role in determining the legal regime governing railroads. This is not to slight the policy making of judges. They adapted common-law rules, such as nuisance, to accommodate railroads and they fashioned such innovative devices as equity receiverships and labor injunctions. But legislators voted generous railroad charters, delegated eminent-domain power, made land grants, and imposed safety regulations. Likewise, legislators took the lead in establishing the comprehensive regulatory regimes of the twentieth century, and subsequently in abandoning this policy in favor of deregulation. Certainly, after 1900, courts played a secondary role, largely upholding legislative decisions. Fourth, as was true in many areas of law, the growth of federal authority displaced the once dominant role of the states with respect to railroads. States developed much of railroad law in the nineteenth century, but it was increasingly evident that an interstate rail system necessitated national legal norms. In 1912 James Bryce correctly observed that "the tendency to enlarge the scope of national control is inevitable and likely to go further."[2]

Railroad regulatory policy has left a cautionary legacy. Rather than a triumph of the Progressive Era, the waves of regulation put the industry in a straitjacket and ultimately proved disastrous. Controls were invariably directed against earlier problems, and failed to anticipate future developments. "Regulatory policy," Maury Klein has observed, "like old generals, seems doomed always to fight the last war, partly because in our system it takes so long to recognize new problems and then to build a consensus for change."[3] Legislators and champions of regulation were loath to admit that their policies had failed. For decades the only solution to continued railroad problems was more regulation. As a result, railroads were turned into a sort of political football to be kicked from all sides. Even worse, regulation took little account of technological change and tended to stifle innovation. Many factors, of course, contributed to the decline of the rail industry, but fossilized regulatory law must bear a large part of the blame.

A study of railroad legal history helps to dispel several myths. There is little evidence to support the contested thesis that courts devised legal rules in the nineteenth century to subsidize economic growth at the expense of the weaker segments of society.[4] The law governing accidents and the exercise of eminent domain—two subjects frequently cited as demonstrating an entrepreneurial bias—were in actuality molded by efforts to adjust railroad interests with deep-seated notions of individual responsibility and respect for private property. There was sufficient financial liability imposed on railroads in both tort and condemnation proceedings to cast doubt on the subsidy thesis. Judges and legislators always understood that individuals and the public had rights important to safeguard.

Similarly, it is impossible to sustain the contention, initially advanced by Populists and Progressives but echoed too casually by modern historians, that the Supreme Court invariably sided with rail enterprise in the nineteenth and early twentieth centuries.[5] The record is too complex for such a one-dimensional portrait. To be sure, the justices acted to vindicate interstate commerce and protect railroad investments against the imposition of confiscatory rates. But in broad areas, encompassing fencing laws, appliance safety measures, grade-crossing removals, and revisions of legal liability for accidents, the Supreme Court readily upheld sweeping laws that governed rail operations. The Court even acknowledged the validity of rate regulation so long as the carriers received a reasonable return. Railroad labor laws likewise passed judicial muster. During the nineteenth and early twentieth centuries, then, the Supreme Court made no persistent attempt to shield railroads from public controls.

The interplay between railroads and the legal system, moreover, is far from complete. Although diminished in size, the industry remains a vital transportation link in the American economy. As such, railroads continue to present new legal questions as they move into the twenty-first century. Several of these emerging issues can only be sketched here.

There was continued merger activity following deregulation.[6] In the 1990s the Burlington Northern combined with the Santa Fe, and the Union Pacific acquired the Southern Pacific to create giant rail networks. Regulators readily approved these extensive merger plans. Then, in 1998, the Surface Transportation Board (STB) sanctioned the division of Conrail between CSX and Norfolk Southern. The number of major carriers was steadily shrinking. At this writing there remain only four large railroads in the United

States. The STB and other observers speculate that in the future there may be just one dominant carrier respectively in the eastern and western sections of the United States. Such concentrated economic power might spur calls for some type of renewed regulation. Yet once again these mega-mergers have seemingly not achieved their goals of enhanced efficiency and greater profitability. Equally troublesome, several of these consolidations produced severe disruptions in service. Viewing merger proposals with a more skeptical eye and concerned about further restructuring of the industry, the STB in 2000 placed a fifteen-month moratorium on merger applications. The board imposed this moratorium in order to assess its criteria for approving mergers in light of changed circumstances.[7]

The deregulation legislation created new opportunities for the emergence of short-line railroads. Starting in the 1970s, small railroad companies were organized to take over light-traffic branch lines dropped by the major carriers. Rather than abandon lines, railroads could sell or lease marginally profitable trackage to short-line operators who are often able to provide better service to small markets and local shippers. The number of short lines grew rapidly in the 1980s and early 1990s, aided by regulatory steps to encourage their operations. Policy makers saw short lines as a useful means of maintaining rail service on trackage that would otherwise be abandoned.

A sensitive issue, however, was the imposition of labor protective provisions in sales to short lines. For short lines to prosper, it was essential to hold down labor costs and adopt flexible work rules. Many operated on a nonunion basis. Reasoning that high labor expense was hampering the development of short-line carriers, the ICC exempted sales to short lines from the labor protective provisions commonly required in merger situations.[8] In a rather murky opinion, a closely divided Supreme Court in 1989 apparently sustained the authority of the ICC to withhold labor protection in short-line spin-offs. Further, the Court ruled that railroads had no duty to bargain with unions over the sale of their business.[9] In 1995 Congress confirmed the elimination of employee protective provisions in transfers to short lines by expressly prohibiting such requirements.[10] The desire to preserve railroad service prevailed over the income guarantee policy dating from the depression decade of the 1930s.

Notwithstanding the growth of short lines, the major carriers have continued to abandon unprofitable trackage. Local recreational groups have felt that abandoned railroad rights-of-way should be converted into a system of nature trails. In a controversial step, Congress authorized the ICC to allow the interim use of otherwise abandoned railroad easements for recreational trails. Adjacent landowners maintained that this legislative policy constituted a taking of property by preventing the land subject to abandoned easements from passing to them by operation of state law. The rails-to-trails controversy has engendered considerable litigation. Although courts have upheld congressional power to encourage conversion of railroad rights-of-way to trails, they have ruled that at least in some situations such change in usage amounted to a taking of property for which compensation must be paid under the Fifth Amendment. But many issues pertaining to this ongoing dispute remain unresolved.[11]

Railroads are also likely to have an impact on environmental law. Rail operations, of course, have long raised environmental concerns. Recall, for instance, how the use of coal in locomotives contributed to urban smoke pollution in the early twentieth century and triggered the passage of anti-smoke laws. As an industry with a history of contamination and sizeable land holdings, railroading faces heightened regulatory scrutiny and increased environmental litigation. Legal problems abound. Railroad yards have been polluted by years of chemical leaks and spills. Some pollutants have even spread into nearby lakes and rivers. In addition to the cost of cleaning up railroad land, there is the unresolved issue of carrier liability for environmental hazards on trackage easements. Proposed mergers or line expansions require an environmental approval by the STB. In passing upon such applications, regulators are concerned about increases in the traffic volume of hazardous waste materials. Lawsuits, moreover, raise the question of whether the transportation of toxic substances constitute a nuisance.

After decades of rail industry contraction, some carriers have begun to consider expansion of their tracks. With the possible construction of new trackage on the horizon, the exercise of eminent domain by railroads has again emerged as a contentious topic. The Dakota, Minnesota & Eastern Railroad, for example, has proposed a new rail line to reach the Powder River coal fields. Environmentalists and landowners along the proposed route across South Dakota and Wyoming objected to this plan and sought to abolish the right of railroads to use eminent domain. In 1999 the South Dakota legislature restricted the availability of condemnation to carriers. It provided that railroads could exercise eminent domain only with the approval of the governor or state transportation commission.[12] Carriers must apply for authority to use eminent domain and demonstrate that such exercise will serve public needs for South Dakota. Moreover, railroads must show that they have negotiated in good faith to acquire land without eminent domain and that they are prepared to mitigate any adverse environmental impact.

The South Dakota statute once more reveals the tension inherent in eminent-domain law—a project that might well benefit society as a whole will surely harm some individual landowners even though they receive compensation.

It is too early to assess how this change in South Dakota law will affect the railroad project. But such restrictions are not novel. As discussed earlier, some states in the antebellum era required railroads to secure governmental sanction in order to exercise eminent domain. During the age of railroad growth, however, these restrictions proved incapable of dealing with the persistent demand for new lines. Nonetheless, based on the reaction in South Dakota, one may anticipate that any major revival of railroad building will generate fresh controversies over eminent domain.

Congested highways and airports have caused some states to consider the expenditure of public funds to upgrade rail passenger service. In addition to subsidizing commuter lines, states from Virginia to California have provided money to build additional trackage and to purchase new equipment in order to accelerate passenger travel. There has been considerable interest in promoting high-speed rail projects. In 2000 Florida voters amended the state constitution to mandate the development of a high-speed train system linking the five largest urban areas of the state.[13] The amendment authorized the legislature to utilize either a private company or a state agency to achieve this goal, but specified no cost limit nor provided a funding source. Construction of the system awaits legislative determination of routes and financing. Other states are working with Amtrak to improve passenger service. As in the nineteenth century, the states have taken the initiative in providing public support to meet transportation needs.

In the nineteenth and early twentieth centuries, railroads occupied a unique place in American society and law. Just as railroads transformed America by forging national markets and undercutting localism, so they pioneered developments in many areas of the legal culture. Railroad law grew prodigiously as rail operations touched nearly every aspect of life. Lawmakers and judges were often protective of rail enterprise, but also recognized that economic growth had to be balanced by other considerations. Given competing modes of transportation, even resurgent railroads are unlikely to regain a preeminent role in the future. However, the rail industry, once a vigorous force for legal change, will doubtless continue to influence the evolution of law.

NOTES

Prologue

1. *Commercial and Financial Chronicle*, March 18, 1882.
2. *Poor's Manual of the Railroads of the United States* (New York, 1900), xliv.
3. W. G. Hammond, "American Law Schools: Past and Future," *Southern Law Review* 7, N.S. (1881), 400, 405–410.
4. *American Railroad Journal*, September 12, 1857.
5. David C. Frederick, *Rugged Justice: The Ninth Circuit Court of Appeals and the American West, 1891–1941* (Berkeley, 1994), 50.
6. See John Phillip Reid, "A Plot Too Doctrinnaire," *Texas Law Review* 55 (1977), 1307–1321.
7. Leonard W. Levy, *The Law of the Commonwealth and Chief Justice Shaw* (Cambridge, Mass., 1957), 118.
8. *Attorney General v. Chicago and Northwestern Railway Company*, 35 Wis. 425, 582 (1874).
9. Morton J. Horwitz, *The Transformation of American Law, 1780–1860* (Cambridge, Mass., 1977), 1–4, 63–108.

1. The Emergence of the Railroad

1. See George Rogers Taylor, *The Transportation Revolution, 1815–1860* (New York, 1951); William F. Gephart, "Transportation and Industrial Development in the Middle West," in 34 *Studies in History, Economics and Public Law* (New York, 1909).
2. Carol Sheriff, *The Artificial River: The Erie Canal and the Paradox of Progress, 1817–1862* (New York, 1996); Carter Goodrich, *Government Promotion of American Canals and Railroads, 1800–1890* (New York, 1960), 52–61.
3. Goodrich, *Government Promotion*, 61–75.
4. Harry N. Scheiber, *Ohio Canal Era: A Case Study of Government and the Economy, 1820–1861* (Athens, Ohio, 1969), 88–119.
5. James D. Dilts, *The Great Road: The Building of the Baltimore & Ohio, the Nation's First Railroad, 1828–1853* (Stanford, Calif., 1993), 25–48.
6. James A. Ward, *Railroads and the Character of America, 1820–1887* (Knoxville, Tenn., 1986), 12–105.
7. *Hentz v. Long Island Railroad Company*, 13 Barb. 646, 658 (N.Y. 1852).
8. *Louisville and Nashville Railroad Co. v. County Court of Davidson County*, 33 Tenn. 637, 665 (1854).
9. *Louisville, Cincinnati and Charleston Rail Road Company v. Chappell*, 10 S.C. Rep. 383, 398 (1838).
10. *Stockton v. Central Railroad Company*, 50 N.J. Eq. 52, 72 (1892).
11. Goodrich, *Government Promotion*, 41–48; Alfred H. Kelly, Winfred A. Harbison, and Herman Belz, *The American Constitution: Its Origins and Development*, 7th ed. (2 vols., New York, 1991), I, 202–203.

12. One historian has concluded: "More than any other judicial figure, Lemuel Shaw formulated the fundamentals of American railroad law." Leonard W. Levy, *The Law of the Commonwealth and Chief Justice Shaw* (Cambridge, Mass., 1957), 118.

13. See Stephen Salsbury, *The State, the Investor, and the Railroad: The Boston & Albany, 1825–1867* (Cambridge, Mass., 1967), 58–79; John Moretta, "The Censoring of Lorenzo Sherwood: The Politics of Railroads, Slavery and Southernism in Antebellum Texas," *East Texas Historical Association* 35 (1997), 39–52.

14. As quoted in D. G. Brinton Thompson, *Ruggles of New York: A Life of Samuel B. Ruggles* (New York, 1946), 103.

15. See generally Robert J. Parks, *Democracy's Railroad: Public Enterprise in Jacksonian Michigan* (Port Washington, N.Y., 1972), 63–234.

16. J. Willard Hurst, *Law and Social Order in the United States* (Ithaca, N.Y., 1977), 167.

17. Louis Hartz, *Economic Policy and Democratic Thought: Pennsylvania, 1776–1860* (Cambridge, Mass., 1948), 145–148, 166–171.

18. Thomas M. Cooley, *A Treatise on the Constitutional Limitations Which Rest Upon the Legislative Power of the States of the American Union* (Boston, 1868, reprint 1972), 537.

19. Wheaton J. Lane, *From Indian Trail to Iron Horse: Travel and Transportation in New Jersey, 1620–1860* (Princeton, N.J., 1939), 284; Christopher Roberts, *The Middlesex Canal, 1793–1860* (Cambridge, Mass., 1938), 154–155.

20. As quoted in Gephart, "Transportation and Industrial Development in the Middle West," 123.

21. For the litigation between the canal and railroad in Maryland, see Dilts, *The Great Road*, 103–121; H. H. Walker Lewis, "The Great Case of the Canal vs. the Railroad," 19 *Maryland Law Review* 1–26 (1959).

22. *Charles River Bridge v. Warren Bridge*, 36 U.S. 420, 552–553 (1837).

23. *Thompson v. New York and Harlem Railroad Company*, 7 Sandf. Ch. 625, 660–661 (1846).

24. E.g., an act to incorporate the Mohawk and Hudson Rail Road Company, Ch. 253, Laws of New York, 1826; an act to incorporate the Utica and Schenectady Rail Road Company, Ch. 294, Laws of New York, 1833.

25. *Tuckahoe Canal Company v. Tuckahoe and James River Rail Road Company*, 38 Va. 43, 74 (1840).

26. *Newburyport Turnpike Corporation v. Eastern Rail Road Company*, 40 Mass. 326, 328 (1839).

27. An act to authorize the formation of railroad corporations, and to regulate the same, Ch. 140, Laws of New York, 1850. Under separate legislation, however, the New York canal commissioners were given supervisory power over railroads crossing any canal in order to preserve the use of the canal.

28. An act to provide for a general system of railroad incorporations, Laws of Illinois, 1849.

29. An act regulating railroad companies, no. 76, Laws of Pennsylvania, 1849; an act in relation to railroad corporations, no. 41, Laws of Vermont, 1849.

30. An act prescribing a tariff of freight on railroads, Laws of Ohio, 1852.

31. E.g., an act in relation to railroads and the organization of railroad companies, Ch. 112, Laws of Wisconsin, 1872.

32. An act to incorporate the Utica and Schenectady Railroad Company, Ch. 294, Laws of New York, 1833.

33. An act to provide for the construction of a railroad from Auburn to Rochester, Ch. 349, Laws of New York, 1836.

34. An act to amend the act incorporating the Utica and Schenectady Railroad Company, Ch. 335, Laws of New York, 1844.

35. *American Railroad Journal*, February 17, 1855; March 20, 1858.

36. An act to abolish tolls on railroads, Ch. 497, Laws of New York, 1851. See David Maldwyn Ellis, "Rivalry Between the New York Central and the Erie Canal," *New York History* 29 (1948), 268–300.

37. Lee Benson, *Merchants, Farmers, & Railroads: Railroad Regulation and New York Politics, 1850–1887* (Cambridge, Mass., 1955), 9–16; Ellis, "Rivalry Between the New York Central and the Erie Canal," 272–284.

38. Hartz, *Economic Policy and Democratic Thought,* 161–177.

39. *Mott v. Pennsylvania Railroad Company,* 30 Pa. 9, 27, 29 (1858). For the *Mott* litigation, see Hartz, *Economic Policy and Democratic Thought,* 177–180, 278–282.

40. Hartz, *Economic Policy and Democratic Thought,* 273–275.

41. An act for the commutation of tonnage duties, no. 100, Laws of Pennsylvania, 1861. See Stanton Ling Davis, *Pennsylvania Politics, 1860–1863* (Cleveland, 1935), 190–200.

42. *Radcliff's Executors v. Mayor of Brooklyn,* 4 N.Y. 195, 207 (1850).

43. *American Railroad Journal,* September 10, 1859.

44. Issac F. Redfield, *The Law of Railways,* 6th ed. (2 vols., Boston, 1888), II, 483–484.

45. E.g., an act to authorize the formation of the Edgefield Rail Road Company, 1834, 8 *Statutes at Large of South Carolina* 396–404.

46. Thomas M. Cooley, "Limits to State Control of Private Business," *Princeton Review* 54 (1878), 233, at 261.

47. *Boston and Lowell Railroad Corporation v. Salem and Lowell Railroad Company,* 68 Mass. 1, 28 (1854). Likewise, in *Pontchartrain Railroad Company v. New Orleans and Carrollton Railroad Company,* 11 La. Ann. 253 (1856), the Court enforced an exclusive right to construct a railroad between New Orleans and Lake Pontchartrain.

48. Lane, *From Indian Trail to Iron Horse,* 284–370.

49. E.g., *American Railroad Journal,* September 8, December 15, 1855.

50. *Delaware and Raritan Canal and Camden and Amboy Railroad v. Camden and Atlantic Railroad Company,* 16 N.J. Eq. 321, 365 (1863), aff'd 18 N.J. Eq. 546 (1867).

51. See Donald A. Grinde, Jr., "Erie's Railroad War: A Case Study of Purposive Violence for a Community's Economic Advancement," *Western Pennsylvania Historical Magazine* 57 (1974), 15–23.

52. An act fixing the gauges of railroads in the county of Erie, no. 122, Laws of Pennsylvania, 1851.

53. An act regulating railroad gauges, no. 36, Laws of Pennsylvania, 1852.

54. *Commonwealth v. Franklin Canal Company,* 21 Pa. 117, 127–128 (1853).

55. An act repealing the acts regulating the gauge of the track of railroads, no. 239, Laws of Pennsylvania, 1853.

56. Grinde, "Erie's Railroad War," 19–21.

57. *American Railroad Journal,* January 14, 1854.

58. *Commonwealth v. Erie and North East Railroad Company,* 27 Pa. 339, 362 (1854–1856).

59. *American Railroad Journal,* February 4, 1854.

60. Id., February 11, 1854.

61. Cecil Kenneth Brown, *A State Movement in Railroad Development* (Chapel Hill, N.C., 1928), 179–182.

62. See Joseph S. Clark, Jr., "The Railroad Struggle for Pittsburgh," *Pennsylvania Magazine of History and Biography* 48 (1924), 1–37; *Commonwealth v. Pittsburg and Connellsville Railroad Company,* 58 Pa. 26 (1868); *Baltimore v. Pittsburg and Connellsville Railroad Company,* 2 Fed. Cases No. 827 (Cir. Ct., W.D. Penn., 1865).

63. J. Willard Hurst, *The Legitimacy of the Business Corporation in the Law of the United States, 1780–1970* (Charlottesville, Va., 1970), 31–39.

64. E.g., Taylor, *The Transportation Revolution,* 97–102; John F. Stover, *American Railroads,* 2nd ed. (Chicago, 1997), 30.

65. Taylor, *The Transportation Revolution*, 100; Augustus J. Veenendaal, Jr., *Slow Train to Paradise: How Dutch Investment Helped Build American Railroads* (Stanford, Calif., 1996), 50–51, 58–63.

66. Carter Goodrich, "The Virginia System of Mixed Enterprise," *Political Science Quarterly* 64 (1949), 355, 378–380.

67. E.g., an act to authorize the formation of the Charleston and All-Saints Rail Road company, Laws of South Carolina, 1836, reprinted in Cooper and McCord, *Statutes at Large of South Carolina*, VIII, 472–480; an act to incorporate the stockholders of the Lynchburg and Tennessee Rail-Road Company, Ch. 111, Laws of Virginia, 1835; an act to incorporate the Georgia Rail Road Company, Laws of Georgia, 1833. See also Redfield, *The Law of Railways*, II, 16–19.

68. An act regulating railroad companies, no. 76, Laws of Pennsylvania, 1849.

69. An act to authorize the formation of railroad corporations, and to regulate the same, Ch. 140, Laws of New York, 1850.

70. *Inhabitants of Worcester v. Western Rail Road Corporation*, 45 Mass. 564, 566 (1842).

71. *Olcott v. Supervisors*, 83 U.S. 678, 694 (1872).

72. Bryon K. Elliott and William F. Elliott, *A Treatise on the Law of Railroads*, 2nd ed. (5 vols., Indianapolis, 1907), I, 58.

73. *American Railroad Journal*, February 14, 1846.

74. *State v. Richmond & Danville Rail Road Company*, 73 N.C. 527, 533 (1875).

75. Robert H. White, *Messages of the Governors of Tennessee, 1835–1845* (Nashville, 1954), 67.

76. Gephart, "Transportation and Industrial Development in the Middle West," 161.

77. Laws of Illinois, 1857, xiii–xiv.

78. The initial general railroad acts authorized any groups of subscribers to form railroad corporations, but required express legislative permission to use eminent domain. E.g., an act to provide for a general system of railroad corporations, Laws of Illinois, 1849; an act to authorize the formation of railroad corporations, Ch. 140, Laws of New York, 1848. This provision greatly limited the utility of the first statutes, and under later laws the mere organization of a railroad carried with it eminent-domain power. E.g., an act to provide for the incorporation of railroad companies, no. 82, Laws of Michigan, 1855; an act to authorize the formation of railroad corporations, and to regulate the same, Ch. 140, Laws of New York, 1850.

79. *Buffalo and New York City Railroad Company v. Brainard*, 9 N.Y. 100, 110 (1853).

80. White, *Messages of the Governors of Tennessee, 1845–1857*, 423.

81. David Herbert Donald, *Lincoln* (New York, 1995), 60–62; Goodrich, *Government Promotion*, 141–147.

82. Goodrich, *Government Promotion*, 231.

83. White, *Messages of the Governors of Tennessee, 1845–1857*, 399–400.

84. Gephart, "Transportation and Industrial Development in the Middle West," 167.

85. *American Railroad Journal*, September 18, 1852; June 18, 1853.

86. *Goddin v. Crump*, 35 Va. 120, 155 (1837).

87. *City of Bridgeport v. Housatonic Railroad Company*, 15 Conn. 475 (1843). For a helpful analysis of this case, see Charles A. Heckman, "Establishing the Basis for Local Financing of American Railroad Construction in the Nineteenth Century: From *City of Bridgeport v. The Housatonic Railroad Company* to *Gelpake v. City of Dubuque*," *American Journal of Legal History* 32 (1988), 236, 241–247.

88. See Hartz, *Economic Policy and Democratic Thought*, 113–123; Ellis L. Waldron, "Sharpless v. Philadelphia: Jeremiah Black and the Parent Case on the Public Purpose of Taxation," *Wisconsin Law Review* (1953), 48–75; Howard Lee McBain, "Taxation for a

Private Purpose," *Political Science Quarterly* 29 (1914), 185, 189–190 (stating that *Sharpless* "became a leading case for innumerable decisions in many jurisdictions").

89. *Sharpless and Others v. Mayor of Philadelphia*, 21 Pa. 147, 158 (1853).

90. Id., 159.

91. E.g., *Cincinnati, Wilmington and Zanesville Rail Road Company v. Commissioners of Clinton County*, 1 Ohio St. 77 (1852); *Louisville & Nashville Railroad Company v. County Court of Davidson*, 33 Tenn. 637 (1854); *Caldwell v. Justices of County of Burke*, 57 N.C. 323 (1858). See Harry H. Pierce, *Railroads of New York: A Study of Government Aid, 1826–1875* (Cambridge, Mass., 1953), 27–29.

92. *Amey v. Mayor, Aldermen and Citizens of Allegheny City*, 65 U.S. 364, 375 (1860). See also *Board of Commissioners of Knox County v. Aspinwall*, 62 U.S. 539 (1858).

93. *Loan Association v. Topeka*, 87 U.S. 655, 660–661 (1874).

94. Edward L. Pierce, *A Treatise on the Law of Railroads* (Boston, 1881), 87–94; Elliott and Elliott, *A Treatise on the Law of Railroads*, 2nd ed., II, 240–241.

95. Salsbury, *The State, the Investor, and the Railroad*, 31–32; Stover, *American Railroads*, 30; Albert Fishlow, *American Railroads and the Transformation of the Antebellum Economy* (Cambridge, Mass., 1965), 189–196.

96. Dilts, *The Great Road*, 46, 176, 211–213.

97. Goodrich, *Government Promotion*, 268.

98. William Z. Ripley, *Railroads: Rates and Regulations* (New York, 1912), 38–39.

99. See Earl S. Beard, "Local Aid to Railroads in Iowa," *Iowa Journal of History* 50 (1952), 1–34.

100. *Dubuque County v. Dubuque and Pacific Railroad Company*, 4 Greene 15–16 (Iowa 1853).

101. *State v. County of Wapello*, 13 Iowa 388, 423–424 (1862).

102. Heckman, "Establishing the Basis for Local Financing of American Railroad Construction," 254–257; Beard, "Local Aid to Railroads in Iowa," 17.

103. Beard, "Local Aid to Railroads in Iowa," 24–25.

104. Harry M. Tinkcom, *John White Geary* (Philadelphia, 1940), 120.

105. Morton Keller, *Affairs of State: Public Life in Late Nineteenth Century America* (Cambridge, Mass., 1977), 165. See, e.g., an act to facilitate the construction of railroads in the state of Missouri, Laws of Missouri, 1868.

106. Harriette M. Dilla, "The Politics of Michigan, 1865–1878" in 47 *Studies in History, Economics and Public Law* (New York, 1912), 108.

107. Alan R. Jones, *The Constitutional Conservatism of Thomas McIntyre Cooley: A Study in the History of Ideas* (New York, 1987), 173–184. Isaac F. Redfield, another leading authority on railroad law, shared Cooley's concern about municipal stock subscriptions in railroads. David M. Gold, "Redfield, Railroads, and the Roots of 'Laissez-Faire Constitutionalism,'" *American Journal of Legal History* 27 (1983), 254, 259–263.

108. *Whiting v. Sheboygan & Fond du Lac Railroad Company*, 25 Wis. 167 (1869).

109. See C. A. Kent, "Municipal Subscriptions and Taxation in Aid of Railroads," *American Law Register* 9 (1870), 649–657.

110. Herbert Hovenkamp, *Enterprise and American Law, 1836–1937* (Cambridge, Mass., 1991), 38–41.

111. Pierce, *Railroads of New York*, 57–59.

112. Lawrence M. Friedman, *A History of American Law*, 2nd ed. (New York, 1985), 182.

113. Robert S. Hunt, *Law and Locomotives: The Impact of the Railroad on Wisconsin Law in the Nineteenth Century* (Madison, Wis., 1958), 44–65.

114. Ulrich Bonnell Phillips, *A History of Transportation in the Eastern Cotton Belt to 1860* (New York, 1908), 389.

115. *American Railroad Journal*, October 27, 1855.

116. Phillips, *A History of Transportation*, 303–334; Goodrich, "The Virginia System of Mixed Enterprise," 372.

117. Goodrich, "The Virginia System of Mixed Enterprise," 362, 374–383.

118. See Cecil Kenneth Brown, *A State Movement in Railroad Development* (Chapel Hill, N.C., 1928).

119. An act to incorporate the North Carolina Rail Road, ch. 82, Laws of North Carolina, 1849. See Allen W. Trelease, *The North Carolina Railroad, 1849–1871 and the Modernization of North Carolina* (Chapel Hill, N.C., 1991).

120. See generally, Milton S. Heath, "North American Railroads: Public Railroad Construction and the Development of Private Enterprise in the South Before 1861," *Journal of Economic History* 10 (Supplement) (1950), 40–67.

121. Phillips, *A History of Transportation*, 189–192, 230–231; Goodrich, *Government Promotion*, 160; Taylor, *The Transportation Revolution*, 89–90.

122. An act to incorporate the Baltimore and Ohio Rail Road Company, Ch. 123, Laws of Maryland, 1827; Dilts, *The Great Road*, 43–45.

123. E.g., an act to incorporate the Boston and Providence Railroad Company, Laws of Rhode Island, 1831, in W. P. Gregg and Benjamin Pond, *The Railroad Laws and Charters of the United States* (2 vols., Boston, 1851), II, 668–677; Lane, *From Indian Trail to Iron Horse*, 311.

124. An act to incorporate the Baltimore and Ohio Rail Road company, Ch. 123, Laws of Maryland, 1827; An act to incorporate the Georgia Rail Road Company, Laws of Georgia, 1833 (partial exemption); an act to incorporate the Wilmington and Raleigh Railroad Company, Ch. 78, Laws of North Carolina, 1833; an act to amend an act . . . to incorporate the Florida, Atlantic and Gulf Central Rail Road Company, Ch. 481, Laws of Florida, 1852. See also an act to incorporate the Cincinnati and Charleston Rail Road Company, 1835, in Cooper and McCord, *Statutes at Large of South Carolina*, VIII, 409–418 (capital stock and property "shall be forever exempt from taxation"); an act to provide for and encourage a liberal system of internal improvements in this state, Ch. 610, Laws of Florida, 1855 (capital stock "forever exempt from taxation").

125. An act to provide for the incorporation of Railroad Companies, Ch. 1, Laws of New Mexico, 1878.

126. *Mayor and City Council of Baltimore v. Baltimore and Ohio Railroad Company*, 6 Gill (Md.) 288, 221–222 (1848).

127. See *Illinois Central Railroad Company v. County of McLean*, 17 Ill. 291 (1855); Howard Gray Brownson, *The History of the Illinois Central Railroad to 1870* (Urbana, Ill., 1915), 39, 152; John F. Stover, *History of the Illinois Central Railroad* (New York, 1975), 28–29, 89–90.

128. See *State v. Berry*, 17 N.J.L. 80 (1839) (holding railroad under charter exempt from local property taxes); Pierce, *A Treatise on the Law of Railroads*, 478–485; Elliott and Elliott, *A Treatise on the Law of Railroads*, II, 140–141.

129. *Inhabitants of Worcester v. Western Rail Road Corporation*, 45 Mass. 564, 566 (1842); Levy, *Law of the Commonwealth*, 121–122; Pierce, *A Treatise on the Law of Railroads*, 479–480.

130. *Raleigh & Gaston Railroad Company v. Reid*, 64 N.C. 155 (1870), rev'd 80 U.S. 269 (1871).

131. *Wilmington Railroad v. Reid*, 80 U.S. 264 (1871) (North Carolina legislature could not impair tax exemption in 1833 charter); *Louisville & Nashville Railroad Company v. Gaines*, 3 Fed. Rep. 266 (M.D. Tenn. 1880).

132. E.g., an act to provide for the incorporation of railroad companies, no. 82, Laws of Michigan, 1855; an act regulating railroad companies, Laws of Ohio, 1848.

133. E.g., an act to incorporate the Florida, Atlantic, and Gulf Central Rail Road Company, Ch. 317, Laws of Florida, 1850 ("such timber, stone, or any materials"); an act to incorporate the Cincinnati and St. Louis Rail Road Company, Laws of Ohio, 1832; an act in relation to railroad corporations, no. 41, Laws of Vermont, 1849 ("any lands or materials"); an act regulating railroad companies, no. 76, Laws of Pennsylvania, 1849 (land and "any stone, gravel, clay, sand, earth, wood, or other suitable material").

134. E.g., *Swan v. Williams*, 2 Mich. 427 (1852); *Beekman v. Saratoga & Schenectady Railroad Co.*, 3 Paige's Ch. 42, 73–76 (N.Y. 1831); *Louisville, Cincinnati and Charleston Rail Road Company v. Chappell*, 10 S.C. Rep. 383, 397–400 (1838); *Concord Railroad v. Greely*, 17 N.H. 47 (1845); *Bloodgood v. Mohawk and Hudson Railroad Company*, 18 Wend. 9 (N.Y. 1837).

135. *Raleigh and Gaston Rail Road Company v. Davis*, 19 N.C. 451, 469–470 (1837).

136. See *Buffalo and New York Railroad v. Brainard*, 9 N.Y. 100, 110 (1853) (legislature "may without doubt lawfully declare that all lands taken for the construction of their roads shall be deemed taken for public use").

137. 20 Mich. at 480. See also *Bloodgood v. Mohawk and Hudson Railroad Company*, 18 Wend. 9, 54–72 (N.Y. 1837) (dissenting opinion of Senator Tracy) (arguing that public use is confined to direct possession by the public, and that legislature cannot confer eminent-domain power on private railroad companies).

138. Edward Chase Kirkland, *Men, Cities and Transportation: A Study in New England History* (2 vols., Cambridge, Mass., 1948), I, 163–164; an act to render railroad corporations public in certain cases, Ch. 128, Laws of New Hampshire, 1844, in Gregg and Pond, *Railroad Laws and Charters*, I, 643–649.

139. *Gillinwater v. Mississippi & Atlantic Railroad Company*, 13 Ill. 1, 4 (1851).

140. E.g., an act to provide for the construction of a rail-road from Auburn to Rochester, Ch. 349, Laws of New York, 1836. An act to provide for a general system of railroad incorporations, Laws of Illinois, 1849. See also an act to Authorize the Formation of Railroad Corporations, ch. 140, Laws of New York, 1848; an act to provide for the incorporation of railroad companies, no. 82, Laws of Michigan, 1855.

141. Harry N. Scheiber, "The Jurisprudence—and Mythology—of Eminent Domain in American Legal History," in Ellen Frankel Paul and Howard Dickman, eds., *Liberty, Property, and Government: Constitutional Interpretation Before the New Deal* (Albany, N.Y., 1989), 227.

142. Dilts, *The Great Road*, 69, 260.

143. Gephart, "Transportation and Industrial Development in the Middle West," 154, 163.

144. Parks, *Democracy's Railroad*, 222.

145. Brown, *A State Movement in Railroad Development*, 79. Likewise, the Atlantic and North Carolina Railroad reported in 1856 that much of the land along its route had been donated. *American Railroad Journal*, September 27, 1856.

146. An act granting to railroad companies the right of way, Ch. 31, Laws of Iowa, 1853.

147. See an act in relation to railroad companies, no. 41, Laws of Vermont, 1849; an act to provide for a general system of railroad incorporations, Laws of Illinois, 1849; an act regulating railroad companies, Laws of Ohio, 1848.

148. *O'Hara and Darlington v. Pennsylvania Railroad*, 25 Penn. 394 (1855). See also Redfield, *The Law of Railroads*, I, 244 (declaring that railroads must comply with all conditions precedent under the law before resorting to eminent domain).

149. Tony A. Freyer, *Producers Versus Capitalists: Constitutional Conflict in Antebellum America* (Charlottesville, Va., 1994), 153–154.

150. Simeon E. Baldwin, *American Railroad Law* (Boston, 1904), 91.

151. Dilts, *The Great Road*, 254.

152. Scheiber, "The Jurisprudence—and Mythology—of Eminent Domain," 226–227.

153. Elliott and Elliott, *A Treatise on the Law of Railroads*, II, 479–480.

154. Sarah H. Gordon, *Passage to Union: How the Railroads Transformed American Life, 1829–1929* (Chicago, 1996), 60.

155. Baldwin, *American Railroad Law*, 15–16; David Rorer, *A Treatise on the Law of Railways* (2 vols., Chicago, 1884), I, 588–593; *Lauman v. Lebanon Valley Railroad Company*, 30 Pa. 42 (1858).

156. An act to authorize the consolidation of certain railroad companies, Laws of New York, 1853.

157. An act to authorize railroad companies to make certain contracts with each other, Ch. 113, Laws of Kentucky, 1858; an act to provide for the incorporation of railroad companies, no. 82, Laws of Michigan, 1855.

158. E.g., an act to provide for the incorporation of railroad companies, Ch. 1, Laws of New Mexico, 1878; an act to provide for the creation and regulation of incorporated companies in the state of Maryland, Ch. 476, Laws of Maryland, 1870.

159. *Thomas v. Railroad Company*, 101 U.S. 71 (1879); Redfield, *The Law of Railways*, I, 634–642; Baldwin, *American Railroad Law*, 453–454; Rorer, *A Treatise on the Law of Railways*, I, 603–604.

160. *Pennsylvania Railroad Company v. Sly*, 65 Pa. 205 (1870).

161. *White v. Syracuse and Utica Railroad Company*, 14 Barb. 559 (N.Y. 1853).

162. E.g., an act relating to certain corporations, no. 379, Laws of Pennsylvania, 1861.

163. E.g., an act to incorporate the New Jersey Rail Road and Transportation Company, Laws of New Jersey, 1832; an act to amend an act . . . entitled an act to incorporate the Wilmington and Raleigh Rail Road Company, Ch. 30, Laws of North Carolina, 1835.

164. Lane, *From Indian Trail to Iron Horse*, 289, 291–292.

165. An act in relation to railroads and the organization of railroad companies, Ch. 119, Laws of Wisconsin, 1872.

166. *American Railroad Journal*, November 9, 1850.

167. See J. Willard Hurst, *Law and the Conditions of Freedom in the Nineteenth-Century United States* (Madison, Wis., 1956), 3–32.

2. Civil War and Federal Land Grants

1. *American Railroad Journal*, December 22, 1860.

2. See George Edgar Turner, *Victory Rode the Rails: The Strategic Place of the Railroads in the Civil War* (Indianapolis, 1953); Sarah H. Gordon, *Passage to Union: How the Railroads Transformed American Life, 1829–1929* (Chicago, 1996), 133–148.

3. Robert C. Black III, *The Railroads of the Confederacy* (Chapel Hill, N.C., 1952); Wayne Cline, *Alabama Railroads* (Tuscaloosa, Ala., 1997), 50–66; John F. Stover, *The Railroads of the South, 1865–1900*, (Chapel Hill, N.C., 1955), 3–14; Charles W. Ramsdell, "The Confederate Government and the Railroads," *American Historical Review* 22 (1917), 794–810; Peter S. McGuire, "The Railroads of Georgia, 1860–1880," *Georgia Historical Quarterly* 16 (1932), 179–213.

4. Black, *The Railroads of the Confederacy*, 294. See also Paul A.C. Koistinen, *Beating Plowshares Into Swords: The Political Economy of American Warfare, 1606–1865* (Lawrence, Kans., 1996), 226–232.

5. Black, *The Railroads of the Confederacy*, 49–50.

6. An act to induce railroad companies in this state to carry troops and munitions of war for the state free of charge, no. 49, Laws of Alabama, 1861.

7. An act still further defining the duties of the Trustees of the Internal Improvement Fund, Ch. 1, 138, Laws of Florida, 1861.

8. Black, *The Railroads of the Confederacy,* 52–54; Ramsdell, "The Confederate Government and the Railroads," 796.

9. Black, *The Railroads of the Confederacy,* 217–219.

10. Black, *The Railroads of the Confederacy,* 149–163; Turner, *Victory Rode the Rails,* 233–239; Ramsdell, "The Confederate Government and the Railroads," 801–803.

11. Wilfred Buck Yearns, *The Confederate Congress* (Athens, Ga., 1960), 129.

12. Cline, *Alabama Railroads,* 51.

13. Black, *The Railroads of the Confederacy,* 72–73; Ramsdell, "The Confederate Government and the Railroads," 797.

14. William T. Joynes to L. P. Walker, July 17, 1861, reprinted in *War of the Rebellion: A Compilation of the Official Records of the Union and Confederate Armies,* series IV, I (Washington, 1900), 485–486.

15. Resolutions of the Common Council of Petersburg, December 10, 1861, Virginia State Library.

16. Message of January 12, 1863, in *War of the Rebellion,* series IV, II, 348.

17. An act to facilitate transportation for the government, May 1, 1863, in Charles W. Ramsdell, ed., *Laws and Joint Resolutions of the Last Session of the Confederate Congress* (Durham, N.C., 1941), 167–169.

18. Black, *The Railroads of the Confederacy,* 164.

19. Frederick W. Sims to Alexander R. Lawton, April 1, 1864, in *War of the Rebellion,* series IV, III, 228.

20. An act to provide for the more efficient transportation of troops . . . upon the railroads . . . in the Confederate States, no. 85, February 28, 1865, in Ramsdell, ed., *Laws and Joint Resolutions,* 60–61.

21. Black, *The Railroads of the Confederacy,* 200–213.

22. An act to aid the Brunswick & Albany Railroad Company, no. 136, Laws of Georgia, 1869.

23. John F. Stover, *American Railroads,* 2nd ed. (Chicago, 1997), 58. See also Cline, *Alabama Railroads,* 58–66.

24. Turner, *Victory Rode the Rails,* 33–38; Stover, *American Railroads,* 50–51; Carl Russell Fish, "The Northern Railroads, 1861," *American Historical Review* 22 (1917), 778–793.

25. An act to authorize the President of the United States in certain cases to take possession of railroad and telegraph lines, ch XV, Stat. 1862.

26. Turner, *Victory Rode the Rails,* 247; Fish, "The Northern Railroads, 1861," 790–791.

27. See John L. Blackman, Jr., "The Seizure of the Reading Railroad in 1864," *Pennsylvania Magazine of History and Biography* 111 (1987), 49–60.

28. Stover, *American Railroads,* 57; Koistinen, *Beating Plowshares Into Swords,* 150–154.

29. Turner, *Victory Rode the Rails,* 90, 111–115; Maury Klein, *History of the Louisville & Nashville Railroad* (New York, 1972), 37–38.

30. John F. Stover, *History of the Illinois Central Railroad* (New York, 1975), 14–28.

31. An act granting the right of way, and making a grant of land to the states of Illinois, Mississippi, and Alabama, in aid of the construction of a railroad from Chicago to Mobile, Ch. LXI, 1850, 9 U.S. Statutes 466.

32. George Rogers Taylor, *The Transportation Revolution, 1815–1860* (New York, 1951), 94–96.

33. *United States v. Union Pacific Railroad Company,* 91 U.S. 72, 81 (1875).

34. An act to aid in the construction of a railroad and telegraph line from the Missouri River to the Pacific Ocean . . . , July 1, 1862, 12 U.S. Statutes 489.

35. An act to amend an act entitled "An act to aid in the construction of a railroad . . . ," July 2, 1864, 13 U.S. Statutes 356.

36. See David Haward Bain, *Empire Express: Building the First Transcontinental Railroad* (New York, 1999); Stephen E. Ambrose, *Nothing Like It in the World: The Men Who Built the Transcontinental Railroad, 1863–1869* (New York, 2000); Albro Martin, *Railroads Triumphant: The Growth, Rejection and Rebirth of a Vital American Force* (New York, 1992), 280–286; Stover, *American Railroads*, 63–71; Gordon, *Passage to Union*, 150–153.

37. Bain, *Empire Express*, 172, 675–710; Ambrose, *Nothing Like It in the World*, 92–93, 320–321, 373–377.

38. An act making appropriations for the legislative, executive, and judicial expenses of the government, March 3, 1873, 17 U.S. Statutes 508.

39. Martin, *Railroads Triumphant*, 287–288; Paul Kens, *Justice Stephen Field: Shaping Liberty from the Gold Rush to the Gilded Age* (Lawrence, Kans., 1997), 220–222; Charles Fairman, *Reconstruction and Reunion, 1864–88*, Part Two (New York, 1987), 604–606; Stuart Daggett, *Chapters on the History of the Southern Pacific* (New York, 1922), 370–394.

40. An act to alter and amend the act entitled "An act to aid in the construction of a railroad . . . ," May 7, 1878, 20 U.S. Statutes 56.

41. *Sinking Fund Cases*, 99 U.S. 700, 722 (1878).

42. Kens, *Justice Stephen Field*, 222–225; Fairman, *Reconstruction and Reunion*, 607–615.

43. Daggett, *Chapters on the History of the Southern Pacific*, 395–396; Daniel W. Levy, "Classical Lawyers and the Southern Pacific Railroad," *Western Legal History* 9 (1996), 177, 221–225.

44. *Report of the Commission and of the Minority Commissioner of the United States Pacific Railway Commission* (Washington, 1887).

45. Daggett, *Chapters on the History of the Southern Pacific*, 397–424; R. Hal Williams, *The Democratic Party and California Politics, 1880–1896* (Stanford, Calif., 1973), 216–223.

46. *Study of Federal Aid to Rail Transportation* (Washington, 1977), III-2–III-8; Stover, *American Railroads*, 82–84.

47. Ambrose, *Nothing Like It in the World*, 376.

48. For the debate over the economic issues involved in the land grant policy, see Martin, *Railroads Triumphant*, 170–174; Robert S. Henry, "The Railroad Land Grant Legend in American History Texts," *Mississippi Valley Historical Review* 32 (1945), 171–194; Lloyd J. Mercer, "Land Grants to American Railroads: Social Cost or Social Benefit?", *Business History Review* 43 (1969), 134–151; Stanley L. Engerman, "Some Economic Issues Relating to Railroad Subsidies and the Evaluation of Land Grants," *Journal of Economic History* 43 (1972), 443–463.

49. David Maldwyn Ellis, "The Forfeiture of Railroad Land Grants, 1867–1894," *Mississippi Valley Historical Review* 33 (1946), 27, 30–31; Alan Furman Westin, "The Supreme Court, the Populist Movement and the Campaign of 1896," *Journal of Politics* 15 (1953), 3, 9–10.

50. Ellis, "The Forfeiture of Railroad Land Grants," 39–55. See also Leslie E. Decker, *Railroads, Lands and Politics: The Taxation of the Railroad Land Grants, 1864–1897* (Providence, R.I., 1964), 38–45; Carter Goodrich, *Government Promotion of American Canals and Railroads, 1800–1890* (New York, 1960), 197–198.

51. David Maldwyn Ellis, "The Oregon and California Railroad Land Grants, 1866–1945." *Pacific Northwest Quarterly* 39 (1948), 253–283.

52. Joint resolution instructing the attorney general to institute certain suits, 31 Stat. 571 (1908).

53. *Oregon and California Railroad Company v. United States*, 238 U.S. 393, 438–439 (1915).

54. An act to alter and amend an act entitled "An act granting lands to aid in the construction of a railroad . . . ," 39 Stat. 218 (1916).

55. *Oregon and California Railroad Company v. United States*, 243 U.S. 549 (1917).

56. Ross R. Cotroneo, "United States v. Northern Pacific Railway Company: The Final Settlement of the Land Grant Case, 1924–1941," *Pacific Northwest Quarterly* 71 (1980), 107–111. See also Resolution authorizing the Northern Pacific Railroad Company to issue its bonds for the construction of its road . . . , 16 Stat. 378 (1870).

57. An act to alter and amend an act entitled "An act granting lands to aid in the construction of a railroad . . . from Lake Superior to Puget Sound . . . ," 46 Stat. 41 (1929).

58. *United States v. Northern Pacific Railway Company*, 311 U.S. 317 (1940).

59. Transportation Act, 54 Stat. 898, 954–955 (1940).

60. Morton Keller, *Affairs of State: Public Life in Late Nineteenth Century America* (Cambridge, Mass., 1977), 389.

61. Westin, "The Supreme Court, the Populist Movement and the Campaign of 1896," 9–13.

62. See Dan B. Dobbs, *Law of Remedies*, 2nd ed. (3 vols., St. Paul, Minn., 1993), I, 83.

63. *United States v. Union Pacific Railroad Company*, 98 U.S. 569, 620 (1878).

64. *Oregon and California Railroad Company v. United States*, 238 U.S. 393, 416 (1915).

65. Id. at 416.

66. See Robert S. Henry, "The Railroad Land Grant Legend," 171–194; David Maldwyn Ellis, "Railroad Land Grant Rates, 1850–1945," *Journal of Land & Public Utility Economics* 21 (1945), 207, 211–216. See also *Study of Federal Aid to Transportation*, III-9-III-10; D. Philip Locklin, *Economics of Transportation*, 7th ed. (Homewood, Ill., 1972), 136–137 (concluding that the value of the reduced transportation rates to the government exceeded the value of the land grants at the time these were made).

67. The different rate provisions are analyzed in Norris Kenny, "The Transportation of Government Property and Troops over Land-Grant Railroads," *Journal of Land & Public Utility Economics* 9 (1933), 368–381.

68. As quoted in Ellis, "Railroad Land Grant Rates," 212.

69. *Atchison, Topeka and Santa Fe Railroad Company v. United States*, 15 Cl. Ct. 126 (1879).

70. *Louisville & Nashville Railroad Company v. United States*, 273 U.S. 321 (1927); *Southern Pacific Co. v. United States*, 307 U.S. 393 (1939).

71. Ellis, "Railroad Land Grant Rates," 216–222.

72. *Repeal of Land Grant Reduced Rates on Railroad Transportation of Government Traffic, Report, Committee on Interstate and Foreign Commerce*, House of Representatives, March 18, 1942.

73. To amend . . . Transportation Act of 1940 with respect to the movement of government traffic, Ch. 573, 59 Stat. 606–607 (1945).

74. Mark W. Summers, *Railroads, Reconstruction, and the Gospel of Prosperity: Aid Under the Radical Republicans, 1865–1877* (Princeton, N.J., 1984), 3–46.

75. An act to provide for the creation and regulation of railroad companies in the state of Alabama, no. 129, Laws of Alabama, 1868; an act to provide a general law for the incorporation of railroads and canals, Ch. 1987, Laws of Florida, 1874.

76. John F. Stover, *The Railroads of the South, 1865–1900*, 59–98; Goodrich, *Government Promotion of American Canals and Railroads*, 207–229; Clive, *Alabama Railroads*, 79–96.

77. Dorothy Houseal Stewart, "Survival of the Fittest: William Morrill Wadley and the Central of Georgia Railroad's Coming of Age, 1866–1882," *Georgia Historical Quarterly* 78 (1994), 39, 45–46.

78. Goodrich, *Government Promotion of American Canals and Railroads*, 213–214.

79. Clive, *Alabama Railroads*, 82.

80. Allen W. Moger, "Railroad Practices and Policies in Virginia After the Civil War," *Virginia Magazine of History and Biography* 59 (1951), 423, 448–449.

81. Summers, *Railroads, Reconstruction, and the Gospel of Prosperity*, 29, 42–43, 155–156; Michael R. Hyman, "Taxation, Public Policy, and Political Dissent: Yeoman Disaffection in the Post-Reconstruction Lower South," *Journal of Southern History* 55 (1989), 49, 56–57.

82. Edward L. Ayers, *Vengeance and Justice: Crime and Punishment in the 19th Century American South* (New York, 1984), 192–193; Paul W. Keve, *The History of Corrections in Virginia* (Charlottesville, Va., 1986), 74–80; Scott Reynolds Nelson, *Iron Confederacies: Southern Railways, Klan Violence, and Reconstruction* (Chapel Hill, N.C., 1999), 169; Stover, *The Railroads of the South*, 145; Clive, *Alabama Railroads*, 87; Moger, "Railroad Practices and Policies in Virginia After the Civil War," 451–452.

83. Martin, *Railroads Triumphant*, 30, 79; Gordon, *Passage to Union*, 166–177.

84. *State of Arkansas v. Little Rock, Mississippi River and Texas Railway Company*, 31 Ark. 701 (1877).

85. Moger, "Railroad Practices and Policies in Virginia After the Civil War," 437–440.

86. Cecil Kenneth Brown, *A State Movement in Railroad Development* (Chapel Hill, N.C., 1928), 43, 62.

87. Stover, *The Railroads of the South*, 122–154. See also Nelson, *Iron Confederacies*.

88. Robert L. Dabney, "The New South," June 15, 1882, Virginia State Library.

3. Regulatory Landscape of the Nineteenth Century

1. *Thomas v. Boston and Providence Rail Road Corporation*, 51 Mass. 472, 475 (1845); Isaac F. Redfield, *The Laws of Railways*, 6th ed. (Boston, 1888), II, 16–19.

2. See, e.g., an act to authorize the formation of the Charleston, Georgetown and All-Saints Rail Road Company, Laws of South Carolina, 1838; an act to incorporate the stockholders of the Lynchburg and Tennessee Rail-Road Company, Ch. 111, Laws of Virginia, 1835; an act to incorporate the Georgia Rail Road Company, Laws of Georgia, 1833.

3. *McDuffee v. Portland & Rochester Railroad*, 52 N.H. 430 (1873).

4. See *Chicago, Burlington and Quincy Railroad Co. v. Parks*, 18 Ill. 460, 464 (1857); *Fitchburg Railroad Company v. Gage*, 78 Mass. 393, 399 (1859); Walter Chadwick Noyes, *American Railroad Rates* (Boston, 1905), 103–104.

5. See Lee Benson, *Merchants, Farmers, & Railroads: Railroad Regulation and New York Politics, 1850–1887* (Cambridge, Mass., 1955), 1–2; James F. Doster, *Railroads in Alabama Politics, 1875–1914* (Tuscaloosa, Ala., 1957), 5; Edward Chase Kirkland, *Men, Cities and Transportation: A Study in New England History, 1820–1900* (Cambridge, Mass., 1948), I, 267–273.

6. *Beekman v. Saratoga & Schenectady Railroad Company*, 3 Paige's Ch. 42, 75 (N.Y. 1831).

7. *Commonwealth v. Fitchburg Railroad Company*, 78 Mass. 180, 187 (1858).

8. Simeon E. Baldwin, *American Railroad Law* (Boston, 1904), 7–9; George E. Reigel, *The Story of the Western Railroads* (New York, 1926), 3; George Rogers Taylor, *The Transportation Revolution, 1815–1860* (New York, 1951), 83; Stephen Salsbury, *The State, the Investor, and the Railroad: The Boston & Albany, 1825–1867* (Cambridge, Mass., 1967), 63–64.

9. *Boyle v. Philadelphia and Reading Railroad Company*, 54 Pa. 310 (1867); Noyes, *American Railroad Rates*, 6–7.

10. An act to incorporate the Rhode Island and Connecticut Railroad Company, 1832, in W. P. Gregg and Benjamin Pond, eds., *The Railroad Laws and Charters of the United States* (2 vols., Boston, 1851), II, 684.

11. An act to incorporate the "Ohio Canal and Steubenville Railway Company," Ohio Laws, 1830. See also an act to incorporate the Richmond, Eaton and Miami Rail Road Company, Ohio Laws, 1831.

12. An act to authorize the formation of the Edgefield Rail Road Company, 1834, reprinted in Thomas Cooper and David J. McCord, *The Statutes at Large of South Carolina* (Columbia, S.C., 1840), VIII, 396–404.

13. *Boyle v. Philadelphia and Reading Railroad Company,* 54 Pa. 310 (1867); Noyes, *American Railroad Rates,* 4.

14. E.g., an act incorporating the Loudoun Rail-Road Company, Ch. 73, Laws of Virginia, 1831; an act to incorporate the Rhode Island and Connecticut Railroad Company, Laws of Rhode Island, 1832, reprinted in Gregg and Pond, *The Railroad Laws and Charters,* II, 682–691; an act to incorporate the Richmond, Eaton and Miami Rail-Road Company, Ohio Laws, 1831.

15. John L. Ringwalt, *Development of Transportation Systems in the United States* (Philadelphia, 1888), 92; Noyes, *American Railroad Rates,* 7.

16. An act to regulate the use of railroads, Ch. 191, Laws of Massachusetts, 1845, reprinted in Gregg and Pond, *The Railroad Laws and Charters,* II, 648–649.

17. E.g., an act to authorize the formation of the Spartanburg and Union Rail Road Company, 1847, reprinted in 11 *Statutes at Large of South Carolina,* 479–488; an act to incorporate the Florida, Atlantic, and Gulf Central Rail Road Company, Ch. 317, Laws of Florida, 1850.

18. An act to incorporate the Cincinnati and Charleston Rail Road Company, Laws of Tennessee, 1835.

19. E.g., an act incorporating the stockholders of the Eastern Shore Rail-Road Company, Laws of Virginia, 1835; an act to incorporate the Georgia Rail Road Company, Laws of Georgia, 1833; an act to charter the Charlotte and South Carolina Rail Road Company, 1846, reprinted in 11 *Statutes at Large of South Carolina,* 397–408.

20. An act for the construction of a rail-road from Attica to Buffalo, Laws of New York, 1836.

21. E.g., Resolve Incorporating Manchester Railroad Company, Laws of Connecticut, 1833, reprinted in Gregg and Pond, *The Railroad Laws and Charters,* II, 907–913; Act to Incorporate the Boston and Providence Railroad Company, Laws of Rhode Island, 1831, reprinted in Gregg and Pond, *The Railroad Laws and Charters,* II, 668–677; Amending Charter of the Hartford and Providence Railroad Company, Laws of Connecticut, 1849, reprinted in Gregg and Pond, *The Railroad Laws and Charters,* II, 918–925.

22. E.g., an act to incorporate the Milan and Columbus Rail Road Company, Laws of Ohio, 1832.

23. Noyes, *American Railroad Rates,* 44 (pointing out that "cost of transportation does not vary in proportion to distance carried"); Salsbury, *The State, the Investor, and the Railroad,* 129.

24. John K. Towles, "Early Railroad Monopoly and Discrimination in Rhode Island, 1835–1855," *Yale Review* 18 (1909), 299, 307–318 (observing that railroads in antebellum Rhode Island disregarded charter clauses that rates should be in proportion to distance and that legislators declined to pass a bill to enforce the per-mile rate); William F. Gephart, "Transportation and Industrial Development in the Middle West," in 34 *Studies in History, Economics and Public Law* (New York, 1909), 122, 166 (pointing out that most railroads in Ohio ignored rate limits).

25. Massachusetts Revised Statutes, Ch. 39, sec. 83, 1835.

26. An act to incorporate the Florida, Atlantic, and Gulf Central Rail Road Company, Ch. 317, Laws of Florida, 1850.

27. An act to incorporate the Bennington and Brattleboro Railroad Company, no. 34, Laws of Vermont, 1835, reprinted in Gregg and Pond, *The Railroad Laws and Charters*, I, 723–732.

28. E.g., an act incorporating the Richmond Rail-Road and South Anna Navigation Company, Ch. 109, Laws of Virginia, 1834. See also an act prescribing certain general regulations for the incorporation of rail-road companies, Ch. 118, Laws of Virginia, 1837.

29. Gephart, "Transportation and Industrial Development in the Middle West," 168 (pointing out that few Ohio railroads paid any dividends before 1870); James D. Dilts, *The Great Road: The Building of the Baltimore & Ohio, the Nation's First Railroad, 1828–1853* (Stanford, Calif., 1993), 208 (noting that investors were unhappy with the meager dividends paid in the 1830s).

30. Shortage of private capital was a particular problem in the southern states, and explains the heavy reliance on public support for railroad projects during the antebellum era. Milton S. Heath, "Public Railroad Construction and the Development of Private Enterprise in the South Before 1861," *Journal of Economic History* 10 (Supplement 1950), 40.

31. Noyes, *American Railroad Rates*, 215.

32. An act to authorize the formation of the Spartanburg and Union Rail Road Company, 1847, reprinted in 11 *Statutes at Large of South Carolina*, 479–488.

33. *Campbell v. Marietta and Cincinnati Railroad Company*, 23 Ohio St. 168, 189 (1872).

34. Noyes, *American Railroad Rates*, 214 ("Generally, maximum rates were prescribed, leaving to the railroads the right to fix the exact rates within the stated limits").

35. There were some exceptions to this general rule. An 1835 Vermont charter authorized the state supreme court, upon application of ten local property owners, to alter and establish the price of transportation. An act to incorporate the Bennington and Brattleboro Railroad Company, no. 34, Laws of Vermont, 1835, reprinted in Gregg and Pond, *The Railroad Laws and Charters*, I, 723–732.

36. For a rare suit to collect a statutory penalty, see *Camden & Amboy Rail Road Company v. Briggs*, 22 N.J. Law 623 (1850). For this litigation see Wheaton J. Lane, *From Indian Trail to Iron Horse: Travel and Transportation in New Jersey, 1620–1860* (Princeton, N.J., 1939), 298–299.

37. Noyes, *American Railroad Rates*, 33, 232–233 (noting that common-law remedy "is entirely ineffectual and inadequate").

38. An act to prevent the taking of unlawful toll or fare on canals and rail roads, Laws of New Jersey, 1839; an act prescribing certain general regulations for the incorporation of rail-road companies, ch. 118, Laws of Virginia, 1837.

39. Towles, "Early Railroad Monopoly and Discrimination in Rhode Island," 307–319.

40. Benson, *Merchants, Farmers & Railroads*, 10–16.

41. Taylor, *Transportation Revolution*, 134–135.

42. *Campbell v. Marietta and Cincinnati Railroad Company*, 23 Ohio St. 168 (1872); *Pennsylvania Railroad Co. v. Sly*, 65 Pa. 205 (1870); David Rorer, *A Treatise on the Law of Railways* (2 vols., Chicago, 1884), I, 32–33.

43. Taylor, *Transportation Revolution*, 88. See also George H. Miller, *Railroads and the Granger Laws* (Madison, Wis., 1971), 30 (declaring that "few of the existing limits had any practical effect" on railroad rates before 1850).

44. An act to incorporate the Columbus, Delaware, Marion and Sandusky Rail Road Company, Laws of Ohio, 1832.

45. E.g., an act to authorize the formation of railroad corporations, Ch. 140, Laws of New York, 1848; an act in relation to railroad corporations, no. 41, Laws of Vermont, 1849.

46. *Annual Report of the Railroad Commissioners of the State of New Hampshire, 1891* (Concord, N.H., 1892), 23.

47. *In re Opinion of the Justices,* 66 N.H. 629, 33 A. 1076 (1891). For a discussion of this decision, see John Phillip Reid, *Chief Justice: The Judicial World of Charles Doe* (Cambridge, Mass., 1967), 376–383.

48. E.g., an act regulating railroad companies, no. 76, Laws of Pennsylvania, 1849.

49. E.g., an act to provide for a general system of railroad incorporations, Laws of Illinois, 1849; an act to authorize the formation of railroad corporations, and to regulate the same, Ch. 140, Laws of New York, 1850.

50. *City of Roxbury v. Boston and Providence Railroad Corporation,* 60 Mass. 424, 430 (1850).

51. An act to authorize the formation of railroad associations, and to regulate the same, Laws of Missouri, 1853.

52. An act to regulate the use of rail-roads, Ch. 191, Laws of Massachusetts, 1845. See *Boston and Worcester Railroad Corporation v. Western Railroad Corporation,* 80 Mass. 253 (1859); *Lexington and West Cambridge Railroad Company v. Fitchburg Railroad Company,* 80 Mass. 266 (1859).

53. An act to provide for the creation and regulation of railroad companies in the state of Alabama, no. 129, Laws of Alabama, 1868.

54. *Boston and Worcester Railroad Corporation v. Western Railroad Corporation,* 80 Mass. 253, 260–261 (1859).

55. *Chicago and Alton Railroad Company v. People ex rel. Koerner,* 67 Ill. 11, 21 (1873).

56. For a discussion of rising anti-railroad sentiment, see John F. Stover, *American Railroads,* 2nd ed. (Chicago, 1997), 96–117; Miller, *Railroads and the Granger Laws,* 3–23; Sarah H. Gordon, *Passage to Union: How the Railroads Transformed American Life, 1829–1929* (Chicago, 1996), 188–198.

57. For perceptive discussion of the rate controversy, see Herbert Hovenkamp, "Regulatory Conflict in the Gilded Age: Federalism and the Railroad Problem," *Yale Law Journal* 97 (1988), 1017–1072; Albro Martin, "The Troubled Subject of Railroad Regulation in the Gilded Age—A Reappraisal," *Journal of American History* 61 (1971), 339–371. See also *First Annual Report of the Interstate Commerce Commission* (Washington, 1887), 1–43.

58. *Proceedings of the Special Committee on Railroads, State of New York* (5 vols., New York, 1879), II, 1268, 1290, 1300.

59. Ari Hoogenboom and Olive Hoogenboom, *A History of the ICC: From Panacea to Palliative* (New York, 1976), 2.

60. For a thoughtful explanation by railroads of why short-haul freight was more expensive to handle and equal mileage rates were unworkable, see *Memorial of the Chicago & North Western and Chicago, Milwaukee & St. Paul Railway Companies to the Senate and Assembly of the State of Wisconsin* (Chicago, 1875). See generally Ralph L. Dewey, *The Long and Short Haul Principle of Rate Regulation* (Columbus, Ohio, 1935).

61. For the impact of steamboat competition on railroad rates into Nashville, see Don H. Doyle, *Nashville in the New South, 1880–1930* (Knoxville, Tenn., 1985), 32–40.

62. Albro Martin, *Railroads Triumphant: The Growth, Rejection, and Rebirth of a Vital American Force* (New York, 1992), 206–210; Stover, *American Railroads,* 109; Julius Grodinsky, *The Iowa Pool* (Chicago, 1950); Maury Klein, "The Strategy of Southern Railroads," *American Historical Review* 73 (1968), 1052, 1057.

63. Although the question was not conclusively resolved, a number of state courts found that pooling was an undue restraint of competition. In *Morrill v. Boston & Maine Railroad,* 55 N.H. 531 (1875), apparently the first decision on the topic, the court found that a state statute prohibiting the consolidation of competing railroads invalidated an arrangement between two carriers to divide a portion of their earnings.

64. Robert E. Riegel, *The Story of the Western Railroads,* 138–139; Frederick Merk, "Eastern Antecedents of the Grangers," *Agricultural History* 23 (1949), 1, 6–7.

65. Martin, "The Troubled Subject of Railroad Regulation in the Gilded Age," 370–371; W. S. McCain, "Railroads as a Factor in the Law," *Arkansas Bar Association Proceedings* (1886), 9, 11.

66. Riegel, *The Story of the Western Railroads,* 141–143; Martin, *Railroads Triumphant,* 191–194.

67. Merk, "Eastern Antecedents of the Grangers," 1–8.

68. Kirkland, *Men, Cities and Transportation,* II, 232–237.

69. Benson, *Merchants, Farmers & Railroads,* 6–9.

70. An act to establish a board of railroad commissioners, Ch. 408, Laws of Massachusetts, 1869; Kirkland, *Men, Cities and Transportation,* 237–243.

71. Charles Francis Adams, Jr., *Railroads: Their Origin and Problems* (New York, 1878), 138.

72. Miller, *Railroads and the Granger Laws,* 81–82, 115; Harold D. Woodman, "Chicago Businessmen and the 'Granger' Laws," *Agricultural History* 36 (1962), 16–24.

73. See Miller, *Railroads and the Granger Laws,* 87–90.

74. Id., 97–160; Earl S. Beard, "The Background of State Railroad Regulation in Iowa," *Iowa Journal of History* 51 (1953), 1–36.

75. Robert S. Hunt, *Law and Locomotives: The Impact of the Railroad on Wisconsin Law in the Nineteenth Century* (Madison, Wis., 1958), 98–130; Robert T. Daland, "Enactment of the Potter Law," *Wisconsin Magazine of History* 33 (1949), 45–54.

76. Charles Francis Adams, Jr., "The Granger Movement," *North American Review* 120 (1875), 394, 416.

77. As quoted in Reid, *Chief Justice,* 256.

78. Adams, "The Granger Movement," 421.

79. Mildred Throne, "The Repeal of the Iowa Granger Law, 1878," *Iowa Journal of History* 51 (1953), 97–130 .

80. See Richard C. Cortner, *The Iron Horse and the Constitution: The Railroads and the Transformation of the Fourteenth Amendment* (Westport, Conn., 1993), 1–18; Alan Jones, "Republicanism, Railroads, and Nineteenth-Century Midwestern Constitutionalism," in Ellen Frankel Paul and Howard Dickman, eds., *Liberty, Property, and Government: Constitutional Interpretation Before the New Deal* (Albany, N.Y., 1989), 239–265.

81. *Chicago, Burlington and Quincy Railroad Company v. Iowa,* 94 U.S. 155, 161 (1877).

82. *Munn v. Illinois,* 94 U.S. 113, 134 (1877).

83. *Railway World,* March 17, 1877.

84. *Munn v. Illinois,* 94 U.S. at 148. See Paul Kens, *Justice Stephen Field: Shaping Liberty from the Gold Rush to the Gilded Age* (Lawrence, Kans., 1997), 153–166.

85. William Deverell, *Railroad Crossing: Californians and the Railroad, 1850–1910* (Berkeley, Calif., 1994), 46–56.

86. Gordon Morris Bakken, *Rocky Mountain Constitution Making, 1850–1912* (Westport, Conn., 1987), 76–78.

87. Maury Klein, *History of the Louisville & Nashville Railroad* (New York, 1972), 378. See also William G. Thomas, *Lawyering for the Railroad: Business, Law, and Power in the New South* (Baton Rouge, La., 1999), 92–96; Mark W. Summers, *The Plundering Generation: Corruption and the Crisis of the Union, 1849–1861* (New York, 1987), 101; Stover, *American Railroads,* 115.

88. Towles, "Early Railroad Monopoly and Discrimination in Rhode Island," 318.

89. Doster, *Railroads in Alabama Politics,* 36–38. See also Thomas, *Lawyering for the Railroad,* 180.

90. Charles F. Adams, Jr., "Railway Problems in 1869," *North American Review* 110 (1870), 116, 123.

91. David M. Gold, "Redfield, Railroads, and the Roots of 'Laissez-Faire Constitutionalism,'" *American Journal of Legal History* 27 (1983), 254, 267.

92. Thomas A. Scott, "The Recent Strikes," *North American Review* 125 (1877), 351, 357.

93. *Wabash, St. Louis & Pacific Railway v. Illinois,* 118 U.S. 557, 577 (1886).

94. An act to regulate commerce, 24 *U.S. Statutes at Large,* Ch. 104 (1887). See also George W. Hilton, "The Consistency of the Interstate Commerce Act,"*Journal of Law and Economics* 9 (1966), 87–113.

95. *First Annual Report of the Interstate Commerce Commission,* 34.

96. Keith T. Poole and Howard Rosenthal, "The Enduring Nineteenth-Century Battle for Economic Regulation: The Interstate Commerce Act Revisited," *Journal of Law and Economics* 36 (1993), 837–860.

97. Gordon, *Passage to Union,* 193.

98. See Gabriel Kolko, *Railroads and Regulation, 1877–1916* (Princeton, N.J., 1965).

99. Hoogenboom and Hoogenboom, *A History of the ICC,* 12–13; Morton Keller, *Affairs of State: Public Life in Late Nineteenth Century America* (Cambridge, Mass., 1977), 428; Edward A. Purcell, Jr., "Ideas and Interests: Businessmen and the Interstate Commerce Act," *Journal of American History* 54 (1967), 561, 575–578; Martin, "The Troubled Subject of Railroad Regulation in the Gilded Age," 339–371; Hovenkamp, "Regulatory Conflict in the Gilded Age," 1017–1072.

100. James Bryce, *The American Commonwealth,* rev. ed. (2 vols., New York, 1912), II, 700–701 ("Little as the railroads relish regulation from either quarter, they prefer that which proceeds from Congress, because it is uniform, it hampers them less, it is less subject to frequent change").

101. Keller, *Affairs of State,* 428.

102. Hoogenboom and Hoogenboom, *A History of the ICC,* 18–31; Alan Jones, "Thomas M. Cooley and the Interstate Commerce Commission: Continuity and Change in the Doctrine of Equal Rights," *Political Science Quarterly* 81 (1966), 602–627.

103. *ICC v. Louisville & Nashville Railway Company,* 73 F. 409, 420 (Cir. Ct., M.D. Tenn., 1896).

104. Martin, *Railroads Triumphant,* 328; James W. Ely, Jr., *The Chief Justiceship of Melville W. Fuller, 1888–1910* (Columbia, S.C., 1995), 91–92.

105. R. Erik Lillquist, "Constitutional Rights at the Junction: The Emergence of the Privilege Against Self-Incrimination and the Interstate Commerce Act," *Virginia Law Review* 81 (1995), 1989–2042.

106. *Seventeenth Annual Report of the Interstate Commerce Commission* (Washington, 1903), 17.

107. As quoted in Gerald G. Eggert, *Richard Olney: Evolution of a Statesman* (University Park, Pa., 1974), 28.

108. Lawrence M. Friedman, *A History of American Law,* 2nd ed. (New York, 1985), 453.

109. Hovenkamp, "Regulatory Conflict in the Gilded Age," 1058–1062.

110. Jones, "Thomas M. Cooley and the Interstate Commerce Commission," 622–623.

111. See Cortner, *The Iron Horse and the Constitution,* passim.

112. *Stone v. Farmers' Loan and Trust Company,* 116 U.S. 307, 331 (1886).

113. *Chicago & North Western Railway Company v. Dey,* 35 F. 866 (Cir. Ct., S.D. Iowa, 1888); Cortner, *The Iron Horse and the Constitution,* 61–65.

114. Cortner, *The Iron Horse and the Constitution,* 77–124; James W. Ely, Jr., "The Railroad Question Revisited: *Chicago, Milwaukee & St. Paul Railway v. Minnesota* and Constitutional Limits on State Regulations," *Great Plains Quarterly* 12 (1992), 121–134.

115. See Eric Monkkonen, "Can Nebraska or Any State Regulate Railroads? *Smyth v. Ames,* 1898," *Nebraska History* 54 (1973), 365–382; Stephen A. Siegel, "Understanding the *Lochner* Era: Lessons from the Controversy over Railroad and Utility Rate Regulation," *Virginia Law Review* 70 (1984), 187, 224–232. For contemporary criticism of *Smyth,* see Barbara H. Fried, *The Progressive Assault on Laissez-Faire: Robert Hale and the First Law and Economics Movement* (Cambridge, Mass., 1998), 175–204.

116. Doster, *Railroads in Alabama Politics,* 85–86, 143–145, 189–191.

117. Gerald D. Nash, "The California Railroad Commission, 1876–1911," *Southern California Quarterly* 44 (1962), 287, 297–298; *Metropolitan Trust Company v. Houston & Texas Central Railroad Company,* 90 F. 683 (Cir. Ct., W.D. Texas, 1898).

118. Mary Cornelia Porter, "That Commerce Shall Be Free: A New Look at the Old Laissez-Faire Court," 1976 *Supreme Court Review* 135, 143. See also Charles Warren, *The Supreme Court in United States History,* rev. ed. (Boston, 1926, 2 vols.), II, 592 (noting that decision applying due process norms to rate regulations strengthened investor confidence in railroad securities).

119. Herbert Hovenkamp, *Enterprise and American Law, 1836–1937* (Cambridge, Mass., 1991), 159–164.

120. E.g., an act to provide for the incorporation of railroad companies, no. 82, Laws of Michigan, 1855.

121. *Morrill v. Boston & Maine Railroad,* 55 N.H. 531, 539 (1875).

122. E.g., *Pearsall v. Great Northern Railway Company,* 161 U.S. 646 (1896).

123. Robert B. Carlson, *Main Line to Oblivion: The Disintegration of New York Railroads in the Twentieth Century* (Port Washington, N.Y., 1971), 29–31. See generally Paul W. MacAvoy, *The Economic Effects of Regulation: The Trunk-Line Railroad Cartels and the Interstate Commerce Commission Before 1900* (Cambridge, Mass., 1965), 110–204.

124. Martin A. Knapp, "Government Regulation of Railroad Rates," *Albany Law Journal* 51 (1895), 151, 155.

125. *United States v. Trans-Missouri Freight Association,* 166 U.S. 290 (1897). See also *United States v. Joint Traffic Association,* 171 U.S. 505 (1898).

126. *United States v. Trans-Missouri Freight Association,* 166 U.S. at 371.

127. Charles F. Adams, Jr., "The Government and the Railroad Corporations," *North American Review* 112 (1871), 31, 36.

128. Collis P. Huntington, "A Plea for Railway Consolidation," *North American Review* 153 (1891), 272.

129. Railroad consolidation proceeded in Wisconsin despite halfhearted legislative efforts to prevent it. Hunt, *Law and Locomotives,* 80–81. For railroad mergers in Virginia, see Allen W. Moger, "Railroad Practices and Politics in Virginia After the Civil War," *Virginia Magazine of History and Biography* 59 (1951), 423.

130. Carlson, *Main Line to Oblivion,* 43–44.

131. Benson, *Merchants, Farmers & Railroads,* 244–245.

132. *Application of Amsterdam, Johnstown and Gloversville Railroad Company,* 86 Hun. 578, 584, 33 N.Y. Supp. 1009, 1012 (Sup. Ct. 1895). Courts, however, occasionally overturned railroad commission decisions declining to grant a certificate of public necessity and convenience for construction of a new line. *In Re Long Lake Railroad Company,* 11 App. Div. 233, 42 N.Y. Supp. 125 (1896).

133. See *Railroad Gazette,* September 11, 1896 (discussing authority of Maine railroad commission to prevent construction of new railroads).

134. An act to provide for the appointment of a commissioner of railroads . . . , no. 79, Laws of Michigan, 1873.

135. Doster, *Railroads in Alabama Politics,* 160.

136. *Wisconsin, Minnesota and Pacific Railroad v. Jacobson,* 179 U.S. 287 (1900).

137. An act in relation to railroad corporations and the transportation of freight and passengers, Laws of Rhode Island, 1855.

138. Gordon, *Passage to Union*, 194–196.

139. See generally Note, "The State Ownership of Railroads," *American Law Review* 28 (1894), 608.

140. Gerald Berk, *Alternative Tracks: The Constitution of American Industrial Order, 1865–1917* (Baltimore, 1994), 79; David Ray Papke, *The Pullman Case: The Clash of Labor and Capital in Industrial America* (Lawrence, Kans., 1999), 86.

141. William Deverell, *Railroad Crossing: Californians and the Railroad, 1850–1910*, 79.

142. Adams, "Railway Problems in 1869," 146–148; Adams, "The Government and the Railroad Corporations," 49–50.

4. Arteries of Commerce

1. An act to incorporate the Wilmington and Raleigh Rail Road Company, Ch. 78, Laws of North Carolina, 1833.

2. An act to authorize the formation of the Spartanburg Rail Road Company, 1849, reprinted in 7 *Statutes at Large of South Carolina* (Columbia, S.C., 1858), 560–570.

3. An act to provide for a general system of railroad transportation, Laws of Illinois, 1849.

4. An act to authorize the formation of railroad corporations, and to regulate the same, Ch. 140, Laws of New York, 1850; an act to authorize the formation of railroad associations, and to regulate the same, Laws of Missouri, 1853.

5. Sarah H. Gordon, *Passage to Union: How the Railroads Transformed American Life, 1829–1929* (Chicago, 1996), 115; Edward Chase Kirkland, *Men, Cities and Transportation: A Study in New England History, 1820–1900* (2 vols., Cambridge, Mass., 1948), I, 172–175.

6. An act authorizing the construction of a bridge across the Hudson River at Albany, Ch. 146, Laws of New York, 1856.

7. *Silliman v. Hudson River Bridge Company*, 66 U.S. 582 (1861).

8. Kirkland, *Men, Cities and Transportation*, I, 137–138.

9. See Elizabeth B. Monroe, "Spanning the Commerce Clause: The Wheeling Bridge Case, 1850–1856," *American Journal of Legal History* 32 (1988), 265–292.

10. *Pennsylvania v. Wheeling and Belmont Bridge Company*, 54 U.S. 518, 577 (1852).

11. Id., 604.

12. *American Railroad Journal*, March 13, 1852.

13. *Pennsylvania v. Wheeling and Belmont Bridge Company*, 59 U.S. 421, 431 (1856).

14. John G. Parke, comp., *Laws of the United States Relating to the Construction of Bridges Over Navigable Waters of the United States*, 2nd ed. (Washington, D.C., 1887).

15. *Devoe v. Penrose Ferry Bridge Co.*, 7 Fed. Cases 566, 568 (Cir. Ct. E.D. Penn., 1854).

16. An act to incorporate a bridge company . . . . , Laws of Illinois, 1853.

17. *American Railroad Journal*, December 4, 1858.

18. *United States v. Railroad Bridge Co.*, 27 Fed. Cases 686 (Cir. Ct., N.D. Ill., 1855).

19. William Edward Hayes, *Iron Road to Empire: The History of 100 Years of the Progress and Achievements of the Rock Island Lines* (n.p., 1953), 43–49; John W. Starr, Jr., *Lincoln and the Railroads* (New York, 1927), 92–116; John T. Richards, *Abraham Lincoln: The Lawyer-Statesman* (Boston, 1916), 30–38.

20. *Mississippi and Missouri Railroad Company v. Ward*, 67 U.S. 485, 496 (1862). See William H. Clark, *Railroads and Rivers: The Story of Inland Transportation* (Boston, 1939), 155–158.

21. Albro Martin, *Railroads Triumphant: The Growth, Rejection, and Rebirth of a Vital American Force* (New York, 1992), 278.

22. Thomas M. Cooley, *A Treatise on the Constitutional Limitations Which Rest Upon the Legislative Power of the States of the American Union* (Boston, 1868; rpt. 1972), 591–593.

23. J. Willard Hurst, *Law and the Conditions of Freedom in the Nineteenth-Century United States* (Madison, 1956), 44–51; James W. Ely, Jr., *The Guardian of Every Other Right: A Constitutional History of Property Rights*, 2nd ed. (New York, 1998), 71–75.

24. Hurst, *Law and the Conditions of Freedom*, 47.

25. Morton Keller, *Affairs of State: Public Life in Late Nineteenth Century America* (Cambridge, Mass., 1977), 425; Lawrence M. Friedman, *A History of American Law*, 2nd ed. (New York, 1985).

26. *Wabash, St. Louis & Pacific Railway Co. v. Illinois*, 118 U.S. 557 (1886).

27. *Nashville, Chattanooga and St. Louis Railway v. Alabama*, 128 U.S. 96, 98–101 (1888); James F. Doster, *Railroads in Alabama Politics, 1875–1914* (Tuscaloosa, Ala., 1957), 40–41.

28. *Southern Railway Company v. King*, 217 U.S. 524 (1910).

29. *Seaboard Air Line Railway v. Blackwell*, 244 U.S. 310, 314–316 (1917).

30. David P. Currie, "The Constitution in the Supreme Court: The Protection of Economic Interests, 1889–1910," *University of Chicago Law Review* 52 (1985), 324, 366–367.

31. *Atlantic Coast Line Railroad Company v. Wharton*, 207 U.S. 328, 334 (1907).

32. *Herndon v. Chicago, Rock Island and Pacific Railway Company*, 218 U.S. 135 (1910).

33. *Gladson v. Minnesota*, 166 U.S. 427 (1897).

34. *Cleveland, Cincinnati, Chicago and St. Louis Railway Company v. Illinois*, 177 U.S. 514, 518 (1900).

35. *Atlantic Coast Line Railroad Company v. Wharton*, 207 U.S. 328, 337 (1907).

36. *Cleveland, Cincinnati, Chicago and St. Louis Railway Company v. Illinois*, 177 U.S. 514, 522 (1900). The significance of competition in determining whether stoppage laws interfered with interstate commerce was also noted in *Mississippi Railroad Commission v. Illinois Central Railroad Company*, 203 U.S. 335, 346 (1906).

37. *St. Louis Southwestern Railway Company v. Arkansas*, 217 U.S. 136 (1910).

38. *Kansas City Southern Railway Company v. Kaw Valley Drainage District*, 233 U.S. 75, 78–79 (1914).

39. See Richard C. Cortner, *The Arizona Train Limit Case: Southern Pacific Co. v. Arizona* (Tucson, Ariz., 1970).

40. *Southern Pacific Co. v. Mashburn*, 18 F. Supp. 393 (D. Nevada, 1937).

41. *Northern Pacific Railway Co. v. State of Washington*, 222 U.S. 370 (1912); *Erie Railroad Company v. New York*, 233 U.S. 671 (1914).

42. *Pennsylvania Railroad Company v. Public Service Commission*, 250 U.S. 566, 569 (1919).

5. Law Governing Railroad Operations

1. *Thorpe v. Rutland and Burlington Railroad*, 27 Vt. 140, 150 (1854).

2. *Nashville and Chattanooga Railroad Co. v. Messino*, 33 Tenn. 220, 224 (1853).

3. *Gorman v. Pacific Railroad*, 26 Mo. 441, 446 (1858).

4. W.W. Thornton, *The Law of Railroad Fences and Private Crossings* (Indianapolis, 1892), 3–17.

5. *Railroad Company v. Skinner*, 19 Pa. 298, 302–303 (1852). See also *Baltimore and Ohio Railroad v. Lamborn*, 12 Md. 257 (1858).

6. *Williams v. Michigan Central Railroad Company*, 2 Mich. 259, 266–267 (1851).

7. R. Ben Brown, "The Southern Range: A Study in Nineteenth Century Law and Society," Ph.D. dissertation. University of Michigan, 1993, 106–175.

8. *Gorman v. Pacific Railroad*, 26 Mo. 441, 446 (1858).

9. An act to provide for the construction of a rail-road from Schenectady to Troy, Ch. 427, Laws of New York, 1836.

10. An act relating to railroads, Ch. 271, Laws of Massachusetts, 1846.

11. See Clarence H. Danhof, "The Fencing Problem in the Eighteen-Fifties," *Agricultural History* 18 (1944), 168, 170–175.

12. *American Railroad Journal*, November 27, 1852.

13. *Corwin v. New York and Erie Railroad Company*, 13 N.Y. 42, 47 (1855).

14. Thornton, *The Law of Railroad Fences*, 19–40; Thomas M. Cooley, *A Treatise on the Constitutional Limitations Which Rest Upon the Legislative Power of the States of the American Union* (Boston, 1868; rpt. 1972), 579.

15. *New Albany and Salem Railroad Company v. Tilson*, 12 Ind. 3, 5 (1859).

16. *Missouri Pacific Railway Company v. Humes*, 115 U.S. 512, 522 (1885). See also *Minneapolis and St. Louis Railway Company v. Beckwith*, 129 U.S. 26 (1889); *Minneapolis and St. Louis Railway Company v. Emmons*, 149 U.S. 364 (1893).

17. *Thorpe v. Rutland and Burlington Railroad*, 27 Vt. 140, 152 (1854).

18. Thornton, *The Law of Railroad Fences*, 102–120, 201–223. See also *New Albany and Salem Railroad Company v. Pace*, 13 Ind. 411(1859); *Talmadge v. Rensselaer and Saratoga Railroad Company*, 13 Barb. 493 (N.Y. Sup. Ct. 1852).

19. *Corwin v. New York and Erie Railroad Company*, 13 N.Y. 42, 47–48 (1855).

20. E.g., *Price v. New Jersey Railroad and Transportation Company*, 31 N.J.L. 229 (1865).

21. Thornton, *The Law of Railroad Fences*, 279–281; *American Railroad Journal*, August 4, 1855.

22. *Danner v. South Carolina Rail Road Company*, 38 S.C.L. 133, 137 (1851).

23. Brown, "The Southern Range," 161.

24. Id., 161–162, 170–174.

25. *Zeigler v. North & South Alabama Railroad Company*, 58 Ala. 594 (1877).

26. *Savannah, Florida and Western Railway Company v. Geiger*, 21 Fla. 669, 695 (1886). See also *Bethje v. Houston and Central Texas Railway Company*, 26 Tex. 604 (1863).

27. *Doggett v. Richmond and Danville Railroad Company*, 81 N.C. 323, 326 (1879).

28. William G. Thomas, *Lawyering for the Railroad: Business, Law, and Power in the New South* (Baton Rouge, La., 1999), 125–127.

29. See Tony A. Freyer, "Law and the Antebellum Southern Economy: An Interpretation," in David J. Bodenhamer and James W. Ely, Jr., eds., *Ambivalent Legacy: A Legal History of the South* (Jackson, Miss., 1984), 59–61; James W. Ely, Jr., and David J. Bodenhamer, "Regionalism and American Legal History: The Southern Experience," *Vanderbilt Law Review* 39 (1986), 539, 549–555.

30. E.g., an act in relation to railroad corporations, no. 41, Laws of Vermont, 1849; an act to provide for the incorporation of railroad companies, no. 892, Laws of Michigan, 1855. See also Robert S. Hunt, *Law and Locomotives: The Impact of the Railroad on Wisconsin Law in the Nineteenth Century* (Madison, Wis., 1958), 73–74.

31. Thornton, *The Law of Railroad Fences*, 32–35.

32. *Gorman v. Pacific Railroad*, 26 Mo. 441, 452 (1858); Thornton, *The Law of Railroad Fences*, 350–352.

33. Hunt, *Law and Locomotives,* 135–136.

34. *Ellis v. Portsmouth and Roanoke Rail Road Company,* 25 N.C. 138, 140 (1841).

35. *Railroad Co. v. Yeiser,* 8 Barr 366, 377 (Pa. 1848). See also *Burroughs v. Housatonic Railroad Company,* 15 Conn. 124 (1842).

36. See *Baltimore and Susquehanna Railroad Company v. Woodruff,* 4 Md. 242 (1853).

37. An act to revise the laws providing for the incorporation of railroad companies, no. 198, Laws of Michigan, 1873.

38. For a sizable verdict against a railroad for damages to a hotel set on fire by a locomotive, see *American Railroad Journal,* August 16, 1856.

39. An act in addition to an act concerning railroad corporation, Ch. 85, Laws of Massachusetts, 1840.

40. *Chapman v. Atlantic and St. Lawrence Rail Road Company,* 37 Me. 92 (1854).

41. *Hooksett v. Concord Railroad,* 38 N.H. 242 (1859).

42. *St. Louis and San Francisco Railway Company v. Mathews,* 165 U.S. 1, 26 (1897).

43. *Ryan v. New York Central Railroad Company,* 35 N.Y. 210, 216 (1866).

44. *Annapolis and Elkridge Railroad Company v. Gantt,* 39 Md. 115 (1873). See also *Hart v. Western Railroad Company,* 54 Mass. 99 (1847).

45. *Fent v. Toledo, Peoria & Warsaw Railway Co.,* 59 Ill. 349, 361–362 (1871).

46. E.g., an act to authorize the formation of railroad corporations, and to regulate the same, Ch. 140, Laws of New York, 1850; an act to authorize the formation of railroad associations, and to regulate the same, Laws of Missouri, 1853. See Edward Chase Kirkland, *Men, Cities and Transportation: A Study in New England History, 1820–1900* (Cambridge, Mass., 1948), I, 317–318.

47. E.g., an act to provide for a general system of railroad incorporations, Laws of Illinois, 1849; an act to provide a general law for the incorporation of railroads and canals, Ch. 1987, Laws of Florida, 1874.

48. *Galena & Chicago Union Railroad Co. v. Loomis,* 13 Ill. 548 (1852); *Pennsylvania Railroad Company v. Ogier,* 35 Pa. 60 (1860) (failure of railroad to sound whistle at crossing place was evidence of negligence); Cooley, *A Treatise on the Constitutional Limitations,* 580.

49. *People v. New York Central Rail Road Company,* 25 Barb. 199 (N.Y. Sup. Ct. 1855); *American Railroad Journal,* March 21, 1857.

50. *Stanton v. Louisville & Nashville Railroad Company,* 91 Ala. 383 (1890).

51. John R. Stilgoe, *Metropolitan Corridor: Railroads and the American Scene* (New Haven, Conn., 1983), 167–177.

52. *Toledo, Wabash and Western Railway Co. v. City of Jacksonville,* 67 Ill. 37, 41, 42 (1873).

53. An act to revise the laws providing for the incorporation of railroad companies . . . , no. 198, Laws of Michigan, 1873.

54. *General Statutes of the State of New Hampshire* (Concord, 1867), 309–310; an act to prevent obstruction of streets, turnpikes and county roads at the crossing of railways, Laws of Virginia, ch. 391, 1884. See also *Richmond & Danville Railroad Company v. Noell,* 86 Va. 19, 9 S.E. 473 (1889) (discussing 1884 Virginia street obstruction law).

55. *Illinois Central Railroad Company v. City of Galena,* 40 Ill. 344, 346 (1866).

56. See *Towle v. Eastern Railroad,* 17 N.H. 519 (1845); *City of Roxbury v. Boston and Providence Railroad Corp.,* 60 Mass. 424 (1850).

57. As quoted in Clyde Olin Fisher, "Connecticut's Regulation of Grade Crossing Elimination," *Journal of Land & Public Utility Economics* 7 (1931), 367, 368.

58. Joseph W. Barnes, "The N.Y. Central Elevates Its Tracks Under Municipal Pressure,"*Rochester History* 33 (1971), 1–24.

59. Fisher, "Connecticut's Regulation of Grade Crossing Elimination," 367–372; *New York and New England Railroad Company v. Bristol,* 151 U.S. 556 (1894).

60. E.g., *Chicago, Milwaukee & St. Paul Railroad Co. v. Minneapolis,* 232 U.S. 430 (1914); *City of Harriman v. Southern Railway Co.,* 111 Tenn. 538, 82 S.W. 213 (1903).

61. *Erie Railroad Company v. Board of Public Utility Commissioners,* 254 U.S. 394, 410 (1921).

62. Stilgoe, *Metropolitan Corridor,* 181–188.

63. *Merrell v. Public Utilities Commission,* 124 Ohio St. 406 (1931).

64. *Southern Railway Company v. Virginia,* 290 U.S. 190 (1933).

65. *Nashville, Chattanooga & St. Louis Railway v. Walters,* 294 U.S. 405, 431 (1935).

66. *Matter of Village of Spencer Grade Crossing,* 254 App. Div. 412 (1938).

67. Compare *Atchison, Topeka and Santa Fe Railway Co. v. Public Utilities Commission,* 346 U.S. 346 (1953), with *City of Winston-Salem v. Southern Railway Company,* 248 N.C. 637, 105 S.E.2d 37 (1958). See also *City of Gainesville v. Southern Railway Company,* 423 F.2d 588 (5th Cir. 1970).

68. *City of Charlottesville v. Southern Railway Co.,* 97 Va. 428, 34 S.E. 98 (1899).

69. *West Chicago Street Railroad Company v. Illinois,* 201 U.S. 506 (1906); *Cincinnati, Indianapolis and Western Railway Company v. City of Connersville,* 218 U.S. 336 (1910).

70. See James W. Ely, Jr., "The Fuller Court and Takings Jurisprudence," 1996 *Journal of Supreme Court History,* 120, 124–125.

71. John F. Stover, *American Railroads,* 2nd ed. (Chicago, 1997), 155; Sarah H. Gordon, *Passage to Union: How the Railroads Transformed American Life, 1829–1929* (Chicago, 1996), 254.

72. E.g., *General Statutes of the State of New Hampshire* (Concord, 1867), 309; an act to provide a general law for the incorporation of railroads and canals, Ch. 1987, Laws of Florida, 1874; an act in relation to railroads and the organization of railroad companies, Ch. 119, Laws of Wisconsin, 1872.

73. *Haas v. Chicago & Northwestern Railway Company,* 41 Wis. 44, 50 (1876).

74. *Railroad Company v. Richmond,* 96 U.S. 521 (1877).

75. David Stradling, *Smokestacks and Progressives: Environmentalists, Engineers and Air Quality in America, 1881–1951* (Baltimore, 1999), 38–39, 69–73, 112–115; Carl W. Condit, *The Port of New York: A History of the Rail and Terminal System from the Grand Central Electrification to the Present* (Chicago, 1981), 1–11.

76. An act . . . in relation to requiring the electrification of railroads in certain cities, Ch. 901, Laws of New York, 1923.

77. E.g., an act to provide for a general system of railroad incorporations, Laws of Illinois, 1849; an act in relation to railroads and the organization of railroad companies, Ch. 119, Laws of Wisconsin, 1872.

78. An act to prevent injuries and the destruction of life upon railroads, and by railroad trains, Ch. 74, Laws of Connecticut, 1853.

79. *American Railroad Journal,* April 10, 1852.

80. E.g., an act to provide for a general system of railroad incorporation, Laws of Illinois, 1849; an act to authorize the formation of railroad associations, and to regulate the same, Laws of Missouri, 1853.

81. *Railroad Company v. Aspell,* 23 Pa. 147, 150 (1854). See also *New Orleans, Jackson, and Great Northern Railroad Company v. Hurst,* 36 Miss. 660 (1859).

82. *Yazoo & Mississippi Valley Railroad Company v. Mitchell,* 83 Miss. 179, 35 So.2d 339 (1903).

83. An act in relation to railroad corporations, no. 41, Laws of Vermont, 1849.

84. Hunt, *Law and Locomotives,* 138.

85. Gordon, *Passage to Union,* 69.

86. E.g., an act to authorize the formation of railroad corporations, Ch. 140, Laws of New York, 1848; an act to provide for the incorporation of railroad companies, no. 82, Laws of Michigan, 1855.

87. *St. Louis, Alton & Chicago Railroad Company v. Dalby*, 19 Ill. 352, 367–368 (1857).
88. *Railroad Company v. Skillman*, 39 Ohio St. 444, 453 (1883). See also *McClure v. Philadelphia, Wilmington and Baltimore Railroad Company*, 34 Md. 532 (1871); David Rorer, *A Treatise on the Law of Railways* (2 vols., Chicago, 1884), II, 960.
89. E.g., an act to authorize the formation of railroad corporations and regulate the same, Ch. 413, Laws of New Jersey, 1873; an act to provide a general law for the incorporation of railroads and canals, Ch. 1987, Laws of Florida, 1874.
90. *Chicago, Burlington & Quincy Railroad Company v. Parks*, 18 Ill. 460, 468 (1857).
91. *Hibbard v. New York and Erie Railroad Company*, 15 N.Y. 455 (1857); *Frederick v. Marquette, Houghton & Ontonagon Railroad Co.*, 37 Mich. 342 (1877); *Jerome v. Smith*, 48 Vt. 230 (1876); *Ripley v. New Jersey Railroad and Transportation Company*, 31 N.J.L. 388 (1866).
92. *Keeley v. Boston & Maine Railroad Company*, 67 Me. 163 (1878); *Southern Railway Company v. Watson*, 110 Ga. 681 (1900).
93. *St. Louis, Alton & Chicago Railroad Company v. Dalby*, 19 Ill. 352 (1857).
94. *American Railroad Journal*, December 10, 1853.
95. *American Railroad Journal*, June 11, 1853.

6. Railroads and Social Conflict

1. Robert S. Starobin, *Industrial Slavery in the Old South* (New York, 1970), 28, 221–223; Richard C. Wade, *Slavery in the Cities: The South 1820–1860* (New York, 1964), 37, 43–44.
2. See Thomas D. Morris, *Southern Slavery and the Law, 1619–1860* (Chapel Hill, N.C., 1996), 132–134; Scott Reynolds Nelson, *Iron Confederacies: Southern Railways, Klan Violence, and Reconstruction* (Chapel Hill, N.C., 1999), 17–19; John Edmund Stealey III, "The Responsibilities and Liabilities of the Bailee of Slave Labor in Virginia," *American Journal of Legal History* 12 (1968), 336–353. See also promissory note by Richmond and Petersburg Railroad Company, October 1, 1853, for hire of six slaves, Ontario County Historical Society, Canandaigua, New York.
3. *Duncan v. South Carolina Rail Road Company*, 2 Rich. 613, 616 (S.C. 1846).
4. *Tallahassee Rail-Road Company v. Macon*, 8 Fla. 299, 304 (1859). Compare *Haden v. North Carolina Railroad Company*, 53 N.C. 362 (1861) (finding no negligence on part of railroad when hired slave died of disease).
5. *Memphis and Charleston Railroad Company v. Jones*, 39 Tenn. 517, 518 (1859).
6. *Herring v. Wilmington and Raleigh Rail Road Company*, 32 N.C. 402, 408–409 (1849). See also *Felder v. Louisville, Cincinnati and Charleston Rail-Road Company*, 2 McMul. 403 (S.C. 1842).
7. *Louisville & Nashville Railroad Company v. Yandell*, 56 Ky. 466, 473 (1856). See Morris, *Southern Slavery and the Law*, 147–158; Mark V. Tushnet, *The American Law of Slavery, 1810–1860: Considerations of Humanity and Interest* (Princeton, N.J., 1981), 183–188.
8. An act prohibiting the transportation of slaves on rail-roads without proper authority, Ch. 117, Laws of Virginia, 1837.
9. Ulrich Bonnell Phillips, *A History of Transportation in the Eastern Cotton Belt to 1860* (New York, 1908), 395; Patricia Hagler Minter, "The Codification of Jim Crow: The Origins of Segregated Railroad Transit in the South, 1865–1910" (Ph.D. dissertation, University of Virginia, 1994), 24–25.
10. Louis Ruchames, "Jim Crow Railroads in Massachusetts," *American Quarterly* 8 (1956), 61–75.

11. *American Railroad Journal*, April 18, 1857. See generally Minter, "The Codification of Jim Crow," 1–22.

12. Earl M. Maltz, "'Separate But Equal' and the Law of Common Carriers in the Era of the Fourteenth Amendment," *Rutgers Law Journal* 17 (1986), 533–568.

13. E.g., *Chicago & Northwestern Railway Company v. Williams*, 55 Ill. 185 (1870); *Gray v. Cincinnati Southern Railroad Company*, 11 Fed. 683 (C.C.S.D. Ohio, 1882); Minter, "The Codification of Jim Crow," 43–52.

14. Charles A. Lofgren, *The Plessy Case: A Legal-Historical Interpretation* (New York, 1987), 9–17; Kenneth W. Mack, "Law, Society, Identity, and the Making of the Jim Crow South: Travel and Segregation on Tennessee Railroads, 1875–1905." *Law & Social Inquiry* 24 (1999), 377, 381–384.

15. *Councill v. Western & Atlantic Railroad Company*, 1 ICC 638 (1887); Ari Hoogenboom and Olive Hoogenboom, *A History of the ICC: From Panacea to Palliative* (New York, 1976), 23–24.

16. Morton Keller, *Affairs of State: Public Life in Late Nineteenth Century America* (Cambridge, Mass., 1977), 451.

17. William G. Thomas, *Lawyering for the Railroad: Business, Law and Power in the New South* (Baton Rouge, La., 1999), 129–133; Linda M. Matthews, "Keeping Down Jim Crow: The Railroads and the Separate Coach Bills in South Carolina," *South Atlantic Quarterly* 73 (1974), 117–129; Maury Klein, *History of the Louisville & Nashville Railroad* (New York, 1972), 331; Minter, "The Codification of Jim Crow," 214–215.

18. E.g., *Smith v. Smith*, 100 Tenn. 494, 46 S.W. 566 (1898); *Louisville & Nashville Railroad Company v. Commonwealth*, 99 Ky. 663 (1896). For evidence of indictments for violation of separate-car laws, see *Railroad Gazette*, September 22, 1899; February 21, 1902. See also Thomas, *Lawyering for the Railroad*, 219–223.

19. *Southern Kansas Railway Company v. State*, 44 Tex. Civ. App. 218, 99 S.W. 166 (1906).

20. *Railroad Gazette*, August 22, 1902; September 12, 1902.

21. E.g., *Chicago, Rock Island and Pacific Railway Company v. Allison*, 126 Ark. 495, 191 S.W. 15 (1917); *Shelton v. Chicago, Rock Island & Pacific Railroad Company*, 139 Tenn. 378, 201 S.W. 521 (1918); *Payne v. Stevens*, 125 Miss. 582, 88 So. 165 (1921).

22. *Missouri, Kansas and Texas Railway Company v. Ball*, 25 Tex. Civ. App. 500, 503, 61 S.W. 327, 329 (1901).

23. *Louisville and Nashville Railroad Company v. Ritchel*, 148 Ky. 701, 147 S.W. 411 (1912).

24. *Southern Railway Company v. Thurman*, 121 Ky. 716, 723, 90 S.W. 240, 241 (1906).

25. Catherine A. Barnes, *Journey from Jim Crow: The Desegregation of Southern Transit* (New York, 1983), 7–8.

26. Lofgren, *The Plessy Case*, 28–60, 148–195; Barnes, *Journey from Jim Crow*, 9–10.

27. *Plessy v. Ferguson*, 163 U.S. 537, 553–554 (Harlan, J., dissenting) (1896).

28. *Chiles v. Chesapeake & Ohio Railway Company*, 218 U.S. 71, 77 (1910).

29. *McCabe v. Atchison, Topeka and Santa Fe Railway Company*, 235 U.S. 151 (1914); Benno C. Schmidt, Jr., "Principle and Prejudice: The Supreme Court and Race in the Progressive Era—Part I: The Heyday of Jim Crow," *Columbia Law Review* 82 (1982), 444, 485–493.

30. Barnes, *Journey from Jim Crow*, 20–34.

31. Id., 86–107

32. Eric Arnesen, "'Like Banquo's Ghost, It Will Not Down': The Race Question and the American Railroad Brotherhoods, 1880–1920," *American Historical Review* 99 (1994), 1601–1633.

33. Paul Michel Taillon, "Culture, Politics, and the Making of the Railroad Brotherhoods, 1836–1916" (Ph.D. dissertation, University of Wisconsin, 1997), 515–516.

34. John Michael Matthews, "The Georgia 'Race Strike' of 1909," *Journal of Southern History* 40 (1974), 613–630.

35. Sterling D. Spero and Abram L. Harris, *The Black Worker: The Negro and the Labor Movement* (New York, 1931), 291–294.

36. Id., 294–300. See generally Eric Arnesen, *Brotherhoods of Color: Black Railroad Workers and the Struggle for Equality* (Cambridge, Mass., 2001), 42–83.

37. Richard A. Epstein, *Forbidden Grounds: The Case Against Employment Discrimination Laws* (Cambridge, Mass., 1992), 124.

38. David Bernstein, *Only One Place of Redress: Labor Regulations, African Americans, Labor Relations, and the Courts from Reconstruction to the New Deal* (Durham, N.C., 2001), 57–65.

39. F. Ray Marshall, *The Negro and Organized Labor* (New York, 1965), 242–245; Arnesen, *Brotherhoods of Color*, 206–209.

40. Herbert Northrup, *Organized Labor and the Negro* (New York, 1944), 100. See generally Howard W. Risher, Jr., *The Negro in the Railroad Industry* (Philadelphia, 1971).

41. Sarah H. Gordon, *Passage to Union: How the Railroads Transformed American Life, 1829–1929* (Chicago, 1996), 84–85.

42. *Memphis & Charleston Railroad Company v. Benson*, 85 Tenn. 627, 4 S.W. 5 (1887); David Rorer, *A Treatise on the Law of Railways* (2 vols., Chicago, 1884), II, 969; Byron K. Elliott and William F. Elliott, *A Treatise on the Law of Railroads* (4 vols., Indianapolis, 1897), I, 284–285.

43. *Councill v. Western & Atlantic Railroad Company*, 1 ICC 638, 641 (1887).

44. Lofgren, *The Plessy Case*, 118–121.

45. See Barbara Y. Welke, "When All the Women Were White and All the Blacks Were Men: Gender, Class, Race, and the Road to *Plessy, 1855–1914*," *Law and History Review* 13 (1995), 261–316; Patricia Hagler Minter, "The Failure of Freedom: Class, Gender, and the Evolution of Segregated Transit Law in the Nineteenth-Century South," *Chicago-Kent Law Review* 70 (1995), 993–1009; Kenneth W. Mack, "Law, Society, Identity, and the Making of the Jim Crow South: Travel and Segregation on Tennessee Railroads, 1875–1905," 377, 387–398.

46. *Bass v. Chicago & Northwestern Railroad Company*, 36 Wis. 450, 464 (1874). After protracted litigation, the plaintiff recovered both compensatory and punitive damages against the railroad. *Bass v. Chicago & Northwestern Railway Company*, 42 Wis. 654 (1877).

47. Robert Edgar Riegel, *The Story of the Western Railroads* (New York, 1926), 83, 277; David Haward Bain, *Empire Express: Building the First Transcontinental Railroad* (New York, 1999), 349–352.

48. An act to aid in the construction of a railroad and telegraph line from the Missouri River to the Pacific Ocean . . . , July 1, 1862, 12 U.S. Statutes 489, 492. The same act also granted "the right of way through the public lands." This language was later construed to include land within Indian reservations. *Kindred v. Union Pacific Railroad Company*, 225 U.S. 582 (1912).

49. Indian Peace Commission Report, January 7, 1868, reprinted in Wilcomb E. Washburn, ed., *The American Indian and the United States: A Documentary History* (4 vols., New York, 1973), I, 134.

50. Treaty between the United States of America and different tribes of Sioux Indians, 15 Stat. 635, 639 (1868).

51. *Johnson v. McIntosh*, 21 U.S. 543 (1823). See Petra T. Shattuck and Jill Norgren, *Partial Justice: Federal Indian Law in a Liberal Constitutional System* (New York, 1991), 34–38.

52. An act to provide for the acquiring of rights of way by railroad companies through Indian reservations, Indian lands, and Indian allotments . . . , Ch. 374, 30 Stat. 990 (1899); an act to grant the right of way through the Oklahoma Territory and the Indian Territory . . . , Ch. 134, 32 Stat. 43 (1902).

53. Robert T. Handy, *Undermined Establishment: Church-State Relations in America, 1880–1920* (Princeton, N.J., 1991), 71–72.

54. *American Railroad Journal*, December 23, 1854; June 7, 1856.

55. Wilbur F. Crafts, *The Sabbath for Man* (New York, 1885), 291. See also W. S. McCain, "Railroads as a Factor in the Law," *Arkansas Bar Association Proceedings* (1886), 9, 11 ("Another feature of railroads is their hostility to the Sabbath.").

56. *Railroad and Engineering Journal*, June 1889, p. 249.

57. Elliott and Elliott, *A Treatise on the Law of Railroads*, 99–100. For the growth of railroad operations on Sunday, see Andrew J. King, "Sunday Law in the Nineteenth Century," *Albany Law Review* 64 (2000), 675, 734–737.

58. *Gilbough v. West Side Amusement Co.*, 64 N.J. Eq. 27, 29, 53 Atl. 289, 290 (1902).

59. E.g., *Sullivan v. Maine Central Railroad Company*, 82 Me. 196, 19 Atl. 169 (1889); *Louisville & Nashville Railroad Company v. Commonwealth*, 17 Ky. L. Reptr. 223, 30 S.W. 878 (1895).

60. E.g., Code of Virginia, sec. 3801 (1904).

61. James F. Doster, *Railroads in Alabama Politics, 1875–1914* (Tuscaloosa, Ala., 1957), 18, 42, 154, 159.

62. *Hennington v. Georgia*, 163 U.S. 299, 318 (1896) (Fuller, C.J., dissenting).

63. *State v. Suncrest Lumber Company*, 186 N.C. 122, 118 S.E. 882 (1923).

64. An act to incorporate the Boston and Providence Railroad Company, Laws of Rhode Island, 1831, reprinted in W.P. Gregg and Benjamin Pond, eds., *The Railroad Laws and Charters of the United States* (2 vols., Boston, 1851), II, 668–677.

65. An act to authorize the formation of railroad associations, and to regulate the same, Laws of Missouri, 1853. See generally, Rorer, *A Treatise on the Law of Railways*, I, 586–587.

66. An act to provide for the incorporation of railroad companies, no. 82, Laws of Michigan, 1855.

67. An act in relation to railroads and the organization of railroad companies, Ch. 119, Laws of Wisconsin, 1872; Revised Statutes of Illinois, Ch. 114, 1874; an act to provide for the incorporation of railroad companies, and the management of the affairs thereof, Ch. 1, Laws of New Mexico, 1878.

68. *American Railroad Journal*, November 8, 1851.

69. E.g., *Hodge v. State*, 82 Ga. 643, 9 S.E. 676 (1889); *State v. Kilty*, 28 Minn. 421, 10 N.W. 475 (1881).

70. *Railroad Gazette*, May 31, 1901.

71. E.g., an act to authorize the formation of railroad corporations and regulate the same, Ch. 413, Laws of New Jersey, 1873.

72. E.g., an act in relation to railroads and the organization of railroad companies, Ch. 119, Laws of Wisconsin, 1872; An act to provide a general law for the incorporation of railroads and canals, no. 12, Laws of Florida, 1874.

73. Railroad journals regularly reported train robberies. E.g., *Railroad Gazette*, June 23, 1899; December 8, 1899; July 20, 1900; September 5, 1902.

74. Gordon, *Passage to Union*, 163–164; John F. Stover, *American Railroads*, 2nd ed. (Chicago, 1997), 156–157.

75. New York *Times*, December 28–29, 1896.

76. E.g., *Railroad Gazette*, March 30, 1900; September 28, 1900; July 18, 1902.

77. E.g., *Railroad Gazette*, February 23, 1900; August 17, 1900; July 19, 1901.

78. E.g., *Hill v. Pullman Company*, 188 F.Rep. 497 (Cir. Ct., E.D. Pa., 1911); *Carpenter v. New York, New Haven and Hartford Railroad Company*, 124 N.Y. 53, 26 N.E. 277 (1891).

79. *Railroad Gazette*, October 26, 1900.

80. *Railway Age and Northwestern Railroader*, September 22, 1893.

81. An act to amend an act . . . and to add a new section . . . relating to train wrecking and the punishment thereof, Ch. 204, Laws of California, 1891.

82. *Territory v. Ketchum*, 10 N.M. 718, 65 P. 169 (1901). See also *People v. Lovren*, 119 Cal. 88, 51 P. 22 (1897); *State v. Stubblefield*, 157 Mo. 360, 58 S.W. 337 (1900). The United States Supreme Court noted that state legislatures had power to adapt penal laws to conditions, and cited the New Mexico death penalty statute as a response to "the circumstances of terror and danger" that accompanied train robbery. *Weems v. United States*, 217 U.S. 349, 379 (1910).

83. *Railroad Gazette*, August 4, 1899.

84. An act for the suppression of train robbery in the Territories of the United States, Ch. 1376, U.S. *Statutes at Large*, 1902.

85. James D. Dilts, *The Great Road: The Building of the Baltimore and Ohio, The Nation's First Railroad, 1828–1853* (Stanford, Calif., 1993), 179, 347, 358–359.

86. An act empowering railroad companies to employ police force, no. 228, Laws of Pennsylvania, 1865. See H. S. Dewhurst, *The Railroad Police*, (Springfield, Ill., 1955), 3–22.

87. E.g., *Tucker v. Erie Railroad Company*, 69 N.J.L. 19, 54 A. 557 (1903); *New York, Chicago & St. Louis Railroad Company v. Fieback*, 87 Ohio St. 254, 100 N.E. 889 (1912).

88. E.g., *King v. Illinois Central Railroad Company*, 69 Miss. 245, 10 So. 42 (1891); *Pennsylvania Railroad Company v. Deal*, 116 Ohio St. 408, 156 N.E. 502 (1927); Elliott and Elliott, *A Treatise on the Law of Railroads*, III, 638–639.

7. Insolvency, Receiverships, and Commercial Practices

1. Albro Martin, "Railroads and the Equity Receivership: An Essay on Institutional Change," *Journal of Economic History* 34 (1974), 685, 688–689.

2. *Dunn v. North Missouri Railroad*, 24 Mo. 493 (1857); *Winslow v. Woodard*, 47 Ky. 431 (1857).

3. *Georgia v. Atlantic & Gulf Railroad Company*, 10 Fed. Cases 243 (Cir. Ct., S.D. Ga., 1879).

4. *Barton v. Barbour*, 104 U.S. 126, 138 (1881) (Miller, J., dissenting).

5. Id., 134–135. See also *Wallace v. Loomis*, 97 U.S. 146, 162 (1877) (upholding issuance of receiver's certificates to raise money, and noting that the "power of a court of equity to appoint managing receivers of such property as a railroad . . . cannot, at this day, be seriously disputed").

6. Warner Fuller, "The Background and Techniques of Equity and Bankruptcy Railroad Reorganizations—A Survey," *Law and Contemporary Problems* 7 (1940), 377, 378.

7. D.H. Chamberlain, "New-Fashioned Receiverships," *Harvard Law Review* 10 (1896), 140–149; Martin, "Railroads and the Equity Receivership," 697–701; Fuller, "Background and Techniques of Equity," 378–379.

8. *Quincy, Missouri and Pacific Railroad Company v. Humphreys*, 145 U.S. 82, 95 (1892).

9. Morton Keller, *Affairs of State: Public Life in Late Nineteenth-Century America* (Cambridge, Mass., 1977), 425–427.

10. Henry Clay Caldwell, "Railroad Receiverships in the Federal Courts," *American Law Review* 30 (1896), 161, 163–167.

11. Id., 178–179.

12. *In re Tyler*, 149 U.S. 164, 180–191 (1893).

13. *Memorial of the General Assembly of the State of South Carolina to the Congress of the United States in the Matter of Receivers of Railroad Corporations and the Equity Jurisdiction of the Courts of the United States,* reprinted in *American Law Review* 28 (1894), 161, 173, 183.

14. Harry N. Scheiber, "Federalism, the Southern Regional Economy, and Public Policy Since 1865," in David J. Bodenhamer and James W. Ely, Jr., eds., *Ambivalent Legacy: A Legal History of the South* (Jackson, Miss., 1984), 78.

15. *Railroad Gazette,* January 6, 1899.

16. For criticism of railroad receiverships, see Chamberlain, "New-Fashioned Receiverships," 146–149; Caldwell, "Railroad Receiverships in the Federal Courts," 178–187; Moorfield Storey, "The Reorganization of Railway and Other Corporations," *American Law Review* 30 (1896), 802–812.

17. See Mary Cornelia Porter, "That Commerce Shall Be Free: A New Look at the Old Laissez-Faire Court," *Supreme Court Review* (1976), 135, 146–147.

18. Martin, "Railroads and the Equity Receivership," 686.

19. Fuller, "Background and Techniques of Equity," 384–392.

20. Douglas G. Baird and Robert K. Rasmussen, "Boyd's Legacy and Blackstone's Ghost," *Supreme Court Review* (1999), 393, 402–406 (noting that equity receiverships were early experiments in corporate restructuring).

21. *Illinois Central Railroad Company v. Morrison and Crabtree,* 19 Ill. 135, 138 (1857). See also *Norway Plains Company v. Boston and Maine Railroad,* 67 Mass. 263 (1854).

22. An act relating to the transportation of freight on certain railroads, Ch. 270, Laws of New York, 1847; Code of the State of Georgia, sec. 2054, 1861.

23. An act to provide for the incorporation of Railroad Companies, no. 82, Laws of Michigan, 1855.

24. *Pittsburgh, Cincinnati and St. Louis railroad company,* 65 Ind. 188, 193 (1879).

25. *Hilliard v. Wilmington & Weldon Rail Road Company,* 51 N.C. 343, 344 (1857).

26. E.g., *Michigan Central Railroad Company v. Ward,* 2 Mich. 538 (1853); *Moses v. Boston & Maine Railroad,* 32 N.H. 523 (1856); *Wood v. Crocker,* 18 Wis. 363 (1864).

27. See generally Robert J. Kaczorowski, "The Common-Law Background of Nineteenth-Century Tort Law," *Ohio State Law Journal* 51 (1990), 1127, 1129–1157.

28. Byron K. Elliott and William F. Elliott, *A Treatise on the Law of Railroads,* 2nd ed. (5 vols., Indianapolis, 1907), IV, 2314–2321.

29. Isaac F. Redfield, *The Law of Railways,* 6th ed. (2 vols., Boston, 1888), II, 114–123.

30. E.g., *Illinois Central Railroad Company v. Morrison and Crabtree,* 19 Ill. 135 (1857).

31. See *Hart v. Pennsylvania Railroad Company,* 112 U.S. 331, 340 (1884) ("It is just to hold the shipper to his agreement, fairly made, as to value, even where the loss or injury has occurred through the negligence of the carrier").

32. *Chicago, Milwaukee and St. Paul Railway Company v. Solan,* 169 U.S. 133, 138 (1898).

33. *North Pennsylvania Railroad Company v. Commercial Bank of Chicago,* 123 U.S. 727, 734 (1887) (discussing duties of carriers in connection with transport of livestock).

34. *Illinois Central Railroad Company v. Morrison and Crabtree,* 19 Ill. 135, 139 (1857).

35. E.g., *Western Railway Co. v. Harwell,* 91 Ala. 340, 8 So. 649 (1890); see also Elliott and Elliott, *A Treatise on the Law of Railroads,* IV, 2399–2400.

36. E.g., *Kimball v. Rutland and Burlington Railroad Company,* 26 Vt. 246 (1854).

37. Elliott and Elliott, *A Treatise on the Law of Railroads,* IV, 2412–2414.

38. An act to prevent cruelty to animals while in transit by railroad . . . , Ch. 252, *Stat. at Large,* 1873.

39. Elliott and Elliott, *A Treatise on the Law of Railroads*, IV, 2302–2311. See also Code of State of Georgia, sec. 2045, 1861 ("The common carrier is bound not only for the safe transportation and delivery of goods, but also that the same be done without unreasonable delay").

40. *Wibert v. New York and Erie Railroad Company*, 12 N.Y. 245, 250 (1855).

41. *Blackstock v. New York and Erie Railroad Company*, 20 N.Y. 48, 52 (1859).

42. E.g., *Pittsburgh, Cincinnati and St. Louis Railroad Company*, 65 Ind. 188 (1879); *Pittsburgh, Fort Wayne and Chicago Railroad Company*, 84 Ill. 36 (1876).

43. E.g., *Lake Shore and Michigan Southern Railway Company v. Bennett*, 89 Ind. 457 (1883); *Geismer v. Lake Shore and Michigan Southern Railway Company*, 102 N.Y. 563, 7 N.E. 828 (1886).

44. Elliott and Elliott, *A Treatise on the Law of Railroads*, IV, 2223–2239.

45. An act relating to the transportation of freight on certain railroads, Ch. 270, Laws of New York, 1847; see *Burtis v. Buffalo and State Line Railroad Company*, 24 N.Y. 269 (1862) (holding that statutory duty applies where one of connecting lines was outside New York). For a similar statutory duty, see "An Act to provide for the Incorporation of Railroad Companies," no. 82, Laws of Michigan, 1855.

46. *Seaboard Air Line Railway v. Seegers*, 207 U.S. 73, 78 (1907).

47. *Adams Express Company v. Croninger*, 226 U.S. 491 (1913).

48. *Charleston & Western Carolina Railway Company v. Varnville Furniture Company*, 237 U.S. 597 (1915).

49. See Albro Martin, *Railroads Triumphant: The Growth, Rejection, and Rebirth of a Vital American Force* (New York, 1992), 324–326.

8. Property and Taxation

1. Tony A. Freyer, *Producers Versus Capitalists: Constitutional Conflict in Antebellum America* (Charlottesville, Va., 1994), 137–166.

2. See James W. Ely, Jr., " 'That due satisfaction may be made': The Fifth Amendment and the Origins of the Compensation Principle," *American Journal of Legal History* 36 (1992), 1–18; *Carr v. Georgia Railroad and Banking Company*, 1 Ga. Rep. 524, 533 (1846) ("If the charter had contained no provision for making compensation to the plaintiff for his land, it would be in direct conflict with the Constitution, and void").

3. *Troy and Boston Railroad Company v. Lee*, 13 Barb. 169 (N.Y. 1852).

4. See generally Morton M. Horwitz, *The Transformation of American Law, 1780–1860* (Cambridge, Mass., 1977), 70–74; Tony A. Freyer, "Reassessing the Impact of Eminent Domain in Early American Economic Development," *Wisconsin Law Review* (1981), 1263–1286; Harry N. Scheiber, "The Road to *Munn*: Eminent Domain and the Concept of Public Purpose in the State Courts," *Perspectives in American History* 5 (1971), 329, 366; Peter Karsten, "Supervising the 'Spoiled Children of Legislation': Judicial Judgments Involving Quasi-Public Corporations in the Nineteenth-Century U.S.," *American Journal of Legal History* 41 (1997), 315, 322–344.

5. An act to amend an act entitled an act to incorporate the Central Railroad and Canal Company of Georgia, Laws of Georgia, 1835. See also an act regulating railroad companies, Laws of Ohio, 1848 (mandating that commissioners "shall consider the benefit as well as the injury which such owners shall sustain by reason of such railroad").

6. E.g., an act incorporating the Goochland and Louisa Rail-Road Company, Ch. 112, Laws of Virginia, 1833. By general legislation in 1837, however, Virginia lawmakers modified this formula and mandated that "not less than the actual value of the land, without reference to the location and construction of the road, shall be given by the commission-

ers." An act prescribing certain general regulations for the incorporation of rail-road companies, Ch. 118, Laws of Virginia, 1837.

7. An act to authorize the formation of railroad associations,? Laws of Missouri, 1853.

8. Harry N. Scheiber, "Property Law, Expropriation, and Resource Allocation by Government, 1789–1910," *Journal of Economic History* 33 (1973), 232, 237 (concluding that in Ohio railroads were often able to acquire land by eminent domain at almost no cost because of benefit offset).

9. *Pennsylvania Railroad v. Heister,* 8 Barr. 445, 450 (Pa. 1848).

10. John D. Majewski, "Commerce and Community: Economic Culture and Internal Improvements in Pennsylvania and Virginia, 1790–1860," Ph.D. diss., UCLA, 1994, 284–307.

11. Debates and Proceedings of the Ohio State Convention (Columbus, Ohio, 1851), 884.

12. E.g., an act to incorporate the Florida, Atlantic, and Gulf Central Rail Road Company, Ch. 317, Laws of Florida, 1850; an act to incorporate the Bennington and Brattleboro Railroad Company, no. 34, Laws of Vermont, 1835, reprinted in W.P. Gregg and Benjamin Pond, *The Railroad Laws and Charters of the United States* (2 vols., Boston, 1851), I, 723–732.

13. Compare Resolve Incorporating Manchester Railroad Company, Laws of Connecticut, 1833, reprinted in Gregg and Pond, *Railroad Laws and Charters,* II, 907–913, with Resolve Incorporating the Fairfield County Railroad Company, Laws of Connecticut, 1835, reprinted in Gregg and Pond, *Railroad Laws and Charters,* II, 928–933.

14. E.g., an act to provide for the construction of a rail-road from Auburn to Rochester, Ch. 349, Laws of New York, 1836; an act to provide for the construction of a rail-road from Attica to Buffalo, Ch. 242, Laws of New York, 1836. See an act to authorize the formation of railroad corporations, Ch. 140, Laws of New York, 1848.

15. See William A. Fischel, *Regulatory Takings: Law, Economics and Politics* (Cambridge, Mass., 1995), 86–87.

16. *Isom v. Mississippi Central Railroad Company,* 36 Miss. 300, 313 (1858).

17. See Karsten, "Supervising the 'Spoiled Children of Legislation,'" 340–342.

18. *Meacham v. Fitchburg Railroad Company,* 58 Mass. 292, 297–298 (1849). See also *Upton v. South Reading Branch Railroad Company,* 62 Mass. 600 (1851).

19. An act to amend the law condemning right of way for purposes of internal improvement, Laws of Illinois, 1852.

20. See *Hall v. Delaware, Lackawanna and Western Railroad Company,* 262 Pa. 292, 105 A.98 (1918).

21. *Southport, Wilmington and Durham Railroad Company v. Owners of Platt Land,* 133 N.C. 266, 45 S.E. 589 (1903); Note, "Eminent Domain in North Carolina—A Case Study," *North Carolina Law Review* 35 (1957), 296, 307.

22. Issac F. Redfield, *The Law of Railroads,* 6th ed. (2 vols., Boston, 1888), I, 270.

23. *Proprietors of Locks and Canals v. Nashua and Lowell Railroad Company,* 64 Mass. 385, 389 (1852). See also *Rogers v. Kennebec & Portland Rail Road Company,* 35 Me. 319 (1853).

24. E.g., *Drake v. Hudson River Railroad Company,* 7 Barb. 508 (N.Y. Sup. Ct. 1849); *New Albany and Salem Railroad Company v. O'Daily,* 12 Ind. 551 (1859).

25. See Karsten, "Supervising the 'Spoiled Children of Legislation,'" 334–340 (maintaining that trend in nineteenth century was toward compensation for consequential damages).

26. An act regulating railroad companies, no. 76, Laws of Pennsylvania, 1849.

27. *Bradley v. New York and New Haven Railroad Company,* 21 Conn. 294, 309, 312 (1851).

28. *Parker v. Boston and Maine Railroad,* 57 Mass. 107 (1849).

29. *Eaton v. Boston, Concord & Montreal Railroad*, 51 N.H. 504, 512 (1872). See also *Lyon v. Green Bay & Minnesota Railway Co.*, 42 Wis. 538 (1877) (awarding damages for injury to land not actually condemned but rendered worthless by cutting off water supply); *Staton v. Norfolk & Carolina Railroad Company*, 111 N.C. 278, 16 S.E. 181 (1892) (diversion of surface water constituted taking of property).

30. John Lewis, *A Treatise on the Law of Eminent Domain in the United States* (Chicago, 1888), 295–297. See also *Chicago v. Taylor*, 125 U.S. 161 (1888) (discussing meaning of language "taken or damaged for public use" in 1870 Illinois Constitution).

31. *Pennsylvania Railroad Company v. Miller*, 132 U.S. 75, 83 (1889).

32. See John F. Stover, *American Railroads*, 2nd ed. (Chicago, 1998), 29 (asserting that eminent domain "tended to keep . . . right-of-way costs low").

33. Freyer, *Producers Versus Capitalists*, 144–158. See also William G. Thomas, *Lawyering for the Railroad: Business, Law, and Power in the New South* (Baton Rouge, La., 1999), 10–16 (noting that railroads turned to eminent domain only as a last resort).

34. E.g., an act to provide for a general system of railroad incorporations, Laws of Illinois, 1849; an act to provide for the incorporation of railroads and canals, Ch. 1987, Laws of Florida, 1874.

35. An act in relation to railroads and the organization of railroad companies, Ch. 119, Laws of Wisconsin, 1872; an act to provide for incorporation of railroad companies, Ch. 1, Laws of New Mexico, 1878.

36. E.g., *Bonaparte v. Camden and Amboy Railroad Company*, 3 Fed. Cases 821 (Cir. Ct. N.J. 1830); *Raleigh and Gaston Rail Road Company v. Davis*, 19 N.C. 451 (1837); *Buffalo Bayou, Brazos and Colorado Railroad Company v. Ferris*, 26 Texas 588 (1863).

37. Horwitz, *The Transformation of American Law, 1780–1860*, 84–85.

38. E.g., an act to authorize the formation of railroad corporations, Ch. 140, Laws of New York, 1850 ("and on the payment or deposit by the company of the sums to be paid as compensation for the land . . . the company shall be entitled to enter upon, take possession of, and use the said land . . .).

39. An act to incorporate the Florida, Atlantic, and Gulf Central Rail Road Company, Ch. 317, Laws of Florida, 1850.

40. *Bonaparte v. Camden and Amboy Railroad Company*, 3 Fed. Cases 821 (Cir. Ct. N.J., 1830); *Oregonian Railway v. Hill*, 9 Or. 377 (1881).

41. *Pratt v. Roseland Railway Company*, 50 N.J. Eq. 150 (1892).

42. *Buffalo Bayou, Brazos and Colorado Railroad Company v. Ferris*, 26 Texas 588, 602 (1863). See also *Carr v. Georgia Banking and Railroad Company*, 1 Ga. 524 (1846).

43. *Cherokee Nation v. Southern Kansas Railway Company*, 135 U.S. 641, 659 (1890).

44. *Raleigh and Gaston Rail Road Company v. Davis*, 19 N.C. 451 (1837).

45. An act to authorize the formation of railroad corporations, Ch. 140, Laws of New York, 1850.

46. An act prescribing certain general regulations for the incorporation of rail-road companies, Ch. 118, Laws of Virginia, 1837.

47. Simeon F. Baldwin, *American Railroad Law* (Boston, 1904), 77.

48. Redfield, *The Law of Railroads* I, 255.

49. *Quimby v. Vermont Central Railroad Company*, 23 Vt. 378 (1851).

50. *Beach v. Wilmington & Weldon Railroad Company*, 120 N.C. 498, 26 S.E. 703 (1897); *Oregon Railway and Navigation Company v. Oregon Real Estate Company*, 10 Or. 444 (1882).

51. Revisal of 1905 of North Carolina, Ch. 61, §2587 (1905); act of 1905, Ch. 48, Laws of Indiana, 1905.

52. E.g., *Westman v. Kiell*, 183 Mich. App. 489, 455 N.W.2d 45 (1990) (1882 order of condemnation construed as granting an easement for railroad purposes).

53. *Missouri Pacific Railway Company v. Nebraska*, 217 U.S. 196, 206 (1910). For a similar result, see *Chicago, St. Paul, Minneapolis & Omaha Railway Company v. Holmberg*, 282 U.S. 162 (1930).

54. E.g., *Chicago, Burlington and Quincy Railway Company v. Drainage Commission*, 200 U.S. 561 (1906); *West Chicago Street Railroad Company v. Chicago*, 201 U.S. 506 (1906); *Cincinnati, Indianapolis and Western Railway Company v. City of Connersville*, 218 U.S. 336 (1910); *Southeast Cass Water Resource District v. Burlington Northern Railroad Company*, 527 N.W.2d 884 (N.D. 1995).

55. *Illinois Central Railroad Company v. Illinois*, 146 U.S. 387 (1892).

56. William Blackstone, *Commentaries on the Laws of England* (4 vols., Oxford, 1765–1769, reprint Chicago, 1979), III, 216–218. See also Louise A. Halper, "Nuisance, Courts and Markets in the New York Court of Appeals, 1850–1915," *Albany Law Review* 54 (1990), 301, 306–307.

57. For the changes in nuisance law during the nineteenth century, see the insightful article by Paul M. Kurtz, "Nineteenth Century Anti-Entrepreneurial Nuisance Injunctions—Avoiding the Chancellor," *William and Mary Law Review* 17 (1976), 621–670. See also Kermit L. Hall, *The Magic Mirror: Law in American History* (New York, 1989), 118–119.

58. *Lexington and Ohio Railroad v. Applegate*, 38 Ky. 239, 305, 309 (1839).

59. *Drake v. Hudson River Railroad Company*, 7 Barb. 508, 547, 551 (N.Y. Sup. Ct. 1849).

60. *Hentz v. Long Island Railroad Company*, 13 Barb. 646, 658 (N.Y. Sup. Ct. 1852).

61. *Grey v. Ohio and Pennsylvania Railroad Company*, 1 Grant's Cases 412, 413 (Penn. 1856).

62. *Geiger v. Filor*, 8 Fla. 325, 332 (1859).

63. *New Albany and Salem Railroad Company v. O'Daily*, 12 Ind. 551, 552 (1859).

64. Most historians have concluded that courts in the nineteenth century modified nuisance law in ways that aided entrepreneurs, even though they debate the causes and effects of this transformation. This prevailing interpretation has been challenged by William J. Novak, who argues that the law of nuisance remained an effective regulatory instrument. Novak, *The People's Welfare: Law and Regulation in Nineteenth-Century America* (Chapel Hill, N.C., 1996), 125–126, 217, 220.

65. *Drake v. Hudson River Railroad Company*, 7 Barb. at 551.

66. Kurtz, "Nineteenth Century Anti-Entrepreneurial Nuisance Injunctions," 649–651; Halper, "Nuisance, Courts and Markets," 309–315.

67. *Williams v. New York Central Railroad Company*, 18 Barb. 222, 247 (N.Y. Sup. Ct. 1854). See also *Hinchman v. Paterson Horse Railroad Company*, 17 N.J. Eq. 75, 77 (1864) (rejecting argument that construction of railroad in city street constituted public nuisance, and declaring that a "work which is authorized by law cannot be a nuisance"); *McLauchlin v. Charlotte and South Carolina Rail Road Company*, 39 S.C.L. 235 (1850).

68. Halper, "Nuisance, Courts and Markets," 337–340 (new liability rules meant that "an injury to property be thought of not as a nuisance, but as a taking for which monetary compensation was required").

69. *Fletcher v. Auburn and Syracuse Rail Road Company*, 25 Wend. 462 (N.Y. 1841).

70. *Brown v. Cayuga and Susquehanna Railroad Company*, 12 N.Y. 486, 494 (1855).

71. *Baltimore & Potomac Railroad Company v. Fifth Baptist Church*, 108 U.S. 317, 332 (1883).

72. *Richards v. Washington Terminal Company*, 233 U.S. 546, 553 (1914).

73. Lawrence M. Friedman, *A History of American Law*, 2nd ed. (New York, 1985), 569.

74. E.g., *Wilmington Railroad v. Reid*, 80 U.S. 264 (1871); *Mobile and Ohio Railroad Company v. Tennessee*, 153 U.S. 486 (1894); *Atlantic and Gulf Railroad Company v. Allen*, 15 Fla. 638 (1876).

75. *Wisconsin and Michigan Railway Company v. Powers*, 191 U.S. 379 (1903).
76. *Board of County Commissioners v. New Mexico & Southern Pacific Railroad Company*, 3 N.M. 116, 120 (1884).
77. *State v. Maine Central Railroad Company*, 66 Me. 488 (1877), aff'd 96 U.S. 499 (1878); *Railroad Company v. Georgia*, 98 U.S. 359 (1878); Bryon K. Elliott and William F. Elliott, *A Treatise on the Law of Railroads*, 2nd ed. (5 vols., Indianapolis, 1907), II, 140–144.
78. E.g., *Wright v. Georgia Railroad and Banking Company*, 216 U.S. 420 (1910); *Atlantic Coast Line Railroad Company v. Phillips*, 332 U.S. 168 (1947). See also Michael R. Hyman, "Taxation, Public Policy, and Political Dissent: Yeoman Disaffection in the Post-Reconstruction Lower South," *Journal of Southern History* 55 (1989), 49, 61.
79. Christopher Grandy, "Can Government Be Trusted to Keep Its Part of a Social Contract? New Jersey and the Railroads, 1825–1888," *Journal of Law, Economics and Organization* 2 (1989), 249, 259–267.
80. *Erie Railroad Company v. New Jersey*, 31 N.J.L. 531 (1864); Frederick Merk, "Eastern Antecedents of the Grangers," *Agricultural History* 23 (1949), 1, 2–4.
81. *Clarke v. Philadelphia, Wilmington and Baltimore Railroad Company*, 9 Del. 158 (1870).
82. *Case of the State Freight Tax*, 82 U.S. 232, 281 (1872).
83. *City of Chattanooga v. Nashville, Chattanooga & St. Louis Railroad Company*, 75 Tenn. 561 (1881).
84. *Kentucky Railroad Tax Cases*, 115 U.S. 321, 339 (1885).
85. *State Tax on Railway Gross Receipts*, 82 U.S. 284 (1873); *Maine v. Grand Trunk Railway Company*, 142 U.S. 217 (1891).
86. See Wilbur O. Hedrick, "The History of Railroad Taxation in Michigan," Ph.D. dissertation, University of Michigan, 1912.
87. *Railroad Gazette*, March 6, 1896.
88. See H. Roger Grant, *Erie Lackawanna: Death of an American Railroad* (Stanford, Calif., 1994), 82, 141–142, 146–147 (discussing heavy taxes on railroad property in New Jersey).
89. E.g., *Department of Revenue of Oregon v. ACF Industries, Inc.*, 510 U.S. 332 (1994); *Burlington Northern Railroad Company v. Oklahoma Tax Commission*, 481 U.S. 454 (1987); *Consolidated Rail Corporation v. Town of Hyde Park*, 47 F.3d 473 (2nd Cir. 1995), cert. den. 515 U.S. 1122 (1995).

9. Liability for Personal Injury

1. *Railroad and Engineering Journal*, February 1890, 71; July 1890, 300–301.
2. *Nashville & Chattanooga Railroad Company v. Messino*, 33 Tenn. 220, 224 (1853); *Perkins v. New York Central Railroad Company*, 24 N.Y. 196, 204 (1862).
3. *Philadelphia and Reading Railroad Company*, 55 U.S. 467, 486 (1852).
4. *Troxler v. Southern Railway Company*, 124 N.C. 189, 195, 32 S.E. 550, 551 (1899).
5. E.g., Morton J. Horwitz, *The Transformation of American Law, 1780–1860* (Cambridge, Mass., 1977), 85–108; Lawrence M. Friedman, *A History of American Law*, 2nd ed. (New York, 1985), 300–302; Ronald L. Lewis, *Transforming the Appalachian Countryside: Railroads, Deforestation, and Social Change in West Virginia, 1880–1920* (Chapel Hill, N.C., 1998), 126–129; James L. Hunt, "Ensuring the Incalculable Benefits of Railroads: The Origins of Liability for Negligence in Georgia," *Southern California Interdisciplinary Law Journal* 7 (1998), 375–425.
6. E.g., Tony A. Freyer, *Producers Versus Capitalists: Constitutional Conflict in Antebellum America* (Charlottesville, Va., 1994), 167–195; Peter Karsten, *Heart versus Head:*

Judge-Made Law in Nineteenth-Century America (Chapel Hill, N.C., 1997), 79–127; Gary T. Schwartz, "Tort Law and the Economy in Nineteenth-Century America: A Reinterpretation," *Yale Law Journal* 90 (1981), 1717–1775; Robert J. Kaczorowski, "The Common-Law Background of Nineteenth-Century Tort Law," *Ohio State Law Journal* 51 (1990), 1127–1199.

7. G. Edward White, *Tort Law in America: An Intellectual History* (New York, 1980), 14–19; Michael Les Benedict, "Victorian Moralism and Civil Liberty in the Nineteenth Century United States," in Donald G. Nieman, ed., *The Constitution, Law, and American Life: Critical Aspects of the Nineteenth-Century Experience* (Athens, Ga., 1992), 91, 103 (asserting that liability rules were based on the assumption that "people were independent moral agents who controlled their own destinies").

8. See Ralph James Mooney and David E. Moser, "Government and Enterprise in Early Oregon," *Oregon Law Review* 70 (1991), 257, 290–297 (finding that neither Oregon courts nor Oregon legislators regularly aided railroads or other tort defendants); Note, "Private Law and Public Policy: Negligence Law and Political Change in Nineteenth-Century North Carolina," *North Carolina Law Review* 66 (1988), 421, 440 (observing that "at least in North Carolina, there was no single judicial response to tort law in the nineteenth century, particularly in the important area of personal injury disputes").

9. *Nashville & Chattanooga Railroad Company v. Messino*, 33 Tenn. at 225 (1853).

10. Freyer, *Producers Versus Capitalists*, 191. My study of the Tennessee Supreme Court in the nineteenth century supports this conclusion.

11. Mark Aldrich, *Safety First: Technology, Labor, and Business in the Building of American Work Safety, 1870–1939* (Baltimore, 1997), 9–16.

12. *Titus v. Bradford, Bordell & Kinzua Railroad Company*, 136 Pa. 618, 626, 20 A. 517, 518 (1890).

13. *Texas and Pacific Railway Company v. Behymer*, 189 U.S. 468, 470 (1903).

14. *Murray v. South Carolina Railroad Company*, 26 S.C. Law 385, 406 (1841).

15. E.g., *Honner v. Illinois Central Railroad Company*, 15 Ill. 550 (1854); *Ponton v. Wilmington & Weldon Rail Road Company*, 51 N.C. 245 (1858); *Ohio and Mississippi Railroad Company v. Tindall*, 13 Ind. 366 (1859); *Young v. West Virginia Central and Pittsburgh Railway Company*, 42 W. Va. 112, 24 S.E. 615 (1896).

16. *Stuber v. Louisville & Nashville Railroad Company*, 113 Tenn. 305, 87 S.W. 411 (1904).

17. E.g., *Dobbin v. Richmond and Danville Railroad Company*, 81 N.C. 314 (1879); *Ohio River and Charleston Railway Co. v. Edwards*, 111 Tenn. 31, 76 S.W. 897 (1903).

18. Peter Karsten, *Heart versus Head*, 122–124; Gordon Morris Bakken, *The Development of Law on the Rocky Mountain Frontier: Civil Law and Society, 1850–1912* (Westport, Conn., 1983), 103–104; Randolph E. Bergstrom, *Courting Danger: Injury and Law in New York City, 1870–1910* (Ithaca, N.Y., 1992), 75–77.

19. *Union Pacific Railway Company v. O'Brien*, 161 U.S. 451, 457 (1896).

20. E.g., *Hough v. Texas and Pacific Railway Company*, 100 U.S. 213 (1879); *Ford v. Fitchburg Railroad Company*, 110 Mass. 241 (1872); *Wedgwood v. Chicago & Northwestern Railway Company*, 41 Wis. 478 (1877).

21. *Smith v. New York and Harlem Railroad Company*, 19 N.Y. 127 (1859); *Troxler v. Southern Railway Company*, 124 N.C. 189, 32 S.E. 550 (1899).

22. *Laning v. New York Central Railroad Company*, 49 N.Y. 521 (1872); *Harper v. Indianapolis and St. Louis Railroad Company*, 47 Mo. 567 (1871); *Tyson v. South & North Alabama Railroad Company*, 61 Ala. 554 (1878).

23. See Robert S. Hunt, *Law and Locomotives: The Impact of the Railroad on Wisconsin Law in the Nineteenth Century* (Madison, Wis., 1958), 152–156.

24. *Missouri Pacific Railway Company v. Mackey*, 127 U.S. 205, 210 (1888). See also

Louisville & Nashville Railroad Company v. Melton, 218 U.S. 36 (1910); *Hancock v. Norfolk & Western Railway Company*, 124 N.C. 222, 32 S.E. 679 (1899).

25. E.g., *Baltimore and Ohio Railroad Company v. Baugh*, 149 U.S. 368 (1893); *New England Railroad Company v. Conroy*, 175 U.S. 323 (1899); *Northern Pacific Railway Company v. Dixon*, 194 U.S. 338 (1904). See generally Edward A. Purcell, Jr., *Litigation and Inequality: Federal Diversity Jurisdiction in Industrial America, 1870–1958* (New York, 1992), 79–82.

26. *Titus v. Bradford, Bordell & Kinzua Railroad Company*, 136 Pa. 618, 20 A. 517 (1890).

27. E.g., *Carrier v. Union Pacific Railway Company*, 61 Kan. 447, 59 P. 1075 (1900).

28. William G. Thomas, *Lawyering for the Railroad: Business, Law, and Power in the New South* (Baton Rouge, La., 1999), 64, 158; Lewis, *Transforming the Appalachian Countryside*, 127–128 (discussing hostility of West Virginia juries toward railroads).

29. Emory R. Johnson, "Railway Departments for the Relief and Insurance of Employees," *Annals of the American Academy of Political and Social Science* 6 (1895), 424–468; Aldrich, *Safety First*, 31; *Railroad Gazette*, May 27, 1898.

30. *Atlantic Coast Line Railroad Company v. Dunning*, 166 F. 850 (4th Cir. 1908).

31. See *Ashman v. Flint & Pere Marquette Railroad Company*, 90 Mich. 567, 51 N.W. 645 (1892); Hunt, *The Impact of the Railroad on Wisconsin Law*, 136.

32. Aldrich, *Safety First*, 25–40; Steven W. Usselman, "Air Brakes for Freight Trains: Technological Innovation in the American Railroad Industry, 1869–1900," *Business History Review* 58 (1984), 30–50.

33. Aldrich, *Safety First*, 35–40; Kurt Wetzel, "Railroad Management's Response to Operating Employee Accidents, 1890–1913," *Labor History* 21 (1980), 351–368.

34. *Johnson v. Southern Pacific Company*, 196 U.S. 1, 17 (1904).

35. *Schlemmer v. Buffalo, Rochester and Pittsburgh Railway Company*, 205 U.S. 1 (1907).

36. *St. Louis, Iron Mountain and Southern Railway Company v. Taylor*, 210 U.S. 281, 295–296 (1908). See also *United States v. Northern Pacific Railway Company*, 254 U.S. 251 (1920).

37. The FELA, initially passed in 1906, was held to be unconstitutional because it covered railroad employees engaged in intrastate as well as interstate commerce. *Employer's Liability Cases*, 207 U.S. 463 (1908). A subsequent measure, limiting application to employees in interstate commerce, was sustained by the Supreme Court. *Second Employer's Liability Cases*, 223 U.S. 1 (1912).

38. Lester P. Schoene and Frank Watson, "Workmen's Compensation on Interstate Railways," *Harvard Law Review* 47 (1934), 389, 397–410.

39. E.g., *Seaboard Air Line Railway v. Horton*, 233 U.S. 492 (1914); *Southern Pacific Company v. Berkshire*, 254 U.S. 415 (1921); Maurice G. Roberts, *Injuries to Interstate Employees on Railroads* (Chicago, 1915), 190–215.

40. Clarence A. Miller, "The Quest for a Federal Workmen's Compensation Law for Railroad Employees," *Law and Contemporary Problems* 18 (1953), 188–207.

41. See *Consolidated Rail Corporation v. Gottshall*, 512 U.S. 532 (1994).

42. For the high degree of care imposed on common carriers to protect passengers, see Kaczorowski, "The Common-Law Background of Nineteenth-Century Tort Law," 1127, 1157–1169.

43. *McElroy v. Nashua and Lowell Railroad Company*, 58 Mass. 400, 402 (1849). See *American Railroad Journal*, April 24, 1858.

44. E.g., *Galena and Chicago Union Railroad Company v. Yarwood*, 15 Ill. 468 (1855).

45. Karsten, *Heart versus Head*, 91–94.

46. *Philadelphia and Reading Railroad Company v. Derby*, 55 U.S. 467, 485–486 (1855) (observing that "the personal safety of the passengers should not be left to the sport of chance or the negligence of careless servants").

47. *Alexandria & Fredericksburg Railroad Company v. Herndon*, 87 Va. 193, 12 S.E. 289 (1890).

48. An act to incorporate the Florida, Atlantic, and Gulf Central Rail Road Company, Ch. 317, Laws of Florida, 1850.

49. Code of the State of Georgia, sec. 2040, 1861.

50. *Boothby v. Grand Trunk Railway*, 66 N.H. 342, 34 A. 157 (1890).

51. *Gorman v. Pacific Railroad*, 26 Mo. 441, 450 (1858). See also *New Albany and Salem Railroad Company*, 12 Ind. 10 (1859); W. W. Thornton, *The Law of Railroad Fences and Private Crossings* (Indianapolis, 1892), 571.

52. *McPadden v. New York Central Railroad Company*, 44 N.Y. 478, 483 (1871).

53. *Illinois Central Railroad Company v. Slatton*, 54 Ill. 133 (1870); *Phillips v. Rensselser and Saratoga Railroad Company*, 49 N.Y. 177 (1872); *Railroad Company v. Aspell*, 23 Pa. 147 (1854).

54. *Pittsburg and Connellsville Railroad Company v. Andrews*, 39 Md. 329 (1874); *Todd v. Old Colony and Fall River Railroad Company*, 85 Mass. 18 (1861); *Richmond and Danville Railroad Company v. Scott*, 88 Va. 958, 14 S.E. 763 (1892).

55. An act to provide for the incorporation of railroad companies, Ch. 1, Laws of New Mexico, 1878.

56. Schwartz, "Tort Law and the Economy in Nineteenth-Century America," 1743. For a contrary view, see Hunt, "Ensuring the Incalculable Benefits of Railroads," 410–413.

57. *American Railroad Journal*, March 22, 1856.

58. Thomas, *Lawyering for the Railroad*, 69–70.

59. *Southern Railroad v. Hankerson*, 61 Ga. 115 (1878).

60. Thomas, *Lawyering for the Railroad*, 79; Bryon K. Elliott and William F. Elliott, *A Treatise on the Law of Railroads*, 2nd ed. (5 vols., Indianapolis, 1907), III, 614–625.

61. *Bradley v. Boston and Maine Railroad*, 58 Mass. 539 (1849).

62. *Thompson v. New York Central and Hudson River Railroad Company*, 110 N.Y. 463, 17 N.E. 690 (1888).

63. *Harding v. New York and Erie Railroad Company*, 13 Barb. 2, 15 (Sup. Ct. N.Y. 1852).

64. *Norfolk and Western Railroad Company v. Stone's Administrator*, 88 Va. 310, 13 S.E. 432 (1891); *Grostick v. Detroit, Lansing & Northern Railroad Company*, 90 Mich. 594, 51 N.W. 667 (1892); *Atchison Topeka & Santa Fe Railroad Company v. Willey*, 60 Kan. 819, 58 P. 472 (1899); Elliott and Elliott, *A Treatise on The Law of Railroads*, 2nd ed., III, 358–360.

65. *Benner v. Philadelphia and Reading Railroad Company*, 262 Pa. 307, 105 A. 283 (1918).

66. Richard M. Nixon, "Changing Rules of Liability in Automobile Accident Litigation," *Law and Contemporary Problems* 3 (1936), 476, 478–481.

67. *Pokora v. Wabash Railway Company*, 292 U.S. 98, 104 (1934).

68. *Louisville and Nashville Railroad Company v. Yniestra*, 21 Fla. 700, 737 (1886).

69. *Fairport, Painesville & Eastern Railway Company v. Meredith*, 292 U.S. 571 (1934).

70. *Norfolk Southern Railway Company v. Shanklin*, 120 S. Ct. 1467 (2000).

71. Kermit L. Hall, *The Magic Mirror: Law in American History* (New York, 1989), 123.

10. Railroads in the Progressive Era

1. Morton Keller, *Regulating a New Economy: Public Policy and Economic Change in America, 1900–1933* (Cambridge, Mass., 1990), 44–45; Harold U. Faulkner, *The Decline of Laissez-Faire, 1897–1917* (New York, 1951), 187–202; William Deverell,

California Crossing: Californians and the Railroad, 1850–1910 (Berkeley, Calif., 1994), 149–171.

2. *Commercial and Financial Chronicle,* August 4, 1906.

3. Ari Hoogenboom and Olive Hoogenboom, *A History of the ICC: From Panacea to Palliative* (New York, 1976), 52–55.

4. Gabriel Kolko, *Railroads and Regulation, 1877–1916* (Princeton, N.J., 1965), 3.

5. Richard H. K. Vietor, "Businessmen and the Political Economy: The Railroad Rate Controversy of 1905," *Journal of American History* 64 (1977), 47–66.

6. George Harrison Gilliam, "Making Virginia Progressive: Courts and Parties, Railroads and Regulators, 1890–1910," *Virginia Magazine of History and Biography* 107 (1999), 189–222; Mansel Griffiths Blackford, "Businessmen and the Regulation of Railroads and Public Utilities in California During the Progressive Era," *Business History Review* 44 (1970), 307–319.

7. The ICC grappled for years with the nature of competition that justified relief from the long haul–short haul rule, and the outcome in individual cases was so varied as to defy easy generalization. See Homer B. Vanderblue, "The Long and Short Haul Clause Since 1910," *Harvard Law Review* 36 (1923), 426–455; Lee A. Dew, "The Owensboro Cattle Cases: A Study in Commerce Regulations," *Filson Club History Quarterly* 49 (1975), 195–203.

8. Albro Martin, *Enterprise Denied: Origins of the Decline of American Railroads, 1897–1917* (New York, 1971), 183–193; Hoogenboom and Hoogenboom, *A History of the ICC,* 60–61.

9. John F. Stover, *American Railroads,* 2nd ed. (Chicago, 1997), 130–131; Richard D. Stone, *The Interstate Commerce Commission and the Railroad Industry: A History of Regulatory Policy* (New York, 1991), 16; Stanley P. Caine, *The Myth of a Progressive Reform: Railroad Regulation in Wisconsin, 1903–1910* (Madison, Wis., 1970), 189–190; T. Lane Moore, "Railroad Valuation Records," *Railroad History* 163 (1990), 93–102.

10. Martin, *Enterprise Denied,* 228.

11. Caine, *The Myth of a Progressive Reform,* 190; S. G. Reed, *A History of the Texas Railroads* (Houston, 1941), 712–718.

12. Keller, *Regulating a New Economy,* 49. See also Hoogenboom and Hoogenboom, *A History of the ICC,* 68.

13. *Illinois Central Railroad Company v. ICC,* 206 U.S. 441 (1907).

14. *ICC v. Illinois Central Railroad Company,* 215 U.S. 452, 470 (1910).

15. *ICC v. Chicago, Rock Island & Pacific Railway,* 218 U.S. 88 (1910).

16. *Intermountain Rate Cases,* 234 U.S. 476 (1914).

17. *Houston, East and West Texas Railway Company v. United States (Shreveport Rate Case),* 234 U.S. 342 (1914). See Reed, *A History of the Texas Railroads,* 622–632.

18. Kolko, *Railroads and Regulation,* 165–166, 217.

19. *Florida East Coast Railway Company v. United States,* 234 U.S. 167 (1914).

20. *ICC v. Chicago Great Western Railway Company,* 209 U.S. 108, 118–119 (1908).

21. *United States v. Pennsylvania Railroad Company,* 242 U.S. 208 (1916).

22. Maury Klein, *The Life & Legend of E. H. Harriman* (Chapel Hill, N.C., 2000), 392–395, 404.

23. *Harriman v. ICC,* 211 U.S. 407, 417–418 (1908). Holmes had little confidence in the ICC and feared that the commission was constantly seeking to expand its delegated power. Liva Baker, *The Justice from Beacon Hill: The Life and Times of Oliver Wendell Holmes* (New York, 1991), 428–429.

24. Jules I. Bogen, *The Anthracite Railroads: A Study in American Railroad Enterprise* (New York, 1927), 206–214; Eliot Jones, *The Anthracite Coal Combination in the United States* (Cambridge, Mass., 1914), 21–32.

25. *Stockton v. Central Railroad of New Jersey*, 50 N.J. Eq. 52 (1892), 50 N.J. Eq. 489 (1892).

26. As quoted in Allen W. Moger, "Railroad Practices and Policies in Virginia After the Civil War," *Virginia Magazine of History and Biography* 59 (1951), 423, 453.

27. An act to prevent railroad companies from buying and selling coal or coke, Ch. 16, Laws of West Virginia, 1895.

28. Bogen, *The Anthracite Railroads*, 218; Kolko, *Railroads and Regulation*, 163.

29. *United States v. Delaware, Lackawanna and Western Railroad Company*, 238 U.S. 516, 527 (1915); Bogen, *The Anthracite Railroads*, 221–222.

30. *United States v. Reading Company*, 226 U.S. 324 (1912); *United States v. Reading Company*, 253 U.S. 26 (1920); *United States v. Lehigh Valley Railroad Company*, 254 U.S. 255 (1920).

31. Bogen, *The Anthracite Railroads*, 227–236.

32. Id., 241.

33. Keller, *Regulating a New Economy*, 47; Kolko, *Railroads and Regulation*, 217–218; James F. Doster, *Railroads in Alabama Politics, 1875–1914* (Tuscaloosa, Ala., 1957), 161; Maxwell Ferguson, *State Regulation of Railroads in the South* (New York, 1916), 51–217.

34. An act to regulate railroads and other common carriers in this state, no. 78, Laws of Ohio, 1906.

35. Bruce W. Dearstyne, *Railroads and Railroad Regulations in New York State, 1900–1913* (New York, 1986), 75–130.

36. Keller, *Regulating a New Economy*, 50.

37. *Northern Pacific Railway Company v. North Dakota*, 236 U.S. 585 (1915).

38. *Norfolk and Western Railway Company v. West Virginia*, 236 U.S. 605 (1915).

39. *Seaboard Air Line Railway Company v. Railroad Commission of Alabama*, 155 F. 792 (Cir. Ct., Ala., 1907); Doster, *Railroads in Alabama Politics*, 164–211.

40. *Ex Parte Young*, 209 U.S. 123, 160 (1908).

41. John V. Orth, *The Judicial Power of the United States: The Eleventh Amendment in American History* (New York, 1987), 121–135; Richard C. Cortner, *The Iron Horse and the Constitution: The Railroads and the Transformation of the Fourteenth Amendment* (Westport, Conn., 1993), 181–211; William F. Duker, "Mr. Justice Rufus W. Peckham and the Case of *Ex Parte Young*: Locknerizing *Munn v. Illinois*," 1980 *Brigham Young University Law Review*, 539–558.

42. *Ex Parte Young*, 209 U.S. at 165 (1908). See also *Hunter v. Wood*, 209 U.S. 205 (1908) (invalidating a similar North Carolina law).

43. *Herndon v. Chicago, Rock Island and Pacific Railway Company*, 218 U.S. 135 (1910); Doster, *Railroads in Alabama Politics*, 161–162, 183–193.

44. *Missouri Pacific Railway Company v. Tucker*, 230 U.S. 340 (1913).

45. Dearstyne, *Railroads and Railroad Regulations in New York State*, 184–291.

46. *Michigan Central Railroad Company v. Michigan Railroad Commission*, 236 U.S. 615 (1915).

47. *Brooks-Scanlon Company v. Railroad Commission of Louisiana*, 251 U.S. 396 (1920).

48. Martin, *Enterprise Denied*, 115, 145; Faulkner, *The Decline of Laissez-Faire*, 209.

49. *Northern Securities Company v. United States*, 193 U.S. 197 (1904); James W. Ely, Jr., *The Chief Justiceship of Melville W. Fuller, 1888–1910* (Columbia, S.C., 1995), 132–133; Alfred S. Neely, "'A humbug based on economic ignorance and incompetence'— Antitrust in the Eyes of Justice Holmes," *Utah Law Review* 1, (1993), 23–31. For criticism of the decision, see Klein, *The Life & Legend of E.H. Harriman*, 311–313 (noting that the *Northern Securities* decision "illustrated the confusion Americans felt over the corporate behemoths that had become so significant a part of their economic life"); Balthasar H. Meyer, *A History of the Northern Securities Case* (Madison, Wis., 1906).

50. Keller, *Regulating a New Economy*, 29–34.

51. Albro Martin, *Railroads Triumphant: The Growth, Rejection, and Rebirth of a Vital American Force* (New York, 1992), 328–329; Stover, *American Railroads*, 128–129.

52. *United States v. Union Pacific Railroad Company*, 226 U.S. 61, 88 (1912).

53. 37 Stat., Ch. 290 (1912); see *Lehigh Valley Railroad Company v. United States*, 243 U.S. 412 (1917).

54. 38 Stat., Ch. 323 (1914); Hoogenboom and Hoogenboom, *A History of the ICC*, 81.

55. Meyer, *A History of the Northern Securities Case*, 305–307; Martin, *Enterprise Denied*, 181.

56. Blewett Lee, "Combination, Not Competition, of Railroads," *Michigan Law Review* 16 (1918), 496, 497–498.

57. Dearstyne, *Railroads and Railroad Regulation in New York State*, 328–350.

58. Martin, *Enterprise Denied*, 194–318; Hoogenboom and Hoogenboom, *A History of the ICC*, 60–81; Keller, *Regulating a New Economy*, 48–51.

59. William F. Herrin, "Government Regulation of Railways," *California Law Review* 2 (1914), 87, 92, 95.

60. Kolko, *Railroads and Regulation*, 235.

61. See Martin, *Railroads Triumphant*, 385.

62. Robert A. Harbeson, "Railroads and Regulation, 1877–1916: Conspiracy or Public Interest?" *Journal of Economic History* 27 (1967), 230, 240–242.

63. Hoogenboom and Hoogenboom, *A History of the ICC*, 66.

11. *World War I and the Expansion of Federal Regulatory Authority*

1. Morton Keller, *Regulating a New Economy: Public Policy and Economic Change in America, 1900–1933* (Cambridge, Mass., 1990), 50.

2. Albro Martin, *Enterprise Denied: Origins of the Decline of American Railroads, 1897–1917* (New York, 1971), 335–340, 345–351; John F. Stover, *American Railroads*, 2nd ed. (Chicago, 1997), 168–172.

3. Harold U. Faulkner, *The Decline of Laissez-Faire, 1897–1917* (New York, 1951), 219.

4. Walker D. Hines, *War History of American Railroads* (New Haven, 1928), 244–249. See also K. Austin Kerr, "Decision for Federal Control: Wilson, McAdoo, and the Railroads, 1917," *Journal of American History* 54 (1967), 550–560.

5. E. I. Dupont De Nemours & Company v. Davis, 264 U.S. 456 (1924). See K. Austin Kerr, *American Railroad Politics, 1914–1920: Rates, Wages and Efficiency* (Pittsburgh, 1968), 83–87.

6. An act to provide for the operation of transportation systems while under federal control, Ch. 25, 40 Stat. 451 (1918). See K. Austin Kerr, *American Railroad Politics*, 83–87.

7. *Report of the Director General of Railroads, 1924* (Washington, 1925), 6–8.

8. S. G. Reed, *A History of the Texas Railroads* (Houston, 1941), 724.

9. Hines, *War History of American Railroads*, 108–120.

10. *Report of the Director General of Railroads*, 20.

11. Hines, *War History of American Railroads*, 116.

12. Ari Hoogenboom and Olive Hoogenboom, *A History of the ICC: From Panacea to Palliative* (New York, 1976), 88–89; Hines, *War History of American Railroads*, 192–210.

13. Hines, *War History of American Railroads*, 152–190; Stover, *American Railroads*, 176–177; Walter M. W. Splawn, *Government Ownership and Operation of Railroads* (New York, 1928), 375–377 ("Labor problems under Federal control were acute").

14. Leonard A. Lecht, *Experience Under Railway Labor Legislation* (New York, 1955), 36; Hines, *War History of American Railroads*, 166–167.

15. Splawn, *Government Ownership and Operation of Railroads*, 377–382.

16. Stover, *American Railroads*, 178–179; Hoogenboom and Hoogenboom, *A History of the ICC*, 91–93.

17. Address of President Wilson to Congress, December 2, 1918, in Hines, *War History of American Railroads*, 265–266.

18. For the Transportation Act, see Stover, *American Railroads*, 170–180; Hoogenboom and Hoogenboom, *A History of the ICC*, 94–97; Kerr, *American Railroad Politics*, 204–227; Richard D. Stone, *The Interstate Commerce Commission and the Railroad Industry: A History of Regulatory Policy* (Westport, Conn., 1991), 20–22.

19. Kerr, *American Railroad Politics*, 231.

20. Maury Klein, *Unfinished Business: The Railroad in American Life* (Hanover, N.H., 1994), 128.

21. *Texas & Pacific Railway Company v. Gulf, Colorado & Santa Fe Railway Company*, 270 U.S. 266, 277 (1926) (declaring "that competition between carriers may result in harm to the public as well as benefit").

22. Note, "The Waning Power of the States over Railroads," *Harvard Law Review* 37 (1924), 888–893 (noting that the Transportation Act "has undeniably reduced the power of the states over traffic charges to a shadow").

23. *Dayton-Goose Creek Railway Company v. United States*, 263 U.S. 456 (1924).

24. Stone, *The Interstate Commerce Commission*, 34; Albro Martin, *Railroads Triumphant: The Growth, Rejection and Rebirth of a Vital American Force* (New York, 1992), 358; Hoogenboom and Hoogenboom, *A History of the ICC*, 104–105.

25. *Dayton-Goose Creek Railway Company v. United States*, 263 U.S. 456, 478 (1924).

26. Whitefoord R. Cole, "The American Ideal," *L & N Employees' Magazine*, January 1927, 7, 8.

27. Klein, *Unfinished Business*, 130.

12. Tangled Labor Relations

1. See Herbert G. Gutman, "Trouble on the Railroads in 1873–1874: Prelude to the 1877 Crisis?" *Labor History* 2 (1961), 215–235.

2. Robert V. Bruce, *1877: Year of Violence* (Indianapolis, 1959), 36.

3. For the strikes of 1877, see Bruce, *1877*; Gerald G. Eggert, *Railroad Labor Disputes: The Beginning of Federal Strike Policy* (Ann Arbor, Mich., 1967), 24–53; Clifton K. Yearley, Jr., "The Baltimore and Ohio Railroad Strike of 1877," *Maryland Historical Magazine* 51 (1956), 188–211; William T. Doherty, Jr., "Berkeley's Non-revolution: Law and Order and the Great Railway Strikes of 1877," *West Virginia History* 35 (1974), 271–289.

4. David O. Stowell, *Streets, Railroads, and the Great Strike of 1877* (Chicago, 1999), 70–145.

5. Eggert, *Railroad Labor Disputes*, 47–51.

6. Id., 35–41; Elwin W. Sigmund, "Railroad Strikers in Court: Unreported Contempt Cases in Illinois in 1877," *Journal of Illinois State Historical Society* 49 (1956), 190–209.

7. Bruce, *1877*, 309.

8. Eggert, *Railroad Labor Disputes*, 54–59.

9. Paul V. Black, "Experiment in Bureaucratic Centralization: Employee Blacklisting on the Burlington Railroad, 1877–1892," *Business History Review* 51 (1977), 444–459; Gutman, "Trouble on the Railroads in 1873–1874," 215, 230.

10. *In re Doolittle*, 23 Fed. Rep. 544, 547 (Cir. Ct., E.D., Mo., 1885).

11. *Chicago, Burlington & Quincy Railroad Company v. Burlington, Cedar Rapids & Northern Railway Company*, 34 Fed. Rep. 480 (Cir. Ct., E.D., Penn., 1888); Donald L. McMurry, *The Great Burlington Strike of 1888: A Case History in Labor Relations* (Cambridge, Mass., 1956), 114–137; Eggert, *Railroad Labor Disputes*, 81–90.

12. Eggert, *Railroad Labor Disputes*, 103–107.

13. For the Pullman strike, see David Ray Papke, *The Pullman Case: The Clash of Labor and Capital in Industrial America* (Lawrence, Kans., 1999); Almont Lindsey, *The Pullman Strike: The Story of a Unique Experiment and of a Great Labor Upheaval* (Chicago, 1942); Eggert, *Railroad Labor Disputes*, 152–191.

14. William Deverell, *Railroad Crossing: Californians and the Railroad, 1850–1910* (Berkeley, Calif., 1994), 61–92.

15. *In re Debs*, 158 U.S. 564, 582 (1895).

16. Papke, *The Pullman Case*, 97–98; James W. Ely, Jr., *The Chief Justiceship of Melville W. Fuller, 1888–1910* (Columbia, S.C., 1995), 136.

17. Herbert Hovenkamp, *Enterprise and American Law, 1836–1937* (Cambridge, Mass., 1991), 231.

18. An act concerning carriers engaged in interstate commerce and their employees, 30 Stat. 424 (1898).

19. Eggert, *Railroad Labor Disputes*, 217–225; Ari Hoogenboom and Olive Hoogenboom, *A History of the ICC: From Panacea to Palliative* (New York, 1976), 59; Shelton Stromquist, *A Generation of Boomers: The Pattern of a Railroad Labor Conflict in Nineteenth-Century America* (Urbana, Ill., 1987), 259–266.

20. Stromquist, *A Generation of Boomers*, 265.

21. Leonard A. Lecht, *Experience Under Railway Labor Legislation* (New York, 1955), 25–28.

22. Albro Martin, *Enterprise Denied: Origins of the Decline of American Railroads, 1897–1917* (New York, 1971), 319–335.

23. *Wilson v. New*, 243 U.S. 332, 347 (1917).

24. Lecht, *Experience Under Railway Labor Legislation*, 38–40; *Pennsylvania Railroad Company v. Railroad Labor Board*, 261 U.S. 72 (1923); *Pennsylvania Railroad System v. Pennsylvania Railroad Company*, 267 U.S. 203 (1925).

25. Colin J. Davis, *Power at Odds: The 1922 National Railroad Shopmen's Strike* (Urbana, Ill., 1997), 48–115.

26. Id., 131.

27. Id., 130–132; Robert H. Zieger, *Republicans and Labor, 1919–1929* (Lexington, Ky., 1969), 137–143.

28. Lecht, *Experience Under Railway Labor Legislation*, 47–59; Zieger, *Republicans and Labor*, 190–215.

29. *Texas & New Orleans Railroad Company v. Brotherhood of Railway and Steamship Clerks*, 281 U.S. 548, 570 (1930).

30. *Terminal Railroad Association v. Brotherhood of Railroad Trainmen*, 318 U.S. 1 (1943); *Elgin, Joliet and Eastern Railway v. Burley*, 325 U.S. 711 (1945).

31. *Virginian Railway Company v. System Federation No. 90*, 300 U.S. 515 (1937).

32. *Brotherhood of Railroad Trainmen v. Jacksonville Terminal Company*, 394 U.S. 369 (1969); *Andrews v. Louisville & Nashville Railway Company*, 406 U.S. 320 (1972).

33. Ludwig Teller, "Government Seizure in Labor Disputes," *Harvard Law Review* 60 (1947), 1017–1029.

34. Lecht, *Experience Under Railway Labor Legislation*, 176–187.

35. Id., 188–208; Maury Klein, *History of the Louisville & Nashville Railroad* (New York, 1972), 474–478.

36. Klein, *History of the Louisville & Nashville Railroad*, 478.

37. *Brotherhood of Locomotive Engineers v. Chicago, Rock Island & Pacific Railroad Company*, 382 U.S. 421, 429 (1966).

38. Lecht, *Experience Under Railway Labor Legislation*, 90–92; Mark Aldrich, *Safety First: Technology, Labor, and Business in the Building of American Work Safety, 1870–1939* (Baltimore, 1997), 173–174.

39. For the struggle over enactment of a full-crew law in New York, see Bruce W. Dearstyne, *Railroads and Railroad Regulations in New York State, 1900–1913* (New York, 1986), 321–328.

40. John F. Stover, *American Railroads*, 2nd ed. (Chicago, 1997), 232–233.

41. *Brotherhood of Locomotive Engineers v. Chicago, Rock Island & Pacific Railroad Company*, 382 U.S. 421 (1966).

42. *Public Service Commission v. New York Central Railroad*, 247 Ind. 411, 216 N.E.2d 716 (1966), cert. den. 385 U.S. 843 (1966); *Chicago & North Western Railroad Company v. LaFollette*, 43 Wis.2d 631, 169 N.W.2d 441 (1969); *New York Central Railroad Company v. Lefkowitz*, 23 N.Y.2d 1, 241 N.E.2d 730 (1968), app. dis. 393 U.S. 536 (1969).

43. H. Roger Grant, *Erie Lackawanna: Death of an American Railroad, 1938–1992* (Stanford, Calif., 1994), 69–70.

44. *Keeler v. Consolidated Rail Corporation*, 582 F. Supp. 1546 (Special Ct., 1984).

45. Lecht, *Experience Under Railway Labor Legislation*, 102–109; Earl Latham, *The Politics of Railroad Coordination, 1933–1936* (Cambridge, Mass., 1959), 259–265.

46. *United States v. Lowden*, 308 U.S. 225, 234 (1939). For the Washington Agreement, see Latham, *The Politics of Railroad Coordination*, 248–257.

47. Lecht, *Experience Under Railway Labor Legislation*, 115–117.

48. Maury Klein, *Unfinished Business: The Railroad in American Life* (Hanover, N.H., 1994), 153.

49. Herbert R. Northrup, "The Railway Labor Act—Time for Repeal?" *Harvard Journal of Law & Public Policy* 13 (1990), 441–515.

13. Legal Problems of Railroad Decline

1. John F. Stover, *American Railroads*, 2nd ed. (Chicago, 1997), 192–196; Albro Martin, *Railroads Triumphant: The Growth, Rejection, and Rebirth of a Vital American Force* (New York, 1992), 362–363; Stephen B. Goddard, *Getting There: The Epic Struggle Between Road and Rail in the American Century* (New York, 1994), 179–206; Mark Reutter, "The Lost Promise of the American Railroad," *Wilson Quarterly* 18 (1994), 10, 22–29.

2. *Nashville, Chattanooga & St. Louis Railway v. Walters*, 294 U.S. 405, 416 (1935).

3. Stover, *American Railroads*, 2nd ed., 198–199.

4. Ari Hoogenboom and Olive Hoogenboom, *A History of the ICC: From Panacea to Palliative* (New York, 1976), 97–102; Richard D. Stone, *The Interstate Commerce Commission and the Railroad Industry: A History of Regulatory Policy* (Westport, Conn., 1991), 31–36.

5. Gustavus H. Robinson, "The Hoch-Smith Resolution and the Future of the Interstate Commerce Commission," *Harvard Law Review* 42 (1929), 610–638.

6. Hoogenboom and Hoogenboom, *A History of the ICC*, 102–103; Harvey C. Mansfield, "The Hoch-Smith Resolution and the Consideration of Commercial Conditions in Rate-Fixing," *Cornell Law Quarterly* 16 (1931), 339–358.

7. *Consolidation of Railroads*, 63 ICC 455 (1921).

8. *Consolidation of Railroads*, 159 ICC 522 (1929); Hoogenboom and Hoogenboom, *A History of the ICC*, 105–108.

9. *United States v. Southern Pacific Company*, 259 U.S. 214 (1922).

10. Neill C. Wilson and Frank J. Taylor, *Southern Pacific: The Roaring Story of a Fighting Railroad* (New York, 1952), 120–122.

11. *Texas v. Eastern Texas Railroad Company*, 258 U.S. 204 (1922); *Colorado v. United States*, 271 U.S. 153 (1926); Charles R. Cherington, *The Regulation of Railroad Abandonments* (Cambridge, Mass., 1948), 41–58.

12. Sarah J. Gordon, *Passage to Union: How the Railroads Transformed American Life, 1829–1929* (Chicago, 1996), 334–345; Robert B. Carlson, *Main Line to Oblivion: The Disintegration of New York Railroads in the Twentieth Century* (Port Washington, N.Y., 1971), 125–131.

13. *ICC v. Oregon-Washington Railroad & Navigation Company*, 288 U.S. 14 (1933).

14. Martin, *Railroads Triumphant*, 364–365; Hoogenboom and Hoogenboom, *A History of the ICC*, 119–125.

15. Earl Latham, *The Politics of Railroad Coordination, 1933–1936* (Cambridge, Mass., 1959), 86–101.

16. Morton Keller, *Regulating a New Economy: Public Policy and Economic Change in America, 1900–1933* (Cambridge, Mass., 1990), 55.

17. Latham, *The Politics of Railroad Coordination*, 116–266.

18. Stover, *American Railroads*, 2nd ed., 201.

19. Leonard A. Lecht, *Experience Under Railway Labor Legislation* (New York, 1955), 118–123.

20. William E. Leuchtenburg, *The Supreme Court Reborn: The Constitutional Revolution in the Age of Roosevelt* (New York, 1995), 26–51.

21. James W. Ely, Jr., *The Guardian of Every Other Right: A Constitutional History of Property Rights*, 2nd ed. (New York, 1998), 119–134.

22. Lecht, *Experience Under Railway Labor Legislation*, 123–153.

23. Hoogenboom and Hoogenboom, *A History of the ICC*, 133–138.

24. Cherington, *The Regulation of Railroad Abandonments*, 99–158, 219–227.

25. *New York Central Railroad Company v. Public Utilities Commission*, 124 O.S. 549, 552 (1932) (upholding commission order).

26. Stover, *American Railroads*, 2nd ed., 184–191; Robert D. Cuff, "United States Mobilization and Railroad Transportation: Lessons in Coordination and Control, 1917–1945," *Journal of Military History* 53 (1989), 33–50.

27. David M. Potter, "The Historical Development of Eastern-Southern Freight Rate Relationships," *Law and Contemporary Problems* 12 (1947), 416–448.

28. Carole E. Scott, "Were Freight Rates Used to Keep the South and West Down?," *Essays in Economic and Business History* 9 (1991), 51–68.

29. Sam Hall Flint, "The Great Freight Rate Fight," *Atlanta Historical Journal* 28 (1984), 5–22.

30. *Georgia v. Pennsylvania Railroad Company*, 324 U.S. 439 (1945). See Robert A. Lively, *The South in Action: A Sectional Crusade Against Freight Rate Discrimination* (Chapel Hill, N.C., 1949), 67–69.

31. *Georgia v. Pennsylvania Railroad Company*, 340 U.S. 889 (1950).

32. Martin, *Railroads Triumphant*, 214–215; Scott, "Were Freight Rates Used to Keep the South and West Down?," 60; Lively, *The South in Action*, 87–88.

33. Hoogenboom and Hoogenboom, *A History of the ICC*, 138–142.

34. George W. Hinton, *The Transportation Act of 1958: A Decade of Experience* (Bloomington, Ind., 1969), 14–21.

35. Id., 31–41.

36. Goddard, *Getting There*, 215.

37. See also *Seaboard Air Line Railroad Company v. United States*, 382 U.S. 154 (1965); D. Philip Locklin, *Economics of Transportation*, 7th ed. (Homewood, Ill., 1972).

38. Richard Saunders, *The Railroad Mergers and the Coming of Conrail* (Westport, Conn., 1978), 76–94.

39. Hoogenboom and Hoogenboom, *A History of the ICC*, 175.

40. See H. Roger Grant, *Erie Lackawanna: Death of an American Railroad, 1938–1992* (Stanford, Calif., 1994), 84–106.

41. Saunders, *Railroad Mergers*, 156–165.

42. Maury Klein, *The Life & Legend of E.H. Harriman* (Chapel Hill, N.C., 2000), 445.

43. Martin, *Railroads Triumphant*, 382.

44. Stover, *American Railroads*, 2nd ed., 235–236.

45. See Stephen Salsbury, *No Way to Run a Railroad: The Untold Story of the Penn Central Crisis* (New York, 1982); Saunders, *Railroad Mergers*, 263–294.

46. Grant, *Erie Lackawanna*, 106.

47. Stover, *American Railroads*, 2nd ed., 236–239.

48. Stone, *The Interstate Commerce Commission*, 55.

49. Stone, *The Interstate Commerce Commission*, 76–78; Comment, "The Railroad Revitalization and Regulatory Reform Act of 1976: Improving the Railroads' Competitive Position," *Harvard Journal on Legislation* 14 (1977), 575–619.

50. Saunders, *Railroad Mergers*, 319–323.

51. An act to reform the economic regulation of railroads, 94 Stat. 1895 (1980).

52. For the Staggers Act, see Stover, *American Railroads*, 2nd ed., 247–248; Frank J. Dooley and William E. Thoms, *Railroad Law: A Decade After Deregulation* (Westport, Conn., 1994), 3–13.

53. Northeast Rail Service Act, 95 Stat. 643 (1981).

54. Conrail Privatization Act, 100 Stat. 1892 (1986).

55. Carlson, *Main Line to Oblivion*, 204–205.

56. Salsbury, *No Way to Run a Railroad*, 60–61.

Epilogue

1. Albro Martin, *Railroads Triumphant: The Growth, Rejection, and Rebirth of a Vital American Force* (New York, 1992), 363.

2. James Bryce, *The American Commonwealth*, rev. ed. (2 vols., New York, 1912), II, 700.

3. Maury Klein, *Unfinished Business: The Railroad in American Life* (Hanover, N.H., 1994), 133.

4. For the leading statement of this thesis, see Morton J. Horwitz, *The Transformation of American Law, 1780–1860* (Cambridge, Mass., 1977), 63–108. See also Ronald L. Lewis, *Transforming the Appalachian Countryside: Railroads, Deforestation and Social Change in West Virginia, 1880–1920* (Chapel Hill, N.C., 1998), 127–128.

5. See Alan Furman Westin, "The Supreme Court, the Populist Movement and the Campaign of 1896," *Journal of Politics* 15 (1953), 3, 5–19.

6. See James B. Burns, *Railroad Mergers and the Language of Unification* (Westport, Conn., 1998), 157–166.

7. See *Western Coal Traffic League v. Surface Transportation Board*, 216 F.3d 1168 (Ct. App. D.C. 2000) (upholding authority of STB to impose moratorium despite statutory language imposing deadlines for review of merger applications).

8. Frank J. Dooley and William E. Thoms, *Railroad Law: A Decade After Deregulation* (Westport, Conn., 1994), 91–96.

9. *Pittsburgh and Lake Erie Railroad Company v. Railway Labor Executive Association*, 491 U.S. 490 (1989).

10. ICC Termination Act, 109 Stat. 803 (1995).

11. See Jon W. Bruce and James W. Ely, Jr., *The Law of Easements and Licenses in Land,* rev. ed. (New York, 1995), and 2001 Supp. No. 1, ¶12.08.

12. An act . . . to revise certain provisions regarding the right of eminent domain for railroads, South Dakota Codified Laws, sec. 49-16A-75 et seq. (2000).

13. Fla. Const., art. X sec. 19.

BIBLIOGRAPHY

Primary Published Sources

BOOKS

Adams, Jr., Charles Francis. *Railroads: Their Origin and Problems.* New York: G. P. Putnam's Sons, 1878.

Bryce, James. *The American Commonwealth.* Rev. ed. 2 vols. New York: Macmillan, 1912.

Crafts, Wilbur F. *The Sabbath for Man.* New York: Funk & Wagnall's, 1885.

Gregg, W. P., and Benjamin Pond, eds. *The Railroad Laws and Charters of the United States.* 2 vols. Boston: Charles C. Little and James Brown, 1851.

Johnson, Donald Bruce, and Kirk H. Porter, comps. *National Party Platforms, 1840–1972.* Urbana: University of Illinois Press, 1973.

Meyer, Balthasar H. *A History of the Northern Securities Case.* Madison: University of Wisconsin, 1906.

Poor, Henry Varnum. *History of the Railroads and Canals of the United States.* New York: John H. Schultz, 1860; reprint, New York: Augustus M. Kelley, 1970.

Poor's Manual of the Railroads of the United States. New York: Henry Varnum Poor and H. W. Poor, 1900.

Ramsdell, Charles W., ed. *Laws and Joint Resolutions of the Last Session of the Confederate Congress.* Durham, N.C.: Duke University Press, 1941.

Ringwalt, John L. *Development of Transportation Systems in the United States.* Philadelphia, 1888; reprint, New York: Johnson Reprint, 1966.

Ripley, William Z. *Railroads: Rates and Regulations.* New York: Longmans, Green, 1920.

War of the Rebellion: A Compilation of the Official Records of the Union and Confederate Armies. series IV, vol. I. Washington: Government Printing Office, 1900.

White, Robert H. *Messages of the Governors of Tennessee, 1835–1845.* Nashville: Tennessee Historical Commission, 1954.

LEGAL TREATISES

Blackstone, William. *Commentaries on the Laws of England.* 4 vols. Oxford, 1765–1769; reprint, Chicago: University of Chicago Press, 1979.

Baldwin, Simeon E. *American Railroad Law..* Boston: Little, Brown, 1904.

Bruce, Jon W., and James W. Ely, Jr. *The Law of Easements and Licenses in Land.* Rev. ed. New York: West Group, 1995 and 2001. Supp. No. 1.

Cooley, Thomas M. *A Treatise on the Constitutional Limitations Which Rest Upon the Legislative Power of the States of the American Union.* Boston: Little, Brown, 1868; reprint, New York: Da Capo Press, 1972.

Dobbs, Dan B. *Law of Remedies.* 2nd ed. 3 vols. St. Paul, Minn.: West Publishing Company, 1993.

Elliott, Byron K., and William F. Elliott. *A Treatise on the Law of Railroads.* 2nd ed. 5 vols. Indianapolis: Bobbs-Merrill, 1907.

Freund, Ernst. *The Police Power: Public Policy and Constitutional Rights.* Chicago: Callaghan, 1904.

Harris, George E. *A Treatise on Sunday Laws.* Rochester, N.Y.: Lawyer's Co-operative Publishing, 1892.

Lewis, John. *A Treatise on the Law of Eminent Domain in the United States.* Chicago: Callaghan, 1888.

Pierce, Edward L. *A Treatise on the Law of Railroads.* Boston: Little, Brown, 1881.

Redfield, Isaac F. *The Law of Railways.* 6th ed. 2 vols. Boston: Little, Brown, 1888.

Roberts, Maurice G. *Injuries to Interstate Employees on Railroads.* Chicago: Callaghan, 1915.

Rorer, David. *A Treatise on the Law of Railways.* 2 vols. Chicago: Callaghan, 1884.

Thornton, W. W. *The Law of Railroad Fences and Private Crossings.* Indianapolis: Bowen-Merrill Co., 1892.

White, Edward J., *The Law of Personal Injuries on Railroads.* 2 vols. St. Louis: F. H. Thomas Law Book Co., 1909.

REPORTS

Indian Peace Commission Report, January 7, 1868. Reprinted in Wilcomb E. Washburn, ed., *The American Indian and the United States: A Documentary History.* 4 vols. New York: Random House, 1973, I, 134.

Memorial of the Chicago & North Western and Chicago, Milwaukee & St. Paul Railway Companies to the Senate and Assembly of the State of Wisconsin. Chicago, 1875.

Memorial of the General Assembly of the State of South Carolina to the Congress of the United States in the Matter of Receivers of Railroad Corporations and the Equity Jurisdiction of the Courts of the United States. 28 American Law Review, 161–195 (1894).

Proceedings of the Special Committee on Railroads, State of New York. 5 vols. New York: Evening Post Steam Presses, 1879.

Repeal of Land Grant Reduced Rates on Railroad Transportation of Government Traffic, Report, Committee on Interstate and Foreign Commerce. House of Representatives, March 18, 1942.

Report of Commissioners Appointed to Investigate Charges Made Against the Directors of the Delaware and Raritan Canal and Camden and Amboy Railroad Transportation Companies. Trenton: Phillips and Boswell, 1850.

Report of the Commission and of the Minority Commissioner of the United States Pacific Railway Commission. Washington: Government Printing Office, 1887.

Report of the Director General of Railroads, 1924. Washington: Government Printing Office, 1925.

First Annual Report of the Interstate Commerce Commission. Washington: Government Printing Office, 1887.

Remonstrance of the President, Directors and Company of the Middlesex Canal. State Library of Massachusetts, 1830.

Seventeenth Annual Report of the Interstate Commerce Commission. Washington: Government Printing Office, 1903.
Study of Federal Aid to Rail Transportation. Washington: U.S. Department of Transportation, 1977.

ARTICLES

Adams, Jr., Charles Francis. "Railway Problems in 1869." *North American Review* 110 (1870), 116–150.
_____. "The Government and the Railroad Corporations." *North American Review* 112 (1871), 31–61.
_____. "The Granger Movement." *North American Review* 120 (1875), 394–424.
Caldwell, Henry Clay. "Railroad Receiverships in the Federal Courts." *American Law Review* 30 (1896), 161–187.
Chamberlain, D. H.. "New-Fashioned Receiverships." *Harvard Law Review* 10 (1896), 140–149.
Clark, Frederick Converse. "State Railroad Commissions and How They May Be Made Effective." *Publications of the American Economic Association* 6 (1891), 11–108.
Cole, Whitefoord R. "The American Ideal." *L&N Employees' Magazine.* January 1927, 7–9, 26–27.
Cooley, Thomas M. "Limits to State Control of Private Business." *Princeton Review* 54 (1878), 233–271.
Dabney, Robert L. "The New South." June 15, 1882, Virginia State Library.
Eastman, Joseph B. "Public Ownership and Operation of Railroads in the United States." *Annals of the American Academy of Political and Social Sciences* 187 (1936), 106–119.
Hammond, W. G., "American Law Schools: Past and Future." *Southern Law Review* 7, n.s. (1881), 400–429.
Hanson, Burton. "Unfair Railway Agitation." Chicago, 1905.
Herrin, William F. "Government Regulation of Railways." *California Law Review* 2 (1914), 87–103.
Huntington, Collis P. "A Plea for Railway Consolidation." *North American Review* 153 (1891), 272–282.
Johnson, Emory R. "Railway Departments for the Relief and Insurance of Employees." *Annals of the American Academy of Political and Social Science* 6 (1895), 424–468.
Kent, C. A. "Municipal Subscriptions and Taxation in Aid of Railroads." *American Law Register* 9 (1870), 649–657.
Knapp, Martin A. "Government Regulation of Railroad Rates." *Albany Law Journal* 51 (1895), 151–155.
Lee, Blewett. "Combination, Not Competition, of Railroads." *Michigan Law Review* 16 (1918), 496–520.
McCain, W. S. "Railroads as a Factor in the Law." *Arkansas Bar Association Proceedings* (1886), 9–30.
Note. "The State Ownership of Railroads." *American Law Review* 28 (1894), 608–611.

Scott, Thomas A. "The Recent Strikes." *North American Review* 125 (1877), 351–362.
Storey, Moorfield. "The Reorganization of Railway and Other Corporations." *American Law Review* 30 (1896), 802–812.
Thelen, Max. "A Just and Scientific Basis for the Establishment of Public Utility Rates, with Particular Attention to Land Values." *California Law Review* 2 (1914), 3–24.

PERIODICALS
American Railroad Journal
Commercial and Financial Chronicle
Railroad and Engineering Journal
Railroad Gazette

Secondary Sources

BOOKS
Adlow, Elijah. *The Genius of Lemuel Shaw: Expounder of the Common Law.* Boston: Court Square Press, 1962.
Aldrich, Mark. *Safety First: Technology, Labor, and Business in the Building of American Work Safety, 1870–1939.* Baltimore: Johns Hopkins University Press, 1997.
Ambrose, Stephen E. *Nothing Like It in the World: The Men Who Built the Transcontinental Railroad, 1863–1869.* New York: Simon & Schuster, 2000.
Arnesen, Eric. *Brotherhoods of Color: Black Railroad Workers and the Struggle for Equality.* Cambridge, Mass.: Harvard University Press, 2001.
Ayers, Edward L. *Vengeance and Justice: Crime and Punishment in the 19th Century American South.* New York: Oxford University Press, 1984.
Bain, David Haward. *Empire Express: Building the First Transcontinental Railroad.* New York: Viking, 1999.
Baker, Liva. *The Justice from Beacon Hill: The Life and Times of Oliver Wendell Holmes.* New York: Harper Collins, 1991.
Bakken, Gordon Morris. *The Development of Law on the Rocky Mountain Frontier: Civil Law and Society, 1850–1912.* Westport, Conn.: Greenwood Press, 1983.
_____. *Rocky Mountain Constitution Making, 1850–1912.* Westport, Conn.: Greenwood Press, 1987.
Barnes, Catherine A. *Journey from Jim Crow: The Desegregation of Southern Transit.* New York: Columbia University Press, 1983.
Benson, Lee. *Merchants, Farmers, & Railroads: Railroad Regulation and New York Politics, 1850–1887.* Cambridge, Mass.: Harvard University Press, 1955.
Bergstrom, Randolph E. *Courting Danger: Injury and Law in New York City, 1870–1910.* Ithaca, N.Y.: Cornell University Press, 1992.
Berk, Gerald. *Alternative Tracks: The Constitution of American Industrial Order, 1865–1917.* Baltimore: Johns Hopkins University Press, 1994.
Bernstein, David E. *Only One Place of Redress: African Americans, Labor Relations, and the Courts from Reconstruction to the New Deal.* Durham, N.C.: Duke University Press, 2001.

Black, Robert C., III. *The Railroads of the Confederacy*. Chapel Hill: University of North Carolina Press, 1952.

Bogen, Jules I. *The Anthracite Railroads: A Study in American Enterprise*. New York: Ronald Press Company, 1927.

Brown, Cecil Kenneth. *A State Movement in Railroad Development*. Chapel Hill: University of North Carolina Press, 1928.

Brownson, Howard Gray. *History of the Illinois Central Railroad to 1870*. Urbana: University of Illinois, 1915.

Bruce, Robert V. *1877: Year of Violence*. Indianapolis: Bobbs-Merrill, 1959.

Burns, James B. *Railroad Mergers and the Language of Unification*. Westport, Conn.: Quorum Books, 1998.

Caine, Stanley P. *The Myth of a Progressive Reform: Railroad Regulation in Wisconsin, 1903–1910*. Madison: State Historical Society of Wisconsin, 1970.

Carlson, Robert B. *Main Line to Oblivion: The Disintegration of New York Railroads in the Twentieth Century*. Port Washington, N.Y.: Kennikat Press, 1971.

Cherington, Charles R. *The Regulation of Railroad Abandonments*. Cambridge, Mass.: Harvard University Press, 1948.

Clark, William H. *Railroads and Rivers: The Story of Inland Transportation*. Boston: L.C. Page, 1939.

Cline, Wayne. *Alabama Railroads*. Tuscaloosa: University of Alabama, 1997.

Condit, Carl W. *The Port of New York: A History of the Rail and Terminal System from the Grand Central Electrification to the Present*. Chicago: University of Chicago Press, 1981.

Cortner, Richard C. *The Iron Horse and the Constitution: The Railroads and the Transformation of the Fourteenth Amendment*. Westport, Conn.: Greenwood Press, 1993.

_____. *The Arizona Train Limit Case: Southern Pacific Co. v. Arizona*. Tucson: University of Arizona Press, 1970.

Daggett, Stuart. *Chapters on the History of the Southern Pacific*. New York: Ronald Press Company, 1922.

Davis, Colin J. *Power at Odds: The 1922 National Railroad Shopmen's Strike*. Urbana and Chicago: University of Illinois Press, 1997.

Davis, Stanton Ling. *Pennsylvania Politics, 1860–1863*. Cleveland, Ohio: Western Reserve University, 1935.

Dearstyne, Bruce W. *Railroads and Railroad Regulations in New York State, 1900–1913*. New York: Garland Publishing, 1986.

Decker, Leslie E. *Railroads, Lands, and Politics: The Taxation of the Railroad Land Grants, 1864–1897*. Providence, R.I.: Brown University Press, 1964.

Deverell, William. *Railroad Crossing: Californians and the Railroad, 1850–1910*. Berkeley: University of California Press, 1994.

Dewey, Ralph L. *The Long and Short Haul Principle of Rate Regulation*. Columbus: Ohio State University, 1935.

Dewhurst, H. S. *The Railroad Police*. Springfield, Ill.: Charles C. Thomas, 1955.

Dilla, Harriette M. "The Politics of Michigan, 1865–1878" in 47 *Studies in History, Economics and Public Law*. New York: Columbia University, 1912.

Dilts, James D. *The Great Road: The Building of the Baltimore and Ohio, The Nation's First Railroad, 1828–1853*. Stanford: Stanford University Press, 1993.

Donald, David Herbert. *Lincoln*. New York: Simon & Schuster, 1995.

Dooley, Frank J., and William E. Thoms. *Railroad Law: A Decade After Deregulation.* Westport, Conn.: Quorum Books, 1994.

Doster, James F. *Railroads in Alabama Politics, 1875–1914.* Tuscaloosa: University of Alabama Press, 1957.

Doyle, Don H. *Nashville in the New South, 1880–1930.* Knoxville: University of Tennessee Press, 1985.

Eggert, Gerald G. *Railroad Labor Disputes: The Beginning of Federal Strike Policy.* Ann Arbor: University of Michigan Press, 1967.

————. *Richard Olney: Evolution of a Statesman.* University Park: Pennsylvania State University Press, 1974.

Ely, James W., Jr. *The Chief Justiceship of Melville W. Fuller, 1888–1910.* Columbia: University of South Carolina Press, 1995.

————. *The Guardian of Every Other Right: A Constitutional History of Property Rights,* 2nd ed. New York: Oxford University Press, 1998.

Epstein, Richard A. *Forbidden Grounds: The Case Against Employment Discrimination Law.* Cambridge, Mass.: Harvard University Press, 1992.

Fairman, Charles. *Reconstruction and Reunion, 1864–88, Part Two.* Vol. 7 of *Oliver Wendell Holmes Devise History of the Supreme Court of the United States.* New York: Macmillan, 1987.

Faulkner, Harold U. *The Decline of Laissez-Faire, 1897–1917.* New York: Rinehart & Company, 1951.

Ferguson, Maxwell. *State Regulation of Railroads in the South.* New York: Columbia University Press, 1916.

Fischel, William A. *Regulatory Takings: Law, Economics and Politics.* Cambridge, Mass.: Harvard University Press, 1995.

Fishlow, Albert. *American Railroads and the Transformation of the Antebellum Economy.* Cambridge, Mass.: Harvard University Press, 1965.

Frederick, David C. *Rugged Justice: The Ninth Circuit Court of Appeals and the American West, 1891–1941.* Berkeley: University of California Press, 1994.

Freyer, Tony A. *Producers Versus Capitalists: Constitutional Conflict in Antebellum America.* Charlottesville: University Press of Virginia, 1994.

Fried, Barbara H. *The Progressive Assault on Laissez-Faire: Robert Hale and the First Law and Economics Movement.* Cambridge, Mass.: Harvard University Press, 1998.

Friedman, Lawrence M. *A History of American Law.* 2nd ed. New York: Simon and Schuster, 1985.

Gephart, William F. *Transportation and Industrial Development in the Middle West.* 34 *Studies in History, Economics and Public Law.* New York: Columbia University, 1909.

Goddard, Stephen B. *Getting There: The Epic Struggle Between Road and Rail in the American Century.* New York: Basic Books, 1994.

Goodrich, Carter. *Government Promotion of American Canals and Railroads, 1800–1890.* New York: Columbia University Press, 1960.

Gordon, Sarah H. *Passage to Union: How the Railroads Transformed American Life, 1829–1929.* Chicago: Ivan R. Dee, 1996.

Grant, H. Roger. *Erie Lackawanna: Death of an American Railroad, 1938–1992.* Stanford: Stanford University Press, 1994.

Grodinsky, Julius. *The Iowa Pool.* Chicago: University of Chicago Press, 1950.

Hall, Kermit L. *The Magic Mirror: Law in American History.* New York: Oxford University Press, 1989.

Handy, Robert T. *Undermined Establishment: Church-State Relations in America, 1880–1920.* Princeton, N.J.: Princeton University Press, 1991.

Hartz, Louis. *Economic Policy and Democratic Thought: Pennsylvania, 1776–1860.* Cambridge, Mass.: Harvard University Press, 1948.

Hayes, William Edward. *Iron Road to Empire: The History of 100 Years of the Progress and Achievements of the Rock Island Lines.* New York: Simmons-Boardman, 1953.

Healy, Kent T. *Performance of the U.S. Railroads Since World War II.* New York: Vantage Press, 1985.

Hines, Walter D. *War History of American Railroads.* New Haven, Conn.: Yale University Press, 1928.

Hinton, George W. *The Transportation Act of 1958: A Decade of Experience.* Bloomington: Indiana University Press, 1969.

Hoogenboom, Ari, and Olive Hoogenboom. *A History of the ICC: From Panacea to Palliative.* New York: W. W. Norton, 1976.

Horwitz, Morton J. *The Transformation of American Law, 1780–1860.* Cambridge, Mass.: Harvard University Press, 1977.

Hovenkamp, Herbert. *Enterprise and American Law, 1836–1937.* Cambridge, Mass.: Harvard University Press, 1991.

Hunt, Robert S. *Law and Locomotives: The Impact of the Railroad on Wisconsin Law in the Nineteenth Century.* Madison: State Historical Society of Wisconsin, 1958.

Hurst, James Willard, *Law and the Conditions of Freedom in the Nineteenth-Century United States.* Madison: University of Wisconsin Press, 1956.

——. *The Legitimacy of the Business Corporation in the Law of the United States, 1780–1970.* Charlottesville: University Press of Virginia, 1970.

——. *Law and Social Order in the United States.* Ithaca, N.Y.: Cornell University Press, 1977.

Jones, Alan R. *The Constitutional Conservatism of Thomas McIntyre Cooley: A Study in the History of Ideas.* New York: Garland, 1987.

Jones, Eliot. *The Anthracite Coal Combination in the United States.* Cambridge, Mass.: Harvard University Press, 1914.

Karsten, Peter. *Heart versus Head: Judge-Made Law in Late Nineteenth Century America.* Chapel Hill: University of North Carolina Press, 1997.

Keller, Morton. *Affairs of State: Public Life in Late Nineteenth Century America.* Cambridge, Mass.: Harvard University Press, 1977.

——. *Regulating a New Economy: Public Policy and Economic Change in America, 1900–1933.* Cambridge, Mass.: Harvard University Press, 1990.

Kelly, Alfred H., Winfred A. Harbison, and Herman Belz. *The American Constitution: Its Origins and Development,* 7th ed. 2 vols. New York: Norton, 1991.

Kens, Paul. *Justice Stephen Field: Shaping Liberty from the Gold Rush to the Gilded Age.* Lawrence: University Press of Kansas, 1997.

Kerr, K. Austin. *American Railroad Politics, 1914–1920: Rates, Wages and Efficiency.* Pittsburgh: University of Pittsburgh Press, 1968.

Keve, Paul W. *The History of Corrections in Virginia,* Charlottesville: University Press of Virginia, 1986.

Kirkland, Edward Chase. *Men, Cities and Transportation: A Study in New England History, 1820–1900.* 2 vols. Cambridge, Mass.: Harvard University Press, 1948.

Klein, Maury. *Unfinished Business: The Railroad in American Life.* Hanover, N.H.: University Press of New England, 1994.

_____. *History of the Louisville & Nashville Railroad.* New York: The Macmillan Company, 1972.

_____. *The Life & Legend of E. H. Harriman.* Chapel Hill: University of North Carolina Press, 2000.

Koistinen, Paul A. C. *Beating Plowshares Into Swords: The Political Economy of American Warfare, 1606–1865.* Lawrence: University Press of Kansas, 1996.

Kolko, Gabriel. *Railroads and Regulation, 1877–1916.* Princeton, N.J.: Princeton University Press, 1965.

Lamoreaux, Naomi R. *The Great Merger Movement in American Business, 1895–1904.* Cambridge: Cambridge University Press, 1985.

Lane, Wheaton J. *From Indian Trail to Iron Horse: Travel and Transportation in New Jersey, 1620–1860.* Princeton, N.J.: Princeton University Press, 1939.

Latham, Earl. *The Politics of Railroad Coordination, 1933–1936.* Cambridge, Mass.: Harvard University Press, 1959.

Lecht, Leonard A. *Experience under Railway Labor Legislation.* New York: Columbia University Press, 1955.

Leuchtenburg, William E. *The Supreme Court Reborn: The Constitutional Revolution in the Age of Roosevelt.* New York: Oxford University Press, 1995.

Levy, Leonard W. *The Law of the Commonwealth and Chief Justice Shaw.* Cambridge, Mass.: Harvard University Press, 1957.

Lewis, Ronald L. *Transforming the Appalachian Countryside: Railroads, Deforestation, and Social Change in West Virginia, 1880–1920.* Chapel Hill: University of North Carolina Press, 1998.

Lindsey, Almont. *The Pullman Strike: The Story of a Unique Experiment and of a Great Labor Upheaval.* Chicago: University of Chicago Press, 1942.

Lively, Robert A. *The South in Action: A Sectional Crusade Against Freight Rate Discrimination.* Chapel Hill: University of North Carolina Press, 1949.

Locklin, D. Philip. *Economics of Transportation,* 7th ed. Homewood, Ill.: Richard D. Irwin, Inc., 1972.

Lofgren, Charles A. *The Plessy Case: A Legal-Historical Interpretation.* New York: Oxford University Press, 1987.

MacAvoy, Paul W. *The Economic Effects of Regulation: The Trunk-Line Railroad Cartels and the Interstate Commerce Commission Before 1900.* Cambridge, Mass.: The M.I.T. Press, 1965.

Majewski, John. *A House Dividing: Economic Development in Pennsylvania and Virginia Before the Civil War.* Cambridge: Cambridge University Press, 2000.

Marshall, F. Ray. *The Negro and Organized Labor.* New York: Wiley, 1965.

Martin, Albro. *Railroads Triumphant: The Growth, Rejection, and Rebirth of a Vital American Force.* New York: Oxford University Press, 1992.

_____. *Enterprise Denied: Origins of the Decline of American Railroads, 1897–1917.* New York: Columbia University Press, 1971.

McMurry, Donald L. *The Great Burlington Strike of 1888: A Case History in Labor Relations.* Cambridge, Mass.: Harvard University Press, 1956.

Miller, George H. *Railroads and the Granger Laws*. Madison: University of Wisconsin Press, 1971.

Morris, Thomas D. *Southern Slavery and the Law, 1619–1860*. Chapel Hill: University of North Carolina Press, 1996.

Nelson, Scott Reynolds. *Iron Confederacies: Southern Railways, Klan Violence, and Reconstruction*. Chapel Hill: University of North Carolina Press, 1999.

Northrup, Herbert R. *Organized Labor and the Negro*. New York: Harper & Brothers, 1944.

Novak, William J. *The People's Welfare: Law and Regulation in Nineteenth Century America*. Chapel Hill: University of North Carolina Press, 1996.

Noyes, Walter Chadwick. *American Railroad Rates*. Boston: Little, Brown and Company, 1905.

Olson, Sherry H. *The Depletion Myth: A History of Railroad Use of Timber*. Cambridge, Mass.: Harvard University Press, 1971.

Orth, John V. *The Judicial Power of the United States: The Eleventh Amendment in American History*. New York: Oxford University Press, 1987.

Papke, David Ray. *The Pullman Case: The Clash of Labor and Capital in Industrial America*. Lawrence: University Press of Kansas, 1999.

Parks, Robert J. *Democracy's Railroad: Public Enterprise in Jacksonian Michigan*. Port Washington, N.Y.: Kennikat Press, 1972,

Pettengill, George W., Jr. *The Story of the Florida Railroads, 1834–1903*. Boston: Railway & Locomotive Historical Society, 1952.

Phillips, Ulrich B. *A History of Transportation in the Eastern Cotton Belt to 1860*. New York: Columbia University Press, 1908.

Pierce, Harry H. *Railroads of New York: A Study of Government Aid, 1826–1875*. Cambridge, Mass.: Harvard University Press, 1953.

Purcell, Edward A., Jr. *Litigation and Inequality: Federal Diversity Jurisdiction in Industrial America, 1870–1958*. New York: Oxford University Press, 1992.

Reed, S.G. *A History of the Texas Railroads*. Houston: St. Clair Publishing Co., 1941.

Reid, John Phillip. *Chief Justice: The Judicial World of Charles Doe*. Cambridge, Mass.: Harvard University Press, 1967.

Richards, John T. *Abraham Lincoln: The Lawyer-Statesman*. Boston: Houghton Mifflin, 1916.

Riegel, Robert E. *The Story of the Western Railroads*. New York: Macmillan, 1926.

Risher, Howard W., Jr. *The Negro in the Railroad Industry*. Philadelphia: Wharton School of Finance and Commerce, 1971.

Roberts, Christopher. *The Middlesex Canal, 1793–1860*. Cambridge, Mass.: Harvard University Press, 1938.

Salsbury, Stephen. *No Way to Run a Railroad: The Untold Story of the Penn Central Crisis*. New York: McGraw-Hill, 1982.

———. *The State, the Investor, and the Railroad: The Boston & Albany, 1825–1867*. Cambridge, Mass.: Harvard University Press, 1967.

Saunders, Richard. *The Railroad Mergers and the Coming of Conrail*. Westport, Conn.: Greenwood Press, 1978.

Scheiber, Harry N. *Ohio Canal Era: A Case Study of Government and the Economy, 1820–1861*. Athens: Ohio University Press, 1969.

Schwantes, Carlos A. *Railroad Signatures Across the Pacific Northwest.* Seattle: University of Washington Press, 1993.

Shattuck, Petra T., and Jill Norgren. *Partial Justice: Federal Indian Law in a Liberal Constitutional System.* New York: Berg, 1991.

Sheriff, Carol. *The Artificial River: The Erie Canal and the Paradox of Progress, 1817–1862.* New York: Hill and Wang, 1996.

Spero, Sterling D., and Abram L. Harris. *The Black Worker: The Negro and the Labor Movement.* New York: Columbia University Press, 1931.

Splawn, Walter M. W. *Government Ownership and Operation of Railroads.* New York: Macmillan, 1928.

Starobin, Robert S. *Industrial Slavery in the Old South.* New York: Oxford University Press, 1970.

Starr, John W., Jr.,*Lincoln and the Railroads.* New York: Dodd, Mead, 1927.

Stilgoe, John R. *Metropolitan Corridor: Railroads and the American Scene.* New Haven, Conn.: Yale University Press, 1983.

Stone, Richard D. *The Interstate Commerce Commission and the Railroad Industry: A History of Regulatory Policy.* New York: Praeger, 1991.

Stover, John F. *The Railroads of the South, 1865–1900.* Chapel Hill: University of North Carolina Press, 1955.

———. *The Life and Decline of the American Railroad.* New York: Oxford University Press, 1970.

———. *History of the Illinois Central Railroad.* New York: Macmillan Publishing, 1975.

———. *Iron Horse to the West: American Railroads in the 1850s.* New York: Columbia University Press, 1978.

———. *American Railroads.* 2nd ed. Chicago: University of Chicago Press, 1997.

Stowell, David O. *Streets, Railroads, and the Great Strike of 1877.* Chicago: University of Chicago Press, 1999.

Stradling, David. *Smokestacks and Progressives: Environmentalists, Engineers and Air Quality in America, 1881–1951.* Baltimore: Johns Hopkins University Press, 1999.

Stromquist, Shelton. *A Generation of Boomers: The Pattern of Railroad Labor Conflict in Nineteenth-Century America.* Urbana: University of Illinois Press, 1987.

Summers, Mark W. *Railroads, Reconstruction, and the Gospel of Prosperity: Aid Under the Radical Republicans, 1865–1877.* Princeton, N.J.: Princeton University Press, 1984.

———. *The Plundering Generation: Corruption and the Crisis of the Union, 1849–1861.* New York: Oxford University Press, 1987.

Taylor, George R. *The Transportation Revolution, 1815–1860.* New York: Holt, Rinehart and Winston, 1951.

Thomas, William G. *Lawyering for the Railroad: Business, Law, and Power in the New South.* Baton Rouge: Louisiana State University Press, 1999.

Thompson, D. G. Brinton. *Ruggles of New York: A Life of Samuel B. Ruggles.* New York: Columbia University Press, 1946.

Tinkcom, Harry Marlin. *John White Geary.* Philadelphia: University of Pennsylvania Press, 1940.

Tomlins, Christopher L. *The State and the Unions: Labor Relations, Law, and the Organized Labor Movement in America, 1880–1960.* New York: Cambridge University Press, 1985.
Trelease, Allen W. *The North Carolina Railroad, 1849–1871 and the Modernization of North Carolina.* Chapel Hill: University of North Carolina Press, 1991.
Turner, George Edgar. *Victory Rode the Rails: The Strategic Place of the Railroads in the Civil War.* Indianapolis: Bobbs-Merrill, 1953.
Tushnet, Mark V. *The American Law of Slavery 1810–1860: Considerations of Humanity and Interest.* Princeton, N.J.: Princeton University Press, 1981.
Veenendaal, Augustus J., Jr. *Slow Train to Paradise: How Dutch Investment Helped Build American Railroads.* Stanford, Calif.: Stanford University Press, 1996.
Wade, Richard C. *Slavery in the Cities: The South, 1820–1860.* New York: Oxford University Press, 1964.
Ward, James A. *Railroads and the Character of America, 1820–1887.* Knoxville: University of Tennessee Press, 1986.
Warren, Charles. *The Supreme Court in United States History,* rev. ed. Boston: Little, Brown, 1926.
White, G. Edward. *Tort Law in America: An Intellectual History.* New York: Oxford University Press, 1980.
Williams, R. Hal. *The Democratic Party and California Politics, 1880–1896.* Stanford, Calif.: Stanford University Press, 1973.
Wilson, Neill C., and Frank J. Taylor. *Southern Pacific: The Roaring Story of a Fighting Railroad.* New York: McGraw-Hill, 1952.
Yearns, Wilfred Buck. *The Confederate Congress.* Athens: University of Georgia Press, 1960.
Zieger, Robert H. *Republicans and Labor, 1919–1929.* Lexington: University of Kentucky Press, 1969.

ARTICLES AND BOOK CHAPTERS

Arnesen, Eric. "'Like Banquo's Ghost, It Will Not Down': The Race Question and the American Railroad Brotherhoods, 1880–1920." *American Historical Review* 99 (1994), 1601–1633.
Baird, Douglas G., and Robert K. Rasmussen. "Boyd's Legacy and Blackstone's Ghost." *Supreme Court Review* (1999), 393–434.
Barnes, Joseph W. "The N.Y. Central Elevates Its Tracks Under Municipal Pressure." *Rochester History* 33 (1971), 1–24.
Beard, Earl S. "The Background of State Railroad Regulation in Iowa." *Iowa Journal of History* 51 (1953), 1–36.
———. "Local Aid to Railroads in Iowa." *Iowa Journal of History* 50 (1952), 1–34.
Benedict, Michael Les. "Victorian Moralism and Civil Liberty in the Nineteenth Century United States." In Donald G. Nieman, ed., *The Constitution, Law, and American Life: Critical Aspects of the Nineteenth-Century Experience.* Athens: University of Georgia Press, 1992, 91–122.
Black, Paul V. "Experiment in Bureaucratic Centralization: Employee Blacklisting on the Burlington Railroad, 1877–1892." *Business History Review* 51 (1977), 444–459.

Blackford, Mansel Griffiths. "Businessmen and the Regulation of Railroads and Public Utilities in California During the Progressive Era." *Business History Review* 44 (1970), 307–319.

Blackman, John L., Jr. "The Seizure of the Reading Railroad in 1864." *Pennsylvania Magazine of History and Biography* 111 (1987), 49–60.

Brown, Canter, Jr. "The Florida, Atlantic and Gulf Central Railroad, 1851–1868." *Florida Historical Society* 69 (1991), 411–429.

Burton, William L. "Wisconsin's First Railroad Commission: A Case Study in Apostasy." *Wisconsin Magazine of History* 45 (1962), 190–198.

Clark, Joseph S., Jr. "The Railroad Struggle for Pittsburgh." *Pennsylvania Magazine of History and Biography* 48 (1924), 1–37.

Comment. "A. Lincoln, a Corporate Attorney and the Illinois Central Railroad," *Missouri Law Review* 61 (1996), 393–428.

Comment. "The Railroad Revitalization and Regulatory Reform Act of 1976: Improving the Railroads' Competitive Position." *Harvard Journal on Legislation* 14 (1977), 575–619.

Cotroneo, Ross R. "United States v. Northern Pacific Railway Company: The Final Settlement of the Land Grant Case, 1924–1941." *Pacific Northwest Quarterly* 71 (1980), 107–111.

Cuff, Robert D. "United States Mobilization and Railroad Transportation: Lessons in Coordination and Control, 1917–1945." *Journal of Military History* 53 (1989), 33–50.

Currie, David P. "The Constitution in the Supreme Court: The Protection of Economic Interests, 1889–1910." *University of Chicago Law Review* 52 (1985), 324–388.

Daland, Robert T. "Enactment of the Potter Law." *Wisconsin Magazine of History* 33 (1949), 45–54.

Danhof, Clarence H. "The Fencing Problem in the Eighteen-Fifties." *Agricultural History* 18 (1944), 168–186.

Dew, Lee A. "The Owensboro Cattle Cases: A Study in Commerce Regulation." *Filson Club History Quarterly* 49 (1975), 195–203.

Doherty, William T., Jr. "Berkeley's Non-revolution: Law and Order and the Great Railway Strikes of 1877." *West Virginia History* 35 (1974), 271–289.

Duker, William F. "Mr Justice Rufus W. Peckham and the Case of *Ex Parte Young*: Lochnerizing *Munn v. Illinois.*" 1980 *Brigham Young University Law Review,* 539–558.

Ellis, David Maldwyn. "Railroad Land Grant Rates, 1850–1945." *Journal of Land and Public Utility Economics* 21 (1945), 207–222.

———. "The Forfeiture of Railroad Land Grants, 1867–1894." *Mississippi Valley Historical Review* 33 (1946), 27–60.

———. "Rivalry Between the New York Central and the Erie Canal." *New York History* 29 (1948), 268–300.

———. "The Oregon and California Railroad Land Grants, 1866–1945." *Pacific Northwest Quarterly* 39 (1948), 253–283.

Ely, James W., Jr. " 'That due satisfaction may be made': The Fifth Amendment and the Origins of the Compensation Principle." *American Journal of Legal History* 36 (1992), 1–18.

_____. "The Railroad Question Revisited: *Chicago, Milwaukee & St. Paul Railway v. Minnesota* and Constitutional Limits on State Regulations." *Great Plains Quarterly* 12 (1992), 121–134.

_____. "The Fuller Court and Takings Jurisprudence." 1996 *Journal of Supreme Court History,* 120–135.

Ely, James W., Jr., and David J. Bodenhamer. "Regionalism and American Legal History: The Southern Experience." *Vanderbilt Law Review* 39 (1986), 539–567.

Engerman, Stanley. "Some Economic Issues Relating to Railroad Subsidies and the Evaluation of Land Grants." *Journal of Economic History* 43 (1972), 443–463.

Fish, Carl Russell. "The Northern Railroads, 1861." *American Historical Review* 22 (1917), 778–793.

Fisher, Clyde Olin. "Connecticut's Regulation of Grade Crossing Elimination." *Journal of Land and Public Utility Economics* 7 (1931), 367–385.

Flint, Sam Hall. "The Great Freight Rate Fight." *Atlanta Historical Journal* 28 (1984), 5–22.

Freyer, Tony A. "Law and the Antebellum Southern Economy: An Interpretation." In David J. Bodenhamer and James W. Ely, Jr., eds., *Ambivalent Legacy: A Legal History of the South.* Jackson: University Press of Mississippi, 1984.

_____. "Reassessing the Impact of Eminent Domain in Early American Economic Development." *Wisconsin Law Review* (1981), 1263–1286.

Fuller, Warner. "The Background and Techniques of Equity and Bankruptcy Railroad Reorganizations—A Survey." *Law and Contemporary Problems* 7 (1940), 377–392.

Gilliam, George Harrison. "Making Virginia Progressive: Courts and Parties, Railroads and Regulators, 1890–1910." *Virginia Magazine of History and Biography* 107 (1999), 189–222.

Gold, David M. "Redfield, Railroads, and the Roots of 'Laissez-Faire Constitutionalism.' " *American Journal of Legal History* 27 (1983), 254–268.

Goodrich, Carter. "The Virginia System of Mixed Enterprise: A Study of State Planning of Internal Improvements." *Political Science Quarterly* 64 (1949), 355–387.

Grandy, Christopher. "Can Government Be Trusted to Keep Its Part of a Social Contract? New Jersey and the Railroads, 1825–1888." *Journal of Law, Economics, and Organization* 2 (1989), 249–269.

Grant, H. Roger. "Railroaders and Reformers: The Chicago & North Western Encounters Grangers and Progressives." *Annals of Iowa,* 3rd ser. 50 (1991), 772–786.

Grinde, Donald A., Jr. "Erie's Railroad War: A Case Study of Purposive Violence for a Community's Economic Advancement." *Western Pennsylvania Historical Magazine* 57 (1974), 15–23.

Gutman, Herbert G. "Trouble on the Railroads in 1873–1874: Prelude to the 1877 Crisis?" *Labor History* 2 (1961), 215–235.

Halper, Louise A. "Nuisance, Courts and Markets in the New York Court of Appeals, 1850–1915." *Albany Law Review* 54 (1990), 301–357.

Harbeson, Robert W. "Railroads and Regulation, 1877–1816: Conspiracy or Public Interest?" *Journal of Economic History* 27 (1967), 230–242.

Heath, Milton S. "North American Railroads: Public Railroad Construction and the Development of Private Enterprise in the South Before 1861." *Journal of Economic History* 10 (Supplement) (1950), 40–67.

Heckelman, Jac C., and John Joseph Wallis. "Railroads and Property Taxes." *Explorations in Economic History* 34 (January 1997), 77–99.

Heckman, Charles A. "Establishing the Basis for Local Financing of American Railroad Construction in the Nineteenth Century: From *City of Bridgeport v. The Housatonic Railroad Company* to *Gelpcke v. City of Dubuque*." *American Journal of Legal History* 32 (1988), 236–264.

Henry, Robert S. "The Railroad Land Grant Legend in American History Texts." *Mississippi Valley Historical Review* 32 (1945), 171–194.

Higgs, Robert. "Railroad Rates and the Populist Uprising." *Agricultural History* 44 (1970), 291–297.

Hilton, George W. "The Consistency of the Interstate Commerce Act." *Journal of Law and Economics* 9 (1996), 87–113.

Hovenkamp, Herbert. "Regulatory Conflict in the Gilded Age: Federalism and the Railroad Problem." *Yale Law Journal* 97 (1988), 1017–1072.

Hunt, James L. "Ensuring the Incalculable Benefits of Railroads: The Origins of Liability for Negligence in Georgia." *Southern California Interdisciplinary Law Journal* 7 (1998), 375–425.

Hyman, Michael R. "Taxation, Public Policy and Political Dissent: Yeoman Disaffection in the Post-Reconstruction South." *Journal of Southern History* 55 (1989), 49–76.

Jeffrey, Thomas E. "An Unclean Vessel: Thomas Lanier Clingman and the 'Railroad Ring.'" *North Carolina Historical Review* 74 (1997), 389–431.

Jones, Alan. "Thomas M. Cooley and the Interstate Commerce Commission: Continuity and Change in the Doctrine of Equal Rights." *Political Science Quarterly* 81 (1966), 602–627.

——. "Republicanism, Railroads, and Nineteenth-Century Midwestern Constitutionalism." In Ellen Frankel Paul and Howard Dickman, eds., *Liberty, Property, and Government: Constitutional Interpretation Before the New Deal.* Albany: State University of New York Press, 1989.

Kaczorowski, Robert J. "The Common-Law Background of Nineteenth-Century Tort Law." *Ohio State Law Journal* 51 (1990), 1127–1199.

Karsten, Peter. "Supervising the 'Spoiled Children of Legislation': Judicial Judgments Involving Quasi-Public Corporations in the Nineteenth-Century U.S." *American Journal of Legal History* 41 (1997), 315–367.

Kawashima, Yasuhide. "Fence Laws on the Great Plains, 1865–1900." In Elisabeth A. Cawthon and David E. Narreth, eds., *Essays on English Law and the American Experience.* College Station: Texas A&M University Press (1994), 100–119.

Kenny, Norris. "The Transportation of Government Property and Troops over Land-Grant Railroads." *Journal of Land & Public Utility Economics* 9 (1933), 368–381.

Kerr, K. Austin. "Decision for Federal Control: Wilson, McAdoo, and the Railroads, 1917." *Journal of American History* 54 (1967), 550–560.

King, Andrew J. "Sunday Law in the Nineteenth Century," *Albany Law Review* 64 (2000), 675–772.

Klein, Maury. "The Strategy of Southern Railroads." *American Historical Review* 73 (1968), 1052–1068.

Kurtz, Paul M. "Nineteenth Century Anti-Entrepreneurial Nuisance Injunctions—Avoiding the Chancellor." *William and Mary Law Review* 17 (1976), 621–670.

Levy, Daniel W. "Classical Lawyers and the Southern Pacific Railroad." *Western Legal History* 9 (1996), 177–226.

Lewis, H. H. Walker. "The Great Case of the Canal vs. the Railroad." *Maryland Law Review* 19 (1959), 1–26.

Lillquist, R. Erik. "Constitutional Rights at the Junction: The Emergence of the Privilege Against Self-Incrimination and the Interstate Commerce Act." *Virginia Law Review* 81 (1995), 1989–2042.

Mack, Kenneth W. "Law, Society, Identity, and the Making of the Jim Crow South: Travel and Segregation on Tennessee Railroads, 1875–1905." *Law and Social Inquiry* 24 (1999), 377–409.

Majewski, John. "Who Financed the Transportation Revolution? Regional Divergence and Internal Improvements in Antebellum Pennsylvania and Virginia." *Journal of Economic History* 56 (1996), 763–788.

Maltz, Earl M. "'Separate But Equal' and the Law of Common Carriers in the Era of the Fourteenth Amendment." *Rutgers Law Journal* 17 (1986), 553–568.

Mansfield, Harvey C. "The Hoch-Smith Resolution and the Consideration of Commercial Conditions in Rate-Fixing." *Cornell Law Quarterly* 16 (1931), 339–358.

Martin, Albro. "The Troubled Subject of Railroad Regulation in the Gilded Age—A Reappraisal." *Journal of American History* 61 (1971), 339–371.

————. "Railroads and the Equity Receivership: An Essay on Institutional Change." *Journal of Economic History* 34 (1974), 685–709.

Matthews, John Michael. "The Georgia 'Race Strike' of 1909." *Journal of Southern History* 40 (1974), 613–630.

Matthews, Linda M. "Keeping Down Jim Crow: The Railroads and the Separate Coach Bills in South Carolina." *South Atlantic Quarterly* 73 (1974), 117–129.

Mcbain, Howard Lee. "Taxation for a Private Purpose." *Political Science Quarterly* 29 (1914), 185–213.

McGuire, Peter S. "The Railroads of Georgia, 1860–1880." *Georgia Historical Quarterly* 16 (1932), 179–213.

Mercer, Lloyd J. "Land Grants to American Railroads: Social Cost or Social Benefit?" *Business History Review* 43 (1969), 134–151.

Merk, Frederick. "Eastern Antecedents of the Grangers." *Agricultural History* 23 (1949), 1–8.

Merkel, Philip L. "Railroad Consolidation and Late Nineteenth-Century Federalism: Legal Strategy in the Organization of the Southern Pacific System." *Western Legal History* 11 (1998), 215–257.

Miller, Clarence A. "The Quest for a Federal Workmen's Compensation Law for Railroad Employees." *Law and Contemporary Problems* 18 (1953), 188–207.

Minter, Patricia Hagler. "The Failure of Freedom: Class, Gender, and the Evolution of Segregated Transit Law in the Nineteenth Century South." *Chicago-Kent Law Review* 70 (1995), 993–1009.

Moger, Allen W. "Railroad Practices and Policies in Virginia After the Civil War." *Virginia Magazine of History and Biography* 59 (1951), 423–457.

Monkkonen, Eric. "Can Nebraska or Any State Regulate Railroads? Smyth v. Ames, 1898." *Nebraska History* 54 (1973), 365–382.

Monroe, Elizabeth B. "Spanning the Commerce Clause: The Wheeling Bridge Case, 1850–1856." *American Journal of Legal History* 32 (1988), 265–292.

Mooney, Ralph James, and David E. Moser. "Government and Enterprise in Early Oregon." *Oregon Law Review* 70 (1991), 257–332.

Moore, T. Lane. "Railroad Valuation Records." *Railroad History* 163 (1990), 93–102.

Moretta, John. "The Censoring of Lorenzo Sherwood: The Politics of Railroads, Slavery and Southernism in Antebellum Texas." *East Texas Historical Journal* 35 (1997), 39–52.

Nash, Gerald. "The Reformer Reformed: John H. Reagan and Railroad Regulation." *Business History Review* 29 (1955), 189–196.

Nash, Gerald D. "The California Railroad Commission, 1876–1911." *Southern California Quarterly* 44 (December 1962), 287–305.

Neely, Alfred S. " 'A humbug based on economic ignorance and incompetence'— Antitrust in the Eyes of Justice Holmes." *1993 Utah Law Review* 1–66.

Nixon, Richard M. "Changing Rules of Liability in Automobile Accident Litigation." *Law and Contemporary Problems* 3 (1936), 476–490.

Northrup, Herbert R. "The Railway Labor Act—Time For Repeal?" *Harvard Journal of Law & Public Policy* 13 (1990), 441–515.

Note. "Record of the Supreme Court of the United States in Railway Cases." *American Law Review* 32 (1898), 897–899.

Note. "Eminent Domain in North Carolina—A Case Study." *North Carolina Law Review* 35 (1957), 296–313.

Note. "Private Law and Public Policy: Negligence Law and Political Change in Nineteenth-Century North Carolina." *North Carolina Law Review* 66 (1988), 421–441.

Note. "The Waning Power of the States Over Railroads: Curtailment of State Regulatory Activities by the Transportation Act." *Harvard Law Review* 37 (1924), 888–893.

O'Brien, Anthony Patrick. "The ICC, Freight Rates, and the Great Depression." *Explorations in Economic History* 26 (1989), 73–98.

Poole, Keith T., and Howard Rosenthal. "The Enduring Nineteenth-Century Battle for Economic Regulation: The Interstate Commerce Act Revisited." *Journal of Law and Economics* 36 (1993), 837–860.

Porter, Mary Cornelia. "That Commerce Shall Be Free: A New Look at the Old Laissez-Faire Court." *Supreme Court Review* (1976), 135–159.

Potter, David M. "The Historical Development of Eastern-Southern Freight Rate Relationships." *Law and Contemporary Problems* 12 (1947), 416–448.

Purcell, Edward A., Jr. "Ideas and Interests: Businessmen and the Interstate Commerce Act." *Journal of American History* 54 (1967), 561–578.

Ramsdell, Charles W. "The Confederate Government and the Railroads." *American Historical Review* 22 (1917), 794–810.

Reid, John Phillip. "A Plot Too Doctrinnaire." *Texas Law Review* 55 (1977), 1307–1321.

Reutter, Mark. "The Lost Promise of the American Railroad." *Wilson Quarterly* 18 (1994), 10–37.

Robinson, Gustavus H. "The Hoch-Smith Resolution and the Future of the Interstate Commerce Commission." *Harvard Law Review* 42 (March 1929), 610–638.

Ruchames, Louis. "Jim Crow Railroads in Massachusetts." *American Quarterly* 8 (1956), 61–75.

Scheiber, Harry N. "The Road to *Munn*: Eminent Domain and the Concept of Public Purpose in the State Courts." *Perspectives in American History* 5 (1971), 329–402.

———. "Property Law, Expropriation, and Resource Allocation by Government, 1789–1910." *Journal of Economic History* 33 (1973), 232–251.

———. "Federalism and the American Economic Order, 1789–1910." *Law and Society Review* 10 (1975), 57–118.

———. "Federalism, the Southern Regional Economy, and Public Policy Since 1865." In David J. Bodenhamer and James W. Ely, Jr., eds., *Ambivalent Legacy: A Legal History of the South.* Jackson: University Press of Mississippi, 1984.

———. "The Jurisprudence—and Mythology—of Eminent Domain in American Legal History." In Ellen Frankel Paul and Howard Dickman, eds., *Liberty, Property, and Government: Constitutional Interpretation Before the New Deal.* Albany: State University of New York Press, 1989.

Schmidt, Benno C., Jr. "Principle and Prejudice: The Supreme Court and Race in the Progressive Era—Part I: The Heyday of Jim Crow." *Columbia Law Review* 82 (1982), 444–524.

Schoene, Lester P., and Frank Watson. "Workmen's Compensation on Interstate Railways." *Harvard Law Review* 47 (1934), 389–424.

Schwartz, Gary T. "Tort Law and the Economy in Nineteenth-Century America: A Reinterpretation." *Yale Law Journal* 90 (1981), 1717–1775.

Scott, Carole E. "Were Freight Rates Used to Keep the South and West Down?" *Essays in Economic and Business History* 9 (1991), 51–68.

Shaw, Robert C. "The Profitability of Early American Railroads." *Railroad History* (1975), 56–69.

Siegel, Stephen A. "Understanding the *Lochner* Era: Lessons From the Controversy Over Railroad and Utility Rate Regulation." *Virginia Law Review* 70 (1984), 187–263.

Sigmund, Elwin W. "Railroad Strikers in Court: Unreported Contempt Cases in Illinois in 1877." *Journal of Illinois State Historical Society* 49 (1956), 190–209.

Stealey, John Edmund, III. "The Responsibilities and Liabilities of the Bailee of Slave Labor In Virginia." *American Journal of Legal History* 12 (1968), 336–353.

Stewart, Dorothy Houseal. "Survival of the Fittest: William Morrill Wadley and the Central of Georgia Railroad's Coming of Age, 1866–1882." *Georgia Historical Quarterly* 78 (1994), 39–65.

Teller, Ludwig. "Government Seizure in Labor Disputes." *Harvard Law Review* 60 (1947), 1017–1059.

Thompson, William Y. "Robert Toombs and the Georgia Railroads." *Georgia Historical Quarterly* 40 (1956), 56–64.

Thorne, Mildred. "The Repeal of the Iowa Granger Law, 1878." *Iowa Journal of History* 51 (1953), 97–130.

Towles, John K. "Early Railroad Monopoly and Discrimination in Rhode Island, 1835–55." *Yale Review* 18 (1909), 299–319.

Ulen, Thomas S. "The Market for Regulation: The ICC from 1887 to 1920." *American Economic Review* 70 (1980), 306–310.

Usselman, Steven W. "Air Brakes for Freight Trains: Technological Innovation in the American Railroad Industry, 1869–1900." *Business History Review* 58 (1984), 30–50.

Vanderblue, Homer B. "The Long and Short Haul Clause Since 1910." *Harvard Law Review* 36 (1923), 426–455.

Vietor, Richard H. K. "Businessmen and the Political Economy: The Railroad Rate Controversy of 1905." *Journal of American History* 64 (1977), 47–66.

Waldron, Ellis L. "Sharpless v. Philadelphia: Jeremiah Black and the Parent Case on the Public Purpose of Taxation." *Wisconsin Law Review* (1953), 48–75.

Ward, James A. "Promotional Wizardry: Rhetoric and Railroad Origins, 1820–1860." *Journal of the Early Republic* 11 (1991), 69–88.

Welke, Barbara Y. "When All the Women Were White, and All the Blacks Were Men: Gender, Class, Race, and the Road to *Plessy,* 1855–1914." *Law and History Review* 13 (1995), 261–316.

Westin, Alan Furman. "The Supreme Court, the Populist Movement and the Campaign of 1896." *Journal of Politics* 15 (1953), 3–41.

Wetzel, Kurt. "Railroad Management's Response to Operating Employees Accidents, 1890–1913." *Labor History* 21 (1980), 351–368.

Woodman, Harold D. "Chicago Businessmen and the 'Granger' Laws." *Agricultural History* 36 (1962), 16–24.

Yearley, Clifton K., Jr. "The Baltimore and Ohio Railroad Strike of 1877." *Maryland Historical Magazine* 51 (1956), 188–211.

DISSERTATIONS

Brown, R. Ben. "The Southern Range: A Study in Nineteenth Century Law and Society." Ph.D. dissertation, University of Michigan, 1993.

Hedrick, Wilbur O. "The History of Railroad Taxation in Michigan." Ph.D. dissertation, University of Michigan, 1912.

Hylton, Joseph Gordon, Jr. "Jim Crow and the Common Law, 1840–1900." M.A. thesis, University of Virginia, 1978.

Majewski, John D. "Commerce and Community: Economic Culture and Internal Improvements in Pennsylvania and Virginia, 1790–1860." Ph.D. dissertation, University of California, Los Angeles, 1994.

Minter, Patricia Hagler. "The Codification of Jim Crow: The Origins of Segregated Railroad Transit in the South, 1865–1910." Ph.D. dissertation, University of Virginia, 1994.

Taillon, Paul Michel. "Culture, Politics, and the Making of the Railroad Brotherhoods, 1863–1916." Ph.D. dissertation, University of Wisconsin, 1997.

Thompson, David W. "A Study of Railroad Police and Social Change." M.A. thesis, Webster College, 1976.

CASES CITED

Smith & Co. v. Western Railway of Alabama, 91 Ala. 455, 8 So. 754 (1891), 181
Smyth v. Ames, 169 U.S. 466 (1888), 97–98, 227, 232
Southern Pacific Co. v. Arizona, 325 U.S. 761 (1945), 114
Southern Railway Company v. Greene, 216 U.S. 400 (1910), 208
Southern Railway Co. v. Reid, 222 U.S. 425 (1912), 115
Southern Railway Co. v. United States, 322 U.S. 72 (1944), 65
Sparhawk v. Union Passenger Railway Company, 54 Pa. 401 (1867), 150
State v. County of Wapello, 13 Iowa 388 (1862), 26
Steele v. Louisville and Nashville Railroad Company, 323 U.S. 192 (1944), 144–145
Stone v. Farmers' Loan and Trust Company, 116 U.S. 307 (1886), 96–97

Tallahassee Rail-Road Company v. Macon, 8 Fla. 229 (1859), 136
Taylor v. Commissioners of Ross County, 23 Ohio St. 22 (1872), 25
Territory v. Ketchum, 10 N.M. 718, 65 P. 169, 154
Texas and Pacific Railway Company v. Behymer, 189 U.S. 468 (1903), 213–214
Thompson v. New York and Harlem Railroad Company, 3 Sandf. Ch. 625 (N.Y. 1846), 5–6
Township of Pine Grove v. Talcott, 86 U.S. 666 (1873), 28
Tuckahoe Canal Company v. Tuckahoe and James River Rail Road Company, 38 Va. 43 (1840), 6

United States v. Central Pacific Railroad Company, 118 U.S. 235 (1886), 57
United States v. Delaware and Hudson Company, 213 U.S. 366 (1909), 230–231
United States v. Delaware, Lackawanna and Western Railroad Company, 238 U.S. 516 (1915), 231
United States v. ICC, 396 U.S. 491 (1970), 276
United States v. Northern Pacific Railway Company, 256 U.S. 51 (1921), 62
United States v. Pacific Railroad, 120 U.S. 227 (1887), 50–51
United States v. Trans-Missouri Freight Association, 166 U.S. 290 (1897), 100–101
United States v. Union Pacific Railroad Company, 91 U.S. 72 (1875), 55–56

Vaughn v. California Central Railway Company, 83 Cal. 18, 23 P. 215 (1890), 216
Vicksburg and Jackson Railroad Company v. Patton, 31 Miss. 156 (1856), 118–119

Wabash, St. Louis & Pacific Railway v. Illinois, 118 U.S. 557 (1886), 91, 96, 110
Washington and Baltimore Turnpike Road v. Baltimore and Ohio Railroad Company, 10 G. & J. 392 (Md. 1839), 5
West Chester and Philadelphia Railroad Company v. Miles, 55 Penn. St. 209 (1867), 138
White v. Syracuse and Utica Railroad Company, 559 (N.Y. 1853), 40
Williams v. New York Central Railroad, 18 Barb. 222 (N.Y. Sup. Ct. 1854), 203
Wilson v. New, 243 U.S. 332 (1917), 257
Woodfolk v. Nashville & Chattanooga Railroad Co., 32 Tenn. 421 (1852), 192

Young, Ex Parte, 209 U.S. 123 (1908), 233–234

SUBJECT INDEX